THE
unofficial GUIDE®
ᴛᴏ Washington, D.C.

14th Edition

COME CHECK US OUT!

Supplement your valuable guidebook with tips, news, and deals by visiting our websites:

theunofficialguides.com
touringplans.com

Sign up for The Unofficial Guide newsletter for even more travel tips and special offers.

Join the conversation on social media:

 @theUGSeries

 theUnofficialGuides

 theUGSeries

 theUGSeries

 TheUnofficialGuideSeries

Other Unofficial Guides

The Disneyland Story: The Unofficial Guide to the Evolution of Walt Disney's Dream

Universal vs. Disney: The Unofficial Guide to American Theme Parks' Greatest Rivalry

The Unofficial Guide to Disney Cruise Line

The Unofficial Guide to Disneyland

The Unofficial Guide to Las Vegas

The Unofficial Guide to Mall of America

The Unofficial Guide to Universal Orlando

The Unofficial Guide to Walt Disney World

The Unofficial Guide to Walt Disney World with Kids

THE *unofficial* GUIDE®
TO Washington, D.C.

14TH EDITION

RENEE SKLAREW

AdventureKEEN

Please note that prices fluctuate in the course of time and that travel information changes under the impact of many factors that influence the travel industry. We therefore suggest that you call ahead or check websites when available for confirmation when making your travel plans. Every effort has been made to ensure the accuracy of information throughout this book, and the contents of this publication are believed to be correct at the time of printing. Nevertheless, the publishers cannot accept responsibility for errors or omissions, for changes in details given in this guide, or for the consequences of any reliance on the information provided by the same. Assessments of attractions are based upon the authors' own experiences; therefore, descriptions given in this guide necessarily contain an element of subjective opinion, which may not reflect the publisher's opinion or dictate a reader's own experience on another occasion. Readers are invited to write the publisher with ideas, comments, and suggestions for future editions.

The Unofficial Guides
An imprint of AdventureKEEN
2204 First Ave. S., Ste. 102
Birmingham, AL 35233

Cover design by Scott McGrew
Cover photo © dibrova/Shutterstock
Text design by Vertigo Design with updates by Annie Long
Index by Joanne Sprott

To contact us from within the United States, please call 888-604-4537 or fax 205-326-1012. You may also email us at info@theunofficialguides.com; on social media, you may contact us at TheUnofficialGuides on Facebook; @TheUGSeries on Twitter, Instagram, and Pinterest; and TheUnofficialGuideSeries on YouTube.

AdventureKEEN also publishes its books in a variety of electronic formats. Some content that appears in print may not be available in electronic formats.

ISBN 978-1-62809-104-5 (pbk.); ISBN 978-1-62809-105-2 (ebook)

Manufactured in the United States of America

5 4 3 2 1

CONTENTS

LIST *of* MAPS

ABOUT *the* AUTHOR

RENEE SKLAREW has lived most of her life in the Washington, D.C., area. She writes about and photographs her hometown for numerous publications, including *The Washington Post, Washingtonian* magazine, *Northern Virginia Magazine,* and *VivaTysons Magazine.* She is the co-author of *60 Hikes Within 60 Miles: Washington, D.C.* and contributed to *Fodor's Washington, D.C.* guidebook in 2013 and 2014. She is thrilled to offer readers her insider's advice about navigating the city. Find frequently updated information about navigating Washington, D.C., and the mid-Atlantic on her website, TravelandDish.com or on TheUnofficial Guides.com, or follow her on Instagram @TravelandDish.

ACKNOWLEDGMENTS

I AM GRATEFUL TO MY INTREPID DAUGHTERS, Allison and Danielle Sklarew, for exploring our hometown's attractions and neighborhoods with me, and to my husband, Eric, my perfect partner. They are enthusiastic travelers who embrace new foods and cultures by my side. I thank my father, Joseph Marchese, who inspired me to see the world, and my mother, Mary Lu Johnston, for encouraging me to pursue my love of writing.

I would like to express my gratitude to AdventureKeen's managing editor Holly Cross, who made the process of writing and producing this book a total pleasure. I deeply value her insightful guidance and support on this journey. I also thank AdventureKEEN's Liliane Opsomer for promoting this valuable resource to readers.

I heartily applaud my former coauthor, Eve Zibart, for writing the witty and highly informative earlier editions. I am also grateful to have friends like Rachel and Brian Cooper, with whom I coauthored *60 Hikes Within 60 Miles: Washington, D.C.* Their joint research helped me discover uncharted corners of our magical region.

I want to acknowledge the team at Smithsonian Associates for allowing me to guide visitors to inspiring sites around the nation's capital.

And lastly, a shout-out to Pumpkin the Cat, who keeps me company at my desk most days.

—*Renee Sklarew*

INTRODUCTION

◆ **WELCOME** *to* **WASHINGTON**

I MOVED TO THE WASHINGTON, D.C., AREA when I was a toddler. As I grew older, I thought everybody's hometown had magical museums (that charged nothing to enter) where you could gaze upon massive dinosaur skeletons and walk underneath a whale as long as your house. I thought every kid wandered through art galleries that looked like palaces, where you could see *in person* paintings by the most famous artists in the world or actually touch a real moon rock.

My parents loved taking my brother and me to the Smithsonian museums, and we were thrilled when guests came to visit. Then we were allowed to climb the legendary steps of "the Lincoln" or ride the paddleboats in the Tidal Basin next to "the Jefferson" (as we called them). I was especially fortunate in that when I was in third grade, my father took a job in Switzerland, and we were able to visit eight countries in two years (Switzerland is centrally located!). We toured the magnificent museums of London, Paris, and Rome, and it was there that I realized my hometown is an exciting destination, just like the European capitals.

I've always been proud of my city and fascinated by the people who live here. They're smart. They care about global issues. They love learning. Having moved around the country after graduating from a Midwestern college, I never found another place that felt just right. I missed my hometown so much, I cried when I watched newscasters standing in front of the White House. I'm still moved today by so many landmarks—the acres of graves at Arlington Cemetery, the state pillars around the World War II Memorial, and the stark black marble wall of names that is the Vietnam Veterans Memorial.

As parents of two daughters, my husband and I believed an early introduction to travel and exploration would put them on the same path that brought the two of us together. When they were young, we exposed them to different cultures and food. Like most American kids, they turned their noses up at falafel and codfish, but today, they'll eat dishes from around the world, which is easy to do when you live where we do.

We were also fortunate to live in a city with an abundance of history, art, music, theater, and sports. It was all right here in our backyard! There is so much to do in Washington; even after half a century, I haven't visited every attraction or toured every park in the metro area. But I have seen a lot, and new sites are introduced every year. In 2018 we saw the opening of the new Museum of the Bible; the dynamic waterfront neighborhood called The Wharf; and a new stadium for D.C. United, Washington's professional soccer team. In 2019 the Kennedy Center expansion, The REACH, increased the performance and event space with new walkways to the monuments and memorials.

Another reason to love D.C. is the constant debut of new restaurants, by renowned chefs and local talents alike. You won't tire of the food here because we have every cuisine—countless Latin American eateries, especially Peruvian and Salvadoran, with Ethiopian and Vietnamese restaurants almost as common as American. There are dozens of Middle Eastern, East Asian, and European places too, but don't miss sampling the seafood from the Chesapeake Bay, or D.C.'s famous half-smoke sausages. This melting pot is one of the reasons Washington remains so interesting to visitors from across the globe.

Adding to the allure is the city's presence in popular culture. The mysterious workings of Washington politics are the inspiration for a lot of television shows, books, and movies. The nation's capital captures the attention of visitors worldwide thanks to the 24/7 news cycle.

Many tourists (and residents) are surprised by the city's mercurial weather. Here, conditions fluctuate from epic blizzards that shut down the entire city to intense heat and humidity. Our delightful spring and fall are the optimum seasons to visit. But don't let weather deter your plans. In winter, you'll have the museums to yourself, and in summer, there are plenty of shady trees and cool fountains to break up your trek across the National Mall.

The most important things to remember are: Wear comfortable shoes, and understand that you can never see everything worth seeing in one visit (not even in 20 visits). Take your time, prioritize, and use this guide to help you plan. Be ready for an unexpected squall or enchanting ethnic festival to deter your progress. It's OK if you don't see all the monuments on this trip; just come back and visit again soon.

—*Renee Sklarew*

ABOUT THIS GUIDE

WHY "UNOFFICIAL"?

MOST GUIDES TO WASHINGTON, D.C., tout the well-known sights, promote local restaurants and accommodations indiscriminately, and don't explain how to find the best value for your vacation. This one is different.

We'll steer you toward high-quality restaurants—whether it's for a quick stop or a special occasion celebration; we'll dissect the museums and neighborhoods so you can tailor your visit to your personal interests; and we'll guide you to hidden gems and interesting day trips near the city. We evaluate and tour each site, eat in the restaurants, perform critical evaluations of the city's hotels, and visit Washington's entertainment venues, including theaters and sporting events. We hope to make your visit more fun, efficient, and economical. We also note which activities are family-friendly so visitors can figure out the best places to take children and teens.

HOW *UNOFFICIAL GUIDES* ARE DIFFERENT

READERS CARE ABOUT AUTHORS' OPINIONS. Authors, after all, are supposed to know what they are talking about. This, coupled with the fact that travelers want quick answers, dictates that authors be honest, prescriptive, and direct. The authors of the *Unofficial Guides* try to be just that. They spell out alternatives and recommend specific courses of action. They simplify complicated destinations and attractions and help travelers feel in control in unfamiliar environments. The objective of the *Unofficial Guide* authors is to give the most accessible, useful information we can inside the pages of a book.

An *Unofficial Guide* is a critical reference work; it focuses on a travel destination that appears to be especially complex. Our experienced authors and research team are completely independent from the attractions, restaurants, and hotels we describe. *The Unofficial Guide to Washington, D.C.* is designed for people traveling for the fun of it, whether they are visiting D.C. for the first time, studying here for a semester, or relocating here. The guide is directed at value-conscious, consumer-oriented travelers who seek a memorable, comfortable, and convenient travel style.

COMMENTS AND QUESTIONS FROM READERS

WE EXPECT TO LEARN FROM OUR MISTAKES and to improve with each new book and edition. Many users of the *Unofficial Guides* write to us asking questions, making comments, or sharing their own discoveries and lessons learned in Washington. We appreciate all such input, both positive and critical, and encourage you to continue writing. Readers' comments and observations will frequently be incorporated into revised editions of the *Unofficial Guides* and will contribute immeasurably to their improvement.

How to Write the Author

Renee Sklarew
The Unofficial Guide to Washington, D.C.
2204 First Ave. S., Ste. 102
Birmingham, AL 35233
reneesklarew@gmail.com
unofficialguides@menasharidge.com

HOW INFORMATION IS ORGANIZED:
BY SUBJECT AND BY LOCATION

TO GIVE YOU FAST ACCESS TO INFORMATION about the *best* of Washington, we've organized the material into several categories:

ACCOMMODATIONS Because most people visiting Washington stay in one hotel for the duration of their trip, we have summarized our coverage of hotels with descriptions, locations, ratings, and amenities that support your decision-making process. We provide a vivid picture of what it's like to stay at a particular hotel—its proximity to attractions and public transportation, its price point, and whether it's pet- and/or kid-friendly (see Part Two: Accommodations, pages 46–83).

ATTRACTIONS Historic buildings, monuments, museums, art galleries, and other attractions draw visitors to Washington, but it's impossible to see them all in a single trip. We list them by location and then describe each one. These descriptions are the heart of this guidebook and help you determine what to see and when.

RESTAURANTS We provide an array of restaurant options because you will probably eat several restaurant meals during your stay. We include fast-casual options and dining venues that are close to sightseeing or are worthy of a special occasion. Although some downtown sandwich and coffee shops are open only on weekdays, there are dozens of food truck options as well (see page 196).

ENTERTAINMENT AND NIGHTLIFE You may want to try out several theaters or nightspots during your stay, but again, where you go depends on your particular interests. We describe a variety of theaters in the area, as well as the most popular nightlife neighborhoods (pages 255–275), and we list some top destinations for beer lovers, cocktail loungers, and club enthusiasts, including rooftop bars.

NEIGHBORHOODS Once you've decided where you're going, getting there becomes the issue. To help you do that, we have divided the city into neighborhoods:

- The Wharf on the Southwest Waterfront
- Capitol Riverfront and Navy Yard
- Capitol Hill and Barracks Row
- H Street Corridor and NoMa
- National Mall and the White House
- Penn Quarter, Chinatown, and Convention Center
- Foggy Bottom
- Georgetown and West End
- Dupont Circle and Logan Circle
- U Street Corridor
- Adams Morgan and Columbia Heights
- Upper Northwest: Woodley Park, Cleveland Park, and Tenleytown
- Rock Creek Park
- The Maryland Suburbs
- The Virginia Suburbs

WASHINGTON, D.C.:
Portrait of a City

WITH HISTORICAL INFORMATION WRITTEN by Eve Zibart; edited by Renee Sklarew

GEORGE WASHINGTON MAY HAVE BEEN, famously, "first in the hearts of his countrymen," but no such claim could have been made for the city that bears his name. In fact, some people refer to the capital city as a "swamp."

It wasn't the first or second or even fifth city to serve as the capital. Philadelphia was first and foremost: The Continental Congress briefly adjourned to Baltimore when the British threatened, but they quickly returned, only to retreat again to York, Pennsylvania, with an overnight session in Lancaster. The representatives returned to Philadelphia in 1778, but an uprising five years later (not by the British but by their own troops, who were still awaiting their promised pay) sent them first to Princeton, New Jersey; then to Annapolis, Maryland; then to Trenton, New Jersey; then to New York; and—inevitably—back to Philadelphia. (There's a good reason that the city's main boulevard is named Pennsylvania Avenue.)

The British were particularly hard on their former colony: on August 24, 1814, the British Army undertook an incendiary approach to renovating the city by setting fire to several streets and buildings, including the U.S. Capitol, which escaped complete destruction thanks to a luckily timed rainstorm. The brand-new White House was also a casualty, but the British soldiers took time to enjoy a meal there before torching the building. Fortunately, the occupants at the time, President James Madison and First Lady Dolley Madison, were unharmed.

In 1842 Charles Dickens ironically called it "the City of Magnificent Intentions," filled with "spacious avenues that begin in nothing and lead nowhere; streets, mile-long, that only want houses, roads, and inhabitants; public buildings that need but a public to be complete." Americans themselves weren't much impressed with their capital. In 1811 Washington Irving, then dabbling in politics as a lobbyist, called it a "forlorn . . . desert City," especially when the "casual population"—meaning Congress—had adjourned and removed themselves for the comforts of home. Even 150 years after Washington burned, John F. Kennedy famously described it as a "city of Northern charm and Southern efficiency."

But in the 21st century, Washington looks every bit the monumental city the founders envisioned. It may have played a limited role in the Revolutionary War, but it has rebounded from the fires of 1814, the too-close-for-comfort battles of the Civil War, riots that nearly erased whole downtown neighborhoods, crime waves, urban renewal, and even controversial gentrification stronger and far more beautiful than ever. The 9/11 attack on the Pentagon altered the landscape literally and figuratively, resulting in physical barriers and security queues, but the tragedy also inspired the moving National 9/11 Pentagon Memorial. While you are here, you will likely see even more museums, memorials, art spaces, and green spaces under construction.

After all, there were those who called the new capital "the American Rome," and while Washington certainly wasn't built in a day, the wait has been worthwhile.

WASHINGTON BEFORE WASHINGTON

THE HISTORY OF WASHINGTON IS THE TALE OF TWO RIVERS, the mighty 400-mile Potomac and the much more modest 9-mile Anacostia. Rock Creek, which is a tributary of the Potomac, is almost 33 miles long. The same confluence of the Anacostia and Potomac that would later attract the city's founders to the site also drew the attention of indigenous peoples. There is archaeological evidence that American Indians moved into the region as many as 10,000 years ago, and tides of immigration overlapped for millennia.

The Algonquian-speaking Piscataway, the largest American Indian nation in the region, had been permanently established here since at least 1300, long before Captain John Smith of Pocahontas fame put them on the map, so to speak. The Powhatan tribal alliance is estimated to have included 15,000 people at the time of the English explorations. *Potomac* is thought to mean something along the lines of "place where people trade." Oddly, *Anacostia*, derived from the name the Nacotchtank tribe gave it, may have a similar meaning: "the trading place."

 CHESAPEAKE BAY OYSTERS are a famous delicacy and the namesake of many prominent Washington restaurants. They have been a mainstay of the local diet for perhaps 5,000 years. So revered was *Crassostrea virginica* that one possible translation of the Algonquian word *Chesapeake* is "Great Shellfish Bay." When the earliest settlers arrived, not only were oysters abundant, but they were also more like lobsters than the single slurpers of today; early settlers described them as "13 inches long" and "four times as large" as those in England. They became so famous that when the harvest got back up to full speed after the Civil War, Maryland took in 5 million bushels, and Virginia, another 2 million. The various cliques of oystermen became so competitive that a series of skirmishes (some violent), nicknamed the Oyster Wars, lasted into the mid-20th century. Oystering also led to another cottage industry on the Delmarva Peninsula: the making of mother-of-pearl buttons. At its height, around the turn of the 20th century, pearl buttons represented half of all buttons made in the world.

The first Europeans to explore the Washington region were not British but Spanish; Admiral Pedro Menéndez de Avilés, who also founded St. Augustine, Florida, may have sailed up the Potomac River (which he dubbed the Espíritu Santo, or Holy Spirit) as far as Occoquan, Virginia. Captain Smith came even closer, to what is now Great Falls, Virginia, in 1608. Foragers from the Jamestown colony raided an Indian village in Anacostia in 1622. A few years later, George Calvert, Lord Baltimore, was granted the tract of Virginia north and east of the river—henceforth to be known as Maryland—as a refuge for British Roman Catholics.

Thanks to the shipping access afforded by the Potomac River, Washington's two most important early cities, "Old Town" Alexandria and Georgetown, were both founded as ports of call, and both had their roots in the region's first great export, tobacco.

Alexandria is located on part of a 6,000-acre grant given in 1669 by the governor of Virginia to a Captain Robert Howson for his services in transporting 120 new colonists to the state. A month later, Howson sold the land to John Alexander for a pound of tobacco per acre. By 1732, the Alexanders and partner Hugh West had built a tobacco warehouse on the bluffs above the river. Lots were auctioned off in 1749, and more were sold in 1763. Even more enterprisingly, in the 1780s the city added a landfill to the Potomac shoreline so that wharves could be built out to the deeper channel of the river, meaning that oceangoing vessels, including foreign imports, could sail all the way to the port.

Meanwhile, a few miles upstream—the farthest point those oceangoing boats could navigate—another tobacco port had taken hold on the Potomac. By the late 1740s, there was already a string of tobacco warehouses and wharves, a tobacco inspection office, and, of course, taverns along the river in Georgetown. Near as it was, Georgetown was actually part of Maryland, not Virginia; in 1751, the provincial legislature approved the purchase of 60 acres from merchants providentially named George Gordon and George Beall. Local legend has it that Georgetown was winkingly named for these "founders."

 HISTORY, AS WELL AS GEOGRAPHY, can often be read on maps. While the memory of the local tribes lingers largely on the map, history is written by the victors, and the close ties of pre-Revolutionary colonists to the mother country are evident in the majority of county and state names: Virginia (for Elizabeth, the Virgin Queen); Maryland (for Queen Henrietta Maria, wife of the Catholic King Charles I); Prince George's County (for the Danish consort of Queen Anne); Charles County and Calvert County (both for Lord Baltimore, as, of course, is that city); Fairfax County (for Thomas Fairfax, sixth Lord Fairfax of Cameron); and so on. Annapolis went through two Anns, first Anne Arundel, wife of Lord Baltimore, and then the future Queen Anne. Old Town Alexandria—which was partly surveyed by none other than

George Washington—has King, Queen, Prince, Duke, Princess, and Royal Streets. Georgetown, or George Towne, as it was then, is another royalist remnant, named not for the father of our country, as many people assume, but for his then-august Hanoverian majesty, King George II. But because Washington adheres in general to the L'Enfant grid (enforced by Congress), it has few resonant street signs.

Alexandria and Georgetown had more in common than timing and mercantile advantage; they became the seed ground for war—wars, in fact—and then, eventually, Washington, D.C.

In 1753, as tensions over trading rights and expansion in the Ohio Valley escalated between the British and French, the Virginia governor sent 22-year-old militia major George Washington to "invite" the French construction commander to remove himself. The commander refused. Washington headed to Williamsburg to report, and then, having been promoted to lieutenant colonel, was instructed to defend a fort near present-day Pittsburgh that the governor had ordered built by any means necessary. Washington led a group of about 50 that ambushed a French and Canadian party of about 30. The commander, Villers de Jumonville, was killed in the action, which came to be known as the Jumonville Affair.

The Jumonville Affair and its repercussions became one of the prime instigations of the French and Indian War. Major General Edward Braddock, the colonial commander in chief, used Carlyle House in Alexandria, now a museum, as his headquarters. Braddock would lose his life in the war, bequeathing his battle sash to his aide-de-camp, Washington.

 IT WAS ROBERT E. LEE'S FATHER, Washington's close aide Major General Henry "Light-Horse Harry" Lee, who coined the famous epitaph "first in war, first in peace, and first in the hearts of his countrymen," written for George Washington.

Washington did indeed sleep at Carlyle House, probably many times, as he was related by marriage to Sarah Fairfax Carlyle, but he also had his own town house on Cameron Street and a private pew at Christ Church. He danced and dined with most of the other founding fathers and mothers at Gadsby's Tavern (still operating as a restaurant today). But he also frequented the popular Suter's Tavern in Georgetown, where much of the planning for the creation of the nation's capital took place. The tavern's exact location is unclear: it was somewhere near 31st and K Streets NW, not far from what is now the Old Stone House Museum, where Suter's son rented a room for many years. The fact that the pre–Revolutionary War structure was never demolished is due in part to the incorrect assumption for many years that it had served as Washington's Georgetown headquarters.

There was plenty more warfare in Alexandria's future. Partially as a diversion from their attack on Washington, British forces sailed up the

Potomac, bombarded the only fort between the Chesapeake Bay and the city, and politely accepted the surrender of the Alexandria mayor. There was so much loot to be had (including sugar, cotton, wine, and, of course, tobacco), combined with shallow waters, that the British naval forces reportedly grounded their ships and were a little late to the Washington bonfire party. This was very good luck for Georgetown because by then the commodore had decided that proceeding up the Potomac to burn the docks in Georgetown was a waste of time.

But Alexandria's later wartime sufferings would be more significant. Only a block from the Carlyle House is the Stabler-Leadbeater Apothecary, also now a museum, where in 1859 then U.S. Army Lieutenant J. E. B. Stuart handed the orders to Colonel Robert E. Lee, also still in the U.S. Army, to quell John Brown's rebellion in Harper's Ferry (90 minutes from here), powder keg of the Civil War. In 1861, one day after Virginia voted overwhelmingly to secede from the Union, Lee and Stuart followed Virginia into the Confederate fold. Union forces took possession of Lee's family home and plantation just across the Potomac from Washington—now Arlington National Cemetery—and then quickly marched down to Alexandria. Union forces occupied the city for four years, the longest occupation of the conflict.

Washington would be invaded once more, in 1864, by Confederate troops under the command of General Jubal A. Early; that raid, which culminated in the battle at Fort Stevens in Northwest Washington, marks the only time in American history that a sitting president of the United States was present at a battle. Abraham Lincoln was reportedly so fascinated that he kept standing up to watch, oblivious to the bullets flying around him. The young captain, who finally yelled, "Get down, you damned fool!" to the civilian he did not recognize, has been identified by some historians as future Supreme Court Justice Oliver Wendell Holmes Jr.

Long after the 1865 Battle of Appomattox, which marked the end of the Civil War, the issues of slavery and segregation continued to haunt the nation's capital and to shape Washington in palpable ways, not all unhappy; these are discussed in more detail starting on page 12.

THE FIRST CITY OF THE NATION (FINALLY)

WELL BEFORE THE CIVIL WAR, the question of whether the nation's capital should be built in the North or the South was a subject of much debate. In fact, while the Congress was in Trenton, some members made an attempt to lay out a site on the Delaware River. Vice President John Adams, voting as president of the Senate, favored Germantown, Pennsylvania. (To some extent, this indicates just how different in culture the two regions of the country already were.) A compromise was finally struck, so the legend goes, at a private dinner Thomas Jefferson hosted for Alexander Hamilton and Washington's ally Light-Horse Harry Lee.

The specific site was selected by George Washington himself, who lived almost his entire life along his beloved Potomac River, first in

Fredericksburg, Virginia, then later at Mount Vernon. The initial design was a diamond shape, 10 miles by 10 miles, or 100 square miles; many of the mile markers around the perimeter, which were laid by Andrew Ellicott and Benjamin Banneker—a farmer, a mathematician, an astronomer, an inventor, and probably the most famous African American in Colonial America—still stand, though they are badly deteriorated.

Incidentally, though the compass points of the District—Northwest, Northeast, Southwest, and Southeast—are taken from the Capitol, the geographical center of the city is nearer the White House, a bit north of the Washington Monument, near 17th Street NW. And the official heart of the District, and hence the point from which all those "miles to Washington" are measured, can be found on the Ellipse.

 DESPITE THEIR ALREADY FAIRLY LONG HISTORY, neither Georgetown nor Alexandria were formally incorporated until after the Revolutionary War. Alexandria was incorporated in 1779 and Georgetown in 1789—just in time, ironically, for both to find themselves surrendered by their states to create the new nation's capital.

Having argued over the location of the new seat of the national government, the founders couldn't even settle on a name for it. The property where the White House sits now once belonged to a man named Francis Pope, who punningly called his 400-acre farm Rome and the bordering stream the Tiber (more on this later).

Designer Pierre L'Enfant called it the Capital City; Thomas Jefferson referred to it as Federal Town. It was officially dubbed Washington City in 1791, but modest George never used that name himself, continuing to refer to it as the Federal City. He did, however, allow the use of his coat of arms for its flag, and it is still used on the D.C. flag today.

Even the casual tourist can understand how important the Potomac and Anacostia Rivers were to the evolution of the Washington area, but what might not be as immediately apparent beneath the sprawl of modern-day development is how formative a role the underlying topography of Washington played.

The entire region—actually, much of the northeastern United States—basically slopes downhill from north to south. The District's highest point, which is Fort Reno Park, a former Civil War defense near the Maryland border off Wisconsin Avenue, is more than 400 feet above sea level. (Its vantage point was the whole point of its location.) The areas around the city's southern boundaries (that is, the rivers) are marshy and soft; hence the name Foggy Bottom.

 WASHINGTON NATIONAL CATHEDRAL is 400 feet tall. Add 300 feet for the tower, and you have the tallest spot and likely best view in Washington, some 150 feet higher than the Washington Monument.

Tiber Creek, which ran from the Potomac just east of Georgetown toward Capitol Hill, was quite a sizable estuary. According to

L'Enfant's plan, which was intended to fulfill Washington's dream of making the city into (yet another) profitable port, it would be dredged into a canal connecting the city to the river and commercial traffic. In the meantime, it was a prominent recreational feature of the city. People swam, fished, and punted along it. President John Quincy Adams and his son John were canoeing on it in 1825 when their vessel sprang a leak and they were forced to swim to shore.

Gradually, however, and especially during the Civil War when there were troops bivouacked there, Tiber Creek became more of an open sewer than a swimming hole. Any serious rainfall turned downtown into a swamp, and the air in the city was famously pestilential: It is almost certain that the typhoid fever that killed 11-year-old Willie Lincoln came from the water around the White House. Although the creek was diverted down into a tunnel beneath Constitution Avenue in the 1870s, the land around and above it remains less than ideal: building the Ronald Reagan International Trade Building at 14th Street and Constitution Avenue required a huge drainage project that unsettled other buildings nearby, and in 2006 the water problem contributed to the flooding of the National Archives and Internal Revenue Service Buildings, many museums, and the entire Mall itself.

NEAR WHAT WAS THE MOUTH OF TIBER CREEK, and briefly the Washington City Canal, there remains a lockkeeper's cottage, a stone building on the southwest corner of 17th Street and Constitution Avenue NW, not far from the World War II Memorial.

In fact, the land underneath much of what is now the heart of Washington—the Washington, Jefferson, Lincoln, MLK, and World War II Memorials; East and West Potomac Parks; and even the Tidal Basin and its famous cherry trees—was originally mudflats or actual waterways, and the Mall extension was created out of sand and gravel dredged from the Potomac. Repeated attempts to alleviate flooding and clear the river also led to the creation of the various channels around the city and even the expansion of what is now Theodore Roosevelt Island and part of the foundation of the Pentagon.

So despite the advantages of water access, the best options for major construction—and the preferred neighborhoods for housing—tended to be higher and drier. Capitol Hill, then called Jenkins Hill or Jenkins Heights, is naturally elevated, nearly 100 feet up, giving the federal offices a built-in prominence: L'Enfant described it as "a pedestal waiting for a superstructure."

Many of Georgetown's residential sections are similarly elevated. Several of the historic mansions are situated so high up that, in the early days, their owners could see straight across to the Mall. Tudor Place, home of Washington's step-granddaughter Mary Custis Peter, is about 100 feet higher than the riverfront. Dumbarton House, where First Lady Dolley Madison paused after fleeing the President's House with the Gilbert Stuart portrait of Washington, is 125 feet up. From their vantage points, both Madison and Peter had unimpeded views of the White House going up in flames. (Although it's usually the White House fire that is remembered, the British also torched the Capitol, Treasury Building, Navy Yard, War Office, and what was then the only bridge across the Potomac between Washington and Alexandria.)

Even Charles Dickens, who was so clearly disillusioned by the state of official Washington, found Georgetown a pleasant exception, writing: "The heights of this neighborhood, above the Potomac River, are very picturesque; and are free, I should conceive, from some of the insalubrities of Washington. The air, at that elevation, was quite cool and refreshing, when in the city it was burning hot."

It's no wonder that the Lincolns, and several of their successors, delighted in moving their households to the summer residence, now the President Lincoln's Cottage museum. Only 3 miles north, it's about 300 feet higher up and enjoys not only cooler but also cleaner breezes.

 LINCOLN'S HABIT OF CANTERING ALONE along 16th Street from the White House north to the cottage was so widely known that, in 1865, a would-be assassin took a shot at him—leaving a gaping hole through his stovepipe hat.

The bad news is the climate is changing and sea levels are rising. Before the latest round of restoration, the Jefferson Memorial and its sea wall were sinking as much as 8 inches a year, and scientists predict the entire Washington area will drop that much over the next century. Just as the current generation cannot imagine Washington as it was a century ago, so visitors 100 years from now may find it quite different.

THE ROAD TO RACIAL EQUALITY

THOUGH WASHINGTON ITSELF SAW NO ACTION during either the French and Indian or Revolutionary War, crucial campaigns in both were conceived here. Created (and debated) by the then newly independent 13 colonies, it arguably remains the 14th colony—home to both houses of Congress but without a vote in either, a fact many observers believe is influenced by the large African American (and presumably Democrat-leaning) population. The phrase "taxation without representation" was in wide use on both sides of the Atlantic by the mid-18th century, and it is alive today, with good reason. Washington was laid out as a perfect diamond but fragmented by the issue of slavery. It showcases monuments to some who did not want them, such as Presidents Franklin Roosevelt and Dwight Eisenhower, and sequesters statues of some who helped shape America's history, such as Benjamin Banneker.

African Americans—freed, enslaved (by one estimate, as many as 20,000), and indentured—served on both sides of the Revolutionary War, as did American Indians; yet nearly half of the original writers of or signatories to the Declaration of Independence, including Washington, Jefferson, Franklin, Lee, Madison, and Monroe, owned slaves, and not all promises of freedom for martial service were honored.

Census figures from the year 1800 indicate that 30% of Georgetown's population was enslaved, with more than 200 free blacks living there as well. Although they represented half the congregation, African American worshippers at Georgetown's Dumbarton Methodist Episcopal Church were relegated to an airless, crowded balcony, so in 1816 they founded Mount Zion United Methodist Church at 27th and Q Streets NW.

There were slave markets all over the Washington area, a couple within view of the Capitol, as Lincoln noted. In 1830, a census of one of Alexandria's markets listed around 150 slaves, two-thirds under 25 years old and five under age 10. Georgetown's slave markets operated until the Civil War; the District's largest slave pen was located a stone's throw from where the National Museum of African Art is now. Even Francis Scott Key, who wrote "The Star Spangled Banner," was a devout Episcopalian, and nearly became a priest instead of a lawyer, owned slaves. Slaves unquestionably were involved in the construction of the White House, Georgetown University, and the Capitol; staffed the hotels and boardinghouses; drove the cabs; hauled the bathwater; and even attended their owners on the floors of Congress.

The issue was as hot, and hypocritical, in Washington as anywhere in the country, especially as Congress and the U.S. Supreme Court repeatedly debated slave vs. free states and slaves as property. Benjamin Banneker, the surveyor of the city, wrote Jefferson a rather scathing letter on the question of slavery. Most people of color in Washington itself in the early 19th century were free—if they could stay that way. In 1841, violinist Solomon Northup, the inspiration for the film *Twelve Years a Slave,* was kidnapped from a hotel (owned by the same James Gadsby as Washington's favorite tavern in Alexandria) on Pennsylvania Avenue, near the Canadian Embassy.

In 1846 the residents of Alexandria, who feared that the capital would outlaw slavery and thus strangle the slave trade in that busy port, voted to ask Congress to return the portion of the District across the river to the state of Virginia. It was just short of a third of the 100 square miles; you can clearly see on a map how the original diamond is cut off at the southwestern corner by the Potomac. (It's even more obvious on the graphically pared-down Metro subway maps.)

Even on the day of Lincoln's inauguration, the sheriff of Alexandria auctioned off "all free Negroes who have failed to pay their [head] tax for the years 1859 and 1860," though what was actually being sold was their labor, if that constituted any real difference. Ironically, perhaps the one upside of the Union's occupation of Alexandria throughout the Civil War was the opportunities it offered escaped slaves to establish businesses, either as laborers of various degrees of expertise or as personal servants. By one estimate, as many as 10,000 African Americans moved into Alexandria in a period of 16 months, between 1862 and 1863, and by 1870 people of color made up roughly half the city.

In some ways Washington was forward-thinking on the issue. A Washington, D.C., resident and former slave, statesman Frederick

Douglass was an influential voice who recruited African Americans as Union soldiers. In 1863 Douglass met with President Lincoln and advocated for equal protection for all soldiers. At the end of the Civil War, United States Colored Troops comprised 10% of the Union Army.

Slavery was finally outlawed in the District of Columbia in 1862, a year before Lincoln issued the Emancipation Proclamation, and Emancipation Day, April 16, is observed as a holiday in Washington. Howard University was founded in 1867. Black men in the District of Columbia were given the right to vote in 1867, three years before the 15th Amendment enfranchised all men. Until the mid-1870s, black officeholders had substantial influence in D.C.

But the imposition of segregation in federal agencies and the banning of interracial marriage under President Woodrow Wilson in 1913 (who had specifically promised to work for equal rights), restarted a long train of tensions, eventually resulting in race riots in 1919. What might be the earliest black sit-in occurred in 1943, during FDR's efforts to desegregate the federal government, in the U Street neighborhood, then part of "Black Broadway" (see Part Six: Entertainment and Nightlife, page 255). The Reverend Martin Luther King Jr. led the March on Washington for Jobs and Freedom in 1963 that culminated in his "I Have a Dream" speech at the Lincoln Memorial; his assassination in 1968 sparked a week of street battles and firefights that, ironically, devastated blocks around 14th and U Streets NW, then one of the central points of African American development in the District, and on H Street NE. Both neighborhoods have recovered and are thriving, in part due to gentrification.

By 1960, white flight and the lure of the new suburbs had upset the old ratios; African Americans represented the majority of Washington residents. A decade later, they represented more than 70%. (One of the District's nicknames, especially in the 1970s and '80s, was Chocolate City.) Black residents remained the majority until 2013.

Finally, in 1967, Congress appointed Walter Washington as mayor, and a few years later, District residents were finally allowed to vote for him as mayor. All elected District mayors since have been African American. In 2008 presidential candidate Barack Obama won the election with 92% of the District vote; four years later, it was still more than 90%.

However, segregation, subtle or overt, remains somewhat visible in Washington today. The overwhelming majority of African American residents live in the eastern half of the city, especially on the other side of the Anacostia River, and questions of real estate values, health care, and quality of education continue to bedevil the city.

BEAUTIFICATION AND MODERN-DAY WASHINGTON

AS NOTED, WASHINGTON WAS NOT ALWAYS A PLEASURE to visit. Despite the fact that it was conceived in 1791 and Congress and President John Adams officially moved into their new quarters in 1800, construction of the less symbolic sort was spotty at best. Many of the great houses that are now museums were built in the very early 19th century by prosperous farmers and developers, and mostly in the then much more desirable towns of Alexandria and Georgetown.

Pennsylvania Avenue, envisioned as Washington's grand promenade and running directly between the President's House, as it was originally called, and the Houses of Congress, wasn't paved even rudimentarily until 1832 and went through cobblestones, bricks, and even wood surfaces before getting a taste of asphalt in 1876—not that it helped much. The city's first sewer was built beneath Pennsylvania Avenue, too, in 1829 (which again says something about the quality of life in the neighborhood).

Even what we now know as the National Mall, one of the most immediately recognizable stretches in the nation, remained far more mud than marble well into the 20th century. The first Smithsonian building, The Castle, opened in 1855, the neighboring Arts and Industries Building in 1881, the National Museum of Natural History in 1910, and the Freer Gallery in 1923, but it was decades before the other buildings were constructed. (And it should be noted that both the Castle and the Freer were primarily funded by bequests, not the federal government.) The Washington Monument wasn't begun until 1848 and was only half a building until 1884. The Lincoln Memorial opened in 1922, and the Jefferson Memorial in 1923.

Even more surprisingly, post–Civil War downtown Washington, including areas near the White House, housed some dangerous neighborhoods, including what was called Hell's Bottom, Bloody Hill, and Murder Bay, which was where the fortress-like Federal Triangle stands today. (Chillingly, President Lincoln's cortege likely at least brushed the edges of Murder Bay on his way to Ford's Theatre.)

Poor architect Pierre L'Enfant, who had discovered his passion for the new nation while serving under Generals Lafayette and Washington in the Revolutionary War, died penniless and brokenhearted in 1825. His vision for the city was considered too grandiose and was repeatedly amended, though he was finally vindicated in 1901 when the McMillan Commission used his original plan to push for the start of Washington's true construction, including the National Mall.

L'Enfant's remains were finally exhumed in 1909 from a farm in Prince George's County, taken to the Capitol rotunda to lie in state, and reburied on a hillside in Arlington Cemetery. His gravestone is engraved with a replica of his original design. Even more fittingly, President John F. Kennedy, who had admired the moving monumental view not long before his assassination, is buried at his widow's request just a few yards away.

Nevertheless, the statue of L'Enfant that was commissioned in the hope it would someday stand in the U.S. Capitol remains, at press time, forbidden to enter the halls of the building he helped put on the map. Instead (somewhat like Banneker), he looks directly west toward the White House and points backward toward the Capitol from the lobby of a very large government building in Judiciary Square.

The heroes of modern Washington, D.C., are Lady Bird Johnson and President Lyndon Johnson, philanthropist David Rubenstein, the Kogod/Smith family, and Abe Pollin.

While Jacqueline Kennedy was rightly praised for restoring the White House to engage Americans in their own history, Lady Bird Johnson campaigned for the beautification of Washington's byways, parks, and side streets, urging volunteers (and eventually, the National Park Service) to plant the smallest traffic triangle with flowers, dogwoods, and azaleas. Her programs became a sort of adjunct to her husband's vision of the Great Society and helped turn the city from a dutiful destination for schoolchildren into a true tourist attraction.

Financier David Rubenstein is to Washington, D.C., as John D. Rockefeller Jr. was to New York. He has almost singlehandedly restored the National Archives, paying for the new visitor center and restoring the Declaration of Independence, the US Constitution, the Bill of Rights, the Emancipation Proclamation, the 13th Amendment, the first map of the United States (Abel Buell map), and the first book printed in the US (the *Bay Psalm Book*), as well as lending an original copy of the Magna Carta.

Rubenstein has chaired the Kennedy Center for the Performing Arts since 2010 (and has donated $50 million to the organization) and has made transformative gifts for the restoration or repair of Arlington House, the Iwo Jima Memorial, the Library of Congress, Monticello, Montpelier, Mount Vernon, the National Museum of African American History and Culture, the Smithsonian, and the Washington Monument. Even the beloved baby pandas of the National Zoo owe him a huge debt: $4.5 million went to fund the panda reproduction program.

Philanthropists from the Kogod/Smith family are also notable investors in their hometown, having made contributions to fund the Kogod Courtyard that connects the Smithsonian American Art Museum and the National Portrait Gallery, as well as donations to the National Gallery of Art, the Phillips Collection, the Shakespeare Theatre Company, the Woolly Mammoth Theatre Company, and the redevelopment of the Arena Stage.

Abe Pollin, owner of the NBA's Washington Wizards (formerly the Bullets), the WNBA Mystics, and the NHL Washington Capitals, was a construction tycoon who built athletic stadiums/concert venues first outside the Beltway and then in the center of town. The construction of the Capital One Arena in the mid-1990s is often credited with igniting the redevelopment of the Penn Quarter sector of downtown, now perhaps the most vibrant neighborhood of the city.

STILL MOVING FORWARD

IN MANY WAYS, Washington is more an international city than an American one, housing as it does the scores of embassies and consulates, the headquarters of the World Bank and International Monetary Fund, the Organization of American States, and so on. And, of course, repeated waves of immigration have made it one of the country's great melting pots. In 1900 only 7% of the residents had come from other countries; a century later a fifth were foreign-born. According to the 2017 Council of Governments report, 23% of the population in the Washington metropolitan area are immigrants. As of late 2018, the entire metropolitan area comprised around 6.2 million residents, making it the fifth-largest city in the United States.

Today, early in its third century, Washington is again at a cultural and architectural crossroads, with substantial developments continuing to change the city's abbreviated skyline—no buildings in the District of Columbia are allowed to be taller than the Washington Monument. The revitalization of the Pennsylvania Avenue neighborhood and the reuse of historical buildings are a belated testament to the vision of Pierre L'Enfant.

Across the Potomac River, tech giant Amazon has opened its second headquarters (known as HQ2) in Arlington, Virginia. Public transportation options continue to expand, with new bike lanes, rapid-transit buses, and the Metrorail Silver Line expansion to Dulles International Airport set to begin operations by 2021. Similarly, the Maryland suburbs will debut a cross-county light-rail transportation system called the Purple Line, expected to open in 2022. The Anacostia River is on its way to health, and the waterfront now consists of miles of protected parkland. Eventually, the 11th Street Bridge Park will become Washington's first elevated public park (similar to New York's High Line).

Thanks to this dynamic renaissance, the nation's capital welcomed more than 22.8 million visitors in 2018, and 2 million were international tourists. They are coming to see world-class museums, enjoy the vibrant dining scene, and explore the city's public parks and monuments. After your visit, we think you'll agree, it's a great place to vacation and to live!

PART ONE

PLANNING YOUR VISIT

WHEN *to* GO

CROWDS

TO PROVIDE YOU WITH the most reliable information on traveling to Washington, D.C., we looked at a number of resources and used our personal expertise. Our research incorporates data published by Destination DC, the city's official destination marketing organization, which tracks visitor statistics annually. They report that Washington, D.C., welcomed 22.8 million visitors in 2018, an increase of 1.2 million from 2017. We also study information provided by The Smithsonian, with 11 museums in Washington, D.C., and the National Park Service, which oversees the memorials and monuments on the National Mall. Last, but in some ways most important, are our own observations. During weekly research trips, we observe crowds (or lack thereof) at D.C.'s most popular museums, neighborhoods, and attractions to compare different days of the week and times of the year.

Washington, D.C.'s tourist attractions are busiest around the National Cherry Blossom Festival, roughly mid-March through mid-April, and from late June through early August, when most US public schools have their summer vacations. The period from late April through late June is also busy. The best times to visit are late September, October, and November (which also have great weather and gorgeous fall foliage), and then January, February, and early March (when the weather is worse but the museums are far less busy).

DAY-OF-WEEK PATTERNS Attractions, monuments, and museums are generally busiest on Saturday and slowest on Tuesday. Ignoring special events, such as legal holidays, here's how each day of the week stacks up in terms of crowds, with Saturday being the busiest, and Tuesday the least busy: Saturday, Friday, Sunday, Thursday, Monday, Wednesday, Tuesday. Note that holidays and school breaks often combine to move crowds around within a given month.

On individual days, crowds generally peak at attractions between 11 a.m. and 3 p.m. If a museum or monument opens at 10 a.m, arrive by 9:45 a.m. to beat the crowds or after 3:30 p.m. Alternatively, if you're touring during summer and a museum has extended hours, it's possible to do a highlights tour of even the largest museum between 3:30 and 7:30 p.m.

If you have no restrictions on your travel time, we suggest you scan the "Calendar of Festivals and Events" starting on page 39 and determine which ones might lure you.

WEATHER

WASHINGTON, D.C.'S WEATHER is best in spring and fall. The city's fabled cherry blossoms bloom at the end of March or early April—not always coinciding with the Cherry Blossom Festival, unfortunately—while fall brings crisp, cool weather and a spectacular display of foliage. Washington is a city of trees, and the urban and suburban parks are resplendent with forests and shrubbery. For an even greater display of natural beauty, head to the Shenandoah Valley to the west or the Appalachian Mountains to the north; both are about 90 minutes from downtown Washington, D.C. For more information on the city's parks, check out my book *60 Hikes Within 60 Miles: Washington, D.C.*

WASHINGTON, D.C., WEATHER AVERAGES						
	JAN	FEB	MAR	APR	MAY	JUN
HIGH	48° F	50° F	59° F	66° F	75° F	85° F
LOW	29° F	32° F	38° F	47° F	58° F	66° F
RAINFALL (inches)	2.7"	2.7"	3.4"	3.5"	4.5"	3.9"
NUMBER OF RAINY DAYS	14	14	14	14	20	18
	JUL	AUG	SEP	OCT	NOV	DEC
HIGH	88° F	86° F	81° F	69° F	60° F	59° F
LOW	72° F	71° F	63° F	51° F	44° F	33° F
RAINFALL (inches)	3.6"	3.5"	3.9"	3.2"	3.4"	3.0"
NUMBER OF RAINY DAYS	17	16	16	16	16	16

The city owes its lush trees to regular rainstorms. But these storms tend to last only part of a day and are often in different parts of town, with some exceptions. We don't get much snow, but when we do, the city stops operating, in part to avoid terrible traffic congestion.

Summers are generally hot and quite humid. Many Washingtonians follow Congress and foreign diplomats and "recess" out of the city in August, but that means that August has its good side: far less traffic, shorter lines, easy restaurant reservations, extended museum hours, and—because so many federal employees are on vacation—less tedious security. Washington is so much less crowded, in fact, that August is when many of the area's most prominent chefs participate in the summer **Restaurant Week,** offering bargain-priced three-course lunch and dinner menus at about $22 and $35, respectively. It really is the best summer month to visit.

Though D.C.'s weather can be erratic in winter, it's an ideal time to avoid crowds. On weekdays especially, the Mall is nearly deserted, and museums, monuments, and normally crowd-intensive hot spots, such as the Capitol, are almost congenial. (There's a winter version of Restaurant Week offered in January, too.) If you take our advice to stay near a Metro station, the subway will get you around town with minimal exposure to the elements.

GATHERING INFORMATION
Before YOU LEAVE

THERE ARE PLENTY OF DEPENDABLE and frequently updated websites that you might want to browse while planning your visit. The official tourism site is washington.org, operated by **Destination DC,** which lists family-friendly and free seasonal options, events, some package deals you might compare, and so on. It also offers an official, downloadable visitors guide, updated twice a year, with maps and local hotel options.

Another good site for lists of special events and regularly updated information on tourist attractions is **Cultural Tourism DC,** with its links to neighborhood heritage trails and tours of embassies (cultural tourismdc.org). The states of Virginia and Maryland also have websites with tourism information. For **Virginia's suburbs,** check fxva .com (Fairfax County), visitloudoun.org (Loudoun County's wine country), visitalexandriava.com (for historic Old Town Alexandria), and stayarlington.com (Arlington). In **Maryland,** check out visit montgomery.com (Montgomery County); visitprincegeorgescounty .com (Prince George's County, which includes the National Harbor); and the state's website, visitmaryland.org/capital. All include historical attractions, along with breweries, vineyards, and theater and sports venues. Lastly, check the deals on groupon.com, culturecapital .com, and goldstar.com. They often feature discounted tickets to museums (the ones that charge an entry fee), as well as deals on boat and bus tours, theater shows, concerts, and festivals.

Several of the major publications in the area have online editions that you can surf while planning your visit, including *The Washington Post* (washingtonpost.com) and *Washington City Paper,* Washington's free weekly alternative newspaper, with lists of arts, theater, clubs, and more (washingtoncitypaper.com). The *Washingtonian,* the area's preeminent magazine, is strong on lists (top 10 restaurants, hot shopping boutiques, and so on) and provides a monthly calendar of events, dining information, and feature articles (washingtonian.com). Check out *Northern Virginia Magazine* (northernvirginiamag.com) for dining, events, and features on the Virginia side of the Potomac River.

Once you arrive, you'll discover that there are dozens of concerts, art shows, and special events going on all the time around Washington, and many of them are free. Check *The Washington Post*'s Going Out Guide and the Friday Weekend section. *The Post* also owns a free quick-read newspaper called *Express*, handed out at Metro stations and many street corners.

Where Washington D.C. lists popular things to do around town; it's usually available in hotels or at airport racks (wheretraveler.com /washington-dc). The *Washington Blade*, the LGBTQ community's weekly, is available in many restaurants and nightspots, especially those around Dupont Circle and Capitol Hill (washingtonblade.com).

If you're planning to visit any of the **Smithsonian museums,** their site, si.edu/visit will give you a quick first look at the exhibits and floor plans; museums have individual sites as well.

MAKING ADVANCE RESERVATIONS FOR MONUMENTS, MUSEUMS, AND TOURS

A LIMITED NUMBER OF SPACES are available for each day's guided tours at some major attractions, including the Washington Monument and the Capitol. These are almost always filled days or weeks in advance. In addition, you'll have to ask a member of Congress and submit to a background check before being admitted to certain locations, and that makes last-minute visits impossible. The table on pages 22–23 shows how far in advance you must make reservations for popular D.C. destinations.

*un*official **TIP**
To arrange a tour through your Congressperson, visit senate.gov or house.gov, locate your representative's page, and fill out a request form. You will need the birthdate and SSN of everyone in your group.

Even if reservations aren't mandatory, it's still a good idea to make them if you can. It's also worthwhile to buy tickets online ahead of time if possible. Visitors with advance tickets and/or reservations get placed at the front of any line, which can save hours of time waiting. Another benefit to buying entry tickets in advance: you're likely to find discounts or discount codes to reduce the admission price. Note that while many tours are free, a small fee of around $1.50 may be assessed for making reservations in advance.

*un*official **TIP**
An alternative to a White House tour is a stop at the new interactive White House Visitor Center (1450 Pennsylvania Ave. NW), run by the National Park Service.

If you don't have time or the inclination for much advance work, there's a sort of one-stop shop for brochures, maps, discount coupons, and hotel/restaurant reservation kiosks: the **Tourist Information Center** in the Ronald Reagan Building/International Trade Center at 1300 Pennsylvania Ave. NW, which also has an excellent food court. The center is located at the Federal Triangle Metro Station, not far from Metro Center and the National Mall. It's open weekdays

continued on page 24

A GUIDE TO ADVANCE RESERVATIONS FOR MAJOR ATTRACTIONS

ATTRACTION/ WHERE TO GET TICKETS	TOUR TIMES
NATIONAL ARCHIVES archives.gov/museum	Self-guided tour, every 15 minutes from 10:30 a.m. until 90 minutes before closing; 1-hour guided tour offered Mon.–Fri. at 9:45 a.m.
THE WHITE HOUSE Must go through member of Congress; whitehouse.gov1.info/visit/tour.html for info	Mon.–Thu., 7:30–11 a.m.; Fri.–Sat., 7:30 a.m.–1:30 p.m.
US HOLOCAUST MUSEUM ushmm.org	Daily, 9:45 a.m.–4:45 p.m.
TREASURY BUILDING Must go through member of Congress	Sat., 9, 9:45, 10:30, and 11:15 a.m.
WASHINGTON MONUMENT recreation.gov or 877-444-6777	Daily, 9 a.m.–5 p.m.
PENTAGON pentagontours.osd.mil	Mon.–Fri., 9 a.m.–3 p.m.
U.S. CAPITOL visitthecapitol.gov	Mon.–Fri., 8:50 a.m.–3:20 p.m.
FORD'S THEATRE NATIONAL HISTORIC SITE fords.org	Daily, 9 a.m.–4 p.m.
DEPARTMENT OF STATE DIPLOMATIC RECEPTION ROOMS diplomaticrooms.state.gov	Mon.–Fri., 9:30 and 10:30 a.m., 2:45 p.m.
FREDERICK DOUGLASS NATIONAL HISTORIC SITE nps.gov/frdo	Daily, 9 a.m., 12:15 p.m., 1:15 p.m., 3 p.m., 3:30 p.m. (walk-ins only), and 4 p.m. (Apr.–Oct.)
PRESIDENT LINCOLN'S COTTAGE lincolncottage.org	Mon.–Sat., 10 a.m.–3 p.m.; Sun., 11 a.m.–3 p.m.
BUREAU OF ENGRAVING AND PRINTING Must purchase day of visit beginning at 8 a.m.	Mon.–Fri, 9 a.m.–6 p.m.
FOLGER SHAKESPEARE LIBRARY folger.edu	Saturday at noon
DEPARTMENT OF THE INTERIOR Call ☎ 202-208-4743	Tue. and Thu., 2 p.m.
ARLINGTON NATIONAL CEMETERY arlingtontours.com	No time or date selection necessary
FBI EXPERIENCE Security approval required; must go through member of Congress	Mon.–Fri., 9 a.m.–4:30 p.m.
NATIONAL MUSEUM OF AFRICAN AMERICAN HISTORY AND CULTURE Timed entry passes available at nmaahc.si.edu; required on Saturday and Sunday	Daily, 10 a.m.–5:30 p.m.

ADULT COST	MAXIMUM DAYS AHEAD	MINIMUM DAYS AHEAD	NOTES
$1	N/A	N/A	Walk-ins allowed, but reservations recommended
Free	180	21	Background check required
Free	Same-day and advance tickets online	N/A	Passes required Mar.–Aug.
Free	180	21	Background check required
$1 processing fee	N/A	N/A	Some same-day passes available on a first-come, first-served basis
Free	90	14	Submit request, must show ID (passport, driver's license, permanent resident card)
Free	90	1	Some same-day passes available; Gallery Passes must be obtained through member of Congress
$3	90	1	Some timed same-day passes available
Free	90	1	Fine arts tour not appropriate for children; background check may be required; tours canceled periodically
$1.50	90	N/A	Same-day passes available
$15, kids $5 (should be age 6 or older)	90	N/A	Advance tickets required; on-site tickets sometimes available
Free	90	N/A	Tickets only required Mar.–Aug.; can pick up at ticket window for other times
Free	60	1	This is for Reading Room Tours; regular tours do not require tickets.
Free	60	N/A	This is for Murals Tours (some same-day tickets for individuals, groups based on staff availability); museum visits do not require tickets
$15, kids $7.25	30	1	This is for bus tour; ANC Explorer App for self-guided tours
Free	35	21	Must be 16 or older with government-issued ID
Free	90	N/A	Walk-in entry Mon.–Fri., 1 p.m.–close Mar.–Aug; walk-in entry Mon.–Fri., 10 a.m.–close Sept.–Feb.

continued from page 22

9 a.m.–5 p.m. (☎ 202-347-7201; dcchamber.org). You can also ask the concierge at your hotel for help obtaining tickets to a show, finding a tour guide, or pointing you to the best nearby restaurants.

HOW TO GET TO WASHINGTON, D.C.

YOU HAVE SEVERAL OPTIONS when it comes to getting to our nation's capital: by car, train, bus, or plane. We explore these in detail in Part Three: Arriving and Getting Around, but here are some quick points to consider:

- **DON'T DRIVE.** The Capital Beltway, which surrounds the city in the Maryland and Virginia suburbs, is only slightly less congested than New York and Los Angeles. Normal traffic on I-95 can include bumper-to-bumper traffic for up to 60 miles around D.C. Inside I-495 (aka the Beltway), D.C. streets are studded with diagonals, traffic circles, one-way streets, massive construction, and reversible lanes. Street parking near popular tourist sites is severely limited, and garage parking is expensive—around $50 per day in many cases—and often inconvenient. If you do drive, park the car and forget it until you leave. Consider using the Spot Hero app to find and reserve a space in the limited parking garages.

- **TAKE THE TRAIN.** Union Station is the area's train, subway, and bus hub. It is convenient to dozens of cities served by **Amtrak** and only minutes from a downtown hotel by subway; the Union Station Metro is right alongside the tracks and protected from the weather. If your hotel isn't near a Metro stop, you can easily hail a cab or use a ride-hailing app such as Uber or Lyft.

- **TAKE A BUS.** If you're looking for a bargain, there are a number of well-equipped, inexpensive, and easily booked bus lines: **MegaBus, BoltBus, DC2NY, Greyhound, Hola, Vamoose, Tripper Bus,** and others will deposit you at Union Station, Penn Quarter, downtown Bethesda, Rockville, and Arlington.

- **FLY.** Washington is well served by the airline industry. **Reagan National** is the closest airport and has a dedicated Metro station; **Dulles International Airport** is about 45–60 minutes outside of town, and it will have Metro service in 2020. **Baltimore/Washington International Thurgood Marshall Airport,** universally known as BWI, is closer to Baltimore than to D.C., but it is accessible by MARC commuter trains and Amtrak, and taking the train to BWI may save you money. See pages 85–89 for full details.

WHERE *to* GO

THE NEIGHBORHOODS

BEFORE YOU CHOOSE WHERE YOU WANT TO STAY, you should also spend a little time thinking about which Washington attractions you are most interested in touring. There are obvious advantages to being within easy reach, or at least easy commute, of major attractions. Following are brief descriptions of the areas most visited by tourists, plus some neighborhoods where you might find less-expensive hotels, but from where you can easily commute into downtown Washington. These descriptions will help you begin to pinpoint an itinerary and a home base. Remember, because there are no distinct lines between each neighborhood, check a Web-based or conventional map of Washington to see where each hotel is located in relation to the museums and other landmarks mentioned in the descriptions below. Most of the attractions are discussed in more detail in Part Four: Attractions. For descriptions of lodging found in the following neighborhoods, see Part Two: Accommodations. The presence of a nearby Metro stop, whether you actually stay in that neighborhood or not, should factor into your plans.

The Wharf on the Southwest Waterfront

The Wharf is a modern neighborhood that straddles the banks of the Washington Channel in Southwest Washington. Shops, offices, apartments, and restaurants border its mile-long boardwalk, with the stunning Arena Stage on one end and the historic Municipal Fish Market on the other. The Wharf's concrete piers provide access to the water taxis, the Wharf Jitney, and sightseeing boats that cruise the Potomac River. You can also rent paddleboards and kayaks here. Three new hotels offer riverfront and parkland views and are within a 20-minute walk of the National Mall. The Wharf has a recreation area for kids, an ice rink in the winter, rooftop bars open in fair weather, and a music venue called The Anthem, which hosts marquee performers. Residents include apartment dwellers and liveaboards, (people who live full-time on their boats). Another notable feature is East Potomac Park, the narrow peninsula on the other side of the Washington Channel. There you'll find National Park Service–operated hiking and biking trails, a golf course, and tennis courts. To get here, take the Waterfront Metro on the Green Line and/or L'Enfant Plaza station (home of the new Spy Museum), served by multiple lines.

Capitol Riverfront and Navy Yard

This neighborhood, a few blocks south of the National Mall at the confluence of the Potomac and Anacostia Rivers, was developed into a dynamic waterfront community in the last decade. Its renaissance was driven by Nationals Park, where Washington's major league baseball team plays, and by the new Anacostia Riverwalk, a hiker-biker trail that follows the shoreline of the Anacostia River. The Capitol Riverfront is anchored by family-friendly Yards Park, a trapeze school, and Blue Jacket Brewery, along with a cluster of popular eateries. You can also rent kayaks, canoes, and paddleboards to navigate the two rivers. It's a 30-minute walk from Yards Park to the Capitol. The Navy Yard Metro

continued on page 28

Washington at a Glance

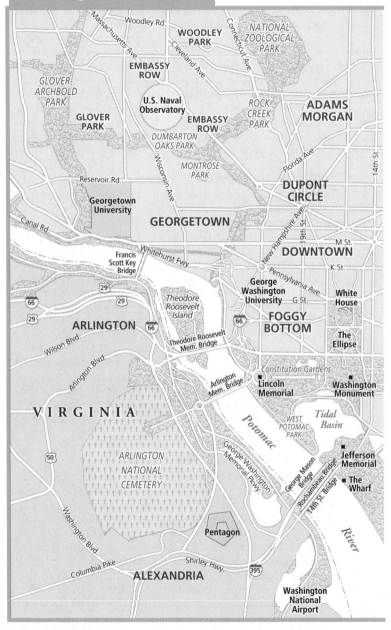

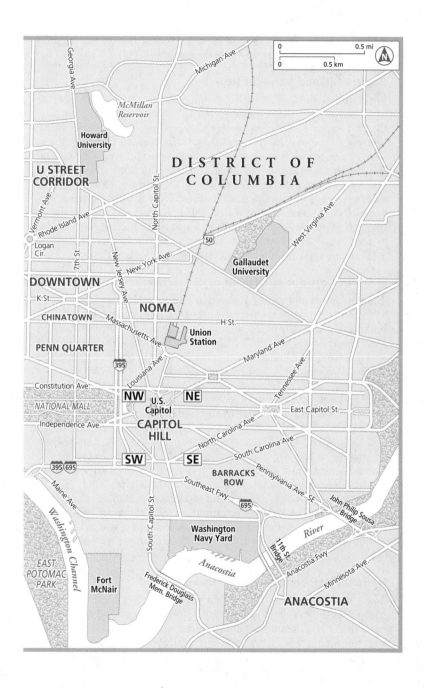

continued from page 25

station is on the Green Line and is named for the historic Washington Navy Yard, an active naval base in the neighborhood.

Capitol Hill and Barracks Row

In addition to the Capitol itself and the sprawling grounds surrounding it, this neighborhood is home to the U.S. Botanic Garden, Supreme Court, Library of Congress, Folger Shakespeare Library, Government Printing Office, and, on the very edges, Congressional Cemetery. Every subway line has at least a couple of stops in the Hill area. Capitol Hill encompasses a residential neighborhood, too, with some of Washington, D.C.'s first homes, dating back to the 1700s. Colorful Eastern Market and the shops and restaurants of Barracks Row function as the neighborhood town center—named for the U.S. Navy members who live in barracks there. On Friday evenings in summer, catch a free performance by the "President's Own" band on their parade deck. Barracks Row is a 25-minute walk from the National Mall and the U.S. Capitol.

H Street Corridor and NoMa

The area north and east of Union Station along H Street NE between 11th and 14th Streets is currently one of the hottest after-hours neighborhoods, with a strip of restaurants, dance clubs, and bars (see Part Six: Entertainment and Nightlife). Although the H Street strip does not have a Metro stop, the D.C. Streetcar connects the neighborhood to Union Station. Politicos live in and around this hipster neighborhood because of the lower rents and its proximity to Capitol Hill. The Atlas Performing Arts Center, nicknamed The Art Beat of H Street, showcases community programs and cultural arts performances. North of H Street NE is NoMa (short for North of Massachusetts Avenue), a neighborhood notable for being diverse and artsy. It's home to Gallaudet University, a prestigious college for students who are deaf or hard of hearing, and Union Market, a mid-20th-century food market with an eclectic mix of vendors, from Rappahannock Oyster Bar to the Capital Candy Jar. The D.C. headquarters of CNN and National Public Radio are also in this neighborhood. The H Street restaurants are a 30-minute walk to the U.S. Capitol. The closest Metro stop is Union Station, while the NoMa neighborhood is served by the NoMa/Gallaudet Metro; both are on the Red Line.

National Mall and the White House

The 1.9 miles between the Capitol steps and the Lincoln Memorial encompasses the most famous museum strip in America and account for more than two dozen attractions, including the National Gallery of Art and the Smithsonian's National Air and Space Museum, National Museum of American History, National Museum of Natural History, National Museum of the American Indian, and National Museum of

African American History and Culture. On a first-time visit, you're likely to want to see the White House, U.S. Capitol, and monuments and memorials positioned in and around the massive National Mall. All these landmarks are spread among parks, including Constitution Gardens (which links the Vietnam Veterans, World War II, and Korean War Memorials) and Potomac Park (which links the Martin Luther King Jr. and the Franklin D. Roosevelt Memorials). The two man-made bodies of water are the Reflecting Pool, in front of the Lincoln Memorial, and the Tidal Basin, a 107-acre reservoir used to harness the power of the tides. The 2.1-mile loop around the Tidal Basin is bordered by the famous cherry trees. The National Park Service operates all the sites and activities that happen on the National Mall, and the area is constantly patrolled by park police. Access the Mall from the Smithsonian (Blue, Silver, and Orange Lines), L'Enfant Plaza (all but the Red Line pass through this huge station), National Archives (Yellow and Green Lines), and Federal Triangle Metro stations (Blue, Silver, and Orange Lines).

Penn Quarter, Chinatown, and Convention Center

North of the National Mall, roughly between 14th Street and Third Street NW, and K Street NW and E Street NW, is the old downtown, which has grown into an effervescent neighborhood with dozens of tourist attractions. Much of the revitalization, like CityCenter DC, grew around the Capital One Arena and the Washington Convention Center. In terms of attractions, this area is also home to the National Portrait Gallery, the Smithsonian American Art Museum, the National Building Museum, the Ford's Theatre museum complex, the Shakespeare Theatre Company at Harman Center for the Arts, and Madame Tussauds wax museum. Many Chinatown restaurants have relocated to suburban Rockville, Maryland, but a few remain. The most notable landmark in D.C.'s Chinatown is the ornate Friendship Arch, a colorful gate that straddles H and Seventh Streets. The neighborhood is a 15-mintue walk to the National Mall. There are several subway stations here, the busiest being Gallery Place/Chinatown (Red Line) and Metro Center (Red Line). There's also Mount Vernon Square, located near the entrance of the Washington Convention Center on the Green and Yellow Lines.

Foggy Bottom

Located west of the White House and north of Constitution Gardens on the National Mall, Foggy Bottom got its funny name from the swampy land on which it was built. The neighborhood is a lively mix of college students, government workers, and businesspeople. The headquarters of the U.S. Department of State and International Monetary Fund are in Foggy Bottom. The neighborhood is the headquarters of George Washington University, the National Academy of Sciences, the Octagon Museum, and the Textile Museum. Other notable sites include Constitution Hall, the Daughters of the American Revolution Museum and Library, The Kennedy Center for the Performing Arts, and, for political junkies, the Watergate complex. Less well known, but worth noting, is the statue of Albert Einstein and the American art collection in the Department of the Interior. The Foggy Bottom Metro houses the Blue, Silver, and Orange Lines and is located on the campus of George Washington University. From the Foggy Bottom Metro station, it's a 15-minute walk to the White House.

Georgetown and West End

Famous in the 1960s and '70s as home to the political establishment and media elite (thanks to the charisma of local residents JFK and Jackie), Georgetown is bustling with upscale boutiques, bars, and a variety of restaurants, some with views of the Potomac River. The historic neighborhood of restored town houses is filled with vintage and familiar name-brand shops and is a good place to shop for antiques and trendy furniture (see pages 282–283 in Part Seven: Shopping for recommendations). Notable historic sites, including the majestic spires of Georgetown University, Dumbarton Oaks, the Old Stone House museum, and Tudor Place, are found among the Federal-style homes here. Spanning the riverfront, the modern Washington Harbour complex, with its dockside restaurants, sits beside Georgetown Waterfront Park. The water taxi and a few cruise tours operate from there. The Chesapeake & Ohio Canal and Towpath begin behind the Four Seasons Hotel and follow the Potomac River upstream for 184 miles to Cumberland, Maryland (see Part Eight: Exercise and Recreation). There is no direct subway service, but both Dupont Circle and Foggy Bottom/GWU Metro stations are a 15-minute walk. The DC Circulator bus runs a regular route from Georgetown to Dupont Circle and Union Station.

Dupont Circle and Logan Circle

Dupont Circle is the center of one of the city's most fashionable neighborhoods, where you'll find elegantly restored town houses, boutiques, restaurants and cafés, bookstores, and art galleries. A stroll down Massachusetts Avenue along Embassy Row leads past embassies and chancelleries, as well as some of Washington's lesser known but exceptional attractions: the Anderson House, the Phillips Collection, and the Woodrow Wilson House. East of Dupont Circle is historic Logan Circle, the only completely residential circle in Washington, where an equestrian statue of General Logan is surrounded by 19th-century Victorian-era brownstones. The neighborhood is the home of Studio Theatre; Duke Ellington grew up playing music in this park. The Dupont Circle Metro station is on the Red Line.

U Street Corridor

Once the heart of black culture in Washington, D.C., U Street offers a plethora of dining, shopping, and nightlife options. Originally nicknamed Black Broadway in the early 20th century, the neighborhood suffered from decades of decline after the riots of 1968. Since the 1990s, it has evolved into a major music district, home to the restored Lincoln and Howard Theaters, U Street Music Hall, DC9, Black Cat, and the 9:30 Club. During the day visitors can peruse the neighborhood's chic boutiques, art galleries, and furniture stores (see Part Seven: Shopping), as well as sample innovative cuisine at some of Washington's finest restaurants. The U Street/African American Civil War Memorial & Museum/Cardozo Metro station is served by the Yellow and Green Lines.

Adams Morgan and Columbia Heights

One of Washington's oldest ethnic-chic neighborhoods, with a heavy emphasis on Hispanic and African cultures, Adams Morgan doesn't offer much in the way of museums or monuments, but the neighborhood features a collection of globally influenced restaurants, eclectic shops, and casual nightclubs. To visit, take a 10-minute walk over Rock Creek Bridge from the Woodley Park/National Zoo Metro station. The majestic Meridian Hill Park, with its acres of terraced gardens and cascading fountains, lies between Adams Morgan and Columbia Heights. The Line DC hotel, built inside a former church, opened in 2017 with a powerhouse lineup of restaurants inside. Along the streets, though, you'll primarily find taquerias, bakeries, and bars, especially on 14th Street NW near the GALA Hispanic Theatre. It's a 35-minute walk from Adams Morgan to the White House. The DC Circulator and multiple Metro buses serve Adams Morgan and Columbia Heights.

Upper Northwest:
Woodley Park, Cleveland Park, and Tenleytown

Everything from Georgetown and Dupont Circle to Friendship Heights is considered the Upper Northwest and is the most affluent quadrant of the city. For this section, we focus on mostly residential neighborhoods that have come to be defined by their Metro stations. Tenleytown Metro serves the American University campus, with its modern Katzen Art Center, and is the closest stop to the Washington National Cathedral. The National Zoo entrance is halfway between the Cleveland Park and Woodley Park Metro stations. Some of the city's most beautiful Victorian homes are in Cleveland Park and Woodley Park, both of which have their own Metro-centered restaurant rows. All Metro stops are on the Red Line.

Rock Creek Park

The great swath of Rock Creek Park—more than twice as large as New York's Central Park—is one of the notable recreational assets of the area. Founded 125 years ago, the park is an oasis in the heart of the city. The Hillwood Museum is located off Beach Drive, on the edge of Rock Creek Park, closest to the Van Ness/UDC Metro station. Also within its borders are Carter Barron Amphitheatre, site of free summer concerts; the National Zoo; Rock Creek Tennis Center, where the Citi Open Tennis Classic is held; a planetarium; a nature center; an equestrian center; a golf course; and numerous playgrounds, picnic areas, hiking trails.

Under the supervision of the National Park Service, Rock Creek Park offers daily programs for families, including nature hikes and mill demonstrations. For more information, see Part Eight: Exercise and Recreation, or go to nps.gov/rocr.

THE MARYLAND SUBURBS

National Harbor

National Harbor is a modern waterfront development that spans more than 350 acres and is located on the shores of the Potomac River, across from Old Town Alexandria. The Marriott Gaylord National Resort & Convention Center is the anchor that draws both vacationers and conventioneers alike, along with special events such as fireworks shows, food festivals, and sporting competitions. The Capitol Wheel, the 175-foot Eye of London–style observation wheel, offers panoramic views of Washington, D.C., and the luxurious MGM National Harbor complex contains a casino, concert venue, boutique mall, and roster of first-rate restaurants. The neighborhood, with its 60 restaurants and 160 stores, is about 6 miles south of Washington, D.C., and offers visitors a resort-like home base. Metrobuses NH1 and NH2 connect National Harbor to multiple Metro stations. A water taxi service departs from the National Harbor Marina for Old Town Alexandria, where you can pick up a free bus to the King Street Metro station. The trip takes about 25 minutes. For more information, visit nationalharbor.com.

Friendship Heights/Chevy Chase

You could call Wisconsin Avenue, which becomes Rockville Pike or MD 355, the Rodeo Drive of Washington—and indeed there was a time when it brought in more retail dollars per square foot than that more-famous Los Angeles address. (Today, CityCenterDC and Tysons Galleria are where you'll find the most exclusive shops.) Western Avenue, which intersects Wisconsin Avenue and Military Road at a five-way intersection, marks the boundary between the District of Columbia and the state of Maryland. The Friendship Heights Metro station, served by the Red Line, is centrally located at that intersection. Along with high-rise luxury apartments and expensive homes, this is a major shopping hub, housing several malls adored by couture and high-end-jewelry addicts alike. See page 285 in Part Seven: Shopping for more on shopping in the Chevy Chase area.

Bethesda and North Bethesda

Bethesda is one of the wealthiest residential communities in the country. You won't find much in the way of attractions, except Strathmore Concert Hall and Rock Creek Park, although in the last few decades, Bethesda and North Bethesda neighborhoods have experienced extensive redevelopment, mostly into multiuse retail centers. These neighborhoods may be good for visitors seeking accommodations that are less expensive yet still feel urban. The area already draws out-of-towners who have business with the National Institutes of Health and Walter Reed military hospitals. Bethesda is a major dining and shopping area and has several large hotels and conference centers. The Bethesda, Grosvenor, and White Flint Metro stations are a 30-minute ride to the National Mall on the Red Line.

Rockville

Continuing up MD 355 (or the Red Line Metro) from Bethesda, you come to Rockville Town Center, with boutiques and excellent ethnic restaurants positioned around county office and judicial buildings. It's a busy area for meetings and corporations, so business lunches and cocktails are quite popular in the neighborhood. Rockville and Twin Brook are on the Red Line for a 50-minute ride to the National Mall.

Silver Spring

The Silver Spring Arts District is another excellent suburban outpost for those who seek easy Metro access to downtown but also wish to save money at less-expensive hotels. Silver Spring is home to the AFI Silver Theatre and Cultural Center, a walkable town center, Montgomery County Community College's Black Box Theatre, and The Cafritz Foundation Arts Center. There's also the Round House Theatre and Education Center, Denizens Brewing Company's Beer Garden, and a collection of modern street art, including a mural of President Harry Truman. The neighborhood is served by Silver Spring Metro station on the Red Line.

THE VIRGINIA SUBURBS
Old Town Alexandria

Like Georgetown, Alexandria is a particularly picturesque area, with waterfront parks and buildings dating back to Colonial times. Streets lined with 18th- and 19th-century homes, along with historic attractions such as the Apothecary Museum, the Carlyle House, and Gadsby's Tavern, are part of this charming community on the shores of the Potomac River. The downtown area is popular with both locals and tourists, who enjoy walking, dining, and shopping. The artist studio/gallery called the Torpedo Factory Art Center and Portside Old Town are popular waterfront destinations. About 20 minutes south of Old Town is George Washington's Mount Vernon property, a must-see if you have time and transportation. Both Metro stops, King Street and Braddock Road on the Yellow Line, are at the edges of the historic district; however, the King Street station provides a free trolley to the waterfront. It's a 50-minute subway ride from the King Street Metro to the Gallery Place Metro.

Tysons Corner and McLean

Tysons is a retail megacenter and will delight visitors who love to shop. After the Tysons Metro station opened, several luxury hotels in the neighborhood became popular options for visitors, thanks to a 30-minute ride to the Metro Center in downtown. The concrete city is anchored by two major shopping malls—Tysons Corner and Tysons Galleria. Along with dozens of restaurants and brand-name stores, American Girl Place is connected to Tysons Corner Mall. Within a short drive is the entry to Great Falls National Park and Scott's Run Nature Preserve, as well as the lovely Wolf Trap Farm Park. The Tysons Metro station is on the Silver Line.

Arlington and Rosslyn

Rosslyn, the high-rise village at the foot of Key Bridge, is a slightly more affordable, convenient option for visitors. Though mostly government and commercial buildings, it's a quick walk to Georgetown, and the area has easy access to waterfront parks and bike paths on the Potomac Heritage Trail. Rosslyn is part of Arlington, which is home to Arlington National Cemetery, the Pentagon, the National 9/11 Pentagon Memorial, and now Amazon's HQ2. Arlington also encompasses Theodore Roosevelt Island, Pentagon City, Crystal City, and Reagan National Airport. The Blue Line Metro stations that serve this area include Arlington Cemetery, Pentagon City, Crystal City/National Place, and Rosslyn. The Yellow Line serves Pentagon, Pentagon City, Crystal City, and Reagan National Airport.

Clarendon and Ballston

Although not as near to D.C. as Rosslyn, these northern Virginia suburbs have been redeveloped around Metro stops as relatively upscale neighborhoods. Clarendon in particular is a dining destination and has an Urban Village Market on Saturdays with vendors and a weekly farmers market on Wednesday afternoons. Ballston is the home of the MedStar Capitals Iceplex, which is open to anyone, and you might get to see the Washington Capitals practicing. See Part Eight: Exercise and Recreation (page 293) for more information.

Reston Town Center

Not far from Dulles International Airport, this compact but sophisticated neighborhood offers shopping, dining, and access to downtown D.C. from two Metro stations. Its urban core is surrounded by homes and parks. The Wiehle/Reston East Metro station has a parking lot; the Reston Town Center Metro does not have parking but is close to development. Both are on the Silver Line.

WHAT *to* PACK

FRANKLY, THE MOST IMPORTANT THING TO CONSIDER when packing is comfortable shoes, and more than one pair of them. This is a culture of concrete and marble, and even if you are using one of the trolleys or shuttles, you're likely to be standing quite a bit. Wearing walking or running shoes during the day is fine, and pick your evening shoes (or boots) with reasonable comfort in mind. Two pairs of comfortable shoes are also useful if it happens to rain or snow—you can wear one pair while the other is drying.

You should plan to walk *a lot* (the National Mall is 2 very long miles), so especially in hot weather, pack double sets of thin socks rather than too-thick ones, and carry some precut moleskin bandages: they offer the best possible protection and won't sweat off.

Washington is a tourist town, but it's also a high-powered center of world politics. Most restaurants have retreated from having a dress code, but a few upscale spots list jackets for gentlemen as "requested." While it's fine to dine in shorts during the day, you'll fit in better dressing up a bit when dining in a moderately upscale restaurant for dinner. In general, polo shirts are fine in spring and fall; a sundress and dress pants will be perfect for evenings out. Also, D.C. buildings are energetically air-conditioned in summer, so consider bringing a sweater to restaurants or museums.

unofficial **TIP**
If you like to read in bed, it might be worth packing one of those mini book lights or using your smartphone flashlight app; hotels are notoriously dim, and your traveling companions may not be on your sleep schedule.

You should bring a raincoat in summer; in winter, you can probably get by with a down coat or a walking coat with a sweater. Gloves and hats are important, of course, but when choosing headgear, make sure to bring something that won't blow off. Washington can get both hot and cold (sometimes in the same day), so in spring and fall, a windbreaker-style coat that you can stuff into a bag is ideal. Many of Washington's museums offer free coat checking, so store those layers and enhance your viewing experience. Women will find a large scarf or shawl a good interim layer in fall and winter, and it will stand in as a sweater (or throw or seat cushion) in an emergency.

Everyone should carry sun protection, including hats and sunscreen, in their travel bag. And seriously consider dressing in layers to deal with changes in weather.

Bring a copy of your passport and other important documents, such as hotel information, as well as a list of any prescription medicines. It's best to store your prescription medicines in carry-on bags, in case your packed bag gets lost. Pacemakers, metal implants, and surgical pins may set off security machines, so a letter from your doctor describing your condition is a wise precaution.

Though over-the-counter medicines are easy to find at local drugstores, you may want to pack travel-size over-the-counter headache and stomach-upset medications. If you're allergic to bee stings, don't forget the antihistamines. Sunscreen and insect repellent are available in individual packets—a great, non-spill space-saver. Stain-removing packets can be helpful too.

Plastic zip-top bags keep soiled and clean clothes separated, keep your underwear together so the luggage inspector doesn't have to sort through them, prevent jewelry from tarnishing and/or snagging your clothes, and prevent shampoos and lotions from leaking out.

SPECIAL TIPS *for*
SPECIAL PEOPLE

TRAVELING WITH CHILDREN
(AND PERHAPS GRANDPARENTS)

WASHINGTON IS SO FULL OF MUST-SEE ICONS—from the U.S. Capitol to the Washington Monument, the White House to President John F. Kennedy's eternal flame, and the Wright Brothers' biplane to giant pandas—that it's easy to get overambitious about an itinerary.

You should consider a few factors when planning a family vacation, especially with small children or seniors. While there are attractions that delight toddlers and preschoolers, many are oriented toward older kids and adults. Consider adding something into your itinerary at least once per day that will please your kids, such as a rest stop at a friendly garden, a visit to a playground, a show for kids, or a ride on the National Mall carousel.

Although the Smithsonian museums have enhanced their exhibits with many more interactive games, children younger than 8 years old might not be enthralled by seeing the entire National Museum of Natural History or National Air and Space Museum. Children age 2 and older will probably enjoy short visits to the art galleries and monuments, but only if you let them outside to walk a bit in between. You might enjoy taking them to the outdoor sculpture gardens, where they can dangle feet in the fountain or walk among the giant art installations. If your child is fussy, the museums have big restaurants and entertaining museum stores where you can find a snack or treat. Most museums are spacious enough for strollers, but they can get very crowded, making it hard to maneuver the big ones.

If your children are younger and you want to minimize the hassle of commuting to and from downtown, look for lodging near—or with short subway commutes to—the Mall and Penn Quarter.

Children and seniors are more susceptible than adults to overheating, sunburn, and dehydration. Be sure to put sunscreen on children in strollers, even if the stroller has a canopy; their exposed foreheads and feet are particularly vulnerable. Small children don't always tell their parents about a developing blister until it's too late; consider using a lunch or bench break to check their feet for hot spots. Similarly, excited children may not inform you or even realize that they're thirsty or overheated. Carry water bottles and drink often.

TIPS FOR INTERNATIONAL TRAVELERS

MOST VISITORS FROM Australia, Chile, Japan, Iceland, Malta, Singapore, South Korea, New Zealand, South Korea, Taiwan, the United Kingdom, and western Europe who stay in the United States fewer than 90 days need only a valid, machine-readable passport, not a visa, and a round-trip or return ticket. Canadian citizens need a passport if arriving by air, but most do not need a visa to enter the United States (though if you have any doubts, you can certainly apply for one). Check the website travel.state.gov under the U.S. Visa Waiver Program.

Citizens of other countries must have a passport good for at least six months beyond the projected end of the visit, as well as a tourist visa, available from any US consulate. Contact consular officials for application forms. There are some countries where, if you visited or were present in that country, you are not eligible for a visa to enter the United States. Check the Terrorist Travel Prevention Act of 2015 for that information. Most current and accurate information can be found by consulting the U.S. Department of State at state.gov/travel or U.S. Customs and Border Protection at cbp.gov/travel/international-visitors.

Check with the local consulate to see whether travelers from your country are currently required to have any inoculations; there are no set requirements to enter the United States, but if there has been any sort of epidemic in your homeland, there may be temporary restrictions.

International visitors should also remember that the United States does not have a national medical program and that if you require medical treatment you will have to pay for it; you may wish to investigate medical and/or travel insurance. However, throughout the United States, if you have a medical, police, or fire emergency, dial 911, free even on a pay telephone, and an ambulance or police cruiser will be dispatched to help you. (For nonemergency police aid in most areas, dial 311.) You can also contact **Traveler's Aid International** in the Washington area at ☎ 202-546-1127 or travelersaid.org. International visitors to Washington who would like a tour conducted in their native language can contact the **Guild of Professional Tour Guides of Washington, D.C.** at washingtondctourguides.com.

If you arrive by air, be prepared to spend as long as 2 hours entering the country and getting through U.S. Customs. US hotels and restaurants generally accept credit and debit cards. Other currencies can be taken to a bank or foreign exchange and turned into dollars.

Two last reminders: The legal drinking age in the United States is 21, something many European travelers forget. And most of Washington's restaurants and all of its cultural facilities are nonsmoking venues.

TRAVELERS WITH SPECIAL NEEDS

WASHINGTON, D.C., IS ONE OF THE MOST ACCESSIBLE CITIES in the world. With the equal-opportunity federal government as the major employer in the area, D.C. provides a good job market for people with disabilities. As a result, the service sector—bus drivers, waiters, ticket sellers, retail clerks, cab drivers, tour guides, and so on—are attuned to the needs of people with disabilities. Check washington.org/dc-information/washington-dc-disability-information for a list of attractions that are particularly welcoming to people with special needs.

For example, the White House has a special entrance on Pennsylvania Avenue for tourists using wheelchairs (you can also borrow one there), and guides frequently allow visually impaired visitors to touch some of the items described during the tour. The U.S. Capitol offers a variety of special services, including wheelchair loans, interpreters for the hard of hearing, Braille and large-type brochures, and sensory aides; for details, go to visitthecapitol.gov and select "Accessibility Services."

The Metro was designed to be accessible from the beginning. As a result, the stations and trains provide optimal services to a wide array of people with special requirements. Elevators provide access to the mezzanine, or ticketing-areas platform, and street level; visit wmata .com/service/elevators-escalators to check whether the elevators at the stations you plan to use are operating. When elevators are out of service (the Metro is constantly struggling with mechanical time-outs and repairs), shuttle buses are provided between the stations that bookend the outage, but depending on your stamina or comfort, you may not wish to go that route.

The edge of the train platform is built with a 14-inch "studded" granite strip that's different in texture from the rest of the station's flooring so that visually impaired passengers can detect the platform edge with a foot or cane. Flashing lights embedded in the granite strip alert deaf or hard-of-hearing passengers that a train is entering the station. Because purchasing a fare card is a strictly visual process, visually impaired passengers must go to the Metro kiosk for assistance. Priority seating for senior citizens and passengers with disabilities is located next to doors in all cars.

Visitors with disabilities who possess a transit ID from their home city can pick up a reduced-fare SmarTrip ID that provides substantial fare discounts. The Metro Disability ID Card is good for a month, but appointments are mandatory at Metro Headquarters, 600 Fifth St. NW near the Judiciary Square Metro's F Street exit. Appointments are available weekdays, 8 a.m.–4 p.m. (until 2:30 p.m. Tuesdays); call ☎ 202-962-1245 or visit wmata.com/accessibility for more information and to download forms for fare discounts.

unofficial **TIP**
In many older parts of Washington, D.C., particularly Adams Morgan, Capitol Hill, Dupont Circle, Georgetown, and Old Town Alexandria, restaurants and museums may not be wheelchair accessible; however, some that were not previously accessible may have been renovated by the time you visit— check in advance.

The Smithsonian and the National Park Service, agencies that run the lion's share of popular sights in Washington, offer top-notch services to people with disabilities: entrance ramps, barrier-free exhibits, elevator service to all floors, and accessible restrooms and water fountains. Visually impaired visitors can pick up large-print brochures, audio tours, and raised-line drawings of museum artifacts at many Smithsonian museums. For special tours or information about accessibility for visitors with disabilities, contact the individual museum or the Smithsonian Accessibility Office at ☎ 202-633-2921, or e-mail the Accessibility Program at access@si.edu. Information is also available at si.edu/accessibility. For information on the National Zoo's provisions for disabled visitors, go to nationalzoo.si.edu/visit/accessibility. For specific information about accessibility on the National Mall, check nps.gov to see what is offered in the way of services for people with disabilities at each of the memorials and at Arlington Cemetery.

Both Old Town Trolleys (trolleytours.com/washington-dc) and Gray Line (graylinedc.com) offer hop-on/hop-off, narrated tours of the Mall, monuments, and other area historic sites. These operators offer handicapped-accessible vehicles if you make a reservation at least 24 hours (Old Town) or 48 hours (Gray Line) in advance.

Unlike the Trolleys or Gray Line, the DC Circulator buses don't provide narration, but they do allow customers to get on and off at all the major monuments and several Smithsonian museums for only $1 (good for 2 hours of riding if you use a SmarTrip card to pay initially; otherwise, you will have to pay $1 each time you board). Circulator buses have designated spaces for wheelchairs, and all have motorized ramps for lifting scooters or wheelchairs on and off the bus. These buses do not require riders to make advance reservations, but they do have restricted hours—summer hours are 7 a.m.–8 p.m., and winter hours are 7 a.m.–7 p.m. For more information, visit dccirculator.com.

In spite of all the services available to disabled visitors, it's still a good idea to call ahead to any facility you plan to visit and confirm that services are in place and that the particular exhibit or gallery you wish to see is still available.

A **CALENDAR** of **FESTIVALS** and **EVENTS**

January

WASHINGTON RESTAURANT WEEK Early to mid-January. More than 150 restaurants offer fixed-price lunch ($22) and dinner ($36) menus; ramw.org or washington.org.

MARTIN LUTHER KING JR. BIRTHDAY EVENTS On the national holiday of January 21, the city hosts a variety of commemorative events at various sites.

MARYLAND POLAR BEAR PLUNGE Late January. At Sandy Point State Park in Annapolis, swimmers take a chilly dip in the Chesapeake Bay to raise money for Special Olympics; plungemd.com.

February

CHINESE NEW YEAR PARADE Mid-February. Marching bands and lion and dragon dancers wind through Chinatown and around the Gallery Place Metro Station; chinesenewyearfestival.org.

ABRAHAM LINCOLN'S BIRTHDAY A wreath-laying ceremony, music, and dramatic readings of Lincoln's speeches inside the Lincoln Memorial; ☎ 202-426-6841, nps.gov/linc.

GEORGE WASHINGTON'S BIRTHDAY PARADE Mid-February. The nation's largest, with marching bands, floats, military reenactors, and other units on the streets of Old Town Alexandria; ☎ 703-829-6640, washington birthday.net.

WASHINGTON DOLLAR DAYS: TOUR FOR A BUCK In honor of George Washington's birthday month, Tudor Place in Georgetown offers tours for $1; tudorplace.org.

March

ST. PATRICK'S DAY PARADE Mid-March. Old Town Alexandria's annual parade of floats, bands, and Irish dancers is usually the first Saturday of March; ballyshaners.org.

SHAMROCK FEST March 17 (St. Patrick's Day). This music festival features carnival rides, dancing, food vendors, and party games. The main attractions are the multiple stages with live bands and DJs, including an occasional big name as headliner. The event includes a separate area for VIPs; shamrockfest.com.

ST. PATRICK'S DAY PARADE Usually held on the Sunday before March 17. Irish dancers, bagpipers, and marching bands salute all things Irish along Constitution Avenue NW from 7th to 17th Streets; ☎ 202-670-0317, dcstpatsparade.com.

BLOSSOM KITE FESTIVAL Late March. Competitions in design, performance, and other categories; ☎ 877-442-5666, nationalcherryblossom festival.org.

WHITE HOUSE EASTER EGG ROLL Colored-egg collecting and entertainment held the Monday after Easter, rain or shine. Open to children age 12 and younger with supervising adults. Free tickets are distributed through an online lottery system; ☎ 202-456-1414, whitehouse.gov1 .info/easter-egg-roll.

EASTER MONDAY: A WASHINGTON FAMILY TRADITION Late March to mid-April. The free annual Easter Monday event offers an Easter egg hunt, field games, live music, and food vendors at the National Zoo; ☎ 202-633-4800, nationalzoo.si.edu/events/easter-monday.

April

THOMAS JEFFERSON'S BIRTHDAY April 13. A military honor guard and a wreath-laying ceremony salute the third president; noon at the Jefferson Memorial; ☎ 202-245-4676; nps.gov/nama.

NATIONAL CHERRY BLOSSOM FESTIVAL The blooming cherry trees surrounding the Tidal Basin are the centerpiece of this two-week festival of concerts, cooking and dance demonstrations, children's activities, restaurant specials, the National Cherry Blossom Parade along Constitution Avenue NW, and the street festival on Pennsylvania Avenue; dates vary each year; ☎ 877-442-5666, nationalcherryblossomfestival.org.

WASHINGTON INTERNATIONAL FILM FESTIVAL Mid- to late April. Scores of new American and foreign films are screened in theaters across town during the annual Filmfest D.C.; ☎ 202-274-5782, filmfestdc.org.

SHAKESPEARE'S BIRTHDAY Mid- to late April. Annual open house with free cake, children's activities, theater tours, dramatic readings, medieval crafts, and entertainment at Folger Shakespeare Library; ☎ 202-544-4600, folger.edu.

EARTH DAY April 22. The celebration on the Mall, one of the nation's largest, includes music, demonstrations of green technology, celebrity speakers, and vendors; ☎ 202-518-0044, earthday.net.

SMITHSONIAN CRAFT SHOW Late April. Juried artists from across the country display their glasswork, furniture, textiles, and other creations at the National Building Museum; smithsoniancraftshow.org.

WHITE HOUSE SPRING GARDEN TOURS Late April (weather permitting). Free, timed tickets distributed each day on a first-come basis at Ellipse Visitor Pavilion, 15th and E Streets NW at 9 a.m.; ☎ 202-456-2200, whitehouse.gov.

GEORGETOWN HOUSE TOUR Last Saturday. Tour private homes in Washington's Georgetown district, with a panel discussion and parish tea. Go to St. John's Episcopal Church at 10 a.m.; tour starts at 11 a.m. and lasts all day; ☎ 202-338-1796, georgetownhousetour.com.

May

PASSPORT DC All of May. D.C.'s embassies open their doors to visitors during this month-long annual event. There are festivals, performances, and the opportunity to sample international cuisine at the open houses of participating embassies; ☎ 202-661-7581, cultural tourismdc.org.

NATIONAL HARBOR FOOD AND WINE FESTIVAL First weekend. Well-known chefs gather for cooking demonstrations, and a wide variety of food and beverage vendors offer samples of at this waterfront festival; nationalharbor.com/event/wine-food-festival.

NATIONAL CATHEDRAL FLOWER MART Early May. With lavish exhibits, floral displays, food vendors, musical performances, and craft sales, this annual fundraising event for the church gardens is held on the grounds of the National Cathedral; ☎ 202-537-6200, cathedral.org.

NATIONAL ZOO ZOOFARI Mid-May. This annual fundraising gala features tastings by more than 100 area restaurants, international wines, entertainment, animal demonstrations, and a silent auction at the National Zoo; ☎ 202-633-4456 (tickets), nationalzoo.si.edu.

MOUNT VERNON SPRING WINE FESTIVAL AND SUNSET TOUR Mid-May. Sample wines from Virginia vineyards, learn more about George Washington's wine-making efforts, and enjoy live jazz at the first president's estate. Advance purchase is recommended; ☎ 703-780-2000 (information), mountvernon.org.

PREAKNESS STAKES Third weekend. This is the second jewel in thoroughbred horse racing's Triple Crown, held at Pimlico Race Course in Baltimore; ☎ 410-542-9400, preakness.com.

NATIONAL MEMORIAL DAY CONCERT Last Sunday. The National Symphony Orchestra and guest performers from Broadway, pop, R&B, country, and more in a free concert on the West Lawn of the U.S. Capitol; ☎ 202-426-6841, pbs.org/national-memorial-day-concert.

MEMORIAL DAY CEREMONIES Last Monday. Commemorative events and wreath layings are scheduled at Arlington National Cemetery and the Vietnam Veterans, World War II, National Law Enforcement Officers, Navy, Air Force, and Women in Military Service for America Memorials. Marching bands and veterans units from all over the country parade down Constitution Avenue, and the U.S. Navy Band performs a free concert at the U.S. Navy Memorial; www.navyband.navy.mil and culturecapital.com.

June

CAPITAL PRIDE FESTIVAL Early to mid-June. A parade Saturday in the Dupont Circle area and a street festival Sunday along Pennsylvania Avenue with crafts and food vendors wind up a weeklong celebration by the area's LGBTQ residents; ☎ 202-719-5304, capitalpride.org.

DC JAZZ FESTIVAL Mid- to late June. Dozens of concerts at nearly 50 venues around town, including the Kennedy Center, The Anthem, and the Mall; dcjazzfest.org.

GIANT NATIONAL CAPITAL BARBECUE BATTLE Last weekend in June. Teams from across the country compete to win prizes for best barbecued pork, chicken, and beef. Entertainment on multiple stages, cooking demonstrations by celebrity chefs, children's activities, and food vendors, along Pennsylvania Avenue between 9th and 14th Streets NW; ☎ 202-488-6990, bbqdc.com.

SMITHSONIAN FOLKLIFE FESTIVAL Late June to early July. Annual festival celebrates the food, music, arts, and culture of a specific nation, region, state, or theme; on the Mall between 7th and 14th Streets; ☎ 202-633-6440, festival.si.edu.

July

SHAKESPEARE THEATRE FREE FOR ALL While the theater offers programs year-round, such as happy hours, book discussions, and readings, during the month of July they offer free performances at Sidney Harman Hall through both same-day and lottery tickets; ☎ 202-547-1122, shakespearetheatre.org.

NATIONAL MALL FOURTH OF JULY CELEBRATION July 4. Independence Day is commemorated with the National Independence Day Parade along Constitution Avenue NW, the Capitol Fourth concert by the National Symphony Orchestra, guest musical celebrities on the West Lawn of the U.S. Capitol, living history actors at the Frederick Douglass Historic Site in Anacostia, and fireworks over the Washington Monument grounds; ☎ 202-426-6841, july4thparade.com.

DC BLACK THEATRE & ARTS FESTIVAL Early July. A multiday festival at the THEARC Theater celebrating stories from around the world through 150 performances with national artists, writers, filmmakers, and musicians; ☎ 202-889-5901, bbardc.org.

USA/ALEXANDRIA BIRTHDAY CELEBRATION Mid-July. The Alexandria Symphony Orchestra celebrates the city of Alexandria's birthday (it's older than D.C.) and America's birthday with a free concert that includes Pyotr Tchaikovsky's "1812 Overture" with cannon fire, followed by fireworks at Oronoco Bay Park on the Potomac; ☎ 703-746-5592, visitalexandriava.com.

August

CITI OPEN TENNIS CLASSIC Late July to first week in August. The US Open men's tennis tour (and young women's pros) stop at FitzGerald Tennis Center in Rock Creek Park in preparation for New York, complete with top-ranked players; citiopentennis.com.

WASHINGTON RESTAURANT WEEK Early to mid-August. More than 150 area restaurants offer fixed-price lunch ($22) and dinner ($35) menus; ramw.org.

September

LABOR DAY CONCERTS Sunday before Labor Day. National Symphony Orchestra performs a free concert featuring patriotic music on the West Lawn of the U.S. Capitol or the Kennedy Center (depending on the weather); ☎ 202-467-4600. Monday, the U.S. Navy Band and Sea Chanters perform at the U.S. Navy Memorial; ☎ 202-433-2525, www.navyband.navy.mil.

LIBRARY OF CONGRESS NATIONAL BOOK FESTIVAL First weekend. More than 70 authors of all types gather for readings, signings, and literacy exhibits; formerly held on the Mall but now inside the Washington Convention Center; ☎ 202-707-5000, loc.gov/bookfest.

DC BLUES FESTIVAL Early September. Concerts and band battles at the American Legion Post 41 in Silver Spring. Event includes performances by several bands. The organization hosts blues concerts year-round; dcblues.org.

DC BEER WEEK Early to mid-September. This eight-day festival celebrates the capital region's craft beer community though events, tastings, and seminars; dcbeerweek.net.

ROSSLYN JAZZ FEST Early to mid-September. Daylong free outdoor concerts by local and national jazz stars at Gateway Park (near the Rosslyn Metro station); ☎ 703-276-7759, rosslynva.org.

ALEXANDRIA KING STREET ART FESTIVAL Second weekend. An outdoor festival features sculptures, paintings, photography, fused glass, jewelry, and other works by nearly 200 artists and artisans along King Street in Old Town Alexandria; ☎ 561-746-6615, visitalexandriava .com and artfestival.com.

ADAMS MORGAN DAY FESTIVAL Second Sunday. Celebrates Washington's most famous multicultural neighborhood with entertainment, children's activities, food vendors, and more; ☎ 502-544-5765, admoday.com.

SILVER SPRING JAZZ FESTIVAL Mid-September. Daylong free outdoor concerts by local and national jazz stars at the Silver Spring Civic Building, Veterans Plaza (near Silver Spring Metro station); ☎ 240-777-5300, silverspringdowntown.com.

WALKING TOWN DC Mid- to late September. Public tours of well-known and lesser-known neighborhoods at various times of the day; cultural tourismdc.org.

H STREET FESTIVAL Late September. Nearly a mile of food vendors, crafts, concerts, performances, and kids' activities, plus a beer garden, positioned along H Street NE; hstreet.org.

October

WHITE HOUSE FALL GARDEN TOURS Mid-October (weather permitting). Free, timed tickets distributed each day on a first-come, first-served basis at the Ellipse Visitor Pavilion, 15th and E Streets NW, at 7:30 a.m.; ☎ 202-456-1111, whitehouse.gov.

TASTE OF DC Third weekend. The mid-Atlantic's biggest food festival offers live music, cooking demos, tastings, art vendors, and a beer garden; thetasteofdc.org.

BOO AT THE ZOO Last weekend. Halloween trick-or-treating, animal demonstrations, and zookeeper talks at the National Zoo; ☎ 202-633-4800, nationalzoo.si.edu.

MARINE CORPS MARATHON Last Sunday. Tens of thousands of runners start at the Iwo Jima Memorial and follow a course along the Mall and back to the memorial; ☎ 800-786-8762 or 800-RUN-USMC, marine marathon.com.

November

VETERANS DAY CEREMONIES November 11. Commemorations and wreath-laying ceremonies at Arlington National Cemetery; the National Marine Corps Museum; and the Navy, Air Force, World War II, Vietnam Veterans, Vietnam Women's, and Women in Military Service for America Memorials; ☎ 202-426-6841, va.gov/opa/vetsday.

GAYLORD NATIONAL RESORT'S ICE! Mid-November through early January. Families love touring the huge ice sculptures housed in a tent at National Harbor; ☎ 301-965-4000, nationalharbor.com/events.

MOUNT VERNON BY CANDLELIGHT Thanksgiving weekend through early December. Tour the first president's estate by candlelight, along with music, holiday cooking, and fireside caroling; ☎ 703-780-2000, mountvernon.org.

LIGHT UP THE WHARF Late November. The waterfront neighborhood kicks off the holidays with a tree lighting and Santa meet and greet at District Pier; wharfdc.com.

D.C. METROPOLITAN COOKING & ENTERTAINING SHOW Late November. Celebrity chefs, demonstrations, book signings, specialty food vendors, and more at the Washington Convention Center; metrocookingdc.com.

December

KENNEDY CENTER HOLIDAY FESTIVAL All of November and December. The Kennedy Center celebrates the holidays with free performances (including popular *Messiah* sing-alongs) and ticketed concerts; ☎ 202-467-4600, kennedy-center.org.

ALEXANDRIA SCOTTISH WALK Early December. Annual parade of Scottish bands in Old Town Alexandria; ☎ 703-549-7078, alexandriasea port.org.

THE WASHINGTON BALLET'S *NUTCRACKER* All month. This classic holiday ballet has elaborate costumes and features the city's premier dance company at the Warner Theatre; ☎ 202-363-3606, washingtonballet.org.

NATIONAL MENORAH LIGHTING Event coincides with the Hanukkah holiday. Families are invited to attend the free annual ceremony of the lighting of the National Menorah on the grounds of the White House; nationalmenorah.org.

PEARL HARBOR DAY December 7. A ceremony commemorates the 1941 attack on Pearl Harbor at the Navy Memorial; navymemorial.org. Friends of World War II Memorial hosts "Remembering Pearl Harbor" on the National Mall; wwiimemorialfriends.org.

PATHWAY OF PEACE Mid-December. The lighting of the National Christmas Tree on the Ellipse, usually by the president and first lady, kicks off a month of free holiday activities, including nightly choral performances and a display of lighted trees representing the states and territories; free passes issued in early November; thenationaltree.org or nps.gov/whho/planyourvisit/national-christmas-tree.htm.

HISTORIC ALEXANDRIA CANDLELIGHT TOURS Mid-December. Tour sites include the Lee-Fendall House, Gadsby's Tavern Museum, and the Carlyle House in Old Town Alexandria, with music, colonial dancing, seasonal decorations, and light refreshments; ☎ 703-746-4554, alexandriava.gov.

NEW YEAR'S EVE Family-oriented, alcohol-free First Night festivals with concerts, children's entertainers, and other activities take place in Alexandria and Annapolis, among others; visitannapolis.org, firstnight alexandria.org.

PART TWO

ACCOMMODATIONS

DECIDING WHERE *to* STAY

BECAUSE THE BEST WAY TO GET AROUND Washington, D.C., is on the Metro, and because most major attractions are also Metro-accessible, we recommend you consider a hotel within reasonable walking distance of a Metro station. Of course, with ride-hailing services such as Uber and Lyft, and multiple bus services, visitors have more flexibility. But the D.C. area is burdened with horrendous traffic, so any opportunity to avoid it just makes sense. To help you decide where to stay, read about Washington's neighborhoods in the "Where to Go" section in Part One: Planning Your Visit (page 24).

WASHINGTON, D.C.'S ICONIC HOTELS

ONE WAY TO SOAK UP THE HISTORY OF THE CITY is to stop by or stay in one of Washington's historic hotels. The following establishments have notable stories to tell, and all treat their guests like VIPs.

THE WILLARD INTERCONTINENTAL HOTEL Located a block from the White House, The Willard was first a row house for journeymen in 1818. In 1901 the hotel was torn down to build an elegant Beaux Arts–style hotel similar to what you see today. US presidents first began staying there in 1853, beginning with Millard Fillmore. In 1861 Abraham Lincoln took up residence with his family for 10 days prior to his inauguration. The hotel fell on hard times but was renovated to its current glory in 1986. The Willard's regal edifice and aristocratic interior are worth seeing, as is the memorabilia from various guests who've stayed there. See notes written by Julia Ward Howe, who penned the lyrics to "The Battle Hymn of the Republic" while staying at the hotel. Dr. Martin Luther King Jr. wrote his legendary "I Have a Dream" speech there. The Willard's Round Robin Bar claims to be the spot where Kentucky senator Henry Clay introduced the bourbon mint julep. The term *lobbyist* came from the many influence peddlers lurking in the hotel's lobby, hoping for an audience with President Ulysses S. Grant.

The hotel's list of guests, from Charles Dickens, Harry Houdini, and the Dalai Lama to George Clooney, is too long to list.

THE HAY-ADAMS Location, location, location . . . but that's not the only reason President Barack Obama and his family spent the fortnight before his inauguration at the famed Hay-Adams. Formerly the home of Lincoln's private secretary, John Hay, and author Henry Adams (the grandson and great-grandson of presidents), it retains much of the look and sophistication of that mid-19th-century era. Located at the corner of Lafayette Park, the view from its west-facing windows is of the White House grounds and President's Park. The cocktail lounge, Off the Record, is a favorite among powerful politicos.

W HOTEL Known for almost a century as Hotel Washington, the W affords views of the White House, as well as the Treasury and Lincoln Memorial. The hotel and POV, its rooftop bar, attract celebrity patrons, including Taylor Swift, Lady Gaga, Calvin Klein, Leonardo DiCaprio, and, in yesteryear, Marilyn Monroe and Elvis Presley. Italianate on the outside, it is ultra mod on the inside.

THE MAYFLOWER HOTEL About four blocks from the White House, The Mayflower has long been nicknamed the Grande Dame of Washington and has hosted a presidential inaugural ball every four years since Calvin Coolidge's day. President Franklin D. Roosevelt rehearsed his "fear itself" speech here; President Harry Truman, who kept a room at the hotel after leaving 1600 Pennsylvania Ave., called it "the second-best address in Washington." Its Edgar Bar & Kitchen was named for FBI director J. Edgar Hoover, who dined on chicken soup and cottage cheese every day here for two decades. In the hotel's Chinese Room, Winston Churchill was once heard from a distance whispering an off-color joke, thanks to the room's unique acoustics.

THE JEFFERSON This Beaux Arts beauty was originally built as an upscale apartment building in 1923. In 1955 the apartments were transformed into a hotel that wins more awards than any other in the city. Inspired by its namesake, Thomas Jefferson, it encompasses Monticello-inspired architectural elements, such as a parquet floor, historical artifacts, and a silk mural of Jefferson's vineyard. Quill, the elegant lounge, has a terrace and an alcove with a library full of signed books by famous guests, like President George W. Bush, who stayed here before his inauguration in 2001, and Barbra Streisand, who is said to be a fan of the hotel.

THE WATERGATE HOTEL Recently reopened after extensive renovations, this luxury hotel is part of the Watergate Complex and has always attracted some of the capital's most glamorous and well-known residents, including Supreme Court Justice Ruth Bader Ginsburg, actress Elizabeth Taylor, and singer Placido Domingo. It offers guests the opportunity to stay in Room 214, where the notorious break-in occurred in 1972 during President Nixon's reelection campaign. The Scandal Room has memorabilia from the 1970s, along with "Cover Up" robes to wear while you're there. It's worth visiting to enjoy cocktails at the Top of the Gate, with the bar's sweeping views of the skyline.

TABARD INN The oldest continuously running hotel in Washington, the Tabard Inn opened its doors in 1922 in the fashionable Dupont Circle neighborhood, and many well-known chefs have gotten their start in the hotel's kitchen. Every room is unique, filled with eclectic furniture and vintage flourishes.

ST. REGIS WASHINGTON, D.C. This glamorous 1926 landmark, with its Renaissance-inspired carved ceiling, opulent lobby, and luxurious guest rooms, feels more European than American. The St. Regis has one of the top afternoon tea programs in the city and is renowned for its impeccable service. Celebrities, dignitaries, and royalty, including Audrey Hepburn, Cher, and President Ronald Reagan, have flocked here over the years.

TRUMP INTERNATIONAL HOTEL (formerly the Old Post Office) The iconic Old Post Office was restored and turned into a luxury hotel in late 2016. The hotel is located a few blocks from the White House and has become a favorite hangout of international visitors and lobbyists. The property retains the historic character of the Old Post Office with its nine-story atrium and Museum & Clock Tower, which is operated by the National Park Service and is open daily, 9 a.m.–5 p.m. Admission to the Museum & Clock Tower is free, and at the top you have a bird's-eye view of the city.

B&BS

B&BS CAN BE PLEASANT OPTIONS and feel more homey than hotels. They offer more of a neighborhood experience—ideally with a subway stop, which generally means dining and services nearby—and with the benefit of a built-in source of information in the hosts. Here are some questions to ask before making a reservation:

- Are young children (or pets) allowed? • Do all the rooms have private baths or showers?
- If applicable, are the facilities wheelchair-accessible? • What is the cancellation policy?

Among the websites with information on Washington-area B&Bs are abba.com, the site of the American Bed and Breakfast Association; bedandbreakfastdc.com; and iloveinns.com. Select Registry (selectregistry.com) is a network of upscale B&Bs and inns that maintain rigorous standards of quality, ambience, and hospitality in order to retain annual membership. The **Embassy Circle Guest House** has achieved this designation, but there are other excellent B&Bs, such as **Akwaaba Inn** (page 69), in the D.C. area.

unofficial **TIP**
If you expect to stay for an extended period, check the B&B websites; some list furnished apartments that are homier than hotel suites and are located in more residential areas.

LUXURY HOTELS AND RESORTS

WHEN YOU'RE LOOKING FOR THE HIGHEST LEVEL of service, amenities, and luxury, there are a few websites worth visiting: In addition to selectregistry.com, mentioned above, **Historic Hotels of America** (historichotels.org) represents historic hotels that meet exemplary standards. Two other options include hotels recognized as AAA Four and Five Diamond Hotels (aaa.com/diamonds/diamond-awards) or Forbes 5-Star Hotels (forbestravelguide.com/award-winners). These hotels are rigorously vetted for location, amenities, style, and service.

VACATION RENTALS

VACATION-RENTAL COMPANIES have millions of live vacation listings and appeal to those seeking longer visits or more space. Three of the most popular and reputable companies offering short-stay rentals are **FlipKey** (from TripAdvisor Rentals), **VRBO,** and **LuxBnB.** Typically, vacation rentals are more spacious than a single hotel room and are often located in residential neighborhoods. Some provide free parking and free laundry facilities. Listings may be sorted by price, dates, location, number of bedrooms, neighborhood, child-friendly accommodations, and so on. The owner of the rental property determines cost. We recommend you read reviews of the property under consideration on the vacation-rental website. Fees vary, but most rentals require advance payment. Many require an additional deposit up front for damages. This deposit should be refunded within 30 days, unless damage occurs. One way to avoid losing your damage deposit is to look around the house when you first arrive and report any problems you encounter directly to the owner. Before you leave on your trip, ask questions of the owner, like "Where do I pick up a key?" "Is the rental near public transportation and, if so, which ones?" and "Where do I park?"

    Airbnb is a community marketplace where individuals offer space in their homes or rental properties to visitors. Rentals can be as small as one guest room in an occupied house or as large as a multi-bedroom apartment or entire home. Airbnb listings are popular in the Washington, D.C., area, and the service has a variety of listings in both downtown and the surrounding suburbs. Some places charge less than any D.C. hotel room would cost, and many have more than one room, which can be especially nice for families. However, look carefully at the additional fees above the quoted rate. These fees are for cleaning, taxes, and damage deposits. Airbnb's community of reviewers help potential customers know what to expect, so it's important to read their comments when making a decision. Prices range from $26 to $520 per night and vary based on the number of bedrooms and bathrooms. Travelers can pay by PayPal or credit card, with a booking fee of 6%–12% added on.

THE BEST HOTELS BY NEIGHBORHOOD

ALL OF THE HOTELS RECOMMENDED BELOW have been vetted by our team. We offer an array of properties in the top neighborhoods, with room rates that vary by season. We rate them as expensive, moderate, and inexpensive; however, the time of year can substantially affect rates (such as increases during cherry blossom season). We've called out our personal favorites with a 🌀 icon.

With so many families visiting D.C., we pay special attention to what makes an excellent family hotel. Roomy accommodations, in-room fridge, great pool (or access to one), complimentary breakfast, and programs for kids are a few of the things we researched when selecting top hotels among hundreds of properties in the area. Look for the 😊 icon for our family-friendly picks.

Although we would all love to stay at one of Washington D.C.'s super-luxury hotels (and there are many), the properties we list here offer the best value, based on access to major attractions, quality of service, tastefulness of furnishings and decor, state of repair, cleanliness, cost, and size of standard rooms. We describe each selection, noting nearby dining options, whether the hotel is pet-friendly and has a refrigerator in the room, and the maximum number of occupants allowed in one guest room. We group the hotels and motels into specific sections of town, noting access to downtown attractions such as the National Mall and subway stations. Our star ratings apply to Washington, D.C., properties only and do not necessarily correspond to ratings awarded by Forbes, AAA, or other travel critics.

OVERALL STAR RATINGS

★★★★★ **Superior hotels** *Tasteful and luxurious by any standard*

★★★★ **Extremely nice hotels** *High-quality rooms, convenient location, excellent service*

★★★ **Nice hotels** *Offers value for a lower price and meets high standards*

★★* **Adequate hotels** *Clean, comfortable, and functional without frills—like a Motel 6*

---

* *Washington, D.C., is an expensive city, so very few hotels in downtown are rated with two stars. To find lower prices, consider staying in suburban Maryland or Virginia.*

THE WHARF ON THE SOUTHWEST WATERFRONT

 ## Hyatt House Washington, D.C./The Wharf
★★★★★   MODERATE

725 Wharf St. SW, ☎ 202-554-1234, hyatt.com

Rate per night $180–$250. **Pool** Yes. **Fridge in room** No. **Pet-friendly** Yes. **Maximum occupants per room** 4. **Nearby dining** Del Mar de Fabio Trabocchi, Kith/Kin, Lupo Marino, Shake Shack, Kirwan's on the Wharf, Hank's Oyster Bar.

THIS MODERN, NEW HOTEL has an array of suites, including a one-bedroom penthouse and one-bedroom suites, some with views of the river and all with sleeper sofas to accommodate additional guests. The hotel is connected to its upscale sister property, Canopy by Hilton. They share a heated rooftop pool and fitness center. The Hyatt House rate includes a buffet breakfast. Staying in the Wharf neighborhood puts you in the middle of pet- and kid-friendly activities like boat trips. You'll also have access to a free shuttle to the National Mall playground, an ice rink in winter, a long boardwalk to explore, and several casual restaurants and shops at your doorstep.

 ## InterContinental Washington, D.C.–The Wharf
★★★★★   MODERATE–EXPENSIVE

801 Wharf St. SW, ☎ 202-800-0844, ihg.com

Rate per night $220–$322. Pool Yes. Fridge in room Yes. Pet-friendly No. Maximum occupants per room 4. Nearby dining Del Mar de Fabio Trabocchi, Kith/Kin, Lupo Marino, Shake Shack, Kirwan's on the Wharf, Hank's Oyster Bar.

IF YOU'RE YOUNG-AT-HEART and looking for a D.C. neighborhood that is lively day and night, then staying at The Wharf is perfect for you. This new hotel pampers guests with sumptuous furnishings; a sparkling fitness center; a rooftop pool; and sweeping views of the marina, East Potomac Park, and the Potomac River. Walk to the new live-music venue, The Anthem; make s'mores on the boardwalk fire pit; and tour the historic Municipal Fish Market.

Mandarin Oriental Washington, D.C.
★★★★★ EXPENSIVE

1330 Maryland Ave. SW, ☎ 202-554-8588, mandarinoriental.com

Rate per night $250–$550. Pool Yes. Fridge in room No. Pet-friendly No. Maximum occupants per room 4. Nearby dining Potbelly Sandwich Shop, Five Guys, Municipal Fish Market, Officina, Rappahannock Oyster Bar.

IF YOU'RE WILLING TO SPLURGE to stay at D.C.'s posh Asian-influenced hotel, with panoramic views of the Potomac River and a quick walk to the National Mall, then this is your hotel. The place is almost always full, due to its location, first-class service, and popularity with business travelers. Yet it's still worth investigating, especially if you're traveling during a quieter time (unfortunately, that's not during school breaks). Guest rooms are luxurious, with marble tubs, Asian-inspired decor, and balconies. It's just steps away from Washington's historic Municipal Fish Market and The Wharf, a sprawling entertainment development on the waterfront. The hotel is also known for its first-class spa and beautiful Empress Lounge, so you can still experience the Mandarin, even if you're not staying there.

CAPITOL RIVERFRONT AND NAVY YARD

kids!
Courtyard Washington Capitol Hill/Navy Yard
★★★½ INEXPENSIVE–MODERATE

140 L St. SE, ☎ 202-479-0027, marriott.com

Rate per night $180–$300. Pool Yes. Fridge in room Yes. Pet-friendly No. Maximum occupants per room 4. Nearby dining BlueJacket Brewery, Five Guys, Starbucks, Gordon Biersch Brewing, Red Hook Oyster Bar, Subway.

JUST A FEW BLOCKS FROM NATIONALS PARK, this Courtyard continues to grow in popularity, thanks to amenities like a spa, nail bar, heated indoor pool, whirlpool, fitness center, and coffee bar. Guests can walk to Washington Canal Park, Nationals Park, or the nearby Anacostia Riverwalk Trail, which stretches for several miles and has water features and play areas for kids. The Navy Yard Metro station is one block away, which makes getting to the National Mall easy and quick. The hotel is quite large, with comfortable, clean rooms. Double rooms have two queen beds, while suites include sleeper sofas and separate living areas. Some rooms even have a view of the Washington Monument. Ask about their Nationals Baseball packages.

continued on page 56

Washington, D.C., Accommodations

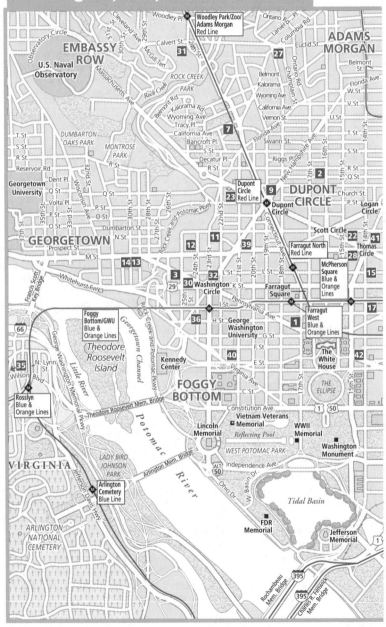

1. AKA White House
2. Akwaaba Inn
3. Avenue Suites Georgetown
4. Capitol Hill Hotel
5. The Conrad Washington DC
6. Courtyard Washington Capitol Hill/Navy Yard
7. Courtyard Washington DC/ Dupont Circle
8. Courtyard Washington/ Downtown Convention Center
9. The Dupont Circle
10. Embassy Suites Washington, D.C. Convention Center
11. Embassy Suites Washington, D.C. Georgetown/The District
12. Fairmont Washington, D.C. Georgetown
13. Georgetown Suites
14. The Graham
15. Hamilton Hotel
16. Hampton Inn & Suites Washington DC Navy Yard
17. Hilton Garden Inn Washington, D.C. Downtown
18. Hilton Garden Inn Washington, D.C./U.S. Capitol
19. Hilton Washington, D.C. National Mall
20. Holiday Inn Washington-Capitol
21. Homewood Suites by Hilton NoMA Union Station
22. Homewood Suites by Hilton Washington
23. Hotel Palomar, A Kimpton Hotel
24. Hyatt House Washington, D.C./ The Wharf
25. InterContinental Washington, D.C.–The Wharf
26. Liaison Washington Capitol Hill
27. The Line Hotel
28. The Madison Washington D.C. by Hilton
29. Mandarin Oriental Washington, D.C.
30. Melrose Georgetown Hotel
31. Omni Shoreham Washington, D.C.
32. One Washington Circle Hotel
33. Phoenix Park Hotel
34. Pod DC Hotel
35. Residence Inn Arlington Courthouse
36. Residence Inn Foggy Bottom
37. Residence Inn Washington Capitol Hill/Navy Yard
38. Residence Inn Washington, D.C. Capitol
39. The St. Gregory Hotel
40. State Plaza Hotel
41. Washington Plaza
42. Willard InterContinental Washington, D.C.

HOW THE HOTELS COMPARE

HOTEL	OVERALL QUALITY RATING	PRICE RANGE	LOCATION
AKA White House	★★★★★	Expensive	National Mall/White House
Conrad Washington DC	★★★★★	Expensive	Penn Quarter/Chinatown/Convention Center
Fairmont Washington, D.C., Georgetown	★★★★★	Expensive	Georgetown/West End
InterContinental Washington, D.C.-The Wharf	★★★★★	Moderate-Expensive	Southwest Waterfront
Mandarin Oriental	★★★★★	Expensive	Southwest Waterfront
Willard InterContinental Washington, D.C.	★★★★★	Expensive	National Mall/White House
The Dupont Circle	★★★★½	Expensive	Dupont Circle/Logan Circle
Gaylord National Resort & Convention Center	★★★★½	Expensive	National Harbor
Kimpton Hotel Palomar	★★★★½	Inexpensive-Moderate	Dupont Circle/Logan Circle
MGM National Harbor	★★★★½	Expensive	National Harbor
Capitol Hill Hotel	★★★★	Inexpensive	Capitol Hill/Barracks Row
Embassy Suites by Hilton Chevy Chase	★★★★	Moderate	Friendship Heights/Chevy Chase
The Graham	★★★★	Moderate	Georgetown/West End
Hamilton Hotel	★★★★	Moderate	National Mall/White House
Hilton Garden Inn Washington, D.C. Downtown	★★★★	Moderate	National Mall/White House
Hilton Washington, D.C. National Mall	★★★★	Moderate	National Mall/White House
Hyatt House Washington, D.C./The Wharf	★★★★	Moderate	Southwest Waterfront
The Canopy by Hilton Bethesda North	★★★★	Moderate	Bethesda
The Madison Washington D.C. by Hilton	★★★★	Moderate	Dupont Circle/Logan Circle
Melrose Hotel	★★★★	Inexpensive-Moderate	Foggy Bottom
Omni Shoreham Hotel	★★★★	Moderate-Expensive	Upper Northwest
Phoenix Park Hotel	★★★★	Moderate	H Street Corridor/NoMa
Residence Inn Washington DC/Foggy Bottom	★★★★	Moderate	Foggy Bottom
Residence Inn National Harbor	★★★★	Moderate	National Harbor
Residence Inn Washington Capitol Hill/Navy Yard	★★★★	Moderate-Expensive	Capitol Riverfront/Navy Yard
Residence Inn Washington DC/Capitol	★★★★	Moderate-Expensive	Capitol Hill/Barracks Row
The St. Gregory Hotel	★★★★	Moderate-Expensive	Dupont Circle/Logan Circle
Avenue Suites Georgetown	★★★½	Moderate-Expensive	Georgetown/West End

HOW THE HOTELS COMPARE *(continued)*

HOTEL	OVERALL QUALITY RATING	PRICE RANGE	LOCATION
Courtyard Washington Capitol Hill/Navy Yard	★★★½	Inexpensive–Moderate	Capitol Riverfront/Navy Yard
Courtyard Washington Downtown/ Convention Center	★★★½	Inexpensive	Penn Quarter/Chinatown/ Convention Center
Embassy Suites Washington, D.C. Convention Center	★★★½	Moderate	Penn Quarter/Chinatown/ Convention Center
Georgetown Suites	★★★½	Moderate	Georgetown/West End
Holiday Inn Washington-Capitol	★★★½	Inexpensive	Capitol Hill/Barracks Row
Homewood Suites by Hilton NoMA Union Station	★★★½	Inexpensive–Moderate	H Street Corridor/NoMA
Hyatt Regency Tysons Corner Center	★★★½	Moderate–Expensive	Tysons Corner
One Washington Circle Hotel	★★★½	Inexpensive–Moderate	Foggy Bottom
Residence Inn Arlington Courthouse	★★★½	Moderate–Expensive	Arlington
Akwaaba Inn	★★★	Inexpensive–Moderate	Adams Morgan/Columbia Heights
Hyatt Regency Bethesda	★★★	Inexpensive–Moderate	Bethesda North
Cambria Hotel and Suites Rockville	★★★	Inexpensive	Rockville
Courtyard Washington DC/ Dupont Circle	★★★	Moderate–Expensive	Adams Morgan/Columbia Heights
Embassy Suites Washington, D.C. Georgetown/The District by Hilton Club	★★★	Moderate	Dupont Circle/Logan Circle
Hampton Inn & Suites Washington DC–Navy Yard	★★★	Inexpensive	Capitol Riverfront/Navy Yard
Hilton Garden Inn Washington, D.C./U.S. Capitol	★★★	Moderate	H Street Corridor/NoMA
Hotel Indigo	★★★	Inexpensive–Moderate	Old Town Alexandria
Liaison Washington Capitol Hill	★★★	Moderate	Capitol Hill/Barracks Row
The Line DC	★★★	Moderate–Expensive	Adams Morgan/Columbia Heights
Pod DC Hotel	★★★	Inexpensive	Penn Quarter/Chinatown/ Convention Center
Residence Inn Alexandria Old Town/Duke Street	★★★	Moderate	Old Town Alexandria
State Plaza Hotel	★★★	Inexpensive	Foggy Bottom
Washington Plaza	★★★	Inexpensive	U Street Corridor
Homewood Suites by Hilton Washington, D.C. Downtown	★★½	Inexpensive	U Street Corridor

continued from page 51

 Hampton Inn & Suites Washington DC Navy Yard
★★★   INEXPENSIVE

1265 First St. SE, ☎ 202-800-1000, hamptoninn3.hilton.com

Rate per night $120–$189. **Pool** No. **Fridge in room** Yes. **Pet-friendly** Yes. **Maximum occupants per room** 4. **Nearby dining** Chopt (fast-casual salads), RASA (fast-casual Indian), Mission Navy Yard, Big Stick Sports Bar, Buffalo Wild Wings.

SPORTS FANS WILL LOVE THIS HOTEL, thanks to its location across the street from Nationals Park and a short walk to Audi Field, home of the DC United soccer team. This Hampton has a lot to offer visitors, including free breakfast, spacious rooms, and a rooftop bar called Top of the Yard with views of the Capitol Riverfront, Washington Monument, and Pentagon. Suites have floor-to-ceiling windows, a microwave, a fridge, and a sleeper sofa. It's about a 25-minute walk to the U.S. Capitol, 5 minutes to the Navy Yard Metro station, and steps from the waterfront entertainment at Yards Park.

 Residence Inn Washington Capitol Hill/Navy Yard
★★★★   MODERATE–EXPENSIVE

1233 First St. SE, ☎ 202-770-2800, marriott.com

Rate per night $168–$375. **Pool** No. **Fridge in room** Yes. **Pet-friendly** Yes. **Maximum occupants per room** 4. **Nearby dining** Buffalo Wild Wings, The Salt Line, Blue Jacket Brewery, Bonchon, Nando's Peri-Peri, Harris Teeter grocery, Ana at District Winery.

THIS ALL-SUITE HOTEL IS LOCATED JUST STEPS FROM NATIONALS PARK. Each room has a kitchenette and sleeper sofa. Choose a studio or one-bedroom suite, with use of laundry facilities, complimentary buffet breakfast, and cooking utensils. On weeknights the hotel offers light meals with free drinks, including wine and beer. The Capitol Riverfront neighborhood has multiple dining options nearby in Barracks Row and Eastern Market. It's also a perfect location—about two blocks to the Navy Yard Metro station, Yards Park, and the picturesque Anacostia Riverwalk Trail.

CAPITOL HILL AND BARRACKS ROW

 Capitol Hill Hotel   ★★★★   INEXPENSIVE

200 C St. SW, ☎ 202-543-6000, capitolhillhotel-dc.com

Rate per night $135–$200. **Pool** No. **Fridge in room** Yes. **Pet-friendly** Yes. **Maximum occupants per room** 4. **Nearby dining** Hank's Oyster Bar, Good Stuff Eatery, We the Pizza, Eastern Market.

THIS FAMILY-FRIENDLY HOTEL IS A CONVENIENT HOME BASE for exploring Washington's must-see landmarks, such as the U.S. Capitol, Library of Congress, Supreme Court, Eastern Market, National Gallery of Art, and U.S. Botanic Garden. Located near a combination of residential and federal buildings, all of the guest rooms are like small apartments—doubles have two queen beds, and all have kitchenettes and roomy closets. Ask about the Family Getaway Package, which comes with four daily Metro passes and free roll-away beds. Breakfast and Wi-Fi are complimentary, and the hotel hosts a weekday wine reception. This neighborhood has a plethora of restaurants and bars within walking distance, as well as Eastern Market. Capitol Hill Hotel is just one block from the Capitol South Metro station, with a friendly staff eager to help plan your day or answer questions.

 Holiday Inn Washington-Capitol ★★★½ INEXPENSIVE

550 C St. SW, ☎ 202-479-4000, ihg.com

Rate per night $123–$180. **Pool** Yes. **Fridge in room** Yes. **Pet-friendly** No. **Maximum occupants per room** 4. **Nearby dining** Mitsitam Native Foods Cafe in the National Museum of the American Indian, McDonald's, Starbucks, Cosmo Cafe, Pizza Autentica, and multiple fast-casual restaurant options in L'Enfant Plaza complex.

STEPS FROM THE NATIONAL MALL, this large hotel has a rooftop pool, a poolside bar with views of the U.S. Capitol, and a relaxing courtyard. It's perfect for families who want to rest and refuel after a long day of sightseeing but who plan to tour the monuments later that night. The hotel is used by many large groups, so expect the lobby to be extremely busy at times. You can't beat the location—one block from the Smithsonian Air and Space Museum, the Museum of the American Indian, and the Hirshhorn Gallery of Art. Small children will love the nearby carousel, and older kids will enjoy renting a bike from Capital Bike-share to tool around the safe paths of the National Mall. Only two blocks from the L'Enfant Plaza Metro and a little farther to the Smithsonian Metro, the hotel also has a McDonald's and a CVS pharmacy right outside the door. Ask for an even-numbered room that faces the courtyard because the street noise can be quite loud. The breakfast buffet is complimentary but can be very crowded; other options include the in-house Starbucks and the Shuttle Express Deli. The hotel gift shop sells tickets for various tour buses, and full-size washing machines are available to guests. Although the decor is dated, the king rooms have sleeper sofas and feel very spacious. All rooms have a microwave, a coffee maker, and standard Wi-Fi access.

Liaison Washington Capitol Hill ★★★ MODERATE

415 New Jersey Ave. NW, ☎ 202-638-1616, yotel.com/en/hotels
/liaison-washington-capitol-hill.com

Rate per night $175–$250. **Pool** Yes. **Fridge in room** No. **Pet-friendly** Yes. **Maximum occupants per room** 4. **Nearby dining** Union Station Eatery, Bistro Bis, Corner Bakery, Charlie Palmer Steak, West Wing Cafe.

THIS IS THE CLOSEST HOTEL TO THE U.S. CAPITOL. It's popular for its party atmosphere at its rooftop bar and pool. With a vibe that's especially appealing to youthful revelers, this prime location is ideal for walking to the National Mall, Supreme Court, and National Gallery of Art and for commuting from Union Station. The hotel's restaurant, Art and Soul, is a D.C. institution. Trendy guest rooms have the latest conveniences, but the hotel does charge a daily resort fee of $28–$30, so factor that into your price.

 Residence Inn Washington, DC/Capitol
★★★★ MODERATE-EXPENSIVE

333 E St. SW, ☎ 202-484-8280, marriott.com

Rate per night $180–$600. **Pool** Yes. **Fridge in room** Yes. **Pet-friendly** Yes; deposit required. **Maximum occupants per room** 6. **Nearby dining** Mitsitam Native Foods Cafe in the National Museum of the American Indian, Milk + Honey Café and Manna at the Museum of the Bible, McDonald's, Good Stuff Eatery, Starbucks, We the Pizza, Tortilla Café, and multiple fast-casual restaurant options in L'Enfant Plaza complex.

THIS RESIDENCE INN HAS FLAIR. The all-suite hotel has standard amenities consistent with others in the chain, but what makes this one so great is the location—it's just two blocks to the Federal Center Metro station, an 8-minute walk to the National Mall, and a 15-minute walk to the U.S. Capitol. The hotel offers a full complimentary breakfast and buffet on weekdays, as well as an indoor saltwater pool, a fitness center, and an outdoor deck adjacent to the pool. Four tribes of American Indians own it, and you'll see touches that salute the nearby Smithsonian Museum of the American Indian, such as the bed covers and the lobby wall.

H STREET CORRIDOR AND NOMA
Hilton Garden Inn Washington, D.C./U.S. Capitol
★★★ MODERATE

1225 First St. NE, ☎ 202-408-4870, hiltongardeninn3.hilton.com

Rate per night $215–$276. **Pool** Yes. **Fridge in room** Yes. **Pet-friendly** No. **Maximum occupants per room** 4. **Nearby dining** Roti Mediterranean, Seoul Spice, Potbelly Sandwich Shop, Starbucks, Uptown Cafe, The Perfect Pita, CaliBurger.

THIS NEW HOTEL NEAR GALLAUDET UNIVERSITY has spacious guest rooms with a microwave, coffee maker, and comfy sleeper sofa. Add in their urban sundeck, fitness center, and indoor pool, and you get a lot for your money, despite being outside the traditional tourist areas. However, you're close to the vibrant H Street/Atlas District, and with only a two-block walk to the NoMa/Gallaudet Metro or a quick cab ride, you can be at the U.S. Capitol and National Mall in minutes. The hotel's Lily & the Cactus restaurant features Southwestern cuisine. This is a transitional neighborhood, with an occasional panhandler and some street noise, but it's also only a 5-minute drive to Union Market and La Cosecha Latin market.

☺ Homewood Suites by Hilton NoMA Union Station ★★★½ INEXPENSIVE–MODERATE
kids

501 New York Ave. NE, ☎ 202-393-8001, homewoodsuites3.hilton.com

Rate per night $166–$353. **Pool** Yes. **Fridge in room** Yes. **Pet-friendly** No. **Maximum occupants per room** 4. **Nearby dining** Union Market, Masseria, Ethiopic, Ta Korean, Dolcezza Gelato Factory & Coffee Lab, Coconut Club, Rappahannock Oyster Bar, Bidwell Restaurant, ArepaZone, DC Dosa.

WHILE THIS HOTEL IS NOT LOCATED IN A TOURISTY AREA, it offers amenities that leisure travelers will appreciate. It's modern, clean, and within walking distance of the Union Market complex, a trendy destination for locals, with hip dining options. To overcome its distance from the National Mall, the hotel offers a free shuttle to Union Station, where you can board the Metro. In addition to a free daily breakfast and evening snacks Monday–Thursday, every studio and suite comes equipped with a kitchenette, two televisions, a separate sitting area, and a sleeper sofa. The indoor pool, fitness room, and whirlpool are nice after a day of touring. The hotel provides free use of washers and dryers, as well as baby equipment upon request. The Gallaudet Metro station is a short walk. This is a good money-saving choice for an extended stay.

 Phoenix Park Hotel ★★★★ MODERATE

520 N. Capitol St. NW, ☎ 202-638-6900, phoenixparkhotel.com

Rate per night $237–$280, $800 for suites. **Pool** No. **Fridge in room** Yes. **Pet-friendly** No. **Maximum occupants per room** 4. **Nearby dining** Bistro Bis, The Monocle, West Wing Café, Corner Bakery, Crumbs Bake Shop, Art & Soul, Shake Shack, dozens of fast-casual restaurants inside Union Station.

THIS HISTORIC HOTEL HAS ICONIC D.C. VIEWS and is near Union Station and the National Postal Museum. Guest rooms are on the smaller side but are sophisticated and attractive; some have views of the U.S. Capitol dome. The suites come in a variety of configurations; some are two stories, with a fireplace, sleeper sofa, and separate sitting room. The hotel features a landmark D.C. restaurant called The Dubliner, an Irish pub that's been a favorite of Hill staffers for decades. The location can't be beat either—enjoy a short and scenic walk to the Library of Congress, National Gallery of Art, and National Mall. Because the hotel caters to business travelers, it often has good deals on weekend rates. The Phoenix Park gets top marks for the staff's attentiveness and service.

NATIONAL MALL AND THE WHITE HOUSE

 AKA White House ★★★★★ EXPENSIVE

1710 H St. NW, ☎ 202-904-2500, stayaka.com/aka-white-house

Rate per night $250–$900. **Pool** No. **Fridge in room** Yes. **Pet-friendly** No. **Maximum occupants per room** 6. **Nearby dining** Luke's Lobster, GCDC Grilled Cheese Bar, Taberna del Alabardero, Wicked Waffle, Bombay Club, Equinox, Le Pain Quotidien.

THE LEADING INTERNATIONAL LUXURY LONG-STAY BRAND, the AKA is two blocks from The White House and historic Lafayette Park, putting you within walking distance. of many major attractions. The guest rooms, with one or two bedrooms, as well as the penthouse suites, are the peak of sophistication and comfort, with full kitchens, dining areas, a dishwasher, a washer and dryer, and marble bathrooms. Many have balconies, where you can watch the street action. The gym is small but has state-of-the-art equipment. AKA is a new brand to D.C., and they are making their mark with their apartment-like suites, rooftop terrace, and cinema. The property is three to four blocks from the McPherson Square, Farragut North, and Farragut West Metro stations.

 Hamilton Hotel ★★★★ MODERATE

1001 14th St. NW, ☎ 202-682-0111, hamiltonhoteldc.com

Rate per night $120–$320. **Pool** No. **Fridge in room** Yes. **Pet-friendly** Yes, on third floor. **Maximum occupants per room** 4. **Nearby dining** Toro Toro, &pizza, Pret a Manger, The Hamilton, Cosi, Woodward Table, Society, Starbucks.

WHAT MAKES THE HAMILTON HOTEL SPECIAL is the beauty of this historic building and the exemplary service provided by the staff. It's also centrally located—McPherson Square is one block away, the White House is three blocks away, and the National Mall is less than a mile away. The hotel looks out on Franklin Square Park, and the higher floors have gorgeous nighttime views of the city. Guest rooms vary in size, but all are beautifully furnished, though with small bathrooms. Partnered with HBO and the Newseum, the hotel has specialty suites with memorabilia from TV shows like *Veep* and *Newsroom* (ask about Selina Meyer's Oval Office). Besides the full-service Starbucks in the lobby, the hotel has a restaurant called 14K that serves a popular weekend brunch. Hamilton now offers Roomcast for streaming content on your TV.

 ### Hilton Garden Inn Washington, D.C. Downtown
★★★★   MODERATE

815 14th St. NW, Washington, D.C.; ☎ 202-783-7800; hiltongardeninn3.hilton.com

Rate per night $149–$250. **Pool** Yes. **Fridge in room** Yes. **Pet-friendly** No. **Maximum occupants per room** 4. **Nearby dining** The Hamilton, Starbucks, Joe's Seafood Prime Steak & Stone Crab, &pizza, Old Ebbitt Grill, Buredo, Cosi, Toro Toro, Café Mozart & Bar.

IT'S HARD TO BEAT THE QUALITY, LOCATION, AND PRICE of this hotel. The spacious rooms have microwaves, fridges, and Keurig coffee makers. More like a boutique hotel than your typical chain, this Hilton provides complimentary coffee/tea in the morning and cookies in the afternoon. Other amenities include an indoor pool, in-room fitness supplies, a 24-hour pantry/gift shop, a laundry room, and baby gear. Across the street from the McPherson Square Metro station, the Trolley stop, and Franklin Square Park, it's a great base for exploring. Parking is pricey, so ask about Parking Panda; it's less expensive and only a few blocks away. To avoid street noise, ask for a room on a higher floor.

Hilton Washington, D.C. National Mall
★★★★   MODERATE

480 L'Enfant Plaza SW, ☎ 202-869-1952, 3hilton.com

Rate per night $149–$250. **Pool** Available summer 2020. **Fridge in room** Yes. **Pet-friendly** No. **Maximum occupants per room** 4. **Nearby dining** L'Enfant Plaza food court, Officina, Mi Vida, Dolcezza, Kith/Kin, Pizza Autentica, Five Guys, Amsterdam Falafelshop.

THIS NEWLY RENOVATED HILTON offers so many benefits. Located in the busy L'Enfant Plaza complex, it feels a bit like a concrete maze; however, that maze leads to a central Metro station on the lower level and food and shopping on the street level. The hotel is also very close to the heart of the National Mall and the exciting Wharf neighborhood; plus, the new spy museum is next door. Furnishings in the large rooms celebrate D.C.'s beloved cherry trees. Some rooms include two king beds, while the one- and two-bedroom suites boast a sleeper sofa, a fireplace, and floor-to-ceiling windows with panoramic city views. Executive rooms have access to a complimentary continental breakfast and evening snacks. The hotel will debut its new pool in the summer of 2020.

 ### Willard InterContinental Washington, D.C.
★★★★★   EXPENSIVE

1401 Pennsylvania Ave. NW, ☎ 202-628- 9100, washington.intercontinental.com

Rate per night $248–$720. **Pool** No. **Fridge in room** No. **Pet-friendly** No. **Maximum occupants per room** 4. **Nearby dining** Old Ebbitt Grill, The Hamilton, MXDC Cocina Mexicana, POV Lounge, Maison Kayser, Starbucks, District Taco, Chopt, Eat at National Place.

THIS REVERED HOTEL HAS A STORY TO TELL. It has been a rest stop for countless celebrities and notable politicians, including Presidents Abraham Lincoln and Ulysses S. Grant. Martin Luther King Jr. wrote his "I Have a Dream" speech here. Just steps from the White House and the National Mall, this elegant but friendly boutique hotel is a good choice for people who want to immerse themselves in the action of Washington's most famous street, Pennsylvania Avenue. The hotel is three blocks from Metro Center and a 10-minute walk to the National Mall, and has easy access to museums, monuments, the National and Warner Theatres, shopping, and dining. The Family Package includes free parking, goodies for the kids upon arrival, and a $75 food and beverage credit. Pamper yourself with a spa treatment at the hotel's Red Door Spa, have cocktails at the famous Round Robin Bar, or enjoy afternoon tea with live harp music in Peacock Alley.

PENN QUARTER, CHINATOWN, AND CONVENTION CENTER

Conrad Washington DC ★★★★★ EXPENSIVE

950 New York Ave. NW, ☎ 202-844-5900, conradhotels3.hilton

Rate per night $290–$470. **Pool** No. **Fridge in room** Yes. **Pet-friendly** No. **Maximum occupants per room** 4. **Nearby dining** Centrolina, Sfoglina Pasta House, Carmine's, Cuba Libre, Momofuku CCDC, Capitol City Brewing Company, Matchbox Pizza, Rare Sweets, Dolcezza, Cure Bar & Bistro.

THIS BRAND-NEW HOTEL IS STEPS from D.C.'s most upscale shopping and dining spots in CityCenterDC. If you want nightlife and culture, you can't beat the location, three blocks from Capital One Arena, the Shakespeare Theatre, the National Portrait Gallery, and two Metro stops. The rooms are equipped with espresso machines and Bluetooth speakers, and the design feels residential, like a chic apartment. The Conrad is also known for offering a unique hotel refuge called the Sakura Club (named after Washington's famous cherry blossoms), with expansive suites that include a gourmet buffet three times a day; evening libations; afternoon tea; and priority access to the rooftop bar and Estuary, a restaurant owned by Top Chefs the Voltaggio brothers that showcases the flavors of nearby Chesapeake Bay. There's no pool, but the fitness center features Precor equipment. The hotel caters to international business travelers, so it's quieter on the weekends, when the rates drop.

Courtyard Washington/Downtown Convention Center ★★★½ INEXPENSIVE

901 L St. NW, ☎ 202-589-1800, marriott.com

Rate per night $150–$250. **Pool** Yes. **Fridge in room** Yes. **Pet-friendly** Yes. **Maximum occupants per room** 4. **Nearby dining** Daikaya, Shake Shack, Hill Street BBQ, Oyamel, Zengo, Proof, Starbucks.

THIS FAMILY-FRIENDLY HOTEL IN PENN QUARTER not only puts you right into the action, but also shelters visitors in comfortable accommodations at a reasonable price. The hotel was once a bank, with thick, solid walls, so you won't hear the lively street noise (check out the old bank vault door in the lobby). The rooms aren't large—double rooms have full-size beds but will fit a rollaway bed or crib. The hotel was recently renovated and has spacious suites, a small pool, a hot tub, a fitness center, and complimentary bottled water and snacks in the lobby daily. It's located near the Gallery Place/Chinatown Metro, Smithsonian Art Museum, and Ford's Theatre and is surrounded by dozens of restaurants and shops. You can catch a sightseeing bus or walk to the National Mall in about 5 minutes. Some guests complain about the sink being outside the bathroom and the lack of bathtubs, but the hotel is clean, and the staff is eager to accommodate your needs. Be sure to make specific requests when you book your reservation. This is a great place to stay if you plan to see a concert or sports event at Capital One Arena.

Embassy Suites Washington, D.C. Convention Center ★★★½ MODERATE

900 10th St. NW, ☎ 202-739-2001, embassysuites3.hilton.com

Rate per night $160–$260. **Pool** Yes. **Fridge in room** Yes. **Pet-friendly** Yes. **Maximum occupants per room** 6. **Nearby dining** Brasserie Beck, Centrolina, Cuba Libre, DBGB, El Rinconcito Café, Kinship, Momofuku CCDC, Potbelly Sandwich Shop, West Wing Café, Zaytinya.

NEAR THE D.C. CONVENTION CENTER this Embassy Suites serves travelers well, with sleeper sofas, a free buffet breakfast, and an evening reception with free drinks and snacks. You get a microwave, a fridge, and an LCD TV in each room. Guests love that every room is a suite; plus they enjoy the indoor pool, Jacuzzi, 24-hour fitness center, and laundry facilities. It's a solid home base for sightseeing, and the neighborhood has an ever-growing list of dining options. It's about seven blocks to the National Mall and the Smithsonian museums, and on the way you'll pass CityCenterDC, with its high-end shops, and Macy's department store. You'll have access to the Circulator bus and the Convention Center Metro; plus, it's only three blocks to the Metro Center station, where many subway lines meet.

Pod DC Hotel ★★★ INEXPENSIVE

627 H St. NW, ☎ 202-847-4444, thepodhotel.com

Rate per night $123–$250. **Pool** No. **Fridge in room** No. **Pet-friendly** No. **Maximum occupants per room** 2. **Nearby dining** Vapiano, Carmine's, Chinatown, Panera Bread, Penny Whisky Bar, Kofuku, Wok & Roll, Hip City Veg, Nando's Peri-Peri, Fado Irish Pub, Cava Mezza Grill.

RIGHT IN THE MIDDLE OF WASHINGTON'S CHINATOWN, this new Pod Hotel is a minimalist's dream. As some guests say, "It has everything you need, and nothing you don't." The rooms are small—some have bunk beds called Bunk Pods—but views of the city are glorious, especially from the hotel's Crimson View rooftop bar. If you're averse to buzzy and sometimes noisy nightlife, you should avoid the Pod. If you want to be in the heart of the action, you'll be happy. The hotel employs a team called The Pod Squad, who are available to advise guests on what to do, where to go, and how to get there. The hotel offers free Wi-Fi and free access to the Washington Sports Club. Rooms are limited to two people, but the price is so reasonable, you can rent a separate room for the kids. You'll share a block with Capital One Arena as well as dozens of restaurants and shops, and it's just a few blocks from the National Mall. Right outside the door is the Gallery Place/Chinatown Metro station.

FOGGY BOTTOM

 Melrose Georgetown Hotel Washington, D.C. ★★★★
INEXPENSIVE–MODERATE

2430 Pennsylvania Ave. NW, ☎ 202-955-6400, melrosehoteldc.com

Rate per night $180–$250. **Pool** No. **Fridge in room** Yes. **Pet-friendly** Yes (dogs). **Maximum occupants per room** 4. **Nearby dining** Marcel's, Sweetgreen, CIRCA, District Commons, One Fish Two Fish, Aroma, Founding Farmers, Trader Joe's, Whole Foods.

THIS HOTEL IS A MIX OF HISTORIC BEAUTY AND MODERN COMFORT. Located on the border of Foggy Bottom and Georgetown, the independent boutique hotel is known for its attractive, luxurious rooms and friendly, courteous staff. Melrose is a 20-minute walk to the National Mall; three blocks to the Foggy Bottom Metro; and a 10-minute walk to the Georgetown Waterfront, restaurants, and shopping. You'll be surrounded by George Washington University students, which is why there are so many takeout and fast-casual restaurants nearby, but the walls are thick, so you will rarely hear street noise. Complimentary coffee is served in the lobby each morning. The elegant Art Deco–style lobby has a wood-burning fireplace and a gym. The hotel restaurant, Jardenea, serves meals all day and has an appealing lounge that attracts locals. Guest rooms are smartly done, with artwork featuring George Washington and the Constitution. For kids, ask about the Munchkin package.

 One Washington Circle Hotel ★★★½
INEXPENSIVE–MODERATE

1 Washington Circle NW, ☎ 202-872-1680, thecirclehotel.com

Rate per night $160–$250. **Pool** Yes (outdoor). **Fridge in room** Yes. **Pet-friendly** No. **Maximum occupants per room** 4. **Nearby dining** Founding Farmers, Prime Rib, District Commons, Marcel's, Burger Tap & Shake, Devon & Blakely, Beefsteak Vegetarian, Ris.

THIS SPACIOUS SUITE HOTEL has the stylish feeling of a pied-à-terre and offers lots of extras. The rooms and bathrooms are a bit dated but may be the largest in the city; they're more like condos than hotel rooms. Choose from studios or one-bedroom suites; each suite has a full kitchen, a separate bedroom, and scenic views from the balcony that will inspire you to spend more time in your room. Some even have pianos! It's a short walk to the Foggy Bottom and Farragut West Metro stations and a six-block walk to the National Mall and the White House. You have access to the fitness center and complimentary passes to the pool at the Washington Plaza Hotel in Thomas Circle. They host a free wine hour in the lobby. If you book directly with the hotel, you get a discount, a complimentary upgrade, and other benefits.

 Residence Inn Washington DC/ Foggy Bottom ★★★★ MODERATE

801 New Hampshire Ave. NW, ☎ 202-785-2000, marriott.com

Rate per night $150–$280. **Pool** Yes, rooftop. **Fridge in room** Yes. **Pet-friendly** Yes. **Maximum occupants per room** 6. **Nearby dining** District Commons, Burger Tap & Shake, Circa at Foggy Bottom, Bangkok Joe's.

THIS NEIGHBORHOOD GETS ITS HIGH ENERGY from the George Washington University college students, and it's busy at all hours of the day and night, making it safe to walk to many destinations, including the Potomac River waterfront and Foggy Bottom Metro. Thanks to the students, there are lots of inexpensive restaurants around, too, and many stay open late. Walk to the Watergate building's grocery store to stock that full kitchen, and go for a swim in the beautiful rooftop pool. The hotel has the usual suite-style rooms—one-bedroom suites with a choice of one king or two queen beds, both with a sleeper sofa. It's only one block to the Foggy Bottom Metro. Georgetown, the National Mall, and the White House are all within a mile of the hotel.

 ## State Plaza Hotel ★★★ INEXPENSIVE

2117 E St. NW, ☎ 202-861-8200, stateplaza.com

Rate per night $100–$150. **Pool** No. **Fridge in room** Yes. **Pet-friendly** No. **Maximum occupants per room** 4. **Nearby dining** Chipotle, Johnny Rockets, Dunkin' Donuts, Potbelly Sandwich Shop, Starbucks, Tonic, Whole Foods.

LOCATED NEAR GEORGE WASHINGTON UNIVERSITY and a few blocks from Georgetown's restaurants and shops, rooms at this all-suite hotel resemble a small apartment rather than a standard hotel room. Suites come in a variety of configurations, all with fully equipped kitchens and eat-in dining areas; some have sleeper sofas in separate sitting rooms, which makes them especially nice for families who want to spread out. The Garden Café serves three meals a day, and after your workout in the fitness center, check out the daily happy hour 4–7 p.m. The neighborhood can be deserted at night because it's surrounded by offices, but you'll still have a choice of several fast-casual restaurants. State Plaza is three blocks from the Foggy Bottom Metro station and just half a mile from the National Mall.

GEORGETOWN AND WEST END

 ## Avenue Suites Georgetown ★★★½
MODERATE–EXPENSIVE

2500 Pennsylvania Ave. NW, ☎ 202-333-8060, avenuesuites.com

Rate per night $200–$310; some weekends require a 2-night minimum. **Pool** No. **Fridge in room** Yes. **Pet-friendly** Yes; $25 per pet. **Maximum occupants per room** 4. **Nearby dining** Charm Thai, Flavors of India, Marcel's, La Perla, Trader Joe's, Whole Foods.

AVENUE SUITES GEORGETOWN has a reputation for enthusiastic service and large guest rooms that resemble apartments, some up to 600 square feet. Located between Georgetown and Foggy Bottom, it's only four blocks to the Foggy Bottom Metro station and within walking distance of popular attractions, such as the White House and the National Mall. Some rooms have beautiful views of the city, and the neighborhood has a youthful vibe thanks to its proximity to George Washington University and Georgetown University. The hotel is also close to dining options in different price points. Because the neighborhood is mostly residential, it's safe at night, with more locals out on the streets than tourists. Guest rooms come in multiple configurations—some have two queen beds and a sleeper sofa; some have private terraces. Bathrooms are small, but every room has a full (but dated) kitchen. Guests are welcome to grill or dine on the outdoor patio at cozy fire pits. In addition to a small gym, the hotel offers Saturday morning yoga on the terrace. For those staying awhile, the staff will pick up groceries for a fee.

Fairmont Washington, D.C. Georgetown ★★★★★ EXPENSIVE

2401 M St. NW, ☎ 202-429-2400, thefairmont.com/washington

Rate per night $170–$380. **Pool** Yes. **Fridge in room** Only in suites. **Pet-friendly** Yes. **Maximum occupants per room** 4. **Nearby dining** Tea Cellar, District Commons, Cafe Deluxe, Rasika West End, Blue Duck Tavern, Marcel's, Ris, Burger Tap & Shake.

ALTHOUGH IT'S NOT IN THE BEATING HEART OF GEORGETOWN (that would be M Street and Wisconsin Avenue NW), the Fairmont is located in the sophisticated West End neighborhood and is about 1 mile from the Dupont Circle and Foggy Bottom Metro stations. What makes the Fairmont special are the extras: free lemonade and board games in the lobby, a beautiful garden courtyard, a safe residential neighborhood, free bicycles, and gracious service. The rooms have luxurious furnishings and marble bathrooms, and some have sleeper sofas or balconies overlooking a courtyard fountain. The hotel stream-lines check-in by providing roving guest-service representatives armed with iPads to facilitate the process. The hotel's Balance Gym Fitness Center and Spa boasts a sauna; a whirlpool; a steam room; a large indoor saltwater pool; and yoga, Spinning, CrossFit, Pilates, barre, and Zumba classes. If you love a good spread and value convenience, consider upgrading to Fairmont Gold level, with daily breakfast and evening hors d'oeuvres. Children age 5 and under eat free; kids ages 6–11 eat for half price.

Georgetown Suites ★★★½ MODERATE

1111 30th St. NW, ☎ 202-298-7800, georgetownsuites.com

Rate per night $160–$200. **Pool** No. **Fridge in room** Yes. **Pet-friendly** Yes. **Maximum occupants per room** 6. **Nearby dining** 1789, Clyde's of Georgetown, Chaia Vegetarian, The Sovereign, Bourbon Steak, Baked & Wired, Filomena Ristorante, Dog Tag Bakery.

THIS HOTEL OFFERS FAMILIES APARTMENT-STYLE SUITES in the heart of charming Georgetown. There are two buildings located half a block apart. Georgetown Suites Courtyard has studios, two-bedroom suites, and bilevel town homes and is located off bustling M Street. Georgetown Suites Harbour is a secluded, quiet building with views of the Potomac River. All suites have full kitchens, and the Courtyard building includes a free Continental breakfast. If you want to splurge, consider the penthouse suite with an outdoor dining area and gorgeous views of the city. From these buildings, you can walk to shops, restaurants, and Georgetown Waterfront Park. This location is especially fun for tweens and teens.

The Graham ★★★★ MODERATE

1075 Thomas Jefferson St. NW, ☎ 202-337-0900, thegrahamgeorgetown.com

Rate per night $160–$200. **Pool** No. **Fridge in room** Yes. **Pet-friendly** Yes. **Maximum occupants per room** 6. **Nearby dining** Georgetown Cupcakes, Baked & Wired, Chez Billy Sud, Il Canale, Filomena Ristorante, Thunder Burger, Dog Tag Bakery, Bodega Spanish Tapas, El Centro, Bourbon Steak.

THIS BOUTIQUE HOTEL HAS SLEEK, MODERN ROOMS; junior suites; and full suites, some with outdoor patios overlooking the neighborhood. The vibe makes this hotel more suited to couples or friends than to families. The

Federal-style architecture harks back to Georgetown's residential history, and the hotel is just steps away from the historic C&O Canal Towpath and the buzzy shops and bars on M Street NW. The hotel pays homage to inventor Alexander Graham Bell, who once lived in Washington, D.C., and the Art Deco lobby displays a gramophone like the one he invented. The Graham's rooftop bar is one of the best addresses in town. It's an idyllic spot to enjoy the sunset over the Potomac River. From the Graham, you can easily walk to shops, restaurants, and Georgetown Waterfront Park.

 NEW AND TRENDY HOTELS TO CONSIDER: If you are looking for a personalized, European-style hotel rather than a large chain or luxury hotel, consider staying at **Hotel Hive** or the recently renovated **Watergate Hotel,** both in Foggy Bottom; **Eaton Hotel** near Penn Quarter; **The Darcy** in Dupont Circle; **District by Hilton Club** near Georgetown (part of Embassy Suites Georgetown); or **Moxy Washington, D.C. Downtown.**

DUPONT CIRCLE AND LOGAN CIRCLE

 The Dupont Circle ★★★★½ EXPENSIVE

1500 New Hampshire Ave. NW, ☎ 202-483-6000, doylecollection.com

Rate per night $200–$850. **Pool** No. **Fridge in room** No. **Pet-friendly** No. **Maximum occupants per room** 4. **Nearby dining** Pizzeria Paradiso, Rakuya, Hank's Oyster Bar, Doyle Bar & Lounge, Bibibop, Ankara, Iron Gate.

IF YOU LOVE AN EXCLUSIVE ADDRESS, luxurious furnishings, and being where the hip people go, this is your spot. The high energy of this boutique hotel draws both visitors and locals, who come to enjoy its outdoor bar. Send your kids on a Capital Space Journey as the hotel sets up an in-room tepee, binoculars, planetarium light, and telescope to transport them to another planet. Try the Bed & Breakfast package, which includes breakfast served in your room.

 Embassy Suites Washington, D.C. Georgetown/ The District by Hilton Club ★★★ MODERATE

1250 22nd St. NW, ☎ 202-857-3388, embassysuites3.hilton.com

Rate per night $170–$280. **Pool** Yes. **Fridge in room** Yes. **Pet-friendly** No. **Maximum occupants per room** 6. **Nearby dining** Bread & Chocolate, Cafe Deluxe, Rasika West End, West End Bistro, Blue Duck Tavern.

EMBASSY SUITES IS KNOWN AND LOVED BY TRAVELING FAMILIES, and this location is no exception. From the cheery lobby to the expansive suites, it's hard to beat this chain hotel situated between Georgetown, Foggy Bottom, and Dupont Circle. One criticism is the thin walls and resulting noise, although that's probably because of the open lobby atrium. Nevertheless, travel with earplugs and don't shy away from this all-suite hotel with the complimentary buffet breakfast For a higher level of service and luxury, upgrade to The District by Hilton Club, which occupies the upper floors of the Embassy Suites. This entitles you to partake in the evening reception. The hotel's location is ideal, just four blocks from the Dupont Circle and Foggy Bottom Metro stations and a Circulator bus stop. Each suite includes a coffee maker, kitchenette, and sleeper sofa. Guests love the indoor pool and fitness center, along with the bountiful koi swimming around in the lobby fountain. Breakfast is usually extremely busy, so try to get there early.

Hotel Palomar, A Kimpton Hotel ★★★★½
INEXPENSIVE–MODERATE

2121 P St. NW, ☎ 202-448-1800, hotelpalomar-dc.com

Rate per night $120–$270. **Pool** Yes. **Fridge in room** No. **Pet-friendly** Yes. **Maximum occupants per room** 4. **Nearby dining** Obelisk, Equinox, Al Tiramisu, Pesce, Ankara, Zorba's Café, Urbana.

HOTEL PALOMAR WILL CONSTANTLY SURPRISE YOU with the whimsy hidden behind the guest room door. Inside the small lobby, you'll see quirky original art, as well as guest-service representatives who welcome you with a glass of wine (wine hour is every evening, 5–6 p.m.). The lobby opens to the courtyard, where a sparkling heated outdoor pool and a sundeck are nestled between the walls of the hotel. Across the street are several restaurants serving takeout and fast food, and it's only a short walk to dozens of sit-down restaurants too. Besides the proximity to the Dupont Circle Metro, there's also the Circulator bus stop nearby that will whisk you away to Georgetown or Union Station. Palomar guests enjoy complimentary morning coffee and tea, a fitness center, and a yoga mat in every room. Urbana, the hotel restaurant, serves outstanding pizzas, cocktails, and healthy entrées. Palomar even provides the use of free bikes (based on availability). If you're uncomfortable with or allergic to animals, be forewarned: you may ride the elevators with someone's furry friend (no size restrictions).

The Madison Washington D.C. by Hilton
★★★★ **MODERATE**

1177 15th St. NW, ☎ 202-785-1255, 3.hilton.com

Rate per night $160–$300. **Pool** No. **Fridge in room** Yes. **Pet-friendly** Yes; 75-pound max and $75 nonrefundable deposit. **Maximum occupants per room** 4. **Nearby dining** Lincoln, Post Pub, The Greenhouse at The Jefferson, Baan Thai, The Pig, DNV Rooftop Lounge.

IN 1963 PRESIDENT JOHN F. KENNEDY was the first to open the doors of the historic Madison, then considered the most modern, sophisticated hotel in the city. While it's no longer the exclusive address it once was, The Madison continues to exude charm and offers visitors a central location from which to explore the nation's capital. Inspired by the legacy of renowned entertainers President James Madison and First Lady Dolley Madison, the decor in this boutique hotel hearkens back to Washington's Federal period in the late 1700s. The hotel garners glowing reviews for its welcoming staff and its full-service concierge. Standard guest rooms tend to be on the small side, but several suites have large terraces that overlook the city. The Madison is conveniently located near the National Geographic Museum, four blocks from the McPherson Square Metro station and two blocks from the Dupont Circle Metro station.

The St. Gregory Hotel ★★★★ MODERATE–EXPENSIVE

2033 M St. NW, ☎ 202-530-3600, stgregoryhotelwdc.com

Rate per night $140–$400. **Pool** No. **Fridge in room** Minibar. **Pet-friendly** Yes. **Maximum occupants per room** 5. **Nearby dining** Bub and Pop's, Blue Duck Tavern, Grill-fish, Rasika West End, Soi 38, District Taco, West Wing Cafe.

THIS BOUTIQUE HOTEL, located in the elegant West End neighborhood between Foggy Bottom and Dupont Circle, is bedecked in posh midcentury modern furnishings that make it feel more like an apartment than a standard hotel. For a daily fee of $30 above the room rate, you'll enjoy complimentary coffee in the lobby, a European-style breakfast buffet, a nightly wine hour, L'Occitane products, and discounts on Bird electric scooters. The executive suites include a separate living area with a sleeper sofa and two TVs; the one-bedroom suites offer the same but are also a very spacious 850 square feet. The swanky Tredici Enoteca Restaurant opens its patio in warmer weather and has a cozy fireplace for when it's cold outside. The hotel is three blocks from the Dupont Circle Metro and a 10-minute walk to Farragut North.

U STREET CORRIDOR

 Homewood Suites by Hilton Washington ★★½
INEXPENSIVE

1475 Massachusetts Ave. NW, ☎ 202-265-8000, homewoodsuites3.hilton.com

Rate per night $130–$225. **Pool** No. **Fridge in room** Yes. **Pet-friendly** No. **Maximum occupants per room** 6. **Nearby dining** Estadio, The Pig, ChurchKey, Le Diplomate, Birch & Barley, Ghibellina.

THIS ALL-SUITE HOTEL IS LOCATED NEAR THOMAS CIRCLE, between the Dupont Circle, Farragut North, McPherson Square, and U Street Metro stations. Although not in the heart of the U Street Corridor's amazing array of restaurants and irresistible boutiques, you will enjoy a pleasant stroll past some of Washington's most beautiful homes to get there. Guests rave about the friendly staff and the two-room configuration in this hotel, with the sleeping and living rooms separated by a wall and door, though some rooms feel a bit cramped. All accommodations have a bedroom ceiling fan, a fully equipped kitchen, two TVs, and a sleeper sofa, making them an excellent place to spread out and prepare meals. A hot breakfast is complimentary, as is the evening social (weeknights only). There's a fitness and business center, laundry facilities, and a gift shop. It's about 10 blocks to the National Mall and 8 to the White House, but close to many restaurants, shops, and exercise studios in the U Street Corridor.

 Washington Plaza ★★★ INEXPENSIVE

10 Thomas Circle NW, ☎ 202-842-1300, washingtonplazahotel.com

Rate per night $150–$200. **Pool** Yes. **Fridge in room** Yes. **Pet-friendly** Service animals only. **Maximum occupants per room** 5. **Nearby dining** City Tap House, DBGB, Dolcezza, The Pig, ChurchKey, B Too, Thaitanic, Lalibela.

A BIG DRAW OF THIS RETRO-STYLE HOTEL is the large outdoor pool with views of the city. Architect Morris Lapidus, who designed the Fontainebleau in Miami Beach, intended the Washington Plaza to feel like a resort in the heart of Washington, D.C. The hotel is located at Thomas Circle, near restaurants, bars, and nightclubs, and is reasonably close to other attractions, such as the convention center, the National Geographic Museum, and Capital One Arena. Guest rooms are decorated in bright contrasting colors, and some lower-level rooms have balconies with city views. The 15 junior suites include a sitting area and two full bathrooms. The hotel's restaurant, Thomas Circle, serves three meals a day, and in warm weather, guests can choose to be served by the pool. In cold weather, the lounge has a cozy fireplace. There's no fitness center, but the hotel can direct guests to a yoga and Pilates studio nearby. Washington Plaza is four blocks from the McPherson Square and Mount Vernon Square/ Convention Center Metro stations.

ADAMS MORGAN AND COLUMBIA HEIGHTS

Akwaaba Inn ★★★ INEXPENSIVE–MODERATE

1708 16th St. NW, ☎ 866-466-3855, akwaaba.com

Rate per night $150–$285. **Pool** No. **Fridge in room** Yes. **Pet-friendly** No. **Maximum occupants per room** 4. **Nearby dining** Hank's Oyster Bar, Dupont Italian Kitchen, Floriana, Logan Tavern, Commissary, Komi, Ted's Bulletin.

THIS CIRCA-1890S INN IS ONE OF THE TOP BED-AND-BREAKFASTS in the city. The elegant town house has eight spacious guest rooms, each with its own bathroom, and each has a theme. Some were named for famous African American authors who lived in Washington, D.C., such as Toni Morrison, Zora Neale Hurston, and Langston Hughes. The proprietors get top marks for hospitality, and guests are treated to a full breakfast, as well as afternoon cocktails and refreshments. The inn does not allow children under age 12 to stay. Limited parking is available, and the hotel is a 10-minute walk to Dupont Circle Metro and dozens of popular restaurants and boutiques.

Courtyard Washington DC/Dupont Circle ★★★ MODERATE–EXPENSIVE

1900 Connecticut Ave. NW, ☎ 202-332-9300, marriott.com

Rate per night $230–$280. **Pool** Yes. **Fridge in room** Yes. **Pet-friendly** No. **Maximum occupants per room** 4. **Nearby dining** Glen's Garden Market, Buca di Beppo, Banana Leaves Asian Restaurants & Sushi Bar, Bistrot du Coin, Teaism.

ALTHOUGH THIS HOTEL ISN'T TECHNICALLY in either Adams Morgan or Columbia Heights, it is one of the closest to both neighborhoods and has much to offer travelers. Located on lively Connecticut Avenue, the hotel is a 10-minute walk to the Dupont Circle Metro and a 10-minute walk to Adams Morgan, with restaurants and shops nearby; the walk to Adams Morgan passes by lovely historic town homes and Kalorama Park. Guest rooms and bathrooms are small but modern, and some feature views of the Washington Monument. The hotel has a fitness center and an outdoor pool, and the restaurant serves breakfast and dinner. In nice weather, the hotel patio has umbrella tables— perfect for eating takeout. The National Zoo is 1 mile from the hotel.

The Line DC ★★★ MODERATE–EXPENSIVE

1770 Euclid St. NW, ☎ 202-588-0525, thelinehotel.com

Rate per night $160–$330. **Pool** No. **Fridge in room** No. **Pet-friendly** Yes. **Maximum occupants per room** 4. **Nearby dining** A Rake's Progress, Spoken English, Brothers and Sisters, Counter Culture Coffee Shop, Tryst, Amsterdam Falafelshop, Mintwood Place, Philz Coffee.

THIS TRENDY, NEW HOTEL was a 110-year-old historic church in Adams Morgan. The founding was a community effort from various local chefs and broadcasters, and it has taken the city by storm. It's a favorite hangout for the locals, too, and the neighborhood gets a little noisy and rowdy on weekends. Rooms are decorated with eclectic touches, and configurations vary from a traditional king to a corner suite with views of the Washington Monument. Guests can enjoy three restaurants, two bars, a coffee shop, and watching the DJ spin tunes from the lobby. The Line also serves high tea in the lobby. If you're looking for a stylish, upbeat, quirky time in D.C., this is your place, but it's not recommended for travelers with children.

UPPER NORTHWEST: WOODLEY PARK, CLEVELAND PARK, AND TENLEYTOWN

  Omni Shoreham Hotel ★★★★
MODERATE–EXPENSIVE

2500 Calvert St. NW, ☎ 202-234-0700, omnihotels.com

Rate per night $150–$375. **Pool** Yes. **Fridge in room** No. **Pet-friendly** No. **Maximum occupants per room** 4. **Nearby dining** Open City Diner, Chipotle, Lebanese Taverna, Hot n Juicy Crawfish, New Heights, Starbucks.

THIS HISTORIC HOTEL WITH A BEAUTIFUL POOL sits regally above bucolic Rock Creek Park and spreads its literal wings a full block on Calvert Street. The lobby is elegant and enormous, with lots of space to relax and people-watch after a busy day of sightseeing. The rooms have a classic look; suites have luxurious living areas, and many rooms have balconies, with views of the hotel gardens. If you're traveling with kids, ask about special treats, such as milk and cookies delivered to your room on the first night. The garden area has a kid-friendly, resort-style pool, with an outdoor bar where parents can sit and watch the little ones splash around. There's also a fire pit, a well-equipped gym, and a coffee and gift shop in the lobby area, so you don't need to go far to jump-start your morning. However, there are some things to consider: prices for breakfast items are sky high, the elevators are cramped, and the bathrooms are unimpressive. Also, this hotel hosts a lot of convention crowds and gets very busy. On the upside, the Woodley Park Metro station is across the street, the National Zoo is a 10-minute walk downhill, and several restaurants and a CVS are within a block of the hotel. You can easily explore Adams Morgan from this location, and although it's not possible to walk to the National Mall from here, it's only three subway stops away.

MARYLAND SUBURBS

National Harbor

  Gaylord National Resort & Convention Center ★★★★½ **EXPENSIVE**

201 Waterfront St., National Harbor; ☎ 301-965-4000; marriott.com

Rate per night $250–$325. **Pool** Yes. **Fridge in room** Yes. **Pet-friendly** No. **Maximum occupants per room** 5. **Nearby dining** Bobby McKey's Dueling Piano Bar, Old Hickory Steakhouse, Succotash, Nando's. MGM (profiled below) has a dozen restaurants worth investigating like Fish, Maryland Fry Bar, Osteria Costa, and Shake Shack.

THE GAYLORD PUT NATIONAL HARBOR ON THE D.C. MAP. The water-front complex of shops, restaurants, and entertainment grew up around this self-contained resort. The beautiful 19-story atrium overlooks the Potomac River, and the sunsets are stunning from the massive open lobby. Some spacious rooms and suites face the atrium, with a variety of configurations, including small suites that face the river. The Relâche Spa and Salon is a soothing escape, with floor-to-ceiling windows of the marina and park. The indoor pool is an oasis, with garage doors that open to a patio. With many reasons to love the Gaylord, the dining venues are a big part of that. Pose Rooftop Lounge is free for guests of the hotel, a big selling point for those seeking nightlife activities. The Belvedere Lobby Bar and Pienza Marketplace are situated inside the atrium, with views of the nightly laser light show.

MGM National Harbor   ★★★★½   EXPENSIVE

101 MGM National Ave., Oxon Hill; ☎ 844-646-6847;
mgmnationalharbor.mgmresorts.com

Rate per night $250–$500. **Pool** Yes. **Fridge in room** No. **Pet-friendly** No. **Maximum occupants per room** 4. **Nearby dining** MGM restaurants: Voltaggio Brothers Steak House, Fish, Osteria Costa, Shake Shack, TAP Sports Bar, National Market, Bellagio Patisserie, Ginger, Maryland Fry Bar.

MGM OPENED THIS MASSIVE COMPLEX that looks like a sleek cruise ship from a distance. The luxurious, modern property features a popular, sophisticated casino with slots and table games. Staying overnight at the MGM hotel allows you to play as late as you like. Also within the complex are a hotel, restaurants, boutiques, and an upscale spa. The theater is another big draw; it has 3,000 seats and welcomes vintage performers like Cher and Aerosmith. The decor and furnishings are first-class, with a nod to the hotel's location in Maryland, near the Chesapeake Bay. The hotel offers a range of rooms, from a Capital View King to suites fit for a celebrity. Hanging out on the outdoor deck is probably one of the highlights—as the fizzy fountain sprays, you'll take in the panoramic views of Old Town Alexandria across the Potomac River and the monuments and memorials on the D.C. side.

Residence Inn National Harbor   ★★★★   MODERATE

192 Waterfront St., National Harbor; ☎ 301-749-4755; marriott.com

Rate per night $190–$300. **Pool** No. **Fridge in room** Yes. **Pet-friendly** Yes. **Maximum occupants per room** 6. **Nearby dining** Rosa Mexicana, Grace's Mandarin, Cadillac Ranch, Public House.

NATIONAL HARBOR IS A SPRAWLING COMPLEX of hotels, shops, restaurants, a marina, and other recreational activities. Although it's about 20 minutes from downtown Washington, staying here has its perks. This hotel has views of the riverfront and is adjacent to the lavish Gaylord resort; a sandy beachfront; a carousel; boat rentals; and the Capital Wheel, a huge Ferris wheel offering a birds-eye view. The large suites have a bedroom and separate living area, which allows guests to relax and spread out. The hotel provides a free breakfast and has a small fitness center. There are multiple options to get into Washington from here. Besides driving, National Harbor has a courtesy shuttle to the King Street Metro station in Alexandria (across the river). It runs every hour 6:30 a.m.–8:30 p.m. Another option, more fun but less convenient, is taking the water taxi from National Harbor to the Alexandria City Marina; the water taxi runs approximately 11 a.m.–11 p.m. during the summer.

Friendship Heights/Chevy Chase

  Embassy Suites by Hilton Chevy Chase ★★★★
MODERATE

4300 Military Rd. NW, Washington, D.C.; ☎ 202-362-9300; embassysuites3.hilton.com

---

Rate per night $220–$350. **Pool** Yes. **Fridge in room** Yes. **Pet-friendly** Yes. **Maximum occupants per room** 6. **Nearby dining** Whole Foods, Maggiano's, Cheesecake Factory, P.F. Chang's, The Capital Grille, Clyde's, Potomac Pizza, Sushiko.

THIS URBAN NEIGHBORHOOD IS KNOWN FOR ITS HIGH-END SHOPS like Neiman Marcus and Saks Fifth Avenue. It will be too far to walk to D.C. attractions, but from this hotel, you're a 15-minute Metro ride from downtown. The hotel is located inside the Chevy Chase Pavilion mall, with the Friendship Heights Metro directly below the building. Many restaurants surround the hotel, too, although a hot buffet breakfast and an evening happy hour are included in your rate. The atrium in the hotel center opens up to mall shops and restaurants below. Each guest room has a full kitchen and separate living area. Whole Foods Market is within walking distance. An indoor pool, a bright bar area, and a large fitness center all add value to this hotel stay. Sign up with the Hilton rewards program to request complimentary Wi-Fi and (sometimes) free parking.

Bethesda and North Bethesda
The Canopy by Hilton Bethesda North ★★★★ MODERATE

940 Rose Ave., Bethesda; ☎ 301-882-9400; canopy3.hilton.com

Rate per night $120–$300. **Pool** No. **Fridge in room** Yes. **Pet-friendly** Yes. **Maximum occupants per room** 4. **Nearby dining** Seasons 52, Nando's Peri-Peri, Summer House Santa Monica, City Perch, Ize's Bagelry, Pho Eatery, Del Frisco's, Bibibop, &pizza, Stella Barra Pizzeria, Owen's Ordinary.

THIS HOTEL IS IN A MINI-CITY CALLED PIKE AND ROSE, and it's an option for tourists who don't mind commuting to downtown. It's located across the street from the White Flint Metro station on the Red Line, so you can be downtown in about 35 minutes. Guest rooms are spacious and were recently renovated with modern fixtures and luxurious linens. The hotel has a coffee shop and a rooftop bar and deck, complimentary bikes, evening wine tastings, and an on-site spa and salon. Marriott rewards customers should ask about complimentary breakfast. Parking is $25 per day.

  Hyatt Regency Bethesda ★★★
INEXPENSIVE–MODERATE

1 Metro Center, Bethesda; ☎ 301-657-1234; hyatt.com

Rate per night $100–$250. **Pool** No. **Fridge in room** Yes. **Pet-friendly** No. **Maximum occupants per room** 4. **Nearby dining** Woodmont Grill, Black's Bar and Kitchen, Original Pancake House, True Food Kitchen, Persimmon, Moby Dick, Don Pollo.

THIS HOTEL WAS RECENTLY REFRESHED, thanks to a multimillion-dollar renovation. Located just above the Bethesda Metro station, this is a terrific choice if you're looking for luxury at a reasonable cost. Most important, it provides easy access to downtown D.C. The hotel has a 12-story atrium, and the stylish rooms have views of downtown Bethesda, an urban neighborhood in Maryland. After a busy day of touring, take a walk or hop on the free Bethesda Trolley to movie theaters, a farmers market, upscale boutiques, dozens of restaurants, and the Capital Crescent Trail for hiking and biking.

Rockville

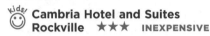

Cambria Hotel and Suites Rockville ★★★ INEXPENSIVE

1 Helen Heneghan Way, Rockville; ☎ 301-294-2200; cambriasuitesrockville.com

Rate per night $90–$150. **Pool** Yes. **Fridge in room** Yes. **Pet-friendly** Yes. **Maximum occupants per room** 4. **Nearby dining** Five Guys, La Canela, Sushi Damo, Peter Chang, World of Beer, First Watch, La Tasca, Bonchon Chicken, Lebanese Taverna, Thai Pavilion.

THIS HOTEL IS LOCATED IN ROCKVILLE TOWN CENTER, a multiuse development anchored by a modern library. Around the town center are dozens of shops and restaurants, a movie theater, the Capitol Limited Amtrak stop, and a Metro stop. You can take the Red Line from Rockville to Washington in about 45 minutes, and then return to a comfortable hotel room with queen beds, a microwave, a sleeper sofa, and room to spread out. There's an indoor pool, and in winter, an outdoor ice-skating rink. A coffee bar and well-equipped gym round out the amenities.

VIRGINIA SUBURBS

Old Town Alexandria

Hotel Indigo ★★★ INEXPENSIVE–MODERATE

220 S. Union St., Alexandria; ☎ 703-721-3800; hotelindigooldtownalexandria.com

Rate per night $104–$350. **Pool** No. **Fridge in room** No. **Pet-friendly** Yes. **Maximum occupants per room** 4. **Nearby dining** Union Street Public House, Virtue Feed & Grain, Fish Market Restaurant, Pizzeria Paradiso, Chart House, Gadsby's Tavern.

THIS IS A PRIME LOCATION FOR VISITORS WHO LOVE HISTORY and want to enjoy the delights of Old Town Alexandria. The hotel's proximity to the Potomac River helps explain how, during its construction, builders unearthed a 50-foot sunken vessel from the 1700s. This boutique-style hotel offers visitors the ability to walk to shops, waterfront parks, and the Torpedo Factory Art Center, along with an endless array of restaurants. While it's not close to the Alexandria Metro station, you can take the Old Town Trolley there, or hearty souls can walk the 16 blocks through the safe and charming neighborhood. You will walk in the footsteps of our founding fathers when you stay in Old Town.

Residence Inn Alexandria Old Town/Duke Street
★★★   MODERATE

1456 Duke St., Alexandria; ☎ 703-548-5474; marriott.com

Rate per night $140–$225. **Pool** No. **Fridge in room** Yes. **Pet-friendly** Yes. **Maximum occupants per room** 6. **Nearby dining** Whole Foods, Brabo, Laporta's, Hard Times Cafe, Table Talk Restaurant, Perfect Pita, Namaste.

SAVE SOME MONEY and still find yourself in one of Washington's most delightful neighborhoods, Old Town Alexandria. Founded around the time of the American Revolution, Old Town features impressive Colonial-era attractions and charming cobblestone streets. Hop the Old Town Trolley to visit shops, restaurants, and the waterfront parks. It's also easy to get to D.C.'s best tourist sites by taking the King Street Metro (Yellow Line), only three blocks away. Each of the Residence Inn's suite-style rooms has a kitchenette, separate living area, and sleeper sofa, and hot breakfast is complimentary. This location is also convenient for visiting Arlington Cemetery, Mount Vernon, and the 9/11 Memorial at the Pentagon. Ask for an upper floor for the best views.

Tysons Corner and McLean

 ### Hyatt Regency Tysons Corner Center
★★★½   MODERATE–EXPENSIVE

7901 Tysons One Place, Tysons Corner; ☎ 703-893-1234; tysonscornercenter.regency.hyatt.com

Rate per night $190–$350. **Pool** Yes. **Fridge in room** No. **Pet-friendly** Yes, small dogs. **Maximum occupants per room** 4. **Nearby dining** Shake Shack, Earl's, Coastal Flats, The Capital Grille, Silver Diner, Brix and Ale, Nostos, American Girl Bistro.

THIS IS ONE OF THE TOP HOTELS IN SUBURBAN VIRGINIA, and it is connected to Tysons Corner (a mega mall) by an open-air plaza with restaurants, a playground, outdoor games such as Ping-Pong and chess, and outdoor seating around fire pits. The rooms have separate seating areas, night-light foot sensors (these are awesome!), spa showers, and luxurious linens. Staying on the club floor entitles guests to a Continental breakfast, snacks, appetizers, and dessert daily. You don't need to go far to find restaurants, however—there are dozens inside Tysons Corner mall, plus a huge multiplex. There's an indoor pool, and the gym is open 24 hours. In partnership with the Tysons American Girl store, Hyatt has a package that includes a doll-bed souvenir and free breakfast for kids under 10 years old. There's a walkway to the Tysons Metro station for a 30-minute ride into Washington.

Arlington and Rosslyn

 ### Residence Inn Arlington Courthouse   ★★★½   MODERATE–EXPENSIVE

1401 N. Adams St., Arlington; ☎ 703-312-2100; marriott.com

Rate per night $260–$500. **Pool** Yes. **Fridge in room** Yes. **Pet-friendly** Yes. **Maximum occupants per room** 6. **Nearby dining** Me Jana, Bayou Bakery, Fire Works Pizza, Asahi, Ambar Clarendon, Cava Mezze Clarendon, Green Pig Bistro.

THIS MODERN ALL-SUITE HOTEL is adjacent to the Arlington Courthouse Metro station, so it's an easy ride into downtown D.C. The neighborhood is mostly office and government buildings, but there are several restaurants nearby in the Plaza. The hotel offers the traditional benefits of a Residence Inn—a kitchenette in every room, evening snacks, and a buffet breakfast. The rooms are not luxurious, but they work well for families. The small pool is a hit with kids, and the area is very walkable. A short Metro ride away is a bonanza of dining and shopping options in Clarendon town center. This is a good location to access attractions such as the Artisphere, the U.S. Marine Corps Memorial, Arlington Cemetery, Theodore Roosevelt Island, the Observation Deck at CEB Tower, and the scenic walk across Key Bridge into Georgetown.

GETTING *a* GOOD DEAL *on a* ROOM

HOTEL PRICING IN WASHINGTON, D.C., is driven not only by tourism but also by business, government, and convention trade, and that translates to high rack rates (a hotel's published room rate). Even in the suburbs, where you might expect lower rates as the trade-off for commuting into town, there are few bargains because, no matter how far you are from the Capitol, you are apt to be close to some agency, airport, university, or research complex. The Bethesda Marriott near Grosvenor-Strathmore, for example, is 30–40 minutes away from the Mall but remains busy year-round because it's close to the National Institutes of Health.

> *un*official **TIP**
> Always use your friendliest voice when asking for favors, and avoid calling between 10 a.m. and 3 p.m., when the staff is busiest dealing with checkout and check-in.

One key factor in getting a better deal is having flexibility on your travel dates. If you're traveling during your kids' school vacation schedule, that, of course, limits your flexibility. But while you're on the phone with the hotel, ask which days may have lower rates.

Another trick is to check the internet to see what aggregate sites, such as trivago.com, kayak .com, and booking.com, offer (more about that in the next section). Then, even if you are considering a chain hotel rather than an independent

> *un*official **TIP**
> In addition to the quoted room rates, the District of Columbia imposes a 15% hotel tax (including sales tax); hotels in the suburbs, once town and state taxes are figured in, can be almost as high, so add that into your budget.

establishment, call the specific Washington location, not the toll-free number, which is likely to be located in some other city. While the central operator may not be aware of local specials, the in-town reservations desk should know about special packages. If you're a member of a loyalty club, such as Marriott Bonvoy or Wyndham Rewards, ask for complimentary services like free breakfast, Wi-Fi, and parking.

If you're staying for several days, ask whether you might stay for any additional nights at a reduced rate or even free. If you're talking to the on-site staff, seek more specific information about quiet rooms, good views, access to a swimming pool, and the nearest Metro stop.

When you call, you can find out how old the hotel is, how recently the rooms—and the bathrooms—were renovated, and whether the photos on the hotel's website are up-to-date. Be sure to ask if there is any ongoing construction, either inside the hotel itself or nearby. Just because the work isn't being done on your floor, it may start before you want to get up in the morning, and dust or paint smells can work their way around through the elevators and ductwork.

If you are driving to Washington, find out if the hotel provides parking, and for how much; valet and overnight fees can be substantial. Ask about alternative parking garages near the hotel to see if the garage offers discounts to hotel guests. You can also check the app **SpotHero** for up-to-the-minute parking information.

If your visit to Washington coincides with a major convention or trade show, hotel rooms are likely to be scarcer and more expensive than if you can avoid the big-business traffic. If you have flexibility with travel dates, you might avoid the conventions and trade shows; check the calendar at dcconvention.com.

Look into weekend, off-season, and corporate rates. In January, February, and August, hotel rates in D.C. are reduced significantly. Hotels often tout cheaper weekend rates if they cater to business travelers who stay during the week and go home on Friday. Others offer corporate rates of 5–20% off-rack, and you may not have to work for a large company to qualify: just ask. Some hotels will guarantee you the discounted rate when you make your reservation; others may make the rate conditional on your providing a fax on your company's letterhead requesting the rate, or a company credit card or business card upon check-in. Membership in AARP or AAA often qualifies you for notable discounts as well.

THE INTERNET ADVANTAGE

ALTHOUGH THE PERSONAL TOUCH IS THE BEST IDEA, once you get to the point of making your reservation, it's worth understanding how the internet affects hotel rates.

Months in advance, hotels establish rates for each day of the coming year, taking into consideration weekend versus weekday demand; holidays, major conventions, trade shows, and sporting events; and the effect of weather on occupancy. If demand is greater than forecast, the rate may rise; if demand is less than expected, the hotel will begin "nudging," or incrementally decreasing the rate for the days in question until bookings rebound to the desired level. A hotel can adjust website rates almost hourly. Consequently, major internet travel sellers, such as Travelocity, Hotels.com, and Expedia, among others, can advertise special deals and rates almost instantaneously. Lower rates and deals are also communicated by email to preferred travel agents, and sometimes directly to consumers. It's a good idea to sign up for a hotel's email blasts if you're thinking about visiting.

An easy way to scout room deals is on **kayak.com,** which scans not only internet sellers but also national hotel chain websites and some individual hotel websites. You can organize your search by price, location, star rating, brand, and amenities; plus, you can see detailed descriptions of each property, photos, customer reviews, and maps. Kayak provides a direct link to the lowest-price sellers. Other websites to scour include **groupon.com, costco.com, oyster.com,** and **jetsetter.com.**

Also consider **priceline.com,** where you see prices not at a specific hotel, but within a neighborhood and quality level. When you make a nonrefundable payment, you will be assigned to a hotel and your credit card charged. Notification of your hotel assignment is the next step. Hopefully the selection lives up to your expectations, but that's a risk you take for reduced rates. **Hotwire.com** is structured similarly— you pay in advance and you may or may not know which hotel you'll be assigned until after payment. They typically show you that it will be one of three hotels or limit the options to certain brands like Westin or InterContinental.

When you book your flight, some major airlines have packages that include airfare and hotels, including JetBlue, Delta, and Southwest. Price the cost of the flight and hotel separately to see if you're getting a good deal when you book your package with an airline.

If you are coming into town for a convention or trade show, and the sponsoring agency has negotiated a special rate with area hotels for a block of rooms, you can use some of these same techniques to figure out whether it really is a good deal. (Afer all, a lot of travelers simply take for granted that the block rate is a bargain.)

Check the rate offered on websites; if you think you can do better, book it on the internet, call one of the (preferably local) reservation services, or try your luck with the hotel directly. Or avoid the crowd altogether; look through our guide for something that suits you better. The earlier you book, the broader your options. Just remember: stay near the Metro.

WEBSITES OFFERING D.C. HOTEL PACKAGES

- groupon.com/travel/washington-dc/hotels   • hotelsneardcmetro.com
- costcotravel.com   • washington.org/hotel-deals   • wdcahotels.com

---

TRAVEL AGENTS AND VACATION PACKAGES

FIRST, FIND OUT WHETHER YOUR TRAVEL AGENT has actually been to Washington, because an agent who doesn't know the territory may turn to a tour operator or wholesaler and then pass that package along to you. That allows the travel agent to set up your whole trip with a single phone call and still collect an 8–10% commission, but it may not be the best bargain for you.

Here's why: package vacations seem like win-win deals for buyers and sellers. The buyer makes one phone call to set up the whole trip: transportation, lodging, meals, tours, attraction tickets, and perhaps even golf or spa services. Similarly, by settling everything in a single conversation, the seller avoids multiple sales calls, confirmations, and billing. In addition, some packagers benefit by buying airfares and hotel rooms in bulk at significant savings, bargains theoretically passed along to the buyer.

In practice, however, the seller may be the only one who benefits. Wholesalers typically work with specific airlines or chains rather than looking for deals. Many packages are padded with extras that cost the bundler next to nothing but grossly inflate the retail price, as with a loaded new automobile. Many of the extras in the package sound enticing but won't get used (most people overestimate how much can be crammed into a single day) or may not be as advertised (we've all had a "hot" hotel breakfast that wasn't).

So you should present your agent with some information up front. Choose a neighborhood you prefer, and maybe a second choice; if possible, specify a hotel. (Check our ratings in the table on pages 54–55, use the websites, and see the local website listings in the "Gathering Information" section of Part One (page 20.) If you see a good package advertised online or in a travel publication, follow up by calling the hotel or package operator for more information—but don't make the reservation yourself. Even if it seems that you're doing all the work yourself, you should still let the agent do the actual booking. He or she might still get a commission (free to you) and is more likely to know whether the deal is too good to be true. And you should always give your agent a chance to match or better the package once you have a baseline to go by.

One word of caution, however: If you make a reservation through anything other than the hotel itself, you must then submit any changes or complaints to that service. The hotel will no longer consider you their customer; rather, they expect your proxy to speak and act on your behalf. This can be frustrating if you can't reach the wholesaler or website.

If you are considering booking a package yourself, choose one that includes at least some features you are sure to use; you'll pay for them all anyway. Spend an hour surfing and estimate what the major components of your trip—airfare, lodging, transportation, museum tickets—would actually cost. If the package costs less, or is even close, go for the convenience factor and book the package. Remember local factors too. For example, if offered a choice of rental car or transportation to and from the airport, free transportation would be more useful in Washington than a car. And if at all possible, be flexible about travel time; some specials do live up to the hype, but you may have to move fast.

Don't forget that if you have a premium credit card, you probably have a "concierge" too. These are basically unpaid travel agents (at least, not paid by you), and because cards tend to be accepted almost everywhere these days, these agents can often scout a variety of hotels and packages, find out whether your rewards or points can be transferred to a hotel or airline, and more. They also keep track of short-term fare deals. Again, just try to have an idea of what going rates are.

WHEN ONLY *the* BEST WILL DO

NOTE: The following are listed in alphabetical order and not by rank.

Best Luxury Boutique Hotels

- **The Alexandrian** Alexandria
- **The Avery Hotel** Georgetown
- **Donovan Hotel** Dupont Circle
- **Hotel Hive** Foggy Bottom
- **Hotel Lombardy** Foggy Bottom
- **Kimpton Hotel Monaco** Penn Quarter
- **Kimpton Lorien Hotel & Spa** Alexandria
- **The Jefferson** Dupont Circle
- **The Line DC** Adams Morgan
- **The Mansion on O Street** Dupont Circle
- **Morrison-Clark Historic Inn** Convention Center
- **Moxy Washington, DC** Downtown/White House
- **Rosewood Washington, D.C.** Georgetown
- **Sofitel Washington, D.C. Lafayette Square** Downtown
- **Tabard Inn** Dupont Circle

Best Family-Friendly Chain Hotels

- **Cambria Hotel and Suites** Rockville, Maryland
- **Comfort Inn Downtown DC/Convention Center**
- **Courtyard Washington Downtown/Convention Center** Penn Quarter
- **Embassy Suites Hotels** Dupont Circle, Friendship Heights, Georgetown, Convention Center
- **Gaylord National Resort & Convention Center** National Harbor
- **Georgetown Suites**
- **Hilton Garden Inn** near McPherson Square
- **Holiday Inn Washington–Capitol** National Mall
- **Holiday Inn Washington–Central/White House** Downtown
- **Holiday Inn Rosslyn** Arlington, Virginia
- **Homewood Suites** Dupont Circle
- **Hyatt Regency Washington on Capitol Hill**
- **Residence Inn National Harbor**
- **Residence Inn Washington, DC/Capitol**
- **Residence Inn Washington, DC/Foggy Bottom**

Best Swimming Pools (INDOOR AND/OR OUTDOOR)

- **Cambria Washington, D.C. Convention Center**
- **Courtyard Washington, DC/Dupont Circle**
- **Courtyard Washington Downtown/Convention Center**   Penn Quarter
- **Courtyard Washington, DC/Foggy Bottom**
- **Courtyard Washington Capitol Hill/Navy Yard**   Capitol Hill
- **Donovan Hotel**   Dupont Circle
- **The Embassy Row Hotel**   Dupont Circle
- **Embassy Suites Chevy Chase Pavilion**   Northwest D.C.
- **Embassy Suites Washington Convention Center**   Penn Quarter
- **Fairmont Washington, D.C.**   Georgetown
- **Four Seasons Hotel Washington, DC**   Georgetown
- **Gaylord National Resort & Convention Center**   National Harbor
- **Grand Hyatt Washington**   Downtown
- **Hampton Inn Washington, D.C.**   White House
- **Hilton Garden Inn**   Bethesda
- **Hilton Garden Inn Washington, D.C./US Capitol**   Capitol Hill
- **Holiday Inn Washington–Capitol**   National Mall
- **Holiday Inn Washington–Central/White House**   Downtown
- **Hyatt Regency Washington on Capitol Hill**
- **Hyatt House Washington, D.C./The Wharf**
- **InterContinental Washington, D.C.**   The Wharf
- **JW Marriott Washington, DC**   Downtown
- **Kimpton Hotel Palomar**   Dupont Circle
- **Liaison Washington, D.C.**   Capitol Hill
- **Mandarin Oriental**   Capitol Hill
- **Marriott Wardman Park**   Woodley Park
- **Mason & Rook Hotel**   Downtown
- **MGM National Harbor**   National Harbor
- **Omni Shoreham Hotel**   Woodley Park
- **One Washington Circle Hotel**   Foggy Bottom
- **Park Hyatt Washington D.C.**   Georgetown
- **Residence Inn Washington, DC/Foggy Bottom**
- **Residence Inn Washington, DC/Capitol**   Capitol Hill
- **Ritz-Carlton Washington, D.C.**   Georgetown
- **Ritz-Carlton Pentagon City**
- **Rosewood Washington, D.C.**   Georgetown
- **Washington Hilton**   Dupont Circle
- **Washington Marriott at Metro Center**   Penn Quarter
- **Washington Plaza**   Thomas Circle
- **The Watergate Hotel**   Foggy Bottom
- **Westin Georgetown**

Best Hotel Restaurants

- **American Son** at Eaton Hotel
- **Bistro Bis** at Kimpton George
- **BLT Prime** at Trump International Hotel
- **Blue Duck Tavern** at Park Hyatt Washington D.C.
- **Bourbon Steak** at Four Seasons Hotel
- **Brabo Brasserie** at Kimpton Lorien Hotel & Spa
- **Café du Parc** at Willard InterContinental
- **Edgar Bar & Kitchen** at Mayflower Hotel
- **Estuary** at Conrad Washington, D.C.
- **Fish by José Andrés** at MGM National Harbor
- **Kingbird/Top of the Gate** at Watergate Hotel
- **Kith/Kin** at InterContinental Washington, D.C.-The Wharf
- **The Lafayette/Off the Record** at Hay-Adams
- **Old Hickory Grill** at Gaylord National Resort & Convention Center
- **Opaline Bar & Brasserie** at Sofitel Washington, D.C. Lafayette Square
- **Plume** at The Jefferson
- **A Rake's Progress** at The Line DC
- **Seasons** at Four Seasons Hotel
- **Tabard** at Tabard Inn
- **Voltaggio Brothers Steak House** at MGM National Harbor

Best Hotel Fitness Centers

- **Club Quarters Hotel Washington, D.C.**   White House
- **The Embassy Row Hotel**
- **Fairmont Washington, D.C.**
- **Four Seasons**
- **Gaylord National Resort & Convention Center**   National Harbor
- **Hyatt Regency Washington on Capitol Hill**
- **The Jefferson**   Dupont Circle
- **Kimpton George**   Capitol Hill
- **Kimpton Glover Park Hotel**
- **Kimpton Hotel Palomar Washington, D.C.**   Dupont Circle
- **Mandarin Oriental**   Capitol Hill
- **Marriott Marquis Washington, D.C.**   Convention Center
- **The Mayflower Autograph Collection.**   White House
- **MGM National Harbor**
- **Omni Shoreham Hotel**   Woodley Park
- **Park Hyatt Washington D.C.**   Georgetown
- **Renaissance Washington, D.C. Downtown Hotel**
- **Ritz-Carlton Georgetown**   Georgetown
- **Ritz-Carlton Washington, D.C.**   Georgetown

Best Hotel Fitness Centers *(continued)*

- **Washington Hilton Hotel** Dupont Circle
- **Willard InterContinental** White House

Best for High Tea

- **Brothers and Sisters at The Line DC** Any day
- **Empress Lounge at the Mandarin Oriental** Friday–Sunday
- **Fairmont Washington, D.C.** Saturday and Sunday
- **Four Seasons Hotel** Saturday and Sunday
- **Henley Park Hotel** Any day with advance reservations
- **The Jefferson** Saturday and Sunday
- **Kingbird at The Watergate Hotel** Saturday and Sunday
- **Mansion on O Street** Advance reservations for groups only
- **Park Hyatt Washington D.C.** Saturday and Sunday
- **Ritz-Carlton Pentagon City** Saturday and Sunday
- **Ritz-Carlton Tysons Corner** Seasonal
- **The St. Regis** Any day with advance reservations
- **Willard InterContinental** Friday–Sunday only

Best Hotel Bars

- **Bar Moxy** at Moxy Washington, DC
- **Barrel & Bushel** at Hyatt Regency in Tysons Corner
- **Benjamin Bar** at Trump International Hotel
- **Blue Bar Lounge** in Henley Park Hotel
- **CUT Bar and Lounge** at Rosewood Washington, D.C.
- **Doyle Bar & Lounge** at The Dupont Circle
- **The Dubliner** at Phoenix Park Hotel
- **Empress Lounge** at Mandarin Oriental (garden)
- **Estuary** at Conrad Washington, D.C.
- **Jardenea Lounge** at Melrose Hotel Washington, D.C.
- **Kintsugi** at Eaton Hotel
- **The Living Room** at W Washington D.C.
- **The Lounge** at Bourbon Steak, Four Seasons
- **Next Whisky Bar** at The Watergate Hotel
- **Off the Record** at The Hay-Adams
- **Opaline Bar & Brasserie** at Sofitel Washington, D.C. Lafayette Square
- **POV** at the W Washington D.C.
- **Quill** at The Jefferson
- **Round Robin Bar** at Willard InterContinental
- **St. Regis Bar** at The St. Regis

Best Views

- **Citybar Rooftop Bar** at Hyatt Place Washington DC/National Mall
- **DNV Rooftop Lounge** at the Donovan Hotel
- **Ellipse Rooftop Bar** at Hyatt Place Washington DC/White House
- **Felt Bar and Lounge** at MGM National Harbor in Maryland
- **The Graham Georgetown Rooftop** at The Graham Georgetown
- **Key Bridge Terrace** at Hyatt Centric Arlington
- **Pose Rooftop Lounge** at Gaylord National Resort & Convention Center in National Harbor, Maryland
- **POV** at W Washington D.C.
- **The Rooftop** at Embassy Row Hotel
- **Sky Bar** at the Beacon Hotel
- **Skydome** at DoubleTree by Hilton Washington DC–Crystal City, Virginia
- **Tony & Joe's Seafood Place** at Key Bridge Marriott in Arlington, Virginia
- **Top of the Yard** at Hampton Inn Navy Yard
- **Top of the Gate** at The Watergate Hotel
- **Waves** at InterContinental Washington, D.C.–The Wharf
- **Whiskey Charlie Rooftop Bar** at Canopy by Hilton Washington, D.C.–The Wharf

PART THREE

ARRIVING *and* GETTING AROUND

COMING *into the* CITY

WE REALIZE THERE ARE MANY FACTORS (cost, number of people traveling together, distance, time) involved in choosing a mode of transportation, and there are plenty of options when it comes to travel to Washington, each with pros and cons. Here are the basics.

ARRIVING BY CAR

IF YOU DRIVE, you will most likely arrive either on one of three interstate highways (I-95 from the north or south, I-66 from the west, or I-70/270 from the northwest); on US 50 from the east; or on the Baltimore-Washington Parkway, which parallels I-95 between Baltimore and Washington.

unofficial **TIP**
You'll hear constant references to the Inner Loop and Outer Loop in directions and traffic reports. These refer to the twin circles of the Beltway. Because Americans drive on the right, the Inner Loop runs clockwise and the Outer Loop counterclockwise.

All the routes connect with Washington's Capital Beltway, I-495, which is where it gets confusing. The Capital Beltway is a 64-mile loop that encircles the District of Columbia through the Maryland and Virginia suburbs. Six major bridges cross over the Potomac River, and they experience nearly constant bottlenecks. The Beltway has a few different names in different parts of town. It's called both I-95 and I-495 because I-95 is rerouted along the southern and eastern half of the Beltway. The signage along the scenic George Washington Memorial Parkway is complicated, but one rule to remember is to follow the Potomac shoreline.

Much of the highway construction in recent years is designed to make life easier for commuters, but it can make driving even more stressful for outsiders. There are **HOV,** or high-occupancy vehicle, lanes on many area highways, but their hours of restriction vary. Express lanes have opened around the Springfield Interchange, where the

Beltway meets I-95, and prepare to be confused by battling signage. It also gets complicated around Tysons Corner, which runs around the southwest quadrant of I-495. There are only a few, sometimes obscure, entrances to the Express lanes, and using them requires an **E-ZPass**. *If you don't have an E-ZPass, don't use the toll lanes on I-495.* You'll incur expensive fines for doing that.

You won't have to pay a fee to use the Dulles Access Road to Dulles International Airport. This express route parallels the Dulles Toll Road from the Beltway, but it has no exits. There is also a toll road in Maryland, between I-270 and I-95, officially MD 200 (locally known as the ICC or Intercounty Connector); it has four intermediate exits and also requires an E-ZPass. For more information, visit 495expresslanes.com or mdta.maryland.gov.

If at all possible, *avoid rush-hour traffic,* especially between 6:30 and 10:30 a.m. and between about 2:30 and 7 p.m. When locals talk about gridlock, they are referring not only to politics, but also to traffic jams. In some bottleneck areas, like where I-95 meets I-495, expect slow traffic, even on the weekends. In particular, avoid what is called the "Friday getaway," noon–7:30 p.m. on summer weekends between Memorial Day and Labor Day. And remember, a majority of commuters have to cross some bridge or other to get into the city; one fender-bender and the highway becomes a parking lot. In the winter, snow and ice can impose a whole new set of challenges, as city drivers are not known for their skills in this area. Expect huge delays on all roads when there's a winter-weather advisory.

ARRIVING BY PLANE

RONALD REAGAN WASHINGTON NATIONAL AIRPORT Of the area's three airports, Reagan National Airport is by far the most convenient, located a few miles south of D.C. on the Virginia side of the Potomac River, and is the favored airport of Congress members headed home to their districts. But its proximity to the capital (with its restricted airspace for security reasons) and so many residential neighborhoods, has resulted in limits on overnight flights and those outside a 1,250-mile perimeter (because larger jets are louder).

unofficial **TIP**
All three Washington regional airports have designated animal relief areas for those traveling with pets and USO lounges for members of the armed services and their families (and service animals). All three also participate in the TSA's PreCheck program.

Reagan National is expanding and adds new airlines every year. There's a very convenient Delta Shuttle to New York's LaGuardia, Chicago's O'Hare, and Boston's Logan Airports multiple times each day. Reagan has an original vintage-looking building and two stunning terminals with domelike ceilings, built to pay tribute to Thomas Jefferson's Monticello.

Reagan National offers several options for getting into the city or suburbs. The airport's own Metro station is the most obvious: Both the Blue and Yellow Lines stop here, offering connections to other lines at several crosspoints in the system. Two pedestrian bridges connect the

Washington, D.C., and Vicinity

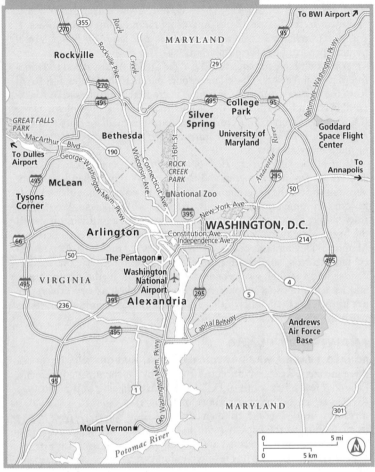

Metro to terminals B and C, although if you have extra baggage or are transferring terminals, you can take a free shuttle. Two ground-transportation centers located on the baggage claim level provide information on the Metro, taxi service, Uber and Lyft, shuttle vans, and rental cars.

Union Station, home of D.C.'s Amtrak trains, is also on the Metro, although you have to transfer at Gallery Place or Metro Center to get to Reagan National Airport. There's also an Amtrak stop in Alexandria by the King Street station.

Cab fares from Reagan National range from about $22 to downtown to $25 to Union Station. We do not recommend renting a car unless you plan to take road trips from D.C.—you'll have to negotiate some of the busiest traffic just to get out of the immediate area. There are trains you can take from Union Station to Baltimore, Philadelphia, New York, and Richmond.

SuperShuttle shared-service vans depart regularly to various destinations in the D.C. area. Fares start at $14 for travel into the District of Columbia. Three SuperShuttle ticket counters are located at Reagan National; look for the WASHINGTON FLYER/SUPERSHUTTLE signs posted throughout the airport. For more information, exact fares, and reservations, call ☎ 800-258-3826 or go to supershuttle .com. Other options include Go Airport Shuttle, The Airport Shuttle, Airport Quick Connection, and Rendez-Vous Limousine Service.

For detailed information about Reagan National Airport, go to flyreagan.com.

THE SMITHSONIAN NATIONAL AIR AND SPACE MUSEUM'S Steven F. Udvar-Hazy annex, 2.5 miles from the Dulles Airport, houses a Concorde, the space shuttle *Enterprise,* and the *Enola Gay,* among other aviation and aerospace legends.

WASHINGTON DULLES INTERNATIONAL AIRPORT is located 26 miles west of downtown in the Virginia suburbs. Housed in a soaring landmark building designed by architect Eero Saarinen, Dulles International is 45 minutes to an hour from the city by car. There is no direct public transportation to downtown yet, but an extension of the Metro on the Silver Line is scheduled to open in late 2020.

Dulles is primarily known as an international hub—more than 30 international airlines fly in and out of here, along with a dozen domestic airlines: United Airlines has a major hub at Dulles.

The building has five terminals, and all are accessible by either AeroTrains, underground passenger trains that travel between three terminals, or elevated, vanlike Mobile Lounges. There are 135 airline gates. For complete information on the airport and services, go to flydulles.com.

Until the Silver Line is complete, Dulles remains the least convenient of the three airports serving Washington, despite the existence of the airport-only Dulles Access Road, which connects with the Capital Beltway and I-66. In fact, Bloomberg recently ranked it the third-most frustrating airport in the country. Cab fare is about $76–$86 to downtown Washington. You'll get a better deal from Uber or Lyft, though it's sometimes hard to meet up with them at this busy Arrivals road. Tip: It's easier to meet your driver on the Departures level, one floor above.

Washington Flyer coach service to the Wiehle/Reston Metro station operates daily and leaves about every 30 minutes ($5 one-way); it takes 15–20 minutes, depending on traffic. For more information, call ☎ 888-927-4359 or visit washfly.com. SuperShuttle shared-ride vans will take you anywhere in the D.C. metropolitan area; there's usually about a 30-minute wait, and fares start at about $29 to the downtown area (additional members of the party are $10 each). Another service called Go Airport Shuttle offers transportation to and from all three D.C.-area airports; visit theairportshuttle.com for details.

 THIS TAKES SOME TIME BUT WILL SAVE YOU MONEY. Metrobus offers transportation from Dulles Airport to three Virginia stops. Metrobus has service from the L'Enfant Plaza Metro station (near the National Mall) with stops at the Rosslyn Metro, Herndon/Monroe Park and Ride, and Tysons West*Park Transit Station, which might be handy for those staying in the Virginia suburbs. The 5A bus leaves L'Enfant Plaza every 25–45 minutes weekdays and on the hour between 6:30 a.m. and 11:40 p.m. on weekends. The trip takes close to an hour and costs $7 each way; you must have exact change if you don't have a Metro SmarTrip Card. Be mindful that the bus may be crowded during peak hours. For more information, visit wmata.com /bus/timetables. For information on SmarTrip cards, see "Taking the Metro," starting on page 94

If you happen to be staying or working near Dulles Town Center, there is also bus service from there to the airport, with five stops in between. The **Dulles 2 Dulles Connector** leaves from the town center every 45–60 minutes between 7 a.m. and 6:30 p.m. weekdays. The trip takes about 45 minutes and costs only $1. (This shuttle also stops at the Udvar-Hazy Air and Space Museum.) For more information, call ☎ 877-777-2708 or go to vatransit.org.

BALTIMORE/WASHINGTON INTERNATIONAL THURGOOD MARSHALL AIRPORT There's a reason that *Baltimore* comes first in the name; it's located only 10 miles south of Baltimore's Inner Harbor but about 35 miles—a 50-minute drive in the best of traffic conditions—from downtown D.C.

Although it is a true international airport, Baltimore/Washington International Airport (BWI) handles primarily domestic air traffic (with the exception of British Airways and Turkish Airways). It's a Southwest Airlines hub, which accounts for more than half the traffic. Its popularity as a lower-cost, high-efficiency airport has kept business booming. Aviation.com has named it one of the Top 10 easiest airports to get to, in great part because, despite its out-of-the-way location, it has public transportation links to Washington via both Amtrak and the MARC Train to Union Station.

Cab fare from BWI to downtown D.C. starts at about $90 without tip. Metrobus B30 offers express service to the Greenbelt Metro station on the Green and Yellow Lines, leaving every 40 minutes daily from about 6 a.m. to 10 p.m. weekdays and 9 a.m.–10 p.m. weekends; the fare is $6 ($3 for seniors and disabled passengers), and the transfer onto the subway system is free. Greenbelt is also a stop for the MARC Camden Line (described on the next psage), which terminates at Union Station. For information, call ☎ 202-637-7000.

Amtrak has a designated station at BWI, and the free shuttle ride from the airport over to the station takes only a few minutes. The shuttle runs every 12 minutes from 5 a.m. to 1 a.m. and every 25 minutes from 1 to 5 a.m. (bwiairport.com/en/travel/ground-transportation). Depending on the time of day, day of week, and particular train, one-way tickets to Union Station range from $13 to $39, but there is also an Amtrak stop at New Carrollton, which is a subway stop and might be closer to some Maryland destinations, such as College Park, home of the University of Maryland. Travel time from BWI to Union Station is about 30 minutes, and it's 15 minutes to New Carrollton; for information call ☎ 800-USA-RAIL (872-7245) or go to amtrak.com. MARC trains, which use the same stations as Amtrak, are inexpensive ($4 from Greenbelt to Union Station), but it's primarily a commuter service that is only available on weekdays and infrequently at that; for schedule information, call ☎ 866-743-3682 or go to mta.maryland.gov/marc-train.

For more information on Baltimore/Washington International Airport, go to bwiairport.com.

ARRIVING BY TRAIN

UNION STATION, LOCATED NEAR CAPITOL HILL, is the major **Amtrak** terminal in Washington. Once inside the restored train station (which also houses restaurants, a food court, and plenty of shopping, in case you missed a meal or need to stock up on shoes), you can jump on the Metro, located on the lower level. To reach cabs, limousines, buses, and open-air tour trolleys, walk through Union Station's magnificent Main Hall to the colonnade entrance.

Amtrak also has a station adjacent to the King Street Metro station in Alexandria, which might be more convenient for Virginia-bound travelers. For information and schedules for Amtrak, call ☎ 800-872-7245 (TTY 800-523-6590) or visit amtrak.com.

In addition to Amtrak, Washington's Union Station is served by the Maryland commuter system (MARC) and the Virginia Railway Express (VRE), which might be useful for those staying with family or friends farther out or who wish to make a day trip to some of the regional attractions.

MARC operates three lines: the Penn Line, which connects to Baltimore's Pennsylvania Station (the Amtrak terminal) with stops at the New Carrollton Amtrak/Metro station and BWI airport; the Camden Line, which terminates in downtown Baltimore near the Inner Harbor and the Baltimore Orioles and Ravens stadiums; and the Brunswick Line, going northwest through the Montgomery County suburbs along the Potomac River into western Maryland with a stop at Harper's Ferry and an extension to Frederick, Maryland. Note, however, that

unofficial **TIP**
A convenient way to compare bus fares among Washington, D.C.; Baltimore; New York; and Philadelphia is to visit godcgo.com, which monitors several bus lines, including Vamoose and Megabus.

MARC operates Monday–Friday only. For schedules and more information, go to mta.maryland.gov/marc-train or call ☎ 800-325-RAIL (TTY 410-539-3497).

VRE operates two commuter lines, one south to Fredericksburg and the other west to Manassas. Most service is inbound in the mornings and outbound in the afternoons, but some trains serve day-trippers as well. VRE also operates weekdays only; ☎ 703-684-1001 (TTY 703-684-0551) or 800-743-3873 or visit vre.org.

ARRIVING BY BUS

GREYHOUND MAY BE THE VETERAN on the block and have the most memorable slogan, but it's not up to the standards of some of the hipper modern bus lines, the routes aren't always direct, and it's not even always a bargain. If you happen to be traveling from New York or Philadelphia, or along the Northeast Corridor, you might also check into some of the new luxury bus lines, which offer free Wi-Fi, bottled water, and/or video screens. Tickets start as low as $1, and though that's obviously a very limited promotional rate, most tickets range from $20 to $50; departure and arrival points vary.

As noted in Part 1: Planning Your Visit, the Greyhound bus terminal is near Union Station, which gives you fairly easy access to the subway or taxis, but if you have much more than a carry-on, it's something of a schlep. Coach lines along the corridor have various arrival points, all of them at or very near major Metro stops. **BestBus** (bestbus.com) stops at Dupont Circle; **Washington Deluxe Bus** (washny.com) runs Lux Bus, a tricked-out bus that makes a 20-minute pit stop and runs family-friendly movies. Deluxe Bus will drop you off near the Pentagon City, Dupont Circle, or Union Station Metro stops (the route depends on the time you leave New York); **Vamoose Bus** (vamoosebus.com) stops in Bethesda, Lorton, and Arlington. **Megabus** (megabus.com) has many more destinations, most notably to college campuses around the region, including Pittsburgh, Durham, and Boston. Megabus terminates at Union Station, provides free Wi-Fi, and sometimes offers fares that dip to the bargain bin if you book several weeks ahead.

GETTING *Around* WASHINGTON

THE LAY OF THE LAND

THE DISTRICT OF COLUMBIA is a city of nearly 711,571 people (2019 estimate), but metropolitan Washington (formally the National Capital Region)—which includes Arlington County; the town of Alexandria; Prince William, Fairfax, and Loudoun Counties in Virginia; and the Maryland counties of Montgomery, Prince George's, and parts of Howard and Frederick—totals more than 6 million residents. Rockville, a few miles north of the D.C. line, is Maryland's second-largest city, after Baltimore. Loudoun County, west of Fairfax County, is the fastest-growing and, according to some surveys, wealthiest county in the nation.

ALTHOUGH IT ISN'T TECHNICALLY ACCURATE, residents generally use "Washington" or "the DMV" (District, Maryland, and Virginia)
to refer to the entire metropolitan region, and "D.C." or "the District"
to indicate the central city.

Washington's most important geographical features, the Potomac
River and, to a slightly lesser degree, the Anacostia River, can be challenges to commuters; the bridges that cross the rivers are rush-hour
bottlenecks. In town there are a number of driving challenges that add
to the confusion: alternating one-way streets; two-way streets that are
one-way at certain hours; and, of course, the two blocks of Pennsylvania Avenue immediately in front of the White House that are closed
to vehicles. Not to mention constant construction obstructions and
detours, accidents, official motorcades. . . .

On the other hand, while it's routinely exhausting to drive around
Washington, the street layout is more logical than it might seem.
Many of Washington's streets, especially downtown, are arranged in a
grid, with numbered streets running north–south and lettered streets
going east–west. The Capitol is the grid's center (although if you look
at the map, you'll see that the White House is much closer to the geographical heart), with North Capitol, South Capitol, and East Capitol
Streets looking like spokes of a wheel protruding out in those directions. What would be West Capitol Street, in effect, is the green swath
of the National Mall.

What takes getting used to are the avenues—Wisconsin, Massachusetts, Florida, New York, New Hampshire, etc.—which are named after
states and cut across the grid diagonally; they tend to lead into traffic circles or park squares that, though picturesque on a map, are the
nemesis of many drivers. To make it worse, those diagonal avenues will
disappear for the length of the square: Vermont Avenue temporarily
vanishes at either end of McPherson Square; Connecticut Avenue runs
toward, and away from, Farragut Square; and so on. Our advice is to
look at the map long enough to understand that underlying pattern.

If you are trying to find a location on a lettered street, the address
number indicates the nearest cross streets. For example, the National
Building Museum, at 401 F St. NW, is on F Street between Fourth and
Fifth Streets NW (the NW is important because there can be multiple
examples of the same address; there are, for instance, Eighth and F
Streets SE). Luckily, you can always refer to a map app like wmata
.com (the DC Metro map) or Google Maps to help you find your way.

 YOU MAY NOTICE THAT THE LETTER J IS MISSING from the lettered street names. Although long-standing legend claims that it was
because city planner Pierre L'Enfant so disliked U.S. Supreme Court
Chief Justice John Jay that he refused to acknowledge even the hom-
onym, it was actually because in those days the letters "I" and "J" were
written so much alike that it would have caused confusion.

This situation remains impossible to understand even after living here nearly five decades, so don't expect to learn it on your first or even fifth visit. Fortunately, there are signs pointing you to important attractions, as well as nice folks on the street who will gladly point you in the right direction. And, of course, you can use GPS to navigate (we natives do it all the time).

IT'S NOT JUST THE DRIVING, IT'S THE PARKING

IF WE HAVEN'T ALREADY MADE IT CLEAR why you don't want to drive around Washington, we'll point out the other problem: you'll have to park somewhere.

Though there are more than 17,000 street meters in D.C. alone, many only allow for 2 hours of parking (at up to $2.30 an hour), and meter attendants are quick to issue tickets for expired meters. Street meters and lots may require you to pay via credit card or smartphone app; adding to the hassle, various neighborhoods use different proprietary apps to allow you to park there. Some neighborhoods have blocks of parking slots to be paid for at a single machine; others have individual meters. Also, note that a lot of legal spaces turn illegal during rush hour; especially beware of this in Georgetown.

unofficial **TIP**
Incredibly, the National Park Service operates two free parking areas with a few all-day and 2-hour maximums. One is on Ohio Drive SW on the Potomac River south of the Lincoln Memorial, and the other is Lots A, B, and C south of the Jefferson Memorial near the Tidal Basin paddleboats. Needless to say, competition for the spaces is fierce, but less so in the evening, after 7 p.m., which is a lovely time to walk around the National Mall in the summer. Since the Mall and memorial parks are open 24 hours a day, the early evening and morning hours are the most tranquil times to visit.

The lingering hope is to find a space after 5:30 p.m.; however, meters in high-demand areas run until 7 p.m. or, in the premium-demand zones of Bethesda, Arlington, Penn Quarter, Adams Morgan, U Street, H Street, Capital Riverfront, and Georgetown, until 10 p.m. Plus, if you are in a restricted zone rather than a garage, it is illegal to add on more money after your time expires. Be sure to check the times on parking signs; they may be at the end of the block. Parking tickets will shock you—they usually start at $40.

Note: Most jurisdictions, especially in the District of Columbia, enforce meter fares on Saturdays. And if your car is in a traffic lane at rush hour, no matter how much you put in that box, you'll be towed, so don't even think about it. Thousands of vehicles are towed each year for rush-hour violations alone.

Parking garages charge anywhere from $12 to $25 a day or $10 an hour, and many of those are moving toward automated or smartphone payment as well. Valet parking for dinner at a hot spot can easily cost you $25. In some residential neighborhoods, such as Georgetown and Adams Morgan, parking is restricted to 2 hours, unless you have a residential parking permit on your windshield.

Every jurisdiction has a different method of assessing fares. For instance, in Arlington, there are color-coded short- and long-term parking meters—allowing everything from a half hour to 10 hours—that cost $1.75 an hour (short term) or $1.50 an hour (long term). Check transportation.arlingtonva.us/parking for more information on meters, garages, and fees.

Parking restrictions in most areas are lifted only on federal holidays and Sundays. You can use your smartphone to pay for all meters in the District of Columbia with the ParkMobile app, used by the District Department of Transportation and other major US cities. For meters in Bethesda, Wheaton, and Silver Spring in Montgomery County, download the MobileNOW! app.

Our best advice: Once you have chosen your accommodations, ask the hotel staff or the parking attendant what method of parking is nearest. But before you leave your car anywhere, be sure to read the signs.

ALTERNATIVE WHEELS

IF YOU FOLLOW OUR ADVICE to avoid driving to Washington but really want to take a day trip or go outside the mass-transit circuit, you can rent your wheels without the rental car counter. If you are already a member of the **Zipcar** auto-sharing nation (which allows you to rent by the hour as well as by the day), there are dozens of pickup locations; go to zipcar.com for details.

The popular bike-sharing network **Capital Bikeshare** has more than 500 stations around the metropolitan area, especially near subway stations. You can join for a month online or get a one-day ($7–$10), 3-day ($17), or 30-day ($28) membership at the kiosk. Once you're a member, you get the first 30 minutes of each trip free, with various hourly rates thereafter; go to capitalbikeshare.com for usage fees and a map showing station locations. You can also download the Bikeshare System Map, or use the Lyft mobile app, to rent one of their 4,300 bikes. When you're done, return the bike to any Bikeshare Station. For information on suggested commuter routes, maps, and expanded bike lanes in Washington, go to ddot.dc.gov/bike or bikewashington.org. However, be aware that as yet only a few dedicated bike lanes have been put in place downtown, and even locals find them tricky.

The Metro transit system is also bike-friendly. Most Metro parking lots have free bicycle racks (available on a first-come basis), but you can actually take your bike—classic two-wheelers only, no tandems, etc.—on the subway at non–rush hours during the week (peak hours are opening–9:30 a.m. and 3–7 p.m.) and all day on weekends and most holidays. (Supercrowded days, such as the Fourth of July, are a no-go.) Use the first and last cars only. Children under age 16 with

*un*official **TIP**
If you prefer that someone else provide the pedal power, check the tourist hot spots around the Mall and nightlife neighborhoods for a pedicab. To schedule a pickup or even a tour, contact DC Pedicab (☎ 202-345-8065, www.dcpedicab.com) or National Pedicabs (☎ 202-269-9090, nationalpedicabs.com).

bikes must be accompanied by a person over the age of 18. For more information, go to wmata.com/service/bikes.

Despite the obvious dangers of riding without a helmet, you can now rent an on-demand motorized scooter or electric bike from **Jump** (jump.com). You'll need to download the Uber app to use them. Please take the time to read the rules. Some places restrict their use. We vigorously encourage you to bring a helmet along in your suitcase if you think you will use these. There are dozens of injuries every day from their use. D.C. drivers are not known for respecting pedestrians. You can rent a helmet from **Bike and Roll DC** (bikeandrolldc.com) and use their well-maintained bikes (see page 115 in Part Four for details).

Recently, D.C. introduced the use of **Revel** e-mopeds at various locations in the city and suburbs, but it's a pilot program that may be gone by the time you read this. The price is $1 to start and 25 cents for every minute of riding. Drivers must be 21 or older and pass a driving background check to ride. For more information, visit gorevel.com.

TAKING THE METRO: *Just Do It*

EVEN IF YOU HAVE A CAR, adopt the park-and-ride method. The Metrorail system—nearly always called the Metro, though that refers to the Metrobus system as well—connects the outer suburbs to the city with 117 miles of track and 91 stations throughout the Washington area, with more stations under construction. It's the second-busiest system in the country after New York City's, transporting about 600,000 passengers every day, and it's fully accessible. Each of the six color-coded lines—Red, Blue, Green, Yellow, Silver, and Orange—run from the outlying counties through downtown D.C. The Silver line, Metrorail's most recent addition, runs west from the District (piggybacking on some Orange Line stations) to Tysons and Reston, with a station under construction at Dulles Airport.

unofficial **TIP**
The new Purple Line, operated by the Maryland Transit Administration, is a 16-mile light-rail line from Bethesda to New Carrollton. It will have 21 stations and provide a connection to the Metrorail Red, Green, and Orange Lines, as well as the MARC train and Amtrak. The Purple Line is expected to begin operation in 2022.

The Metro is a relatively clean, generally safe, and efficient system that saves visitors time, money, and energy. The trains are fairly quiet, with a mix of seats and straphangers, and heating and air-conditioning that is relatively reliable. The stations are clean, if somewhat stark, with signature arching concrete panel ceilings; in many stations the electrified tracks run along the wall and the platform is in the middle, so this helps protect the walls from graffiti. The wide-open design also explains why Metro is less susceptible to the sort of pickpocketing and petty crime often associated with subways: there are few places for thieves to hide, especially with the extensive closed-circuit TV and car-to-operator intercoms. Metro also has its own police/security force.

Trains operate Monday–Thursday, 5 a.m.–11:30 p.m.; Friday, 5 a.m.–1 a.m.; Saturday, 7 a.m.–1 a.m.; and Sunday, 8 a.m.–11 p.m. (Holiday schedules vary; check the schedule at wmata.com.) During peak hours (weekdays 5–9:30 a.m. and 3–7 p.m., but can be affected by severe weather conditions), trains run every 4–6 minutes; off-peak hours, the wait averages 12 minutes and can go to 30 minutes late at night and on weekends. Fortunately, the stations have signs indicating when the next train is expected. Check the brown poles for a list of stops that a train/line makes to ensure you're on the right one. The system is always undergoing track work and repairs, so be prepared to adjust your plans around possible station and rail closures.

Many, though unfortunately not all, street signs in Washington indicate the direction and number of blocks to the nearest Metro station. Station entrances are identified by brown columns with an *M* on all four sides, and the newer ones are marked with a combination of colored stripes in red, yellow, orange, green, silver, or blue that indicate the line or lines serving that station. (The pylon at the entrance nearest the elevator will have a wheelchair symbol on it.)

Because most stations, especially in D.C., are underground, passengers usually have to descend to the mezzanine to ride, buy passes, or add money. Stations have stairs, escalators, and elevators; the escalators in particular have been dogged in recent years with mechanical troubles, and the system is undergoing a vast maintenance and improvement program, but breakdowns do happen. If an elevator is out at a particular station, wheelchair users can ride to the next station, and shuttle service will be available.

 FOR TRIVIA BUFFS, Washington's Metro system might be a tourist attraction in its own right: The Wheaton station boasts the Western Hemisphere's longest single-span escalators, 230-foot-long behemoths that take 2.75 minutes to ride. The Forest Glen station, nearly 200 feet underground, doesn't even have escalators, only elevators.

First-time visitors should get an official **Metro Visitor's Kit,** which includes a pocket-size Metro map, sites of interest near Metro stations, and hours and fare information. You can download the kit, along with Metrobus routes for the District, Virginia, and Maryland, at wmata.com/schedules/maps. The Metro Pocket Guide and map is available for download in English and six additional languages; several others can be read in translation on the website. If you prefer to have it snail-mailed, call ☎ 888-SMARTRIP (762-7874), but you need to allow about 5 days for delivery (the sales office will ship 4–6 weeks from date of purchase). However, there is a service kiosk just inside every station entrance, and the attendants will be happy to help you sort out your directions. Or ask a local; many will volunteer assistance if you look bewildered.

unofficial **TIP**
Although it is not an actual rule, when standing on the Metro escalators, position yourself on the right side. The left side is reserved for those who are walking or climbing. If you block the left side of the moving stairs, expect to hear "Stand to the right!" (or another utterance that might be less pleasant).

You can also purchase your **SmarTrip cards** in advance at smartrip.wmata.com/storefront; they are available in denominations of $10 and $30. Other online options include a one-day pass for $15, a three-day unlimited pass for $30, and a couple of seven-day plans for $28 (during off-peak times only). For more information on SmarTrip cards, including how to purchase them, see pages 97–99.

There are several rules you must follow. Some international visitors (and New Yorkers) are accustomed to eating and drinking on their subway systems, but consumption of any sort is illegal in Metro stations, buses, and trains. You may carry water or coffee in a mug or a burger in a bag, but keep it closed. Smoking is also illegal. You must use earbuds for music and/or video devices. Also, observe the signs for seating reserved for seniors and disabled riders. If you see a parent with a child or a pregnant woman, please offer your seat. *Always let the passengers off the train before trying to board yourself, and report any unattended bags to station managers.*

Warning: Do not shove your arm between subway car doors as they are closing. These do not respond like elevator doors and *will*

unofficial **TIP**
Backpacks and suitcases take up a lot of room. It is not polite to rest them on the seat or block the aisles. Leave space available next to you unless there are ample seats available.

not reopen because of the obstruction. Make sure you don't let a purse strap or briefcase get caught, either, because you're likely to see it dragged away.

Finally, although Metro in general is very safe, it is a major people-mover, which means that you may have to endure loud or rambunctious teenagers, sports fans, or concert-goers. Isolated incidents of violence are rare, but as is the case anywhere you travel, you

should remain alert. Don't flash cash, and keep your purse tucked under your arm and zippered and your wallet in a secure place. If you feel concerned for your safety on a train, move closer to other passengers, or get out and take the next one.

PARKING AT THE METRO

THERE ARE A FEW THINGS TO KNOW before you drive to the Metro station. First, only 42 stations have parking lots, and most of those stations are outside the Beltway. (All have bicycle and motorcycle parking as well.)

None of the 91 stations accept cash at the parking lot exit; you must have a SmarTrip card or credit card to get your car out of the lot on weekdays. Occasionally, the gate will go up, but it's best to assume you're going to pay. (A major exception is Grosvenor/Strathmore; whenever there is a concert or event at Strathmore Hall or the concert center, the bars go up for 30 minutes after a show.) Parking fees vary slightly, depending on the station, but are generally $4.50–$6 a day, except on Saturdays, Sundays, and federal holidays, when you can get out of jail (so to speak) for free.

Most Metro lots and garages have close-in areas of parking spaces marked RESERVED. These require a monthly permit but are reserved only until 10 a.m., after which you may grab an empty space. Don't try to slip in too early; Metro police keep an eye out for that, and you'll likely have competition from locals.

There are a limited number of metered spaces that you may be able to grab that let you pay in coin (follow the SHORT-TERM PARKING signs), but these are usually limited to 2 hours and cost $1 per hour. In a few cases, such as Grosvenor, Rockville, and Twinbrook, there are meters on the streets and in lots just outside the main parking lot as well; though these have longer allowable hours, they are still $1 for 60 minutes. Even trickier, they accept only quarters and $1 coins.

Very few stations allow multiday or longer-term parking (up to 10 days). Those that do—New Carrollton, Union Station, Franconia/Springfield, Greenbelt, Huntington, and Wiehle/Reston East—are all likely farther out than most tourists will be staying, but you could park there and take the Metro into town with your luggage.

PREPARING, AND SQUARING, THE FARE

METRO EMPLOYS A FARE SYSTEM BASED ON DISTANCE, unlike New York, for example, where all trips cost the same regardless of how many stops you pass. One-way fare is a minimum of $2.25 and a maximum of $6 at rush hour, and a minimum of $2 and a maximum of $3.85 at non–rush hour times. Everyone over the age of 5 must have a fare pass; up to two toddlers per paying adult ride free.

Fares between specific stations are listed at the bottom of the color-coded system maps posted throughout the station, along with the estimated time of travel.

unofficial **TIP**
You are required to buy a SmarTrip card for an initial cost of $10 ($2 for the rechargeable card, plus $8 worth of travel), even if you use it only once. You can recharge the card at any Metro station.

SmarTrip Cards

For the past several years, Washington-area transit authorities have been working toward a unified system for paying fares. SmarTrip is already a mainstay of the subway system and can be used to exit any Metro station parking lot and on any Metrobus and nearly every regional bus and shuttle system (including the DC Circulator, described on pages 101–102).

The card can be reused indefinitely, which can be a great convenience for business travelers who return frequently or visitors who have family members in the area.

Metro stations have vending machines for SmarTrip cards, but you can also purchase cards (though not the seniors' version) at CVS pharmacies and many Safeway and Giant grocery stores in the Washington area. The cards are the size of a credit card and have an electronic chip rather than a strip; the screens read out the balance as you enter or exit a station. Though the vending machines can seem rather imposing in their long, square-shouldered ranks, the procedure for buying a pass is actually fairly simple: you insert cash or a credit card, and out comes the SmarTrip card that you will use to get in and out of the subway.

Notice that we said in *and* out. If you are used to a subway system that has a one-price fare for all trips, you may be in the habit of stashing the ticket or even disposing of it once you're on board. Here you must swipe your SmarTrip card again to exit. If you lose your SmarTrip card at this point, consult the gate attendant for assistance.

To buy a fare pass from the vending machine, you start with the large orange circle marked, not surprisingly, "1." Next to that are buttons that point to lighted choices on a screen (pretty much like an ATM); if you're using cash, the machine allows you to adjust the actual value—i.e., after your initial purchase of $10 ($2 for the rechargeable card and $8 worth of travel), you may insert change or cash into the machine, and then choose the amount you want on your card. (At times, we have found it useful to consult our children, who seem to understand technology much faster than adults often do.)

Like all machines that accept paper money, these occasionally turn snarky, spitting back bills they don't like, so use new, stiffer greenbacks whenever you can, or try smoothing wrinkled bills before inserting them. You can save yourself both time and aggravation by inserting or charging $10–$20 at a time, which means you're buying a ticket good for several trips at least. Be forewarned that all change is distributed back to you in coins, not dollar bills.

If you register the card when you buy it, you can replace a lost card for $2, and all the money that was still on it will be restored. If you buy your card online or by mail, it is automatically registered; otherwise, you can register it by going to smartrip.wmata.com.

SmarTrip Card Quick Reference

- Metro fare cards are like debit cards; they can be recharged and reloaded.
- You may buy a SmarTrip card with a credit card or cash at the blue "Dispense" machines in the station.
- Your initial purchase costs $10 up front; $2 goes toward the purchase of the card, while $8 goes toward your future travel within the Metro system (you can also start with $30, with $28 to travel on).
- SmarTrip cards can be used to pay at Metro parking lots and on all regional buses. They enable discounted bus transfers too (Circulator, DASH, RideOn, Fairfax Connector, TheBus, Light Rail, ART, etc.).
- To use your SmarTrip card, touch the entrance emblem at the gate, and touch your exit at the departing gate.

- Only one card per person; you can't pass a card back to another passenger.
- All passengers need a SmarTrip card, except for children under 5 years old, who may ride free with a paying adult.
- Any balance left over can be reimbursed by sending in your SmarTrip card to WMATA (less the $2 fee for the card).

For more information, visit wmata.com/fares/smartrip.

NEGOTIATING THE STATION

NOW THAT YOU HAVE YOUR SMARTRIP CARD IN HAND, you can pass the gate into the Metro station proper. Walk up to one of the waist-high gates with the green "Enter" light and white arrow (red-light turnstiles marked DO NOT ENTER do not work both ways), and press your card against the magnetic reader on the right side of the gate (clearly marked with an image of the card).

Once you're inside the gate, escalators with the name of the end station indicate which platform your train will be on. Most stations have a single, middle platform, though some have dual platforms framing the tracks. You can confirm that you're on the correct side of the platform by reading the list of stations printed on the pylons located there. (The Wheaton and Forest Glen stations are the anomalies, so far underground that they have individual tunnels for the north- and southbound trains, so you have less chance of getting on the wrong train.) The route and the appropriate stations are marked with the route color; if there are two routes that use that station but diverge farther on, make sure the station you want to get off at is marked with the correct color, or both.

If you do find that you are headed in the wrong direction, simply reverse course by walking across the platform, if it is in the middle, or go up the escalator over and down. Just don't go through the turnstile; the computer doesn't know if you're directionally challenged or not.

unofficial **TIP** As a train approaches a station, lights embedded in the floor along the granite edge of the platform begin flashing. As the train comes out of the tunnel, look for a sign over the front windshield or on the side of the train that states the train's line (Blue, Red, Green, Orange, Yellow, or Silver) and sometimes the destination. The terminus, but not the color, is also shown on the side of the train.

Some lines have shorter internal routes at rush hour, so that the busiest stations get more service. If you are staying in Bethesda, for example, you can take a Red Line train marked either Grosvenor/Strathmore or Shady Grove because both are beyond Bethesda. If you are going to Rockville, however, you may have to disembark at Grosvenor/Strathmore and wait for a Shady Grove–bound train. Also, some stations are served by more than one line—both the Blue and Yellow Lines will bring you from Reagan National Airport into town; and the Orange and Blue Lines, Silver and Orange Lines, and Yellow and Green Lines run together for several stops. Check the map or ask the agent. To be quite honest, it's confusing even to locals (I've occasionally ended up on the wrong train, or going the wrong way, and I've lived here most of my life).

Above the platform are electronic signs that tell you how long the wait will be for the next several trains—the estimations are pretty accurate—and how far each train is going (Grosvenor vs. Shady Grove, Glenmont vs. Silver Spring, etc.) APPROACHING means the train has left the previous station and is within about a minute of arriving; ARRIVING means just that. Trains go in one direction only, so you can tell which way your train is coming.

All trains have live operators who announce the next station over a PA system and give information for transferring to other lines, but you can't always hear them over the din and the static. The newer cars have electronic signs at the front and rear that list the next station. Also, those large station signs on the walls over the tracks are visible through the car windows, so if you check the map and note which stop is just before the one where you want to get off, you'll have a couple of minutes to gather your belongings (or kids) and make your way toward the doors.

Directions are always given as if you are facing forward, even though some seats face the side or the back. So if the conductor says, "Doors opening on the right," he or she means the right if you are facing forward. If you can't hear what the conductor is saying, watch the crowd shifting to one side or the other.

unofficial **TIP**
Transfers between route lines are free but usually require going up or down a level. A straight-ahead arrow means go forward, but an upward arrow at an angle means look for an escalator.

When you get off the train, in most stations, you will have a choice of turning left or right to an escalator, and the signs are not always terribly instructive. At the Smithsonian station, for example, the choices are THE MALL (which is almost certainly the one you want) and INDEPENDENCE AVENUE, which means you tunnel beneath the street and come up over on the side with federal buildings. That's not too hard to figure out. At Dupont Circle, on the other hand, one says Q STREET—which brings you out north of the circle—and the other says DUPONT CIRCLE, which lets you up south of it. So if you aren't sure of the exit in advance, it might be a good idea to ask the kiosk attendant at the first station so you don't have to go through the turnstile before discovering you're taking the long way around. But if worse comes to worst, you'll be only a few blocks away from your intended destination.

Remember, you'll have to use your SmarTrip card to exit. Touch the SmarTrip card to the image on the inside of the gate. The lighted sign on the turnstile will flash to indicate how much the fare cost and how much money is left on your card. You will just walk through and out. If you don't have enough money on your SmarTrip card, the gate will not open and you'll need to go to the exit-fare machines inside the station (they look pretty much like a fare-card vending machine). Press the SmarTrip card to the reader light, and the digital readout will tell you how much more money you need to exit the station. You'll be able to add on as much as you like, but note: exit-fare machines only accept cash (carry some change for this, if possible). To add value with a credit card, you'll have to go back to the main fare-card machines. If you don't have enough money, consult the train station operator. He or she will grudgingly accompany you through the turnstile to the machines and make you re-touch your card to pay with a credit card.

Before you enter Washington's Metro stations, you may find it useful to download Metro's Trip Planner, an app that helps you determine where you want to go and how much it will cost. It announces upcoming departures at various stations, informs you of elevator or escalator outages, indicates when the next bus is coming, and describes any disruptions that are ongoing.

Metrobuses, DASH, RideOn, Fairfax Connector, ART, CUE, Loudoun County Connector, Omniride, TheBus, DC Circulator, and Maryland Transit and Light Rail are all equipped with SmarTrip readers that work the same way—touch and go—except that you only touch it once and the fare is automatically counted. If you have used the card at a Metrorail station or other Metrobus within the past 2 hours, the SmarTrip box automatically registers your fare as a transfer, and the second trip is free. And anytime you use the SmarTrip card on Metrobus or another related shuttle, you save 20 cents over the cash price.

METROBUS *and* OTHER BUS SYSTEMS

WASHINGTON'S EXTENSIVE BUS SYSTEM, known as **Metrobus,** serves Georgetown, downtown, and the suburbs, but with 400 routes and more than 1,500 buses, it is complicated. However, it can be a good option if you're trying to reach places that don't have a Metro station. You should consult your hotel concierge about buses to places like Georgetown, the National Cathedral, and H Street Corridor and have them write down your route for you.

Similarly, while most of Washington's suburbs have good subsidiary bus or shuttle systems that connect to the subway and the District, they're probably too complicated, unless you are staying with friends who can show you the nearest stop (however, you can also consult your GPS for on-the-fly bus information).

The **DC Circulator** is the most useful bus for tourists, especially those staying downtown or doing sustained sightseeing. These comfortable, convenient buses arrive at their stops every 10 minutes, so you won't need a timetable (except during extremely busy times such as the Cherry Blossom Festival, when downtown

unofficial **TIP**
Circulator stop signs are also marked with a fish-shaped red-and-gold logo, while Metrobus stop markers are red, white, and blue. They are often, but not always, at the same intersections. Streetcars on the DC Trolley system resemble the Circulator buses.

traffic is legendary). To board the bus, look for the station signs posted on the sidewalk. Confirm that this bus is going in the direction you want to go. You're allowed to bring strollers if there's enough room, but you must fold it up when a person using a wheelchair needs to board, as they have priority. The cost of a single trip is $1. Should the fares increase, Circulator buses accept SmarTrip cards.

Circulator has a **National Mall route** (red) that loops around, connecting passengers to key attractions. It originates at Union Station and then stops at the National Gallery of Art; National Museum of American History; Washington Monument; Holocaust Memorial Museum; and Thomas Jefferson, Martin Luther King Jr., and Lincoln Memorials. It continues to the Vietnam Veterans and World War II Memorials, Smithsonian Visitor Center, National Air and Space Museum, and U.S. Capitol, and then returns to Union Station. You can get on and off at any of these stops.

The DC Circulator's yellow route connects Union Station to Georgetown by way of the Washington Convention Center and K Street NW; the section between downtown (17th and K Streets NW) and Georgetown runs until midnight weekdays and 3 a.m. Fridays and Saturdays. The routes are referred to by their names, but on the Circulator map, the light-blue route (**Dupont Circle–Georgetown–Rosslyn**) travels between Dupont Circle and Rosslyn via Georgetown, primarily along M Street NW; and the green route connects McPherson Square (called **Woodley Park–Adams Morgan–McPherson Square,** i.e., the Farragut North Metro station) with Woodley Park and Adams Morgan via the trendy 14th Street area and has service until 3 a.m. Fridays and Saturdays and midnight the rest of the week. The dark-blue route (called **Eastern Market–L'Enfant Plaza**), which connects L'Enfant Plaza to Eastern Market and the Navy Yard by way of M Street, stays open late when the Nationals or DC United play a home game. The orange route travels from Union Station through Capitol Hill (**Congress Heights–Union Station**) to the Navy Yard.

These bright-red Circulator buses, with silver and yellow stripes on the side, are a public service provided by the City of Washington, and visitors can sign up for live Twitter alerts that announce route changes or service disruption on @DCCirculator.

TAXIS *and* CAR SERVICES

WASHINGTON TAXIS ARE PLENTIFUL and relatively cheap; there are more than a dozen companies registered with the Department of For-Hire Vehicles (dfhv.dc.gov). Many companies also have wheelchair-accessible vans, which you should reserve a day in advance (and get a confirmation number).

In the District of Columbia, meter fares start at $3.50 for the first few blocks (an eighth of a mile), with each additional mile costing $2.16. Shared rider rates are $1.20 per mile (up to $3), and the wait rate is $25 per hour. The suburban taxi companies have their own rates; if you expect to use them, it is probably a good idea to call or go online to see what they are. D.C. cabs are required to have charge-card machines installed; most suburban cabs have them as well.

Cabbies can pick up other fares as long as the original passenger isn't taken more than five blocks out of the way of the original destination. That's good news if you're the second or third rider and it's raining; it's not so hot if you're the original passenger and are trying to catch a train.

Washington is currently saturated with **Uber** and **Lyft** car services. Download the Lyft or Uber app on your phone to set up an account, which includes submitting your credit card number and allowing the app to know your location. In the case of Uber, there are multiple levels of service. Low-cost **UberX** service involves rides in everyday cars driven by individuals. **UberPool** means sharing your ride with others. **UberXL** costs more but involves a professional driver and larger vehicle (best for when you're traveling with a group of up to six people). **UberBlack** means you selected a Black Car, with its private driver in a high-end sedan, guaranteed to arrive within minutes of your request.

Using Uber or Lyft involves providing your pickup location and your destination upon your request. At that time, you will see a range of pricing you can expect to pay for that ride. You can include the tip on your payment, with options of 15%–20%. During periods of intense demand, rates may fluctuate, and if tolls or fees are required by the city government, these are passed on to the passenger.

THINGS *the* NATIVES
Already KNOW

WHERE THERE'S SMOKE, THERE'S FINES

IF YOU HAVEN'T ALREADY REALIZED IT, WASHINGTON—the District of Columbia, in particular—is predominantly public territory. And since the federal government and the surrounding jurisdictions (even tobacco-proud Virginia) have finally conceded that indoor tobacco smoke is as hard on the human body as it is on art, archival materials, and even infrastructure, smoking is prohibited in all public facilities, including but not limited to: federal offices; the Smithsonian museums (and all other museums as well) and major memorials; Metrorail and Metrobus, as well as most smaller transit services; performing arts venues and cinemas; Capital One Arena; airports and train terminals; stores and shopping malls; restaurants; and hotels. Consequently, if you are a habitual smoker, you'll need to factor that in to your itineraries, or at least calculate where and when you can light up.

In February 2015, the District of Columbia approved their citizens' (age 21 and older) right to possess small amounts (2 ounces or less) of marijuana. Residents over 21 years old are also allowed to grow up to six plants in their home and possess no more than 2 ounces of marijuana. They may also possess drug paraphernalia; however, it's still a crime to sell marijuana and to smoke it anywhere other than inside the home. This means the people you may see smoking pot on the street are not allowed to do so and are committing a crime. You may still see and smell smoke, but it's not recommended. Marijuana use is not legal in Maryland or Virginia, but possession of 10 grams or less in Maryland will incur only a small fine, and possession of 10–50 grams is a misdemeanor. Maryland allows the sale of medical marijuana, and you'll see a few dispensaries around. In contrast, Virginia's laws are much tougher, and anyone in possession of less than half an ounce is eligible for a misdemeanor charge involving up to 30 days in jail and a $500 fine. Above half an ounce, and in Virginia, you could be charged with distribution, which is a felony.

Hookah smoking, especially with the large number of restaurants serving Middle Eastern cuisine, is available in many D.C. and Virginia restaurants. Vaping is also legal in the District, Virginia, and Maryland; however, anyone under the age of 21 is prohibited from buying or being in possession of smoking devices such as vape pens. Vaping is not allowed in common areas, libraries, or food businesses or on transportation platforms.

TIPPING

IS THE TIP YOU NORMALLY LEAVE appropriate in Washington? Probably, but bear in mind that while a tip is a reward for good service, people in the service industries depend on tips for their livelihood. If you have a problem, let them know so they can remedy it. Also, consider your hotel's schedule: if your room is serviced twice a day, it would be nice to leave a tip for both the day and night staff—and it might earn you extra attention. Following are some general guidelines, but in truth, we recommend the high end, especially if you are hanging out at one of the area's high-end cocktail bars. Many of the mixologists at these places have become celebrities in their own right, so if you want to command their attention, expect to flash the bigger bucks.

- **Porters, redcaps, and bellhops** At least $1–$2 per bag and $5 for a lot of baggage
- **Cab drivers** 15%–20% of the fare; add an extra dollar if the cabbie does a lot of luggage handling
- **Valet parking** $2–$5 • **Hotel housekeeping** $3–$5 per day
- **Waiters** 20% of the pretax bill • **Bartenders** 10%–15% of the pretax bill
- **Checkroom attendants in restaurants or theaters** $1 per garment
- **Shoeshine** $2 for shoes, $3–$4 for boots

MAKING A CALL

THE WASHINGTON AREA IS SERVED BY SEVERAL AREA CODES: ☎ 202 inside the District; ☎ 301 and 240 for the Maryland suburbs; ☎ 703 and 571 for the closer Northern Virginia suburbs across the Potomac River; ☎ 540 for the outer Virginia suburbs; and ☎ 410 and

443 for Baltimore, Annapolis, and the ocean resorts. The Delaware ocean resorts use the ☎ 302 area code. All calls require the full 10-digit number; depending on your phone or calling plan, you may or may not have to dial 1 first. Most pay phone calls are 50¢—if you can still find one.

RESTROOMS

THE UNOFFICIAL GUIDE FAMILY is legendarily on guard for travelers with small bladders and those who've been recently potty-trained. When we enter a marble edifice, we're not just scrutinizing the layout, the flow of the crowd, and the aesthetics: we're checking for the nearest public restrooms.

So how does Washington rate in the restroom department? Really well. That's because of the huge number of museums, monuments, federal office buildings, restaurants, bars, department stores, and hotels that cover the city, nearly all of which have clean and conveniently located restrooms.

Leading any list of great restroom locations should be the National Air and Space Museum on the National Mall. For women who claim there's no justice in the world when it comes to toilet parity, consider this: there are three times as many women's restrooms as there are men's restrooms. Most facilities have family and gender-neutral restrooms as well.

Facilities of note on the Mall include those at the National Gallery of Art, the Arthur M. Sackler Gallery, the Hirshhorn Museum and Sculpture Garden, and the National Museum of African Art. At the Arts and Industries Building, facilities are located far away from the front entrance (which means they aren't as frequently, um, frequented). The restrooms in The Castle are easier to find, not to mention they're usually not very crowded—perhaps because tourists tend to go there earlier in the day.

Nearly all the monuments have restrooms equipped for wheelchair users, including the Martin Luther King Jr., Lincoln, and Jefferson Memorials (the last two are downstairs by the museum stores), and the Washington Monument (in the ticket lodge). The restrooms at the National World War II Memorial on the Mall and the FDR Memorial are acceptable. The U.S. Capitol Visitor Center has more than two dozen restrooms, and there are more at the Ellipse Visitor Pavilion, Sylvan Theater, Botanic Garden, and White House Visitor Center. There is a stand-alone facility in Constitution Gardens. During events, port-a-potties are set up temporarily in various locations. Ask a national park ranger for specific directions while on the National Mall.

Downtown hotels, restaurants, department stores, coffee shops, and bars are good bets, although some require a purchase to receive a code to the locked doors. You won't find restrooms in Metro stations, although a few stations are located in complexes that do provide restrooms, including Union Station, Metro Center, Farragut North, Friendship Heights, and L'Enfant Plaza; ask the attendant which exit to take.

STREET LIFE

YOU MAY SEE A NUMBER of homeless people in Washington. Street corners and medians contain people asking for money or food and sleeping on the street, with their possessions piled up next to them. Occasionally, drivers are approached at stoplights by people carrying cardboard signs reading HOMELESS—WILL WORK FOR FOOD. Metro exits are sometimes populated by people begging for money. Although there are more than 4,000 people living in D.C. homeless shelters, the number of homeless people continues to climb, partially due to the high cost of living in the Metro area.

Many are lifelong D.C. residents who are poor or have disabilities, according to homeless advocacy groups. Studies show that individuals who are homeless have lower conviction rates for violent crimes than the population at large. Please be polite; look the person in the eye, and say calmly that you can't help right now. If you want to give, it's up to you, just be alert. They are almost always harmless, but they might be unstable.

Following are some recommendations for staying safe from the Metropolitan Police Department: Don't engage in lengthy conversations with a stranger, stay in well-lit areas, keep valuables close, don't walk alone at night, don't wear headphones while walking, and avoid carrying large sums of cash.

CRIME IN WASHINGTON

ALMOST 30 YEARS AGO, Washington was slammed as the "Murder Capital of the United States"—a slight exaggeration even then. Since that time, however, most of the neighborhoods that were associated with violence have been redeveloped and gentrified, and networks of surveillance cameras have been mounted in high-crime areas. Violent crime and property crime rates in D.C. have dropped by half since 1995, and local law enforcement officials call Washington very safe for tourists.

In fact, there are so many law enforcement layers, public and private, that the District might well be the most closely patrolled 68 square miles in the United States. In addition to the Metropolitan Police Department, there are the U.S. Park Police, who patrol all the monuments and parks, including the Mall; the U.S. Capitol Police, who have jurisdiction over not only the Capitol itself but also the 20-square-block area around it; the Secret Service, who patrol the area around the White House, including the Treasury Building, as well as the vice president's residence and foreign embassies and diplomats; the Marshals Service, who ensure the safe conduct of the federal judiciary, jurors, and any judicial proceedings; and the D.C. Protective Services, who guard all city buildings and agencies. The Metro transit system has its own police force. Many federal agencies—the FBI, ICE, the TSA, and the now-famous NCIS, among others—have their own armed officers. On top of that, many museums hire their own police and security guards—the Smithsonian has its own federally trained police force patrolling inside the buildings and around the grounds—as do most embassies, corporations, and international associations (which is why you should get in the habit of traveling light and security gate–friendly).

Aside from all the officers on the ground (and horseback, bicycles, motorcycles, Segways, etc.), a network of security cameras has been added around the Mall by the Park Police, and the Metropolitan Police Department has installed a similar network in high-traffic areas, such as Georgetown, the U.S. Capitol, Union Station, and around the White House. And none of that even takes into account the ever-upgraded high-tech security measures that have become standard since 9/11.

Note: It is legal to carry concealed handguns in Virginia, even in bars, though some restaurants and malls, including Potomac Mills, have opted to prohibit weapons. In theory, bar patrons who are packing aren't supposed to be consuming alcohol, but that's hard to enforce. Neither Maryland nor the District recognizes out-of-state gun licenses or permits; the District does not issue any unless the applicant has received the required amount of firearms training.

Regardless of the level of security, random violence and street crime are facts of life in any large city. You just need to be reasonably cautious and consider preventive measures that will keep you out of harm's way, as well as an escape plan just in case. Don't make yourself an easy target—or, put another way, you should make potential assailants see you as too much of a risk. Good general strategies include:

- **Don't play solitaire.** You're always less appealing as a target if you're with other people. If you're traveling alone, try to stay in well-populated areas.

- **Be alert, and always have at least one of your arms and hands free.** Washington is not known for pickpocketing, theft, or assault. I have lived here nearly all my life and have never experienced any threatening behavior or had anything stolen from my person. However, it's important to consider that thieves gravitate toward people who are staring at a smartphone, which marks you as preoccupied, or who are encumbered by luggage or packages. Billfolds are harder to snatch from a front trouser or breast coat pocket; purses should be hung across the chest. Police will tell you that a would-be thief has the least amount of control in the first few moments, so short-circuit the crime scenario as quickly as possible. If someone demands your money, take out your wallet and hurl it in one direction while you run shouting for help in the other. Always try to press the emergency button on your smartphone. Under no circumstance allow yourself to be taken to another location—a "secondary crime scene" in police jargon—without a battle. This move, police warn, provides the assailant more privacy and consequently more control. However, in a worst-case scenario, you may have to submit in hopes of finding a way of escaping; keep your cool as much as possible.

- **Know where you're going in advance,** and if you get lost, ask a shopkeeper, theater manager, bartender—what *aren't* bartenders good for?—Metro station attendant, or one of those various patrol officers for directions. Be aware of all the public and federal facilities around you. If you think you're in trouble, head to any federal office building for help. They are all patrolled by armed guards who can offer assistance, and even though many (such as embassy guards) are forbidden to leave their posts in case the "emergency" is a ruse, you'll be safe in their presence.

- **Carry a limited amount of cash.** Nearly every business accepts credit cards. If you need to use an ATM, either choose one that is inside a bank lobby or station a friend or family member behind you to make sure nobody reads your PIN. If you are making a transaction requiring you to tell the last four numbers of your Social Security number, punch it in rather than speak it out loud. And stay away from any ATM that looks temporary (at a festival), exposed, or in any way odd; sophisticated scammers have figured out how to put false fronts and magnetic-strip readers on less closely guarded machines.

- **Guard your personal information.** If you are an international visitor and need to use your passport for identification or cash-exchange purposes, you should make a photocopy and keep the original in the hotel safe or at least your room safe. If you bring your laptop or tablet—and this is equally applicable to smartphones and the like—don't have any bank account or charge-card password information on it. As an extra precaution, double-check that you haven't checked "remember me" after entering your computer username and password, either. Avoid purchasing items when using public Wi-Fi; unsecured Wi-Fi is easier to hack.

- **Be careful hailing cabs and cars.** While it's fairly easy to hail a cab on the street, late at night it's best to hail one along the busier commercial routes or approach the doorman of a hotel with a dollar or so and ask him to summon one for you. Otherwise, call a reliable cab company or order an Uber or Lyft, and stay inside while they dispatch a car to your door. Always ask the name of the driver to confirm you have the correct vehicle. When your cab arrives, check the driver's certificate, which must be posted on the dashboard, and make note of the name and cab number. Absolutely never accept an offer for a cab or limo made by a stranger in the terminal or baggage claim area; stick to the official queue. Don't be tricked by people standing at the airport arrival area who offer to give you a ride in a limo and then insist on being paid in cash. Stand in the designated cab or transportation-network-company area only.

- **Scam I am.** Every tourist city has its particular scams, and Washington is no exception. One involves charging for a map or brochure, an especially popular dodge around the top of the Smithsonian Metro. Brochures are free in Smithsonian museums. And then there are always those asking for money for train fare or the like: Use your common sense. If they look like they need money, make your own choice. You may occasionally encounter people outside sports and entertainment venues who want to give you a free hat or water bottle, as they will promptly request a donation "for the children." Just say "no thank you" and continue on your way.

PART FOUR

SIGHTSEEING TIPS, TOURS, *and* ATTRACTIONS

SO MUCH *to* SEE, SO LITTLE TIME

WE'VE ALREADY DISCUSSED the when and the how of visiting Washington, but there is also the staggering number of whats you have to choose from.

Most visitors to Washington, especially first-timers, know the places they want to visit. The four must-sees are typically the National Mall museums, the monuments, the U.S. Capitol, and the exterior of the White House. It's a reasonable itinerary when the average tourist has only two or three days.

The first thing to do is decide whether you just want to see the famous sights or the ones of personal interest. I recommend you take a bus tour first to get the lay of the land. This way you can catch a glimpse of the most famous sights, and then return to see the ones that are most compelling to you. You can tour by day or by night; get around via taxi, Uber, Lyft, bike, scooter, or Segway; relax on the hop-on/hop-off trolley or bus; or hoof it yourself.

Or design an itinerary around a theme: American history, ethnic roots, architecture, decorative arts, etc. (we have listed special-interest tours on page 117). You can hire an expert guide or try using the many helpful apps like Washington DC Travel Guide, US Capitol Visitor Guide, or DC Metro. The abundance of information online makes DIY tours easier than ever.

One advantage of exploring on your own is avoiding crowds around the same famous places at the same time. My favorite time to visit the monuments is around dinner and into the evening. These white marble landmarks are lit brilliantly, and you'll encounter fewer tourists at night. And for those seeking hidden gems, here are some less famous off-the-Mall collections in Washington:

- A collection of miniature Revolutionary soldiers fighting a mock battle (*Anderson House*)
- The finest castle in Washington. It's not the Smithsonian, and you can talk about beer. (*Heurich House Museum*)
- A four-sided Colonial-era mousetrap that guillotines rodents (*Daughters of the American Revolution building*)
- A lush tropical rainforest-type garden located just off the Mall (*Organization of American States building*)
- A jewel-encrusted Fabergé egg designed for Czar Nicholas II (*Hillwood Museum and Gardens*)
- Renoir's iconic *Luncheon of the Boating Party* (*The Phillips Collection*)
- The electric "shock box" constructed to try to revive President Woodrow Wilson's paralyzed limbs following his (highly secret) stroke (*the Woodrow Wilson House*)
- The head of Darth Vader looking down upon the relatively faithful from an almost heavenly 290 feet up (*the northwest tower of the Washington National Cathedral*)
- A 350-year-old miniature white pine tree in a bountiful Bonsai Garden (*National Arboretum*)
- Abraham Lincoln's top hat with a bullet hole through it (*President Lincoln's Cottage*)
- A 200-year-old drugstore that demonstrates how Colonial-era Americans sought medical treatment (*Stabler-Leadbeater Apothecary Museum*)

unofficial **TIP**
It's important to check the websites of the major government sites before you arrive. The list of forbidden items may change, but as of this writing you can't take DSLR cameras (cell phones are OK), oversize purses, food, water bottles, strollers, backpacks, or any sharp objects into the White House or the Capitol. Travel light, and just get used to security lines—dump those 10-gallon belt buckles.

We profile most of the area attractions mentioned here, particularly those that are easily accessible. But we also list museums and collections of special interest, along with "if you like this" options at the end of most profiles.

Remember that prices, times, and exhibits change frequently, and smaller museums may have to close occasionally to mount new exhibitions. Note that Washington is sensitive to inclement weather, especially snow, so check the attraction's website to make sure it's open before setting out.

BUT NOT SO FAST . . .

WHILE IT'S TRUE THAT most federally supported attractions don't charge admission, just because something is free doesn't mean it's easy. In the post-9/11 era, there are a lot of places we, the people, are not welcome to walk in, at least not without a reservation and—not infrequently—a government-issued photo ID. As mentioned in Part One, tickets to the White House tours must be obtained in advance through a member of Congress; the limited passes are first come, first served (whitehouse.gov/about/tours-and-events). You can, however, tour the White House Visitor Center at 15th and E Streets NW without a reservation, and it's open daily, 7:30 a.m.– 4 p.m. You'll need reservations to tour the Treasury Building, the Diplomatic Rooms of the State Department, The Pentagon, and certain sections of the U.S. Capitol and U.S. Supreme Court—see more under "The Best Tours in Town" (page 118).

Unless you're taking a tour with a Pentagon employee, you'll need a reservation to tour the Pentagon, with 14–90 days advance notice. Again, your member of Congress can be helpful, but you can make your own arrangements online at pentagontours.osd.mil. Be sure to fill out all security information. You are welcome to visit the Pentagon 9/11 memorial, however; see page 163.

Tours of the U.S. Capitol are arranged at the Capitol Visitor Center, but you should book them online in advance whenever possible. Multiple tours are available, such as the Halls of Senate, the Freedom Fighters Collection, and Family Programs. To see Congress in session, contact your representative for passes, or you can book them at visit thecapitol.gov. Passes for international visitors are issued at the House and Senate Appointment Desks on the upper level of the Capitol Visitor Center (bring your passport).

The Washington National Cathedral offers so many fascinating tours that you could spend a whole day there. The highlights include the Gargoyle Tour, Behind the Scenes Tour, and Tower Climb (see profile on page 183).

 THE WASHINGTON MONUMENT reopened in September 2019, after repairs were made from damage that occurred during an earthquake in 2011. Today you can ride the state-of-the-art elevator to the observation level in the 555-foot marble obelisk. In just 1 minute, you'll travel 50 stories to the top of the world's tallest freestanding stone edifice. On a clear day, you can see as far as 25 miles in every direction, with views of the major monuments, the Capitol, and Arlington Cemetery. Some same-day tickets are available beginning at 8:30 a.m. at the Washington Monument Lodge located on 15th Street. You can also reserve tickets online through recreation.gov. Hours of operation are 9 a.m.–5 p.m.

HAPPY HOURS
(The Sightseeing Kind)

BY AND LARGE, Washington's major attractions keep typical business hours. Smithsonian museums on the Mall are open daily, 10 a.m.–5:30 p.m., except December 25. (During summer, hours at certain museums may be extended.) There are, however, a few exceptions: The National Portrait Gallery and the Smithsonian American Art Museum, which are sort of twin museums in Penn Quarter, are open daily, 11:30 a.m.–7 p.m., except December 25. The Museum of Natural History stays open until 7:30 p.m. in summer. The National Zoo is open 8 a.m.–7 p.m. April–October and until 5 p.m. the rest of the year.

The National Gallery of Art, not part of the Smithsonian, is open Monday–Saturday, 10 a.m.–5 p.m., and Sunday, 11 a.m.–6 p.m. The Sculpture Garden stays open late from about Memorial Day through Labor Day and hosts jazz on Fridays, 5–8:30 p.m. During the coldest months, when its fountain becomes an ice rink, it's open even later. In both cases, the Pavilion Café stays open late as well.

Although the most lavishly decorated of the three Library of Congress buildings, the Jefferson, opens at 8:30 a.m. and closes at 4:30 p.m., the Madison building stays open until 9:30 p.m. weekdays, and the Adams is open that late Monday, Wednesday, and Thursday. (All three are closed on Sunday.)

The clock tower at Trump International Hotel (formerly the Old Post Office), which is independently operated by the National Park Service, is open daily, 9 a.m.–4:30 p.m., except Thanksgiving and December 25. The entrance is located behind the hotel; the tower offers one of the finest views in Washington, D.C.

The Bureau of Engraving and Printing offers a 40-minute tour Monday–Friday, 9 a.m.–6 p.m. late March–late August. You'll need timed tickets, released at 8:30 a.m. in the visitor center and gift shop.

Private museums, such as The Phillips Collection, the National Museum of Women in the Arts, and the relaunched International Spy Museum, are generally open daily, 10 a.m.–5 p.m., with extended hours once a week.

All the Smithsonian museums and National Zoo are closed on December 25 only—and during any government shutdowns. Many other attractions are closed on Thanksgiving, December 25, and January 1—and double-check whether the site you plan to visit is subject to weather closures. Mount Vernon, the Kennedy Center for the Performing Arts, and the U.S. Botanic Garden are open 365 days a year.

The majority of monuments are open 24 hours a day. We recommend you visit the memorials at the Tidal Basin end of the Mall—Lincoln, MLK Jr., FDR, and Jefferson—at dusk. Lit up by floodlights, they have an even more powerful effect than in daylight, and park rangers are on duty as late as midnight to answer questions. The Korean War Veterans Memorial, which is near the Lincoln Memorial, and the National 9/11 Pentagon Memorial were designed with darkness in mind. If you don't want to walk the area by yourself, most of the organized tour companies offer sunset and moonlight tours.

EARLY BIRD SPECIALS

AS WE MENTIONED, crowds at major attractions have somewhat discernible traffic patterns. In general, mornings are the least crowded time (another reason to stay near a Metro station—you can easily arrive at any Mall museum by 10 a.m.), and there's another slowdown in midafternoon. This is especially true of the most popular attractions, such as the National Air and Space Museum, the National Museum of Natural History, and the National Museum of African American History and Culture. If you get in and out early, you can enjoy the less-traveled galleries of the Sackler or Freer and bide your time until the family groups tail off. The first part of the week is generally the slowest, so if possible, use Thursday, Friday, and the weekend to visit attractions outside the Mall or Penn Quarter.

Whenever you can, buy tickets in advance online. In many cases, prepaid tickets save you money, speed you through lines, and can guarantee your admission time as well. This is especially true for Ford's Theatre, the National Museum of African American History and Culture, the National Archives, the U.S. Holocaust Museum, and the Museum of the Bible. The Smithsonian Castle and Holocaust Museum cafés open at 8:30 a.m., so you can easily be at the door of any of the Mall museums before 10 a.m.

If you're hoping to duck the usual noontime crush, tour through midday and make late-lunch reservations at a downtown restaurant. Many of the museums have attractive dining options; see "The Best Museum Restaurants" on page 251 in Part Five: Dining.

TAKING *an* ORIENTATION TOUR

FIRST-TIME VISITORS TO WASHINGTON can't help but notice the regular procession of open-air, multicar tour buses—motorized trolleys is probably a more accurate term—that prowl the streets along the Mall, the major monuments, Arlington Cemetery, Georgetown, and Upper Northwest Washington. These regularly scheduled shuttle buses drop off and pick up paying customers along a route that includes the town's most popular attractions. Between stops, passengers listen to a tour guide point out the city's monuments, museums, and famous buildings.

These are helpful for first-time visitors who want to get the general layout in their head first and then focus in on the specifics. They're also nice for visitors with children, restricted time, or mobility or respiratory problems. Standardized tours are also handy if you don't like to read and ride at the same time, as the conductor or driver passes along the primary facts about each building or memorial and tosses in some intriguing trivia.

unofficial TIP
Tours are not cheap, so ask whether your AAA or AARP card is good for a discount; it often is. And buying online in advance will often get you a discount. You may even be able to find an online coupon.

They can be expensive—all-day mobile tours can run $45–$55 for adults (here again, buying in advance online may save you a few dollars; check Groupon)—and they can feel like packages of postcards if they just drive by the major sights (although "premium" and "deluxe" Big Bus Tours include admission to Madame Tussauds Wax Museum). If you're pretty familiar with the major monuments, you should look into the special-interest tours, whether guided or do-it-yourself.

What follows is a broad sampling of tours, and while there are plenty of options, make sure there's some form of license attached either to the person or the vehicle.

BUS TOURS

IF YOU CHOOSE one of the big drive-around tours, you can either stick to the bus for the whole circuit or hop on and off at more than a dozen hot spots. These on/off tours circulate every 20–30 minutes, so you can pretty much set your own rhythm. On the other hand, even tour operators suggest not trying to see more than six sites in a day. So you might want to make a list of the ones you really care about. Also, although most of the bus drivers have credit card machines on board and some take Metro cards, you might want to have cash just in case.

In addition to the all- or half-day tours and even two-day itineraries, the larger companies also offer nighttime tours of the monuments and some seasonal tours (ghosts in particular).

The hop-on/hop-off **Old Town Trolley** has been around more than 30 years, and the narration is live, not prerecorded. The routes feature stops at the National Mall, downtown, at the Waterfront, and at Arlington Cemetery. They also sell round-trip boat cruises on the Potomac River to visit Georgetown, Alexandria, The Wharf, and National Harbor. Tickets for Old Town Trolley tours are available at many hotels and online at trolleytours.com/washington-dc.

DC Trails (dctrails.com) has a hop-on/hop-off double-decker bus with an open top. You can choose from one- and two-day tours, a twilight tour, and one that includes Mount Vernon.

Big Bus Tours (bigbustours.com) operates a hop-on/hop-off double-decker service, with tickets for one or two days and a prerecorded narration. The nighttime tours to see the monuments with live narration are especially popular.

Gray Line (graylinedc.com) offers some of the longest, farthest-ranging tours, such as the 8-hour version that takes in Mount Vernon, Old Town Alexandria, Arlington Cemetery, and the Iwo Jima Memorial, and The Battle of Gettysburg day trip from D.C., but they cater primarily to groups.

All About Town (allabouttown.net) provides chartered bus tours with an expert guide in a variety of vehicles and offers pickup from many downtown hotels.

The **DC Circulator** bus is not a tour shuttle, and you won't hear any stories, but the six tour routes will carry you to dozens of attractions at the Mall, Penn Quarter, Georgetown, Woodley Park, and Adams Morgan. The price is right too—only $1; see pages 101–102 for more information on the Circulator or visit dccirculator.com.

BOAT TOURS

MOST WATER TOURS go up and down the Potomac River, offering pretty passing views of the Lincoln and Jefferson Memorials, the Washington Monument, and the Kennedy Center. Some even make their way to Old Town Alexandria, National Harbor, The Wharf, and Mount Vernon (read their maps carefully so you know where they go). You don't even have to make advance reservations; although, here again, it will likely save you time and money. Be sure to read the guidelines and restrictions (alcohol included) on each company's website.

From May through September, **Capitol River Cruises** (capitolrivercruises.com) leave on the hour starting at 11 a.m. and depart from Washington Harbour in Georgetown for a 45-minute cruise past the Kennedy Center, the Capitol building, the LBJ and Maritime Memorials, the Custis-Lee Mansion, and other points of interest.

Potomac Riverboat Company (potomacriverboatco.com) has a varied and intriguing fleet, including a couple of double-deckers, an authentic split sternwheeler, and a 1906 skipjack that takes 90-minute cruises from National Harbor. PRC also operates the water taxi between Georgetown, The Wharf, Old Town Alexandria, and the National Harbor complex. They are known for their quirky canine cruise and their popular fireworks and cherry blossom tours as well.

If you can stand the "wise quacks" or if your party includes kids, consider the **DC Ducks** (dcducks.com) tour aboard renovated WWII amphibious vehicles. The Ducks leave Union Station between 10 a.m. and 4 p.m., roll through the Mall, and then plop into the Potomac River near Georgetown and cruise down to Gravelly Point, under the National Airport flight path. Tours run from April through October, and only if the weather permits.

Spirit Cruises (spiritcruises.com) offers a variety of tours in D.C. The *Spirit of Washington* yacht tour incorporates a 3-hour lunch or dinner cruise departing from 580 Water St. near The Wharf. Some have a live DJ and dance floor. Reservations are required and prices range from $55 to $109. The *Spirit of Mount Vernon,* which also leaves from The Wharf, is another upscale option that runs from March through October and includes admission to Mount Vernon with 3 hours to explore the estate and gardens.

A local family favorite is the **National Park Service**'s hour-long barge trips (nps.gov/choh), drawn 19th century–style by mules through the locks of the C&O Canal at Great Falls Visitor Center in Potomac, Maryland. Park Service rangers in costume explain the workings of the lock system and the history of the canal.

The recently refurbished *Odyssey* (odysseycruises.com) offers entertaining options, such as a Bottomless Mimosa Brunch Cruise, a Mother's Day cruise, festive holiday cruises, and traditional dinner cruises. The glass-topped luxury ship departs year-round from Southwest Waterfront, near The Wharf, and most passengers dress for the occasion. The three-course plated dinners range from $113 to $135 per person.

WHEELING AROUND WASHINGTON

WHILE BIKE TOURS COVER basically the same territory (monuments, Capitol Hill, and the Mall, and, by prior arrangement, private tours down to Mount Vernon), they have a few advantages. You get some exercise, you really can hop off and on at will, you don't need equipment (bikes and helmets are included), and, with some companies, you can bring kids on tandems. On the other hand, they are subject to the weather, are generally not offered in January and February, and require advance booking.

Bike and Roll DC's approximately 3.5-hour family-friendly tours of the National Mall depart from L'Enfant Plaza and traverse sidewalks and bike paths. Choose from private and group tours; pedals or electric bikes; cruisers; mountain bikes; and Segways. Their 9-mile trek from Mount Vernon is a favorite. Visit bikeandrolldc.com for more information. For details on bike-sharing with the Capital Bikeshare network, see page 93 in Part Three.

unofficial **TIP**
Most Segway tours require reservations, and many require a security deposit. D.C. law prohibits riders under age 15, and companies impose weight limits as well.

Speaking of Segways, they are great fun and make it easy to cover a lot of ground in a very spread-out city. But you do have to learn how to drive one first, so tours begin with training sessions and safety checks. **City Segway Tours'** 3-hour tours leave from the office at 23rd and E Streets NW, near the Foggy Bottom/GWU Metro ($75; dc.citysegwaytours.com). City Segway also allows you to bundle two tours, providing the opportunity to see the National Mall during the day and then monuments and memorials in the evening. **Segs in the City** (segsinthecity.com), at 1300 Pennsylvania Ave. NW, offers five routes, such as the Cherry Blossom Safari and Monumental Safari. **Capital Segway** (capitalsegway.com) trains in and rolls out from McPherson Square (which has its own Metro station) and offers tours that stop at 25 historic buildings and monuments. Tours are offered in English, French, and German.

Go green on a pedicab. **Capitol Pedicabs,** (capitolpedicabs.com), **DC Pedicab** (dcpedicab.com), and **National Pedicabs** (nationalpedicabs.com) are bicycle rickshaw services that can handle three adults and some baggage. You can reserve them in advance, but they can also be hailed like taxis. They generally hang out around sightseeing and nightlife areas, such as Gallery Place, Dupont Circle, Adams Morgan, and the Mall. And, of course, they are social media–accessible. You can ask them to stop wherever you wish, and some are equipped with a canopy for shade on sunny days. Check out the Lincoln Assassination Tour and the Lost DC Tour through National Pedicabs. Rides are about $60 an hour per person.

WALKING TOURS

THERE ARE PLENTY OF WALKING TOURS around Washington—and as with everything else in life, some of the best are free.

Washington Walks (washingtonwalks.com) is an established organization with popular tours such as Memorials by Moonlight, Women Who Changed America, and Hamilton's D.C., as well as various neighborhood tours; check the website for a full list. You can also book any Washington Walks tour for times and/or days other than the regularly scheduled ones. Most tours are $20 per person.

If you're on a budget, you can get a free tour—although you should be prepared to tip generously—from **DC Free Tours by Foot** (freetoursbyfoot.com). These daily group tours give you a 90-minute presentation by a knowledgeable guide while you walk, or you can rent GPS-enabled audio for a self-guided tour. Once you have a feel for the area, you may want to do it alone, taking it one attraction or area at a time. The organization offers tours of Capitol Hill, the National Mall, Georgetown, and Arlington National Cemetery, as well as ghost tours.

*un*official **TIP**
If you do have a special interest, such as black history or military history, look at the profile of a major attraction in that field below; we have included leads to sites on similar topics.

One extensive online resource is **Cultural Tourism DC** (culturaltourismdc.org), which offers information on local attractions by neighborhood (Barracks Row, U Street, the Southwest Waterfront, etc.); by cultural niche (religious sites, museums, and so on); by historical themes, such as black history and the Civil War; and by a few specialized interests, including gardens, cemeteries, and historic houses. If you're seeking a private tour of a museum or wish to arrange a group tour, check out DC Insider Tours (dcinsidertours.com). Another outstanding option is to find out where and when the **National Park Rangers** (nps.gov/nama/planyourvisit) are offering their free tours; they have a wide variety of topics.

GET UP CLOSE AND PERSONAL

IF YOU'RE SERIOUS ABOUT A PARTICULAR FIELD of interest or neighborhood, you may want to hire an expert. The most elaborate of customized tours are likely to be expensive, and you should be sure to ask whether transportation or admission fees and/or gratuities are included (most tours last 3–4 hours and are available in multiple languages). But rates are generally the same for a solo tour or a small group, so if you have a friend who shares your passion, it might help with the bill.

With a personal guide, you can set your own timetable and mode of transportation, so there's more flexibility. The **Guide Service of Washington, Inc.** (dctourguides.com) and the **Guild of Professional Tour Guides of Washington, D.C.** (washingtondctourguides.com) can steer you to former government employees, professors, historians, and even ex-spies who will spill the beans on Washington history and gossip for about $40–$60 an hour. They will also design a customized itinerary based on your interests. If you're looking for a guide offering private transport from local hotels, consider Bi-Partisan Tours (bi-partisantourcompany.com).

Reserve a weekday evening tour through the **Capitol Historical Society.** The guides spend 90 minutes pointing out the architecture and landscaping around the Capitol building, as well as discuss the political history of the neighborhood ($30 per adult and $15 per child, March–November; uschs.org).

A Tour de Force (atourdeforce.com) is a collection of private guided tours planned by Jeanne Fogel, a Master Tour Guide and author of books on the regional history of the Washington area. Several local attractions offer free or inexpensive tours, including Mount Vernon, Arlington Cemetery, and the Congressional Cemetery.

The BEST TOURS *in* TOWN

IF YOU'RE MORE INCLINED to enjoy a few places in-depth than to try to make the Big Circuit all over the National Mall, you can pretty much have your pick of interesting tours. Government agencies may have tighter restrictions, but almost all the museums, historic homes, and religious sites offer guided tours, detailed brochures, and audio recordings that you can use. Many offer apps too. Or you can just wander about at your leisure.

Here are some lesser-known sites, most of which you can walk into on the spur of the moment. For details on hours and access, see the profiles later in this chapter.

The Thomas Jefferson Building of the Library of Congress (page 147) is an example of lavish public construction, with its mythological murals and sculptures, gilded ceilings, stained glass skylights, mosaics, allegorical friezes, and grand staircases—and that's not even counting the Gutenberg Bible or President Jefferson's book collection from his library at Monticello. It's not just a library; it's a work of art. There are multiple free tours available, some in Spanish and French.

Dumbarton Oaks Museum and Gardens (pages 135–136) is not only an extraordinary mansion filled with medieval and Renaissance tapestries, and Asian and European art and sculpture, but it's also a treasure trove of Byzantine and pre-Columbian art and rare books. As if that weren't enough, the grounds—a dozen specialized formal gardens, a swimming pool, and a bathhouse with tile mosaics—are one of the most underrated oases in the area.

The **Daughters of the American Revolution Museum** (page 133) is another of Washington's underrated beauties. It has 31 period rooms, and even though you can only peek in from the doors, the wealth of decorative pieces, ceramics, paintings, silver, costumes, and oddities is wonderful. It may not sound kid-friendly, but there is a space upstairs where children can play with 18th- and 19th-century toys and flags.

The **U.S. Department of State's Diplomatic Reception Rooms** (page 178) are another lesser-known delight, a stunning geode of 18th- and 19th-century decorative arts worth more than $100 million hidden inside that boulder of an office building. You have to reserve a spot in advance, but it's worth it. Not recommended for kids younger than 12.

The **Society of the Cincinnati Museum at Anderson House** (page 174) in Dupont Circle is a turn-of-the-20th-century fantasia of Florentine architecture, built for an American diplomat whose patriotic fervor extended to hiring muralists and decorators to install historic scenes and symbols throughout the house. The upper floors have their original furnishings and tapestries—check out the crystal chandeliers in the two-story ballroom and the Revolutionary War artifacts.

The **Hillwood Estate Museum and Gardens** (page 142) was the home of cereal heiress, socialite, and collector Marjorie Merriweather Post. One of Post's husbands was the equally wealthy E. F. Hutton, and another was ambassador to the Soviet Union, so they came in handy when she began collecting art and confiscated Romanov treasures. If you love exquisite silver, ornate Imperial china, impressive portraits with crowns, and—oh yes—Fabergé eggs, this is the place. Reservations are not required, but are recommended during busier seasons.

The **Heurich House Museum** (pages 141–142) is an intriguing look at the personal lifestyle of one of Washington, D.C.'s richest entrepreneurs during the late 19th to early 20th century. His German castle-style home is a well-preserved example of Richardsonian Romanesque residential architecture. The Heurich House is also a popular gathering place for beer and German-inspired events, and they offer free guided tours (but recommend a $10 donation).

There's a lot more to **Mount Vernon** (page 150) than 2 hours' worth, including a view over the Potomac so fine it explains why Washington was so eager to retire. An impressive orientation and education center was added to the mansion, stables, greenhouses, working farm, distillery, and slave quarters. This visitor center complex offers interactive displays; films; life-size re-creations of Washington at three points in his life; and rooms full of china, rare books, and private letters, as well as Revolutionary War artifacts. The specialty tours include Herstory: Women of Mount Vernon, National Treasure Tour, and The Enslaved People of Mount Vernon, so expect to spend at least half a day.

Washington National Cathedral (page 183) offers docent-led tours throughout the day, and you can certainly wander about on your own (unless some special event or ceremony is in progress, of course). But the most fun tour combines a special in-depth cathedral tour with traditional English tea in the seventh-floor tower, which affords a scenic view of Washington. Reservations are required (Tuesdays and Wednesdays at 1:30 p.m., $37; price to increase to $40 in March 2020).

▌ WASHINGTON'S ATTRACTIONS

NOW WE GET TO THE SPECIFICS of many of the city's most popular or most interesting attractions. But because visitors come to Washington from all over the world and for a lot of different reasons, it's difficult for a guidebook to decree where they should spend their time. Is the National Gallery of Art better than the Air and Space Museum? Yes, if your interests and tastes range more toward van Gogh than Von Braun. Should you visit the International Spy Museum or the Library of Congress? We offer up the best clues we have to your own personal treasure map.

We have profiled the most prominent spots, plus a variety of specialty attractions, to help you select. In each case, we've included an author's rating from one star (skip it unless you're particularly interested) to five stars (not to be missed); ratings based on age groups that reflect the sort of exhibits and relative sophistication of the attraction; and a physical description. Sometimes we refer to other attractions whose proximity might appeal to those with extra time, repeat visitors, or those who have special interests, and we've added touring tips when possible.

unofficial **TIP**

Some of the attractions featured list "suggested donations" rather than admission fees. If you are genuinely on a tight budget or have a big family, you may wonder about taking advantage of the loophole, but we urge you to be honest and as generous as possible.

Even before you walk in the door, use your brains. Most museums allow you to photograph items from the permanent exhibit—for personal use only, not commercial—but may have rooms that are off-limits to cell phones. Put your phones on mute, and if you're using a downloaded tour guide app, wear headphones. All bags will be inspected, and in most cases, you'll need to pass through security. If you have small children, check websites for prohibitions on strollers. Food and drink? Only in designated areas.

Occasionally, an attraction's relative accessibility—possibly due to the challenges of reaching it on public transportation—weighs into the decision to list it here or not. Some lesser-known attractions may be found in our "Hidden Gems" section on pages 193–194. And there are new memorials and museums going up all the time. Washington is a city worth seeing, so do your research in advance to enjoy the atmosphere and scenic beauty.

THE NATIONAL MALL AND ARLINGTON MEMORIALS

THE EAST HALF OF THE MALL IS MUSEUMS, and the west side is mostly monuments. Many are open-air, some classical, some modern, some abstract.

But there is a quite strong generation gap visible among them. While the older memorials tend to be valedictory and solemn—Washington's Egyptian-Masonic monolith, Jefferson's Roman Pantheon, and Lincoln's impressive Athenian Parthenon—those erected in the late 20th century are more realistic. The **Korean War Veterans Memorial,** with its platoon of dogged soldiers, and the two sculptural appendages to the otherwise stark **Vietnam Veterans Memorial,** one honoring soldiers and the other the female medical and support troops who tended them, evoke an essentially different emotional response from visitors than do the great temples of the Founding Fathers. The **Martin Luther King Jr., Franklin Delano Roosevelt,** and **Pentagon 9/11 Memorials** are large-scale meditation sites. (All of the above are profiled below.)

The **National Museum of African American History and Culture** (profiled on pages 157–158) opened in 2015, and the crowds keep

The National Mall Area Attractions

N

0   0.125 mi
0   0.1 km

1. Arlington National Cemetery
2. Arthur M. Sackler Gallery
3. Bureau of Engraving and Printing
4. Daughters of the American Revolution (DAR) Museum
5. Ford's Theatre/Petersen House
6. Franklin Delano Roosevelt Memorial
7. Freer Gallery of Art
8. Hirshhorn Museum and Sculpture Garden
9. International Spy Museum
10. Jefferson Memorial
11. John F. Kennedy Center for the Performing Arts
12. Korean War Veterans Memorial
13. Lincoln Memorial
14. Madame Tussauds
15. Martin Luther King Jr. Memorial
16. Museum of the Bible

17. National Air and Space Museum
18. National Archives
19. National Building Museum
20. National Children's Museum
21. National Gallery of Art
22. National Museum of African American History and Culture
23. National Museum of African Art
24. National Museum of American History
25. National Museum of Natural History
26. National Museum of the American Indian
27. National Museum of Women in the Arts

28. National Portrait Gallery–Smithsonian American Art Museum
29. National World War II Memorial
30. Old Post Office Tower and Pavilion
31. The Renwick Gallery
32. Smithsonian Institution Building (aka the Castle)
33. U.S. Department of State Diplomatic Reception Rooms
34. U.S. Department of the Treasury
35. U.S. Holocaust Memorial Museum
36. Vietnam Veterans Memorial
37. Washington Monument
38. The White House
39. The White House Visitor Center

Northern D.C. Attractions

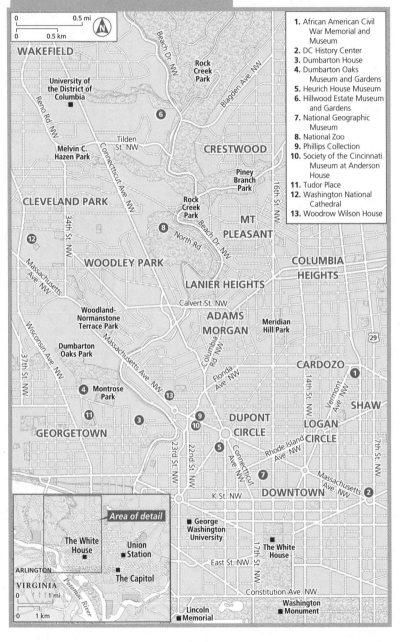

1. African American Civil War Memorial and Museum
2. DC History Center
3. Dumbarton House
4. Dumbarton Oaks Museum and Gardens
5. Heurich House Museum
6. Hillwood Estate Museum and Gardens
7. National Geographic Museum
8. National Zoo
9. Phillips Collection
10. Society of the Cincinnati Museum at Anderson House
11. Tudor Place
12. Washington National Cathedral
13. Woodrow Wilson House

Capitol Hill Attractions

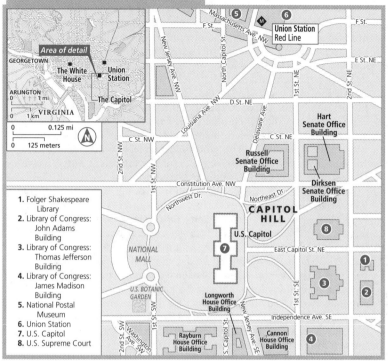

1. Folger Shakespeare Library
2. Library of Congress: John Adams Building
3. Library of Congress: Thomas Jefferson Building
4. Library of Congress: James Madison Building
5. National Postal Museum
6. Union Station
7. U.S. Capitol
8. U.S. Supreme Court

coming. Unless you visit in the off-season during the week, you must reserve a timed pass in advance. The **Belmont-Paul Women's Equality National Monument** was designated in 2016, and although it is still a work in progress, the historic home portrays American women's struggle for voting rights and their unsuccessful effort to pass the Equal Rights Amendment of 1972.

Notable for its restrained elegance, the **District of Columbia War Memorial** is an open-sided Doric temple with the names of D.C. residents killed in World War I engraved upon its outer walls. Above the circular colonnade is another inscription, subtle but striking in its irony: a reference to "*the* World War"—the one after which Americans believed there would be no other. President Herbert Hoover and General John Pershing both took part in the dedication ceremony in 1931, and the bandleader, John Phillip Sousa, played not only his own "Stars and Stripes Forever" but also "The Star-Spangled Banner," which had just been named the US national anthem by an Act of Congress. As befits a monument to what was in some ways the last 19th-century war, the memorial is about halfway between the

Lincoln and World War II memorials, on the south side of Constitution Gardens facing Independence Avenue.

Just south of Constitution Avenue is a pretty, figure eight–shaped lake with a small island that houses the **56 Signers of the Declaration of Independence Memorial.** The memorial features the final phrase of the Declaration: "We pledge to each other our Lives, our Fortunes, and our sacred Honor," and the 56 signatures reproduced in the granite blocks of a semicircle.

On the southeast edge of the Tidal Basin is the seated figure of the oft-underappreciated founding father **George Mason;** he rests, his cane leaning on the bench alongside, near the memorial to Thomas Jefferson, who borrowed so many ideas from Mason but wound up with most of the credit. The **Albert Einstein Memorial,** on 2100 Constitution Ave. NW, is a bronze statue of the famous scientist; it was dedicated in 1979 on his 100th birthday.

At the opposite end of the Memorial Bridge from the Lincoln Memorial, just outside the entrance to Arlington National Cemetery, is the little island comprising **Lady Bird Johnson Park.** Though not technically a memorial, it is a fittingly green tribute to the first lady who turned her energies to the beautification of the capital. About a mile south of the Memorial Bridge along the George Washington Parkway is the **Lyndon Baines Johnson Memorial Grove,** which consists of a commemorative monolith and a grove of 500 white pines. (The stream between Lady Bird Johnson Park and the cemetery is **Boundary Channel,** which marks the border between D.C. and Virginia.)

The **National 9/11 Pentagon Memorial** (profiled on pages 163–164), opened to the public on September 11, 2008, and is accessible via the Pentagon Metro. Those arriving by car must park in public lots at Pentagon City, about 0.5 mile away, and walk to the site.

The **U.S. Air Force Memorial,** which opened in October 2006, is a triad of soaring (270-foot-tall) stainless-steel arcs that are illuminated at night and are visible from many of the approaches to Washington. The memorial is also accessible to pedestrians via the Pentagon Metro station (it's about a 0.5-mile walk).

The **U.S. Marine Corps Memorial,** popularly known as the Iwo Jima Memorial and the subject of Clint Eastwood's 2006 motion picture, *Flags of Our Fathers,* is about a 20-minute walk from the Arlington Cemetery subway stop. The 32-foot-long sculpture, capped by a 60-foot-tall flagpole, was dedicated by President Eisenhower on Veterans Day in 1954. Alongside the memorial is the **Netherlands Carillon,** a gift from the Dutch people in gratitude for American aid during and after World War II. It plays recorded music—mostly armed-forces themes, marches, "The Star-Spangled Banner," and the like—hourly 10 a.m.–6 p.m., with some longer concerts in the summer. This location offers a panoramic view of the National Mall and is especially stunning at night.

Located at the Archives/Navy Memorial Metro station, the **U.S. Navy Memorial and Visitor Center** immerses visitors in the heritage and culture of the U.S. Navy.

WASHINGTON ATTRACTIONS BY TYPE

CEMETERIES

Arlington National Cemetery ★★★★★ NATIONAL MALL | largest US military cemetery

CHURCHES/HOUSES OF WORSHIP

Basilica of the National Shrine of the Immaculate Conception ★★½ NORTHEAST | largest Catholic church in US

Washington National Cathedral ★★★★★ UPPER NORTHWEST | 6th-largest cathedral in the world

GOVERNMENT BUILDINGS OPEN FOR TOURS

Bureau of Engraving and Printing ★★★ NATIONAL MALL | where US dollars and stamps are printed

National Archives ★★★½ NATIONAL MALL | home of the nation's important records

U.S. Capitol Visitor Center ★★★★★ CAPITOL HILL | path to the Capitol

U.S. Department of State Diplomatic Reception Rooms ★★★★ FOGGY BOTTOM | decorative arts; reservation only

U.S. Department of the Treasury ★★★★ NATIONAL MALL | restored 19th-century landmark

U.S. Supreme Court ★★★★ CAPITOL HILL | nation's highest court

HISTORIC BUILDINGS AND HOMES

Dumbarton House ★★★ GEORGETOWN | historic mansion

Ford's Theatre/Petersen House ★★★★ DOWNTOWN | where Lincoln was assassinated and died

Frederick Douglass National Historic Site ★★★ SOUTHEAST | preserved Victorian home

Gunston Hall ★★★★ VIRGINIA SUBURBS | George Mason's plantation

Heurich House ★★★★ DUPONT CIRCLE | a true Victorian castle

Mount Vernon Estate and Gardens ★★★★★ VIRGINIA SUBURBS | George Washington's river plantation

Old Town Alexandria ★★★★ VIRGINIA SUBURBS | restored Colonial port town

President Lincoln's Cottage ★★★★★ UPPER NORTHWEST | Lincoln's summer home

Society of the Cincinnati Museum at Anderson House ★★★ DUPONT CIRCLE | lavish mansion and Revolutionary War museum

Tudor Place ★★★ GEORGETOWN | mansion built by Martha Washington's granddaughter

Union Station ★★★ CAPITOL HILL | transportation hub in a Beaux Arts palace with food and shopping

The White House ★★★½ NATIONAL MALL | the Executive Mansion; reservation only

Woodrow Wilson House ★★★★ DUPONT CIRCLE | final home of the 28th president

LIBRARIES

Folger Shakespeare Library ★★★ CAPITOL HILL | Bard museum and library

Library of Congress ★★★★ CAPITOL HILL | world's largest library

MONUMENTS AND MEMORIALS

Franklin Delano Roosevelt Memorial ★★★★★ NATIONAL MALL | open-air memorial

Jefferson Memorial ★★★★ NATIONAL MALL | classical-style monument on Tidal Basin

Korean War Veterans Memorial ★★★★ NATIONAL MALL | platoon memorial

Lincoln Memorial ★★★★★ NATIONAL MALL | memorial to 16th president

Martin Luther King Jr. Memorial ★★★★ NATIONAL MALL | meditation garden and walk

National 9/11 Pentagon Memorial ★★★★ VIRGINIA SUBURBS | outdoor memorial to victims of 9/11 attacks

National World War II Memorial ★★½ NATIONAL MALL | tribute to "The Greatest Generation"

continued on next page

WASHINGTON ATTRACTIONS BY TYPE *(continued)*

MONUMENTS AND MEMORIALS *(continued)*

Old Post Office Tower ★★½ NATIONAL MALL | food court with a view

Vietnam Veterans Memorial ★★★★ NATIONAL MALL | US soldier memorial on the Mall

Washington Monument ★★★★ NATIONAL MALL | 555-foot memorial to first US president

MUSEUMS AND GALLERIES

African American Civil War Memorial and Museum ★★★ NORTHWEST | from Civil War to civil rights

Arthur M. Sackler Gallery ★★★ NATIONAL MALL | Asian art

Belmont-Paul Women's Equality National Monument House and Museum ★★★ CAPITOL HILL | exhibits chronicling the National Woman's Party

Daughters of the American Revolution (DAR) Museum ★★★★ NATIONAL MALL | US decorative arts and antiques

DC History Center ★★½ DOWNTOWN | documents everyday life in D.C.

Freer Gallery of Art ★★★★ NATIONAL MALL | Asian and American art

Glenstone ★★★ MARYLAND SUBURBS | premier modern-art collection

Goddard Space Flight Visitor Center ★★★ MARYLAND SUBURBS | space museum

Hillwood Estate Museum and Gardens ★★★★ UPPER NORTHWEST | mansion with fabulous art treasures; reservation only

Hirshhorn Museum and Sculpture Garden ★★★★ NATIONAL MALL | modern art

International Spy Museum ★★★★ SOUTHWEST | history and gadgetry of espionage

Kreeger Museum ★★★ UPPER NORTHWEST | modern-art museum

Madame Tussauds ★★★ DOWNTOWN | wax-sculpture museum

Museum of the Bible ★★★★★ NATIONAL MALL | biblical history through technology

National Air and Space Museum ★★★★★ NATIONAL MALL | chronicles manned flight

National Building Museum ★★★ DOWNTOWN | architectural marvel and exhibits

National Children's Museum ★★★★ DOWNTOWN | educational fun for the kids

National Cryptologic Museum ★★★½ MARYLAND SUBURBS | National Security Agency's museum of code making and code breaking

National Gallery of Art ★★★★★ NATIONAL MALL | 20th-century art; European and American classical art

National Geographic Museum ★★★ DOWNTOWN | like flipping through the magazine

ATTRACTION PROFILES

African American Civil War Memorial and Museum ★★★

PRESCHOOL ★	GRADE SCHOOL ★★½	TEENS ★★★
YOUNG ADULTS ★★★½	OVER 30 ★★★½	SENIORS ★★★★

Location 1925 Vermont Ave. NW and 1000 U St. NW. **Nearest Metro stations** U Street/ African American Civil War Memorial/Cardozo or Shaw. **Contact** ☎ 202-667-2667, afroamcivilwar.org. **Admission** Free. **Hours** Tuesday–Friday, 10 a.m.–6:30 p.m.; Saturday, 10 a.m.–4 p.m.; Sunday, noon–4 p.m.; closed December 25 (museum); statue open 24/7.

DESCRIPTION AND COMMENTS Though it mostly focuses on the war itself, the museum traces "The Glorious March to Liberty," from the Civil War to the civil rights struggle, and is a combination of family stories, documents, newspapers, and artifacts. Though small in size—the collection is housed in a former school gymnasium marked by an iron gate with images of black soldiers—it contains gripping exhibits, such as shackles used to imprison

WASHINGTON ATTRACTIONS BY TYPE (continued)

National Museum of African American History and Culture ★★★★★ NATIONAL MALL | from slavery to Civil War, civil rights, and today

National Museum of African Art ★★★½ NATIONAL MALL | traditional arts of Africa

National Museum of American History ★★★★★ NATIONAL MALL | American experience

National Museum of Health and Medicine ★★½ MARYLAND SUBURBS | medical museum

National Museum of Natural History ★★★★★ NATIONAL MALL | treasure chest of the natural sciences

National Museum of the American Indian ★★★½ NATIONAL MALL | American Indian art and artifacts

National Museum of the Marine Corps ★★★★ VIRGINIA SUBURBS | immersive, modern exhibits honoring US Marines

National Museum of Women in the Arts ★★★½ DOWNTOWN | modern and classical art by women

National Portrait Gallery–Smithsonian American Art Museum ★★★★★ DOWNTOWN | Two important art collections in a beautifully restored building

National Postal Museum ★★★ CAPITOL HILL | philately (stamp collections) and exhibits

The Phillips Collection ★★★★★ DUPONT CIRCLE | first US modern-art museum

The Renwick Gallery ★★★★★ NATIONAL MALL | American crafts and decorative arts

Smithsonian Institution Building (The Castle) ★★★ NATIONAL MALL | museum information and display

Udvar-Hazy National Air and Space Museum ★★★★★ VIRGINIA SUBURBS | mind-blowing collection of air- and spacecraft

U.S. Holocaust Memorial Museum ★★★★★ NATIONAL MALL | graphic memorial to the World War II Holocaust

PARKS, GARDENS, AND ZOOS

Dumbarton Oaks Museum and Gardens ★★★★ GEORGETOWN | mansion/museum and a beautiful garden

Kenilworth Park and Aquatic Gardens ★★★★ NORTHEAST | national park for water plants

National Zoo ★★★★★ UPPER NORTHWEST | world-class zoo

U.S. Botanic Garden ★★★ CAPITOL HILL | huge greenhouse and living museum

U.S. National Arboretum ★★★ NORTHEAST | 446-acre collection of trees and flowers

THEATERS/PERFORMANCES

John F. Kennedy Center for the Performing Arts ★★★ FOGGY BOTTOM | stunning venue on the Potomac

---

abducted men and women on slave ships. An efficient way to understand the collection is to see the movie and then move through the exhibits. You may be surprised to learn that the U.S. Colored Troops provided one-tenth of all the manpower for the Union Army. Located at the foot of the U Street/Cordoza Metro station is the 10-foot-tall *Spirit of Freedom* memorial itself, a tribute to the USCT, 36,000 of whom died during the war. A Wall of Honor lists more than 209,000 USCT who served in the Civil War.

TOURING TIPS There is no food available on site, but there is a small dining area outside, and the U Street neighborhood is one of the booming dining areas of the city.

IF YOU LIKE THIS See the **Martin Luther King Jr. Memorial** (page 149); **President Lincoln's Cottage** (page 172); the **National Museum of African American History and Culture** (page 157); and Cedar Hill, the **Frederick Douglass National Historic Site** (page 138). The *Records of Rights* exhibit at the **National Archives** (pages 152–153) showcases black-history documents

WASHINGTON ATTRACTIONS BY LOCATION

NATIONAL MALL AND WHITE HOUSE	
Arlington National Cemetery	U.S. Department of Treasury
Arthur M. Sackler Gallery	U.S. Holocaust Memorial Museum
Bureau of Engraving and Printing	Vietnam Veterans Memorial
Daughters of the American Revolution (DAR) Museum	Washington Monument
	The White House
Franklin Delano Roosevelt Memorial	The White House Visitor Center
Freer Gallery of Art	**CAPITOL HILL**
Hirshhorn Museum and Sculpture Garden	Belmont-Paul Women's Equality National Monument House and Museum
Jefferson Memorial	
Korean War Veterans Memorial	Folger Shakespeare Library
Lincoln Memorial	Library of Congress
Martin Luther King Jr. Memorial	National Postal Museum
Museum of the Bible	Union Station
National Air and Space Museum	U.S. Botanic Garden
National Archives	U.S. Capitol Visitor Center
National Gallery of Art	U.S. Supreme Court
National Museum of African American History and Culture	**DOWNTOWN**
National Museum of African Art	DC History Center
National Museum of American History	Ford's Theatre/Petersen House
National Museum of Natural History	Madame Tussauds
National Museum of the American Indian	National Building Museum
National World War II Memorial	National Children's Museum
Old Post Office Tower	National Geographic Museum
The Renwick Gallery	National Museum of Women in the Arts
Smithsonian Institution Building (The Castle)	National Portrait Gallery–Smithsonian American Art Museum

going back to the Revolutionary War. The lunch counter from the Greensboro, North Carolina, F.W. Woolworth store where four black college students launched the first sit-in on February 1, 1960, is on display at the **National Museum of American History** (page 159). **Mt. Zion United Methodist Church and Heritage Center** on 29th Street NW between Dumbarton and Q Streets in Georgetown was founded in 1816 and served as a stop on the Underground Railroad in the years before and during the Civil War (☎ 202-234-0148). Also, Cultural Tourism DC has an African American Heritage Trail guide, which lists almost 100 sites of historical interest ($5; trails@culturaltourismdc.org).

 Arlington National Cemetery ★★★★★

PRESCHOOL ★	GRADE SCHOOL ★★	TEENS ★★★
YOUNG ADULTS ★★★★	OVER 30 ★★★★	SENIORS ★★★★

Location Across the Potomac from Washington via Arlington Memorial Bridge, which crosses the river near the Lincoln Memorial. **Nearest Metro station** Arlington Cemetery. **Contact** ☎ 703-607-8000, arlingtoncemetery.mil. **Admission** Free. **Hours** April–September, daily, 8 a.m.–7 p.m.; October–March, daily, 8 a.m.–5 p.m.

WASHINGTON ATTRACTIONS BY LOCATION (continued)

FOGGY BOTTOM	NORTHEAST
John F. Kennedy Center for the Performing Arts	Basilica of the National Shrine of the Immaculate Conception
U.S. Department of State Diplomatic Reception Rooms	Kenilworth Park and Aquatic Gardens
GEORGETOWN	U.S. National Arboretum
Dumbarton House	**SOUTHWEST**
Dumbarton Oaks Museum and Gardens	International Spy Museum
Tudor Place	**SOUTHEAST**
DUPONT CIRCLE	Frederick Douglass National Historic Site
Heurich House	**MARYLAND SUBURBS**
The Phillips Collection	Glenstone
Society of the Cincinnati Museum at Anderson House	Goddard Space Flight Visitor Center
Woodrow Wilson House	National Cryptologic Museum
UPPER NORTHWEST	National Museum of Health and Medicine
African American Civil War Memorial and Museum	**VIRGINIA SUBURBS**
	Gunston Hall
Hillwood Estate Museum and Gardens	Mount Vernon Estate and Gardens
Kreeger Museum	National Museum of the Marine Corps
National Zoo	National 9/11 Pentagon Memorial
President Lincoln's Cottage	Old Town Alexandria
Washington National Cathedral	Udvar-Hazy National Air and Space Museum

DESCRIPTION AND COMMENTS It's not really accurate to call a visit to Arlington National Cemetery mere sightseeing; as Americans, our lives are too intimately attached to the 400,000 men and women buried here. They include the famous, the obscure, and the unknown. The most famous of all is the gravesite where the Eternal Flame burns in honor of President John F. Kennedy. The fallen president is buried beside his wife, Jacqueline Kennedy Onassis; brothers Robert, Joseph, and Edward Kennedy; and two of his children who died in infancy. President William Howard Taft has a notable marker, along with war heroes like General George C. Marshall and Audie Murphy, civil rights martyr Medgar Evers, boxing champ Joe Louis, baseball's popularizer Abner Doubleday, and Supreme Court Justices Thurgood Marshall and Oliver Wendell Holmes.

Among the iconic sites in the cemetery's 612 rolling acres are the Tomb of the Unknowns (guarded 24 hours a day; witness the changing of the guard every half hour March–September and on the hour October–February); memorials to the crew of the space shuttle *Challenger;* the Iran Rescue Mission Memorial; and Arlington House, built in 1802.

If it's open, stop in at Arlington House for a tour of this historic home, where Robert E. Lee and Mary Anna Randolph Custis once lived. Adjacent to Arlington House are the South Slave Quarters, with exhibits about the generations of slaves who lived and worked on this estate before the Civil War.

Arlington National Cemetery

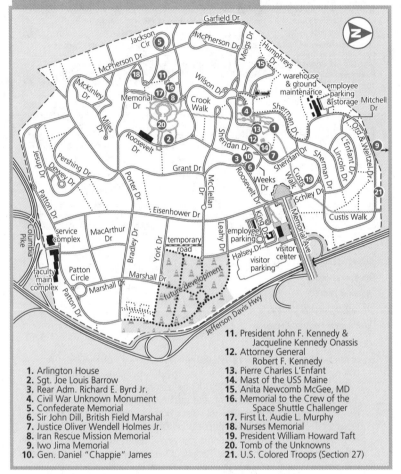

1. Arlington House
2. Sgt. Joe Louis Barrow
3. Rear Adm. Richard E. Byrd Jr.
4. Civil War Unknown Monument
5. Confederate Memorial
6. Sir John Dill, British Field Marshal
7. Justice Oliver Wendell Holmes Jr.
8. Iran Rescue Mission Memorial
9. Iwo Jima Memorial
10. Gen. Daniel "Chappie" James
11. President John F. Kennedy & Jacqueline Kennedy Onassis
12. Attorney General Robert F. Kennedy
13. Pierre Charles L'Enfant
14. Mast of the USS Maine
15. Anita Newcomb McGee, MD
16. Memorial to the Crew of the Space Shuttle Challenger
17. First Lt. Audie L. Murphy
18. Nurses Memorial
19. President William Howard Taft
20. Tomb of the Unknowns
21. U.S. Colored Troops (Section 27)

TOURING TIPS No food is allowed on site, but you can find restrooms, a bookstore, and water fountains in the welcome center. The hop-on/hop-off tours leave from the welcome center about every 15–30 minutes, and you can get off at all the major sites and reboard at your leisure. The cost is $15 for adults, $7.25 for children, and $11 for seniors. If you want to save a little money and tour the cemetery by foot, just take the subway to the Arlington Cemetery Metro station and walk the short distance to the welcome center. The website has a downloadable map; you can also download a free iTunes guide called ANC Explorer and buy the cemetery-only ticket.

IF YOU LIKE THIS The **National 9/11 Pentagon Memorial** (page 163) and the **Air Force Memorial** (page 124) are not far, but you'll need to take another subway leg to the Pentagon station. The **Iwo Jima Memorial** (page 124) and the

Netherlands Carillon (page 124) are also nearby. Consider visiting the **Congressional Cemetery**, accessible from the Potomac or Stadium/Armory Metro stations; among its "residents" are J. Edgar Hoover; Senate orators Henry Clay and John C. Calhoun; Speaker of the House Thomas "Tip" O'Neill; march composer John Phillip Sousa; and Belle Youngs, who conducted the séances at the White House after the death of young Willie Lincoln.

Arthur M. Sackler Gallery *(a Smithsonian museum)* ★★★

| PRESCHOOL ★ | GRADE SCHOOL ★★ | TEENS ★★½ |
| YOUNG ADULTS ★★★ | OVER 30 ★★★ | SENIORS ★★★ |

Location On the Mall near the Castle. **Nearest Metro stations** Smithsonian or L'Enfant Plaza. **Contact** ☎ 202-633-1000, asia.si.edu. **Admission** Free. **Hours** Daily, 10 a.m.–5:30 p.m.; closed December 25.

DESCRIPTION AND COMMENTS This museum is dedicated to Asian art from antiquity to modern times. Descend through a granite-and-glass pavilion to view a collection of Asian (mostly Chinese and Persian) treasures, many of them made of gold and encrusted with jewels. The gallery is full of exotic statuary, paintings, calligraphy, and textiles that will catch the eye of older children, teens, and adults.

TOURING TIPS Stop at the information desk and ask about the free guided tours, talks, family programs, and workshops, generally offered midday. The gift shop is an exotic bazaar featuring paintings, textiles, ancient games, Zen-rock garden kits, and plenty of other Asian-influenced items. No food is available on site.

IF YOU LIKE THIS The Sackler is connected with its twin, the **National Museum of African Art** (page 158), belowground, so that's the logical next stop—especially if it's rainy or blazingly hot outside. Another underground corridor connects the Sackler to the **Freer Gallery** (page 139), making this complex an Asian-art lover's dream.

Basilica of the National Shrine of the Immaculate Conception ★★½

| PRESCHOOL ★ | GRADE SCHOOL ★ | TEENS ★ |
| YOUNG ADULTS ★ | OVER 30 ★½ | SENIORS ★★ |

Location 400 Michigan Ave. NE, on the campus of the Catholic University of America. **Nearest Metro station** Brookland/CUA. **Contact** ☎ 202-526-8300, nationalshrine.org. **Admission** Free. **Hours** November 1–March 31, daily, 7 a.m.–6 p.m.; until 7 p.m. the rest of the year.

DESCRIPTION AND COMMENTS Though not widely publicized, this is the largest Catholic church in the United States and one of the 10 largest religious structures in the world. A blue-and-gold onion dome lends Byzantine overtones to this massive cathedral, as does the wealth of colorful mosaics and stained glass throughout its interior. But its more formal style is not as generally accessible as the awe-inspiring Washington National Cathedral across town (page 183), and it is huge, floored in hard marble, and requires a lot of walking. Visited by Pope Francis, Pope Benedict, Saint John Paul II, and Saint Theresa of Calcutta, it hosts about 1 million visitors annually and offers six Masses daily.

TOURING TIPS Guided tours are conducted Monday–Saturday at 9 a.m., 10 a.m., 11 a.m., 1 p.m., 2 p.m., and 3 p.m. and Sunday at 1:30, 2:30, and 3:30 p.m.;

but these tours stop in what seems to be every one of the 70 chapels. Instead, grab a map at the information desk on the ground (crypt) level and enter Memorial Hall, which is lined with chapels and houses the great organ. Then go upstairs to the Upper Church. There is a small cafeteria open 7:30 a.m.–2 p.m. on the ground level. The gift shop offers an array of relics, books, and rosaries.

IF YOU LIKE THIS The **Franciscan Monastery** (myfranciscan.org) is a brisk 20-minute walk away: continue past the Metro station on Michigan Avenue to Quincy Street, turn right, and walk about four blocks. The **Saint John Paul II National Shrine** (jp2shrine.org), an interactive museum in honor of Pope John Paul, is open to all faiths and is also nearby.

Belmont-Paul Women's Equality National Monument House and Museum ★★★

PRESCHOOL ★	GRADE SCHOOL ★	TEENS ★★★
YOUNG ADULTS ★★★	OVER 30 ★★★½	SENIORS ★★★★

Location 144 Constitution Ave. NE, near the U.S. Capitol. **Nearest Metro station** Union Station. **Contact** ☎ 202-543-2240, nps.gov/bepa. **Admission** Free. **Hours** Wednesday–Sunday, 9 a.m.–5 p.m.; closed on federal holidays and the week between December 25 and January 1.

DESCRIPTION AND COMMENTS The National Woman's Party (NWP) purchased the historic home in 1929 to use as their headquarters, and it became ground zero for American women's quest for voting rights. The museum is named for Alice Paul and Alva Belmont, leaders of the movement. The house was recently named a national monument and is operated by the National Park Service. The exhibits contain artifacts from suffragettes working to convince Congress to award women the right to vote, and there's a helpful video explaining the history of suffrage in the United States. The house beautifully blends into the Capitol Hill neighborhood and gives you a sense of how proximity to the Capitol helped the women accomplish their mission. It also depicts later efforts by feminists to pass the Equal Rights Amendment in 1972.

TOURING TIPS The museum hosts programs on women's equality efforts, both in history and current day. Ranger-led tours are offered Wednesday–Sunday at 9:30 a.m., 11 a.m., 2 p.m., and 3:30 p.m. No reservations are required for individuals or groups of fewer than 10 people.

IF YOU LIKE THIS You might want to look into the **Hillwood Estate** (page 142) in Rock Creek Park, owned by Marjorie Merriweather Post, a prominent businesswoman, socialite, and heiress. The **DAR Museum** (pages 133–134), which showcases American women's experiences since the American Revolution, might also be of interest.

Bureau of Engraving and Printing ★★★

PRESCHOOL ★★	GRADE SCHOOL ★★★★	TEENS ★★★½
YOUNG ADULTS ★★★	OVER 30 ★★★½	SENIORS ★★★★

Location Raoul Wallenberg Place (15th St.) and C St. SW, just south of the Mall. **Nearest Metro station** Smithsonian. **Contact** ☎ 866-874-2330 or 202-874-2330, moneyfactory .gov. **Admission** Free. **Hours** Monday–Friday, 9 a.m.–2 p.m.; closed on federal holidays and the week between December 25 and January 1.

DESCRIPTION AND COMMENTS This is a 35- to 45-minute guided tour through the rather cramped glass-lined corridors that overlook the government's immense currency and stamp-printing plant. Visitors look down and gape at the printing presses that crank out the dough and at pallets of greenbacks in various stages of completion. The sign hung on a press, however, says it all: YOU HAVE NEVER BEEN SO CLOSE YET SO FAR AWAY. Kids love this place, so it's a tourist site families should plan on hitting, even if you're in town for only a short period. However, small children may have trouble looking over the ledge and down into the press rooms below.

TOURING TIPS In early spring and summer, get to the ticket booth before 8 a.m. to avoid disappointment. The ticket office, located on Raoul Wallenberg Place, distributes about 80 tickets for every tour, which start at 15-minute intervals between 9 and 10:45 a.m. and 12:30 and 2 p.m. You have about a 30-minute grace period if you're running late. When all tickets are gone—which can be as early as 9—the ticket office closes. (No tickets are required September–February.) However, if you do miss out on tickets for the tour, you can still see the exhibits in the visitor center, which stays open late in summer. There is no food available on site. Check out the bags of shredded money for sale in the visitor center; they make great souvenirs (or wedding confetti).

A valid ID is required. No book bags, backpacks, or sharp objects are allowed. For a VIP guided tour, contact your congressperson's office at least two months before your trip. Also be aware that when the Department of Homeland Security threat level is elevated to high, all general public tours are canceled.

IF YOU LIKE THIS You might want to check out the **National Postal Museum** (page 165) on Capitol Hill.

Daughters of the American Revolution (DAR) Museum
★★★★

PRESCHOOL ★	GRADE SCHOOL ★★	TEENS ★★★
YOUNG ADULTS ★★★	OVER 30 ★★★★	SENIORS ★★★★

Location 1776 D St. NW, across from the Ellipse. **Nearest Metro stations** Farragut West or Farragut North. **Contact** ☎ 202-879-3241, dar.org. **Admission** Free. **Hours** Monday–Friday, 8:30 a.m.–4 p.m.; Saturday, 9 a.m.–5 p.m.; closed on Sundays and federal holidays.

DESCRIPTION AND COMMENTS This Beaux Arts building, completed in 1910, is a knockout. The huge columns that grace the front are solid marble; a special railroad spur was built to transport them to the building site. The museum emphasizes the role of women throughout American history, mostly before 1840, and the 31 period rooms each represent a different time and place in America. Each contains a cornucopia of decorative arts and antiques, including furniture, ceramics, glass, paintings, costumes, doll houses, and textiles. Expect to do a lot of stair climbing on the tour.

Because so many items are authentic, the rooms are roped off, and only two or three visitors at a time can squeeze into doorways to peer inside. Fashion enthusiasts will enjoy the Colonial-period clothing and accessories.

TOURING TIPS Docent-led tours are often available on the hour and half hour (Monday–Friday, 10 a.m.–2:30 p.m. and Saturday, 9 a.m.–4:30 p.m.), but it's easy to explore the museum on your own. Although the building faces the Ellipse, the museum entrance is half a block down D Street on the side of the building. The museum closes for a week in late June or early July for a national DAR convention. There is no food available on site.

IF YOU LIKE THIS You'll have to make a reservation in advance (☎ 202-303-4233 or tours@redcross.org or), but decorative-arts lovers should visit the national headquarters of the **American Red Cross,** next door to the DAR Museum on 17th Street. You can visit Wednesdays and Fridays at 10 a.m. and 2 p.m. A grand staircase leads to the second-floor ballroom, which holds three 25-foot Tiffany stained glass Memorial Windows, reputed to be the largest suite of Tiffany panels still in their original location (except in churches). The windows, which represent the organization's three missions—Hope, Charity, and Love—were donated to the Red Cross by Union and Confederate nursing agencies, and their theme is ministry to the sick and wounded.

The elegant **Octagon House** (architectsfoundation.org/octagon-museum) museum, which served James and Dolley Madison as a temporary executive mansion after the British burned the White House in 1814, is a short walk from the DAR Museum and Red Cross headquarters at 18th Street NW and New York Avenue. It's open Thursday–Saturday, 1–4 p.m. and at other times by prior reservation; $10 suggested donation.

DC History Center ★★½

PRESCHOOL —	GRADE SCHOOL ★	TEENS ★★
YOUNG ADULTS ★★	OVER 30 ★★★	SENIORS ★★★

Location Carnegie Library, 801 K St. NW, near the convention center. **Nearest Metro stations** National Archives/Navy Memorial or Mt. Vernon Square. **Contact** ☎ 202-516-1363, dchistory.org. **Admission** Free. **Hours** Tuesday–Saturday, 10 a.m.–5 p.m.; Sunday, noon–5 p.m.; closed on federal holidays.

DESCRIPTION AND COMMENTS During the spring of 2019, the Historical Society of Washington, D.C., reopened its doors as the DC History Center. Located in the beautiful Beaux Arts building known as the Carnegie Library, the museum is dedicated to preserving and documenting the city's stories of everyday life, in some cases with new technology. The museum strives to tell the story of how the Capitol City has intersected with US history. Exhibits rotate periodically, but one example is a collection of drawings and photographs of notable Washington, D.C., events and people.

TOURING TIPS The museum sells many books on Washington, D.C. history. On the lower level of the building is a sprawling Apple Store.

IF YOU LIKE THIS You might want to check out the **Anacostia Community Museum** (page 194), which displays artifacts and multimedia collections representing Washington, D.C.'s evolving history. Also, don't miss the **National Museum of American History** (pages 159–160) and the **National Museum of African American History and Culture** (pages 157–158).

Dumbarton House ★★★

PRESCHOOL —	GRADE SCHOOL —	TEENS ★★
YOUNG ADULTS ★★	OVER 30 ★★★	SENIORS ★★★

Location 2715 Q St. NW. **Nearest Metro station** Dupont Circle. **Contact** ☎ 202-337-2288, dumbartonhouse.org. **Admission** $10; children and students with ID free. **Hours** February–December, Tuesday–Sunday, 10 a.m.–2:45 p.m.; closed all of January, July 4, Thanksgiving, and December 24 and 25.

DESCRIPTION AND COMMENTS This turn-of-the-19th-century Georgetown mansion is not only a particularly fine example of early Federal architecture, but it also originally had an unimpeded view of the President's House (as the White House was then known) and of its burning by British forces in 1814. It belonged to a high-level Cabinet member, and First Lady Dolley Madison, having rescued Gilbert Stuart's portrait of George Washington and other papers, stopped here to await word from her husband before evacuating across the Potomac to Virginia. The collection features more than 1,000 items, including furniture, art, documents, and more. The walk from the Dupont Circle Metro is about a mile, but it's a lovely neighborhood to explore.

TOURING TIPS You can book online for Saturday and Sunday guided tours at 10:30 a.m. and 1:30 p.m., but you must call the number above to book a tour during the week. There is a smallish formal garden behind and alongside the museum. Strollers are not allowed, and staff recommends kids be at least age 6 for the tour. An elevator allows wheelchair access. No food is available on site. Nearby **Oak Hill Cemetery,** at 30th and R Streets, boasts a Gothic Revival chapel designed by James Renwick and fabulous 19th-century funeral sculptures.

IF YOU LIKE THIS An even finer mansion with more-elaborate gardens and exhibits is **Tudor Place** (pages 174–175), about four blocks away. See also **Dumbarton Oaks Museum and Gardens** (below), which, though of a different era, is nearby and has a lovely garden.

Dumbarton Oaks Museum and Gardens   ★★★★

PRESCHOOL ★	GRADE SCHOOL ★★	TEENS ★★★
YOUNG ADULTS ★★★★	OVER 30 ★★★★	SENIORS ★★★★

Location 1703 32nd St. NW,. **Nearest Metro station** Dupont Circle. **Contact** ☎ 202-339-6400, doaks.org. **Admission** Museum: free. Gardens: March 15–October, $10 adults, $8 seniors and military, $5 children; November–mid-March, free. **Hours** Museum: Tuesday–Sunday, 11:30 a.m.–5:30 p.m. Gardens: November–March 14, 2–5 p.m.; March 15–October, 2–6 p.m. Both the museum and gardens are closed on federal holidays.

DESCRIPTION AND COMMENTS Though many people associate Dumbarton Oaks with the conference held here in 1944 that led to the formation of the United Nations, it's also a major research center for Byzantine and pre-Columbian studies owned by Harvard University. The Byzantine collection is one of the world's finest, featuring bronzes, ivories, and jewelry. The exquisite pre-Columbian art collection is housed in eight interconnected, circular glass pavilions lit by natural light. It's a stunning museum. The terraced 10-acre garden is rated one of the top gardens in the United States. It features an orangery, a rose garden with more than 100 roses, wisteria-covered arbors, and, in fall, a blazing backdrop of trees turning orange, yellow, and red—not to mention elaborate ironwork, a swimming pool, an amphitheater, and a tennis court (now a pebble garden).

TOURING TIPS The entrance to the museum and Music Room are on 32nd Street NW between R and S Streets; the gardens entrance is around the corner on R Street. Guided tours are available every other Friday at 3 p.m. April 12–August 16. Architectural tours are available on the second and fourth Saturday of every month but are limited to 15 people. Brief garden tours are offered seasonally Tuesday–Saturday at 2:10 p.m. There is no food available on site, and picnics are not allowed. Though the Dupont

Circle Metro station is about a mile away, and the Foggy Bottom/GWU station more like 1.5 miles, you'll appreciate both the architecture and the sights along the way.

IF YOU LIKE THIS Nearby **Oak Hill Cemetery,** at 30th and R Streets, boasts a Gothic Revival chapel designed by James Renwick and fabulous 19th-century funeral sculptures. If it's the mansion that grabs you, see the profile of the **Heurich House Museum** on pages 141–142.

Folger Shakespeare Library ★★★

PRESCHOOL ★	GRADE SCHOOL ★	TEENS ★★
YOUNG ADULTS ★★	OVER 30 ★★	SENIORS ★★★

Location 201 E. Capitol St. SE. **Nearest Metro stations** Capitol South or Union Station. **Contact** ☎ 202-544-4600, folger.edu. **Admission** Free. **Hours** Monday–Saturday, 10 a.m.–5 p.m.; Sunday, noon–5 p.m. The Reading Room is open Monday–Friday, 8:45 a.m.–4:45 p.m. and Saturday, 9 a.m.–noon and 1–4:30 p.m. Garden is open Monday–Saturday, 10 a.m.–5 p.m. Closed federal holidays.

DESCRIPTION AND COMMENTS The Folger Shakespeare Library is the world's largest collection of Shakespeare's printed works, as well as a vast array of other rare Renaissance books and manuscripts. One of its treasures, a copy of the *First Folio,* published in 1616, is on permanent display at the east end, open to the title page. (The Folger owns 79 copies of the *First Folio,* about a third of those in existence.) Be sure to look up at the nine bas-relief carvings across the front facade, all depicting scenes from Shakespeare plays. Stroll the Great Hall, featuring hand-carved, oak-paneled walls and priceless displays from the museum's collection. You may also visit the three-tiered Elizabethan Theatre, with walls of timber and plaster and carved oak columns, where three full productions are mounted each season, along with concerts, lectures, and readings. The Bard's birthday is celebrated with a popular open house with performances, kids' activities, and stage combat workshops each year on the Saturday closest to April 23.

TOURING TIPS Free walk-in guided tours of the building and exhibits are conducted Monday–Saturday at 11 a.m., 1 p.m., and 3 p.m. and Sunday at noon and 3 p.m. Reading-room tours are offered only Saturday at noon and Sunday at 1 p.m., with a limit of 15 people, and you must make reservations in advance. Tours of the garden, featuring herbs and flowers grown in Shakespeare's time, are not available at this writing. At the west end of the building, a statue of Puck from *A Midsummer Night's Dream* genially presides over a fountain and pool while grinning toward the U.S. Capitol. The inscription reads, "Lord, what fools these mortals be"—an increasingly popular opinion.

IF YOU LIKE THIS The **Library of Congress** (pages 147–148) and its equally impressive collection of manuscripts is across the street.

Ford's Theatre/Petersen House ★★★★

PRESCHOOL ★	GRADE SCHOOL ★★½	TEENS ★★½
YOUNG ADULTS ★★★	OVER 30 ★★★½	SENIORS ★★★★½

Location 511 10th St. NW. **Nearest Metro stations** Metro Center or Federal Triangle. **Contact** ☎ 202-347-4833, fords.org. **Admission** Free, but only limited numbers of same-day tickets at the box office, and only 6 per pickup; advance tickets $3. **Hours** Daily, 9 a.m.–4:30 p.m. (last entrance at 4); Peterson House, 9:30 a.m.–5:30 p.m. (last entrance at 5); both closed December 25.

DESCRIPTION AND COMMENTS This site is a showcase of programs, performances, and an expanded collection focused on the lead-up to and aftermath of Lincoln's assassination. The National Park Rangers offer tours of the stage and then lead you to the museum belowground. The display includes the size 14 boots and the blood-spattered overcoat that Lincoln was wearing when he was assassinated on April 4, 1865 (ironically, it was Good Friday); the derringer that John Wilkes Booth used to kill him; and other memorabilia.

Across the street is the town house, owned by the Petersen family, where President Lincoln was taken after he was shot and where he eventually died. It leads to the Aftermath Museum next door, which follows Lincoln's funeral train, illuminates the capture of his assassins, and demonstrates Lincoln's impact on the world.

TOURING TIPS No food is available on site. If a matinee or play rehearsal is scheduled, the theater (but not the museum) will be closed to visitors. Occasionally, Ford's offers a tour that involves an actor playing detective James McDevitt on a walking tour of downtown Washington as he investigates the assassination conspiracy. It is conducted by the National Park Service daily, but as this is a regular stop on every eighth-grade class trip, you might try to work around those groups by going early or late in the day. Reservations are recommended, but you can try stopping by for a free timed ticket.

IF YOU LIKE THIS You should visit not only the **Lincoln Memorial** (page 148) but also **President Lincoln's Cottage** (pages 172–173). The **National Portrait Gallery** (page 164) displays life masks, casts of his hands, and photographic portraits. You'll also find a statue of Lincoln as the Great Emancipator, called the Freedmen's Memorial, in Lincoln Park, centered on East Capitol Street and 12th Street NE.

Franklin Delano Roosevelt Memorial ★★★★★

PRESCHOOL ★★★	GRADE SCHOOL ★★★	TEENS ★★★
YOUNG ADULTS ★★★★	OVER 30 ★★★★★	SENIORS ★★★★★

Location West Potomac Park, between the Tidal Basin and the Potomac River. **Nearest Metro stations** Smithsonian, Foggy Bottom/GWU, or Arlington Cemetery (across Memorial Bridge in Virginia). **Contact** ☎ 202-426-6841, nps.gov/fdrm. **Admission** Free. **Hours** Open 24/7; staffed daily, 9:30 a.m.–10 p.m., except on December 25.

DESCRIPTION AND COMMENTS Unlike the nearby imposing marble edifices to Lincoln and Jefferson, the $52 million, 7.5-acre memorial to the 32nd president on the Tidal Basin tells a story: Four interconnected open-air rooms represent each of Roosevelt's four terms. His words are carved on granite walls, bronze images depict the programs and agencies he created to help millions of Americans devastated by the Depression, and statues depict the average citizens whose lives he touched. One shows a man listening intently to a radio, evoking the days before television—and a time when FDR's strong and vibrant voice gave hope to Americans in his fireside chats.

Roosevelt himself is represented in the third room in a larger-than-life bronze statue. The president is seated, his body wrapped in a cape, his face lined with weariness as he approaches the final year of his life. His Scottish terrier Fala is at his feet. The fourth room features a statue of Eleanor

Roosevelt, widely regarded as America's greatest first lady for her service as a delegate to the United Nations and as a champion for human rights.

This is a hands-on memorial: The slightly-larger-than-life figures of FDR and Mrs. Roosevelt, as well as statues of five men in an urban bread line and a rural couple outside a barn door, are placed at ground level. Visitors can easily drape an arm around the first lady, pose by Franklin as he delivers a fireside chat, or join the men in line for a souvenir snapshot. The many waterfalls (FDR considered himself a Navy man) attract splashers, and kids enjoy climbing on giant, toppled granite blocks inscribed with the words "I hate war."

TOURING TIPS While you can enter the memorial from either end, try to start your tour at the official entrance (the one on the Lincoln Memorial side) so you can stroll through the outside rooms in chronological order. Restrooms are located at both entrances. No food is available on site, but there is a bookstore. The memorial is an ideal spot for a picnic by the water, so you might want to bring a lunch. People with mobility challenges may find it difficult to visit the memorial; nearby parking is scarce (see the website for details), and the walk from the nearest Metro stations is about a mile.

IF YOU LIKE THIS The **Korean War Veterans Memorial, Vietnam Veterans Memorial,** and **World War II Memorial** are nearby.

Frederick Douglass National Historic Site ★★★

PRESCHOOL ★	GRADE SCHOOL ★★	TEENS ★★★
YOUNG ADULTS ★★★	OVER 30 ★★★	SENIORS ★★★

Location 1411 W St. SE, in Anacostia. Nearest Metro station Anacostia. Contact ☎ 202-426-5961, nps.gov/frdo. Admission $1 per person; school groups $5. Hours April–October, daily, 9 a.m.–5 p.m.; November–March, daily, 9 a.m.–4:30 p.m. Closed January 1, Thanksgiving, and December 25.

DESCRIPTION AND COMMENTS Cedar Hill, the preserved Victorian home of abolitionist, statesman, and orator Frederick Douglass, sits on a hill overlooking Washington and is preserved as it was when Douglass died in 1895; more than 70% of the items in the house are original. The former slave—who, among other achievements, became US ambassador to Haiti—spent the final 18 years of his life in this house. Douglass lived here when he wrote the third volume of his autobiography, *Life and Times of Frederick Douglass.* For people interested in the history of the civil rights movement and genteel life in the late 1800s, Cedar Hill is a find. National Park Service guides provide a detailed commentary on Douglass' life and times.

A late-afternoon visit is almost like stepping back into the 19th century because there's no electricity and the gathering shadows in the house evoke the past. Look for the photographs of his two wives, Anna Murray Douglass and white abolitionist Helen Pitts Douglass, whom he married after Anna's death. A look into his library is especially moving.

TOURING TIPS Guided tours are the only way to enter the historic house. Space is limited, so make a reservation in advance at recreation.gov. Tours run daily at 9 a.m., 12:15 p.m., 1:15 p.m., 3 p.m., 3:30 p.m., and 4 p.m. (April–October only). From the Anacostia Metro station, take the B2 bus toward Mt. Rainier. No food is available on site.

IF YOU LIKE THIS Visit the **National Museum of African American History and Culture** (pages 157–158) and the **National Museum of American History** (pages 159–160). The Smithsonian's **Anacostia Community Museum** (1901 Fort Place SE., ☎ 202-633-4820, anacostia.si.edu) features exhibitions on black culture and looks at the lives of local Washingtonians.

Freer Gallery of Art *(a Smithsonian museum)* ★★★★

PRESCHOOL ★	GRADE SCHOOL ★★	TEENS ★★★
YOUNG ADULTS ★★★	OVER 30 ★★★★	SENIORS ★★★★

Location 12th St. SW and Independence Ave., on the Mall. **Nearest Metro station** Smithsonian. **Contact** ☎ 202-633-1000 or 202-357-1729 (TDD), asia.si.edu. **Admission** Free. **Hours** Daily, 10 a.m.–5:30 p.m.; closed December 25.

DESCRIPTION AND COMMENTS Well-proportioned spaces, galleries illuminated by natural light, and serenity are the hallmarks of this elegant landmark on the Mall, with its unusual blend of American paintings (including the world's most important collection of works by James McNeill Whistler) and Asian paintings, sculpture, porcelains, scrolls, and richly embellished household items.

Don't miss the Peacock Room, designed by Whistler; a local favorite, it's widely considered to be the most important 19th-century interior in an American museum. The ornate room was painted by Whistler in blue and gold "feathers" to house a collection of blue-and-white Chinese porcelain. Charles Lang Freer, a wealthy 19th-century industrialist who bequeathed this collection to the Smithsonian, bought the entire room in 1904 and had it moved to his Detroit mansion; it was installed in the Freer Gallery after his death. However, Freer believed that "all works of art go together," so he filled the elaborate shelves with pots from Korea, Egypt, Japan, and Iran, as well as China. The room has been restored to its original splendor and is open to the sunlight only once a month, on the third Thursday from noon to 5:30 p.m.

TOURING TIPS An underground link to the nearby Sackler Gallery serves as public exhibition space, as well as convenient passage between the two museums. Free walk-in tours of the Freer are offered almost daily, generally around midday; check the website or stop at the reception desk (these are not recommended for K–12 students). This is a good place to stop if you're looking for a restroom while walking on the Mall.

IF YOU LIKE THIS See the profile of the **Arthur M. Sackler Gallery** on page 131. These two museums are often referred to as if they were a single entity.

Glenstone ★★★

PRESCHOOL —	GRADE SCHOOL —	TEENS ★★
YOUNG ADULTS ★★	OVER 30 ★★★	SENIORS ★★★

Location 12100 Glen Rd., Potomac, MD, 30–45 minutes from Washington. **No Metro access. Contact** ☎ 301-983-5001, glenstone.org. **Admission** Free. **Hours** Appointments available Thursday–Sunday, 10 a.m.–5 p.m. **Special comments** No children under 12 allowed.

DIRECTIONS AND COMMENTS Although it will require advance planning and a car, Glenstone is a unique museum in Potomac, Maryland, that marries art, architecture, and landscape as it seeks to provide a contemplative experience for visitors. Founded as the personal collection of Mitchell and Emily Wei Rales, Glenstone's expansive exhibit space showcases modern-art pieces and installations. Visitors are allowed by appointment only and must follow a curator who describes the artists and their intent for each room.

Tickets are released three months in advance, but the museum sometimes has last-minute openings, so call first. The 170,000-square-foot expansion quadrupled the existing exhibit space, and the lush landscape encompasses multiple outdoor sculptures, a sustainable meadow, and a lily pond.

TOURING TIPS Allow plenty of time to get there, as driving out to Glenstone will take you along some heavily traveled routes, and plan to arrive 15 minutes early. Tours leave promptly on the hour. There is no seating in the gallery; however, wheelchairs are available with advance notice. No food is allowed on site.

IF YOU LIKE THIS See profiles of the **Hirshhorn Museum** (pages 142–143) and **Kreeger Museum** (pages 146–147).

Goddard Space Flight Visitor Center ★★★

| PRESCHOOL ★ | GRADE SCHOOL ★★★ | TEENS ★★★ |
| YOUNG ADULTS ★★★ | OVER 30 ★★★ | SENIORS ★★★ |

Location 8800 Greenbelt Rd., Greenbelt, MD, about 30 miles from Washington. **No Metro access. Contact** ☎ 301-286-8981, nasa.gov/goddard. **Admission** Free. **Hours** July–August: Tuesday–Friday, 10 a.m.–5 p.m.; Saturday and Sunday, noon–4 p.m. September–June: Tuesday–Friday, 10 a.m.–3 p.m.; Saturday and Sunday, noon–4 p.m.; closed January 1, Easter Sunday, July 4, Thanksgiving, and December 25.

DESCRIPTION AND COMMENTS NASA's 1,100-acre facility in suburban Maryland includes a small museum inside the visitor center that's loaded with space hardware, a space capsule kids can play in, space suits, and real satellites, plus dozens of short animated videos on space exploration, climate tracking, the James Webb Space Telescope, and more. It's a mini National Air and Space Museum. The most fun might be outside, where real rockets and jets used to put the hardware into outer space are on display. There is also a sycamore tree grown from a seed that went to space in 1971 aboard *Apollo 14.*

TOURING TIPS The small gift shop offers interesting NASA-related items, such as postcards, 35mm color slides, posters, and publications.

IF YOU LIKE THIS As this requires a car, it may be only for those with a real hankering for space travel. In that case, you'll be happy at the **National Air and Space Museum** (pages 151–152) or the **Udvar-Hazy National Air and Space Museum** in Chantilly, Virginia (pages 175–176).

Gunston Hall ★★★★

| PRESCHOOL ★½ | GRADE SCHOOL ★★ | TEENS ★★ |
| YOUNG ADULTS ★★★ | OVER 30 ★★★½ | SENIORS ★★★½ |

Location 10709 Gunston Rd., Mason Neck, VA (just off I-95 and US 1), about 20 minutes south of Washington. **No Metro access. Contact** ☎ 703-550-9220, gunstonhall .org. **Admission** $10 adults, $5 ages 6–18, $8 seniors 60+; grounds-only passes $5 (prices tend to fluctuate). **Hours** Daily, 9:30 a.m.–4:30 p.m., except January 1, Thanksgiving, and December 25; 45-minute guided house tours every 30–60 minutes, with last tour at 4:30 p.m.; grounds close at 6 p.m.

DESCRIPTION AND COMMENTS This is the home of George Mason, a fascinating character whose role, like those of several other early activists, has only recently been fully appreciated. He was highly influential in the years leading up to the American Revolution: He cowrote, with George Washington, the protest instruments later known as the Virginia Association and the Fairfax County Resolutions, and many of the provisions he constructed for the Virginia Declaration of Rights were adopted by Thomas Jefferson for the Declaration of Independence, including these: "That all men are by nature equally free and independent, and have certain inherent rights . . . namely, the enjoyment of life and liberty, with the means of acquiring and possessing property, and pursuing and obtaining happiness and safety." After the revolution, however, as a delegate to the Constitutional Convention, Mason came to feel that the Constitution as drafted was flawed. He urged the inclusion of a Bill of Rights, opposed the extension of slave importation, and disagreed on various fine points (such as majority versus two-thirds votes). Ultimately, he was unable to bring himself to put aside his principles and sign, despite the resulting vilification.

The complex includes Mason's house, a first-class example of Georgian Colonial architecture constructed in 1755–1760 with a view of the Potomac River and elaborate interior carvings and then-trendy British architectural fashions, such as Gothic and Rococo; gardens and grounds, where archaeological programs are uncovering slave quarters, fences, and other elements; outbuildings (some replicas) such as a kitchen, dairy, schoolhouse, laundry, and smokehouse. The museum shop has a collection of hand-blown glass, hand-turned wooden accessories from the plantation's 200-year-old boxwoods, scented soaps, silver and jewelry, and books.

TOURING TIPS No food is available on site. Although the first floor of the mansion is accessible by a wheelchair lift, reaching the second floor requires taking the stairs. Most of the grounds are relatively flat. If you buy the grounds-only pass, you can use it for a $5 discount ticket to the mansion another day.

IF YOU LIKE THIS **Mount Vernon** (page 150) is only about 12 miles away, with **Woodlawn Plantation** and the **Pope-Leighey House** (see the section on Virginia suburbs, pages 187–188) only a few miles farther, so history buffs could make a day of it.

Heurich House Museum ★★★★

| PRESCHOOL ★ | GRADE SCHOOL ★½ | TEENS ★★½ |
| YOUNG ADULTS ★★★½ | OVER 30 ★★★★ | SENIORS ★★★★½ |

Location 1307 New Hampshire Ave. NW, 1 block south of Dupont Circle. **Nearest Metro station** Dupont Circle. **Contact** ☎ 202-429-1894, heurichhouse.org. **Admission** $10 suggested donation. **Hours** Open for tours by reservation Thursday–Saturday; closed January and federal holidays. **Special comments** No children under 10 allowed.

DESCRIPTION AND COMMENTS This might be the most impressive exterior in town, with the possible exception of the nearby Indonesian Embassy at 2020 Massachusetts Ave. (which was the home of wealthy socialite Evalyn Walsh McLean). A true Victorian castle, with turret, balconies, and all, it was also absolutely state of the art when it was constructed in the early 1890s for local beer baron Christian Heurich: full indoor plumbing, hot water, an elevator, gas and electric lights, a skylight that aided in cooling, and even an early intercom system. Most of the decorations and furnishings are original, including the elegant hand-carved mantels over the marble fireplaces, carved balconies, lamps that look as if they could have come from the Paris Metro, painted ceiling panels, toys, gilded mirrors, rugs, chandeliers, and inlaid floors. In fact, aside from the limited availability of tours, this is a five-star attraction.

TOURING TIPS Guided tours are offered Thursday–Saturday at 11:30 a.m., 1 p.m., and 2:30 p.m. Like some other private museums, it will arrange tours for groups of 10 or more.

IF YOU LIKE THIS See the profiles of **Hillwood Estate Museum and Gardens** (below) and the nearby **Woodrow Wilson House** (page 185).

Hillwood Estate Museum and Gardens ★★★★

PRESCHOOL —	GRADE SCHOOL ★	TEENS ★★
YOUNG ADULTS ★★★	OVER 30 ★★★★★	SENIORS ★★★★★

Location 4155 Linnean Ave. NW. **Nearest Metro station** Van Ness/UDC (20-minute walk). **Contact** ☎ 202-686-5807, hillwoodmuseum.org. **Admission** Suggested donations of $18 adults, $15 seniors 65+, $5 children 6–18, and $10 college students; children under 6 admitted free. **Hours** Tuesday–Sunday, 10 a.m.–5 p.m.; closed most of January and most federal holidays.

DESCRIPTION AND COMMENTS She was a girl from Michigan who inherited two things from her father: good taste and General Foods. That, in a nutshell, is the story of Marjorie Merriweather Post, who bought this 25-acre Rock Creek Park estate in 1955. She remodeled the mansion and filled it with exquisite 18th- and 19th-century French and Russian decorative art. *Fabulous* is the word required to describe the collection of Imperial Russian objects on display. Raisa Gorbachev, then wife of the Russian premier, is said to have wept with joy when she saw Catherine the Great's huge 1791 gold chalice. Post was married to the US ambassador to Russia in the 1930s—a time when the Communists were unloading decadent pre-Revolution art at bargain prices. Post bought warehouse loads of stuff: jewels, dinner plates commissioned by Catherine the Great, Easter eggs by Carl Fabergé, and chalices and icons. She then had the loot loaded onto her yacht, *Sea Cloud* (then the largest private ship in the world), for shipment home. The very best of the booty is on display here. The formal gardens cover 13 acres, and one of the special treats is the dacha (cottage), which Post once used for her own collection of 19th- and 20th-century Russian decorative arts but now houses traveling exhibits and special programs.

TOURING TIPS Seasonal docent-led garden tours, generally April–July, are available Tuesday–Saturday at 10:30 a.m. and 2:30 p.m. The estate also has a café that serves lunch (sometimes with a special menu inspired by the current exhibition) and tea 11:30 a.m.–3:30 p.m.; a gift shop; and a greenhouse you can tour. Most of the complex is wheelchair-accessible, and a few wheelchairs are available at the visitor center.

IF YOU LIKE THIS See the profiles of **Dumbarton Oaks Museum and Gardens** (pages 135–136) and the **Society of the Cincinnati Museum at Anderson House** (page 174).

Hirshhorn Museum and Sculpture Garden
(a Smithsonian museum) ★★★★

PRESCHOOL ★	GRADE SCHOOL ★★	TEENS ★★★
YOUNG ADULTS ★★★	OVER 30 ★★★★★	SENIORS ★★★★

Location Seventh St. SW and Independence Ave., on the Mall. **Nearest Metro stations** Smithsonian or L'Enfant Plaza. **Contact** ☎ 202-633-4674, hirshhorn.si.edu. **Admission**

Free. **Hours** Daily, 10 a.m.–5:30 p.m.; closed December 25. Sculpture Garden open daily, 7:30 a.m.–sunset.

DESCRIPTION AND COMMENTS The innovative art found inside this cylindrical fortress is often as forward-looking (and unique) as the spiral building that houses it. Works by 19th- and 20th-century contemporary artists, such as Auguste Rodin, Winslow Homer, Mary Cassatt, Alberto Giacometti, and Willem de Kooning, line the easy-to-walk galleries. Its special exhibitions are among the most important in America: Imprisoned Chinese activist/artist Ai Weiwei has been represented, along with Yayoi Kusama's sold-out *Infinity Mirrors* (her iconic polka-dotted pumpkin remains on the grounds). Mark Bradford's *Pickett's Charge* is on display through 2021. The outdoor **Sculpture Garden** (set below Mall level) contains works by Rodin, Yoko Ono, and Alexander Calder, among many others. If you are a modern-art fan, the Hirshhorn is a must-see. The recently redesigned lobby by Hiroshi Sugimoto contains tables made from enormous tree trunks with glass tops and round white leather chairs.

TOURING TIPS Docents offer free 45-minute gallery tours daily at 12:30 and 3:30 p.m. While in the galleries look for anyone wearing a "?" badge. Hirshhorn/DRAW is a drop-in sketching program held on weekends, 2–3 p.m. The museum's Dolcezza Café & Gelato is a locally owned shop that sells specialty coffee drinks, gourmet pastries, and seasonal gelato; open daily, 9 a.m.–5 p.m.

IF YOU LIKE THIS Read the profiles of **Glenstone** (page 139) and the **Kreeger Museum** and **The Phillips Collection** (pages 146 and 172, respectively).

International Spy Museum ★★★★

| PRESCHOOL ★ | GRADE SCHOOL ★★★ | TEENS ★★★ |
| YOUNG ADULTS ★★★★ | OVER 30 ★★★★ | SENIORS ★★★★ |

Location 700 L'Enfant Plaza. **Nearest Metro station** L'Enfant Plaza or Smithsonian. **Contact** ☎ 202-393-7798, spymuseum.org. **Admission** $24.95 adults ages 13–64; $19.95 seniors age 65+, military, law enforcement, and college students; $14.95 children ages 7–12; discounted tickets available online. **Hours** Daily, 10 a.m.–6 p.m.; closed January 1, Thanksgiving, and December 25.

DESCRIPTION AND COMMENTS This is the only public museum in the country that focuses on spycraft. The museum recently reopened in a brand-new space at L'Enfant Plaza directly adjacent to the National Mall. The Spy Museum showcases the motivations, tools, and techniques used by real spies in a high-tech and engaging way for all ages.

More than 400 artifacts are on display, dating from Biblical times to the modern age of terror. What you'll see: tools of the trade, such as a lipstick pistol developed by the KGB, two Enigma cipher machines used by the Allies to break German secret codes during World War II, an Aston Martin DB 5 sports car decked out like the one used by James Bond in *Goldfinger,* and tributes to celebrity spies such as dancer Josephine Baker (who worked for the French resistance) and late TV chef Julia Child (who worked for the OSS), as well as African American spies' intelligence contributions during the Revolutionary and Civil Wars. The new Briefing Room film introduces visitors to the realities that spies face in their work. The School for Spies shows how people are recruited to become spies and how they're trained to use observation and analysis, surveillance, disguise, and clandestine photography. The museum explores topics such as the Navajo Codebreakers used during World War II, 50 years of Bond movies, and the challenges facing today's spies like cyberwars and other newer forms of disruption.

TOURING TIPS The museum is part of the L'Enfant Plaza Metro station complex and a short walk from The Wharf. Start on the upper floors, with the history of spycraft, and work your way down. The museum has a food court nearby, and the gift shop contains some entertaining gadgets inspired by real-life spy gear. The exhibit space is very dark, and at times cramped, so keep this in mind and use caution.

IF YOU LIKE THIS Check out the real-life **National Cryptologic Museum** (pages 154–155).

 ## Jefferson Memorial ★★★★

PRESCHOOL ★★	GRADE SCHOOL ★★★	TEENS ★★★★
YOUNG ADULTS ★★★★	OVER 30 ★★★★	SENIORS ★★★★

Location Across the Tidal Basin from the Washington Monument. **Nearest Metro station** Smithsonian. **Contact** ☎ 202-426-6841, nps.gov/thje. **Admission** Free. **Hours** Open 24 hours; staffed daily, 9:30 a.m.–10 p.m., except on December 25.

DESCRIPTION AND COMMENTS The neoclassical, open-air design of this monument to the third U.S. president and author of the Declaration of Independence reflects Jefferson's taste in architecture. In fact, the dome is representative of Jefferson's Virginia home Monticello and the University of Virginia's rotunda (the university that he founded). It's usually less crowded than the monuments on the Mall, except when the cherry trees around the Tidal Basin bloom. (Here's a semi-secret for you: Beneath the memorial is a vast archive of historical info that the park service and scholars study.)

TOURING TIPS Visitors can walk to the memorial along the rim of the Tidal Basin from Independence Avenue or along 14th Street SW. No food is available on site, except during the Cherry Blossom Festival, when there are temporary vendors. The open-air patio in front of the memorial is a fun place for kids to run around and play. Just keep them away from the edge.

IF YOU LIKE THIS Check out the **Martin Luther King Jr. Memorial** (page 149) and the **Franklin Delano Roosevelt Memorial** (pages 137–138) located at the Tidal Basin. You can see them from the steps of the Jefferson.

John F. Kennedy Center for the Performing Arts ★★★

PRESCHOOL ★	GRADE SCHOOL ★	TEENS ★
YOUNG ADULTS ★★	OVER 30 ★★★	SENIORS ★★★

Location 2700 F St. NW. **Nearest Metro station** Foggy Bottom/GWU. **Contact** ☎ 202-467-4600, kennedy-center.org. **Admission** Free. **Hours** Daily, 10 a.m.–9 p.m. Free tours begin every 10 minutes Monday–Friday, 10 a.m.–5 p.m. and Saturday and Sunday, 10 a.m.–1 p.m.

DESCRIPTION AND COMMENTS The white rectilinear Kennedy Center has always been D.C.'s cultural hub. The facility boasts four major stages; a film theater; a sumptuous interior shimmering with crystal, mirrors, and deep-red carpets; and a huge terrace with a grand view of the Potomac River up to Georgetown. Inside the building is the Grand Foyer, which is longer than two football fields. Nations from around the world contributed art and artifacts such as African art, Boehm porcelain, tapestries, and sculptures. If rehearsals aren't in progress, peek inside the intimate Eisenhower Theater, the Opera House, and the Concert Hall. Admirers of JFK will love the tour, but you don't have to take the tour to enjoy the view; take the elevators to the Rooftop Terrace Restaurant. That 360-degree view, which includes many major monuments and the infamous Watergate Hotel next door, is one of the city's best.

The REACH campus greatly expanded the facility, offering visitors new ways to enjoy the iconic building. The REACH consists of a welcome center and immersive collaborative art experiences, but the game-changer is the walkway from the Kennedy Center to the Potomac River waterfront. The bridge allows people to cross above a busy parkway and gain pedestrian access to the National Mall. The REACH's plaza serves as an outdoor gathering space for movie nights during summer, and the lower lawn features outdoor sculptures and a reflecting pool. The garden area is a sanctuary where visitors can relax and take in the sunset.

TOURING TIPS Tour guides in a number of foreign languages, both live and printed, are available; see website. Signed, touch, and assisted-listening tours are available with two weeks' notice (☎ 202-416-8727 or email access@kennedy-center.org). Free round-trip shuttle service from the Foggy Bottom/GWU Metro station is offered every 15 minutes, Monday–Friday 9:45 a.m.–midnight, Saturday 10 a.m.–midnight, Sunday noon–midnight, and 4 p.m.–midnight on federal holidays. If you can't book a show, be sure to drop in on the free performance given daily at 6 p.m. at the Millennium Stage in the Grand Foyer. The Roof Terrace Restaurant has a pre-performance bar and serves dinner and Sunday brunch. A biking and jogging path along the Potomac River is just below the Kennedy Center; follow it upriver to Thompson's Boat Center and through there to Washington Harbour and into Georgetown, a 5-minute walk.

Kenilworth Park and Aquatic Gardens ★★★★

PRESCHOOL ★	GRADE SCHOOL ★★	TEENS ★★½
YOUNG ADULTS ★★★	OVER 30 ★★★½	SENIORS ★★★★

Location 1550 Anacostia Ave. NE, just across the Anacostia River from the U.S. National Arboretum. **Nearest Metro station** Deanwood. **Contact** ☎ 202-692-6080, nps.gov/keaq. **Admission** Free. **Hours** April–October: daily, 9 a.m.–5 p.m.; November–March: daily, 8 a.m.–4 p.m.; closed January 1, Thanksgiving, and December 25.

DESCRIPTION AND COMMENTS Originally a wetlands area, Kenilworth is a mix of meadow gardens and water gardens—it's actually the only national park for the propagation of water plants. In addition to pools filled with water lilies, water hyacinth, lotus, and bamboo, the gardens teem with wildlife, such as opossums, raccoons, beavers, muskrats, and even coyotes. It's also a bird-watcher's paradise—bald eagles nest here, as do great blue herons. Kenilworth is an amazing place to visit anytime, but it's especially enchanting when the lilies and lotus are in bloom during July and early August. The **Anacostia Riverwalk Trail** (see Part Eight, page 294) passes by the edge of the park and is a perfect place to go for a hike.

TOURING TIPS Ranger-led tours are offered daily at 9:30 a.m. and 2 p.m. On Sundays, catch the popular Bird Walk at 8 a.m. Remember that flowers tend to close up early in hot weather, so go early if that's your main interest. The park is unfenced and marshy in places, so keep a close eye on small children. You'll need a car to get here, but it's truly spectacular and worth the effort if you love gardens and wildlife.

IF YOU LIKE THIS See the profiles of the **U.S. Botanic Garden** (pages 176–177) and the **U.S. National Arboretum** (pages 180–181).

Korean War Veterans Memorial ★★★★

PRESCHOOL ★★	GRADE SCHOOL ★★½	TEENS ★★½
YOUNG ADULTS ★★★½	OVER 30 ★★★★	SENIORS ★★★★

Location Between the Lincoln Memorial and the Tidal Basin. **Nearest Metro stations** Smithsonian or Foggy Bottom/GWU. **Contact** ☎ 202-426-6841, nps.gov/kowa. **Admission** Free. **Hours** Open 24 hours; staffed daily, 9:30 a.m.–10 p.m., except on December 25.

DESCRIPTION AND COMMENTS This three-dimensional freeze-frame of troops crossing a battlefield consists of several distinct parts, though it's not particularly large as a whole. The most obvious elements are sculptor Frank Gaylord's 19 larger-than-life steel statues representing 14 Army troops, three Marines, one Navy recruit, and one Air Force serviceman; 12 are white, three are black, two are Hispanic, one is Asian, and one is American Indian. All are heavily laden with packs and weapons and covered in ponchos; their attire and boots suggest it is winter, an impression that is even stronger at night, when the statues are individually illuminated and seem to move.

The second major component is a black granite wall, which complements the Vietnam Veterans Memorial almost directly across the Mall (though not visible from this point). Instead of names, however, this wall is covered with 2,400 images created from 15,000 photos. Etched into the wall are guns, rescue helicopters, ambulances, bridges being built, mines being defused, and doctors operating. Combined with the reflections of onlookers, the effect is as if you were looking through a window. The wall is made up of 38 panels, symbolizing both the 38th Parallel—the original boundary between North and South Korea—and the 38 months of the war's duration. The small garden planted with Rose of Sharon hibiscus, the national flower of South Korea, was dedicated in 1995 by President Clinton and South Korean President Kim Young Sam.

TOURING TIPS The entire site is particularly striking at night.

IF YOU LIKE THIS The other war memorials, including the **Vietnam Veterans Memorial, Women's War Memorial,** and **World War II Memorial,** are all around you on the National Mall.

Kreeger Museum ★★★

PRESCHOOL ★½	GRADE SCHOOL ★	TEENS ★★
YOUNG ADULTS ★★★½	OVER 30 ★★★½	SENIORS ★★★

Location 2401 Foxhall Rd. NW. **No Metro access. Contact** ☎ 202-337-3050, kreeger museum.org. **Admission** $10 adults, $8 students, seniors age 65+, and military with ID. **Hours** Tuesday–Saturday, 10 a.m.–4 p.m. Closed in August and on all federal holidays.

DESCRIPTION AND COMMENTS Philanthropist David Lloyd Kreeger and his wife, Carmen, began collecting art in the early 1950s, primarily works from the 1850s to the 1970s by such artists as Monet, Picasso, Renoir, Cézanne, Chagall, Gauguin, van Gogh, Kandinsky, Miró, Calder, Noguchi, Moore, David

Smith, and Gene Davis. The museum also showcases notable Washington artists like Sam Gilliam. The sculpture garden fits beautifully into the surrounding 5.5 landscaped acres. In addition to arts fans, anyone interested in modern architecture should be certain to see this museum: Phillip Johnson designed it in 1963 as the Kreegers' residence, museum, and recital hall all in one. In addition to the modern art, the collection includes some traditional Asian and African pieces.

TOURING TIPS   Guided tours occur Tuesday–Friday at 10:30 a.m. and 1:30 p.m. and Saturday at 10:30 a.m., noon, and 2 p.m.; no reservations required. The museum is one of D.C.'s hidden gems; it requires a car to get there. The main level of the museum, the sculpture terrace, and the restrooms are wheelchair accessible, but the lower galleries are down a staircase. Some wheelchairs are available by arrangement. No food is available on site.

IF YOU LIKE THIS   Though transportation to the Kreeger is a little tedious, the collection is among the three best in the area: see also profiles of the **Hirshhorn Museum** (pages 142–143) and **Glenstone** (page 139).

 Library of Congress ★★★★

| PRESCHOOL — | GRADE SCHOOL ★ | TEENS ★★ |
| YOUNG ADULTS ★★★½ | OVER 30 ★★★★½ | SENIORS ★★★★ |

Location First St. SE, on Capitol Hill. **Nearest Metro stations** Capitol South or Union Station. **Contact** ☎ 202-707-8000, loc.gov. **Admission** Free. **Hours** Exhibition areas in the Jefferson Building are open Monday–Saturday, 8:30 a.m.–4:30 p.m. The library is closed Sundays, federal holidays, January 1, Thanksgiving, and December 25.

DESCRIPTION AND COMMENTS   The Library of Congress—the largest library in the world—comprises three buildings, the Jefferson, Madison, and Adams Buildings; but the main exhibitions, and the wow factor, are at the Jefferson. To get the most out of your visit, take one of the guided tours. After the tour, which lasts about an hour, you can look at other exhibits in the Jefferson and Madison Buildings on your own. Because it's a lecture tour, it may not be suitable for young children or visitors on a tight schedule. But you should at least go in to admire the Jefferson Building itself; it's a masterpiece, filled with allegorical murals, statuary, mosaics, memorials, and the incredible domed Reading Room, famous from the opening sequence of *All the President's Men.*

The rotating exhibition in the Great Hall features 200 of the library's rarest and most significant items, such as Thomas Jefferson's rough draft of the Declaration of Independence, Abraham Lincoln's first and second drafts of the Gettysburg Address, a Gutenberg Bible, Wilbur Wright's telegram to his father announcing the first heavier-than-air flight, and Bernard Hermann's manuscript score for the film classic *Citizen Kane.*

Library materials available here go way beyond books. For instance, the Library of Congress has an extensive collection of recorded music, broadcast material, posters, and films. For musical material, go to the Recorded Sound Research Center, located on the first floor of the Madison Building, where helpful librarians are ready to assist.

TOURING TIPS   Free guided tours are offered every hour Monday–Saturday, 10:30 a.m.–3:30 p.m. (no tours at 12:30 and 3:30 p.m. on Saturdays). Check in at the Visitor Tour area 20 minutes in advance. Although the most famous exhibits and elaborate design are in the Jefferson Building, both the Madison and Adams Buildings are open weekdays until 9:30 p.m. Grab lunch at the sixth-floor cafeteria in the Madison Building; it's a good deal for visitors and has a million-dollar view.

IF YOU LIKE THIS The **National Archives** (pages 152–153), which is directly across the Mall, has the country's most important documents.

Lincoln Memorial ★★★★★

PRESCHOOL ★★	GRADE SCHOOL ★★★	TEENS ★★★
YOUNG ADULTS ★★★★★	OVER 30 ★★★★★	SENIORS ★★★★

Location At the west end of the Mall. **Nearest Metro stations** Smithsonian or Foggy Bottom/GWU. **Contact** ☎ 202-426-6841, nps.gov/linc. **Admission** Free. **Hours** Open 24 hours; staffed daily, 9:30 a.m.–10 p.m., except on December 25.

DESCRIPTION AND COMMENTS Almost everyone knows what the iconic Lincoln Memorial looks like, but getting up close and inside will truly inspire awe. The contemplative, almost otherworldly Lincoln is 19 feet tall (he would be 28 feet tall standing up). The murals—60 feet wide, 12 feet tall, and 37 feet above some of Lincoln's most important quotations—are neo-classical allegories, with angels, muses, and goddesses representing Unification (on the north wall) and Emancipation (on the south). The Angel of Truth strikes the shackles from a slave, as Justice and Immortality stand as witnesses. Some of the most historic moments of the civil rights struggle took place on the steps: Soprano Marian Anderson sang here in 1939 after being barred from DAR Constitution Hall and Martin Luther King Jr. gave his "I Have a Dream" speech here in 1963 (look for the five lines from that speech carved into the steps). President Obama's inauguration kicked off here with an all-star concert that drew nearly 400,000.

TOURING TIPS Rangers offer interpretive tours between 10 a.m. and 10 p.m., and there is so much symbolism built into the memorial that it is worth hearing. The Legacy of Lincoln museum in the memorial's basement deserves a brief peek. You'll find exhibits about demonstrations held at the memorial and a video recounting the building's history. No food is available on site, though there are restrooms in the circle. From the steps at dusk, it's especially lovely to watch the sunset illuminate the World War II Memorial and the U.S. Capitol across the Mall.

IF YOU LIKE THIS Make your next stops the **Martin Luther King Jr. Memorial** (page 149) and the **Jefferson Memorial** (page 144).

Madame Tussauds ★★★

PRESCHOOL ★½	GRADE SCHOOL ★★★	TEENS ★★★
YOUNG ADULTS ★★★	OVER 30 ★★★	SENIORS ★★★

Location 1001 F St. NW. **Nearest Metro stations** Metro Center or Gallery Place/Chinatown. **Contact** ☎ 202-942-7300, madametussaudsdc.com. **Admission** $22 ages 13 and over, $17 ages 3–12; discounted tickets available online. **Hours** Vary; check the website for the time of your visit.

DESCRIPTION AND COMMENTS If you've seen one Madame Tussauds—and with 22 locations worldwide, it's getting a lot easier to do—you've pretty much seen them all, so there aren't many surprises here. However, if you're an American-history buff, there's a lot to learn about the American presidents, all of whom are displayed with summaries of their time in office. Visitors are not just invited but actively encouraged to take photos with the figures. In some cases, there are special setups, such as the empty seat alongside President Lincoln in his box at Ford's Theatre, the Oval Office desk with President Donald Trump, the entire Obama family, and a table where you can hold hands with George Clooney. The hottest figures are the astronauts from *Apollo 11*, Taylor Swift, First Lady Melania Trump, and Prince William and his wife, Kate. There is an intriguing description of how the figures are made, and interactive games will challenge your knowledge of American history, specifically Alexander Hamilton.

TOURING TIPS Make sure your cell phone is charged up; you're likely to find someone you'd like to have your picture snapped with. Madame Tussauds and the **Big Bus** sightseeing tour (page 114) offer a two-day discounted combo ticket. If you can travel midweek, the online discounts are even better.

IF YOU LIKE THIS If you like seeing lifelike figures, head over to the **National Museum of Natural History** (pages 160–161), where you can pose with a few wild animals.

Martin Luther King Jr. Memorial ★★★★

| PRESCHOOL ★ | GRADE SCHOOL ★★ | TEENS ★★½ |
| YOUNG ADULTS ★★★½ | OVER 30 ★★★★ | SENIORS ★★★★ |

Location Southwest of the Mall on the Tidal Basin. **Nearest Metro station** Smithsonian. **Contact** ☎ 202-426-6821, nps.gov/mlkm. **Admission** Free. **Hours** Open 24 hours; staffed daily, 9:30 a.m.–10 p.m., except December 25.

DESCRIPTION AND COMMENTS This is one of the new generation of walk-through sites, symbolizing Reverend King's personal journey, as well as that of the civil rights struggle in general, with markers of sorrow, inscriptions from some of his speeches, and the culminating statue of Reverend King emerging from the Stone of Hope. Depending on how you approach the site, you may not even see his face at first, which adds to the impact; some people find his expression as stern as thoughtful, but it is definitely impressive. How much you like this park probably depends on your personal experiences or interest in the history of the civil rights movement. Some find it overwhelmingly moving.

TOURING TIPS The official address of this park is 1964 Independence Avenue SW, recalling the year of the signing of the Civil Rights Act, but this is one of those Washington landmarks that is harder to find by GPS (or car at all) than on foot, as much of the traffic around West Potomac Park is one-way and parking is extremely scarce (though some is reserved for handicapped vehicles). On a map, look for the intersection of Independence Avenue and West Basin Drive SW. The memorial site is on the opposite side of the Tidal Basin from the Jefferson Memorial, on a line between the FDR Memorial and the D.C. War Memorial. Remember that during cherry blossom season, the entire area will be mobbed. A bookstore and restrooms are on site, but no food is available.

IF YOU LIKE THIS This could be thought of as part of a personal tour of freedom because it lies along a path that connects it to three major presidential memorials: Lincoln, Franklin Delano Roosevelt, and Jefferson. In fact, the major "mountain" of the statuary is visible from the **Jefferson Memorial** (page 144), a symbol of the Declaration of Independence.

Mount Vernon Estate and Gardens ★★★★★

| PRESCHOOL ★★ | GRADE SCHOOL ★★★★ | TEENS ★★★ |
| YOUNG ADULTS ★★★★★ | OVER 30 ★★★★★ | SENIORS ★★★★★ |

Location 3200 Mount Vernon Memorial Hwy./George Washington Pkwy., Alexandria, VA, about 16 miles south of Washington. **No Metro access. Contact** ☎ 703-780-2000, mountvernon.org. **Admission** $20 adults, $12 children ages 6–11, free for children age 5 and under. *Note:* Advance tickets are timed. **Hours** April–October, 9 a.m.–5 p.m.; November–March, 9 a.m.–4 p.m.; open 365 days, though some sites or tours may be closed seasonally.

DESCRIPTION AND COMMENTS Touring the complex takes nearly a whole day. The 30-acre plantation includes a 4-acre Colonial-style farm site where visitors can view costumed interpreters using 18th-century farm methods and tools, as well as see hogs, mules, horses, cattle, and sheep (though this is *not* a petting zoo). George and Martha's tomb is here, as well as a working blacksmith's shop and a 1770 gristmill and rye distillery 3 miles away (you'll need a car). Historic interpreters are stationed throughout the estate and mansion to answer questions and give visitors an overview of the property and Washington's life. One of the major attractions is the $110 million, state-of-the-art visitor center, with its videos, 23 galleries of artifacts, interactive exhibits, and several real-life models of Washington based on forensic and computer-modeling advances.

TOURING TIPS A number of special tours are available, some seasonal, such as landscape and garden tours: Enslaved People of Mount Vernon covers the slave quarters, workplaces, and burial ground; a behind-the-scenes mansion tour details ongoing preservation; National Treasure: Book of Secrets highlights places used in the filming of the movie; Gardens & Groves explores the landscape; and there's even a tour that focuses on the dogs of Mount Vernon. Tours are $10–$30. April–October, there are 10 a.m. and 3 p.m. wreath-laying ceremonies at the tomb. During the holiday season, the decorated mansion's seldom-seen third floor is open to the public with dinner by candlelight, but not surprisingly, these reservations are very popular, so plan well in advance.

Also note that a variety of package tickets add on a brief river cruise, audio tour, discount at the shops, and more. Both Gray Line bus tours and Spirit Cruises (on the *Spirit of Mount Vernon*) have package tours; visit grayline.com and spiritcruises.com for details. Although the nearest Metro station is Huntington, about 7.5 miles away, there is a Fairfax Connector bus; see fairfaxcounty.gov/connector/routes for information.

IF YOU LIKE THIS Visit **Woodlawn Plantation,** 3 miles away, which was built by the Custis granddaughter George and Martha raised (see "Virginia Suburbs," pages 187–188). Visit **Old Town Alexandria** (pages 169–171) to walk in Washington's footsteps. Stopping for a meal at **Gadsby's Tavern** (page 171) is also appropriate—that's what George used to do.

Museum of the Bible ★★★★★

| PRESCHOOL ★½ | GRADE SCHOOL ★★ | TEENS ★★★ |
| YOUNG ADULTS ★★★ | OVER 30 ★★★★★ | SENIORS ★★★★★ |

Location 400 Fourth St. SW. **Nearest Metro station** Federal Center SW. **Contact** ☎ 866-430-6682, museumofthebible.org. **Admission** $19.99 adults, $9.99 children ages 7–17. **Hours** Daily, 10 a.m.–5 p.m.; closed January 1, Thanksgiving Day, and December 25.

DESCRIPTION AND COMMENTS This new museum, just steps from the National Mall, immerses visitors in the impact and history of the Bible. Six floors of exhibits use innovative technology to showcase elements of Biblical history, such as a time-lapse view of Jerusalem and the Western Wall. On the fourth floor, the museum displays rare artifacts in a library-like exhibit that includes a first-edition King James Bible, the Pagnini Bible, Elvis Presley's Bible, an autographed letter written by Martin Luther, a Slave Bible used by British missionaries, and ancient Torah scrolls. Probably the most family-friendly exhibit is *Stories of the Bible,* located on the third floor. Here you enter rooms with immersive multimedia portrayals of stories from the Old Testament, with a recreation of a Nazareth village during Jesus's time. The second floor focuses on the impact of the Bible on American culture, throughout the world, and now. The fifth floor presents Israeli antiquities obtained through archaeological discoveries, such as an ancient Roman date flask and hand-blown glass vessels found in tombs from the Roman periods. A 12-minute movie on the New Testament is also included in admission.

TOURING TIPS This is a big museum, so expect to do a lot of walking and set aside at least half a day to see all the exhibits. Two special exhibits require an additional fee of $9.99—the virtual-reality tour of the Holy Lands and *Washington Revelations,* a multisensory flyover tour of Washington, D.C. Adults can save $5 by purchasing tickets online in advance. Guided tours are available for an additional $9.99 and last 45 minutes. The Manna and Milk + Honey Café dining venues are excellent. Views from the open atrium on the top floor are stunning and not to be missed. Be aware that no bags bigger than 8x17x19 inches are allowed, so plan to use the complimentary coat check. Kids will love the interactive play area called *Courageous Pages* on the ground floor.

IF YOU LIKE THIS Consider a visit to the **National Archives** (pages 152–153) and the **National Museum of Natural History** (pages 160–161) to see additional collections of notable artifacts and documents.

kids! ☺ **National Air and Space Museum**
(a Smithsonian museum) ★★★★★

PRESCHOOL ★★★★   **GRADE SCHOOL** ★★★★★   **TEENS** ★★★★★
YOUNG ADULTS ★★★★★   **OVER 30** ★★★★★   **SENIORS** ★★★★

Location Sixth St. SW at Independence Ave., on the Mall. **Nearest Metro stations** Smithsonian or L'Enfant Plaza. **Contact** ☎ 202-633-2214, airandspace.si.edu. **Admission** Free. **Hours** September–March: daily, 10 a.m.–5:30 p.m.; April–Labor Day: daily, 10 a.m.–7:30 p.m.; closed December 25.

DESCRIPTION AND COMMENTS Air and Space holds the world's greatest collection of flying machines. Its galleries contain more of the aviation world's "firsts"—first airplane, first to land on the moon—than anywhere else. What Air and Space does especially well is tell the story of the pilots and engineers whose inventions, bravery, and risk-taking took humans from their first flight of 120 feet in 1903, to the first moon landing and back in 1969.

Visitors can touch a moon rock and gaze up at the Wright Brothers' plane, the *Apollo II* command module, and the *Spirit of St. Louis,* which Lindbergh flew across the Atlantic in 1927. In **Space Hall,** you can tour Skylab and check out the *Apollo-Soyuz* spacecraft; look through a 16-inch telescope; and experience cockpit simulations of takeoff and landing at Reagan National

Airport and even of aerial combat. The **Moving Beyond Earth Gallery** has modern spacesuits used in the shuttle missions, parts of the Hubble Space Telescope, and a replica of the space shuttle crew compartment. The most kid-friendly section, called **How Things Fly,** is filled with hands-on displays demonstrating the principles of airplane and rocket flight. **Exploring the Planets** covers man's discovery of the planets in our solar system. **World War II Aviation** features famous aircraft used in battles over Europe and Japan.

The museum remains open as it undergoes a major renovation, but expect to see phased closures of galleries, shops, and theaters, which can limit access to key artifacts and activities. Check the website for a full list of exhibitions that are available during construction.

TOURING TIPS A quick tour of Air and Space can be done in 2–3 hours, though a comprehensive tour, including lunch and an IMAX movie, takes about 4 hours, depending on how much time you spend reading the details in each gallery. Admission to the museum is free, but the IMAX theaters and planetarium shows are not; visit airandspace.si.edu/visit/imax-and-planetarium for show choices and times. The café has to-go options such as salad, soup, and sandwiches. Especially while the museum is under renovation, flight enthusiasts should visit the museum's other facility, the Udvar-Hazy National Air and Space Museum in Chantilly, Virginia.

IF YOU LIKE THIS The expansive **Udvar-Hazy National Air and Space Museum,** outside Dulles International Airport, houses more than 80 aircraft and dozens of space artifacts, including the Space Shuttle *Discovery,* and has its own flight simulators and IMAX theater. Its air traffic–style observation tower has a 360-degree view. There is no shuttle service between the museums. For more information, see pages 175–176. Also check out the profile of the **Goddard Space Flight Visitor Center** (page 140).

National Archives ★★★½

Location Seventh St. between Pennsylvania and Constitution Aves. NW, adjoining the Mall. **Nearest Metro stations** Archives/Navy Memorial/Penn Quarter or Smithsonian. **Contact** ☎ 202-357-5061, archives.gov/nae. **Admission** Free. **Hours** Daily, 10 a.m.–5:30 p.m. (last admission at 5 p.m.); closed Thanksgiving and December 25.

DESCRIPTION AND COMMENTS Thanks to a $13.5 million gift from David M. Rubenstein, owner of the original 1297 Magna Carta on display here, the Archives has an accessible entrance plaza and a gallery devoted to *Records of Rights,* documents ranging back to the Revolutionary War and related to women's suffrage, slavery and civil rights, immigrant prejudice, union and labor injustice, and more. Just as impressive, the gallery, which sits right below the 75-foot-high magnificent Rotunda, where the Big Three of American government—the Declaration of Independence, the U.S. Constitution, and the Bill of Rights—are displayed, has a trompe l'oeil painting on the ceiling that makes it seem as if you are looking through the floor all the way to the Rotunda itself.

Don't be surprised to find the real Rotunda somewhat dim and cool because of the fragility of the documents. (An elaborate, invisible security system lowers them into a deep, nuclear explosion–proof vault each night.) Fortunately, you can still see the two immense murals, each 14 by 35 feet, that illustrate Jefferson presenting the Declaration to John Hancock and the Continental Congress, and James Madison offering the Constitution to Washington. Each is only a single canvas, so large a special studio above Grand Central Station in New York had to be constructed for their painting.

The general admission entrance is at Ninth Street NW and Constitution Avenue; you just get in line. However, this is one of those times when it's worth making advance arrangements (think six weeks) to take a guided tour, not only because you see more, but also because having a reservation allows you to enter at Seventh and Constitution and avoid standing outside (sometimes for as long as an hour). There is a service charge of $1, and the tours are offered weekdays at 9:45 a.m. (reserve on the website or by calling ☎ 877-444-6777). If you happen to be in Washington on July 4, you can catch costumed patriots reading the Declaration aloud on the steps. Also, if you have been bitten by the genealogical bug, and have the time to devote to it, this is a wonderful place to do research: use the research entrance on Pennsylvania Avenue.

TOURING TIPS If you have a tour or timed-entry reservation, show up early; security here is understandably tight. Armed Forces personnel in uniform or with ID can skip the line and go to the Seventh and Constitution entrance. The café is open weekdays, 10 a.m.–2:30 p.m.; you're also allowed to bring in your own lunch and eat it here.

IF YOU LIKE THIS Several of America's treasured documents, such as drafts of the Declaration and Gettysburg Address, are on rotating display in the rotunda of the Jefferson Building at the **Library of Congress** (pages 147–148) and the exhibition hall at the **U.S. Capitol Visitor Center** (page 177).

National Building Museum ★★★

| PRESCHOOL ★★ | GRADE SCHOOL ★★★ | TEENS ★★★ |
| YOUNG ADULTS ★★★★ | OVER 30 ★★★★ | SENIORS ★★★★ |

Location 401 F St. NW. **Nearest Metro stations** Judiciary Square or Archives/Navy Memorial/Penn Quarter. **Contact** ☎ 202-272-2448, nbm.org. **Admission** $10 adults; $7 children ages 3–17, students with ID, and seniors age 60+. **Hours** Monday–Saturday, 10 a.m.–5 p.m.; Sunday, 11 a.m.–5 p.m.; closed January 1, Thanksgiving, and December 25.

DESCRIPTION AND COMMENTS The ideal way to visit this museum would be to walk in blindfolded, then have the blindfold removed. Rather unimposing on the outside, the former Pension Building offers one of the most imposing interiors in Washington, if not the world. The Great Hall measures 316 feet by 116 feet, and at its highest point the roof is 159 feet above the floor. Eight marbleized Corinthian columns adorn the interior. It's worth seeing, even if all you do is poke your head inside the door. But if you're interested in architecture and building construction, check out the permanent and temporary exhibits on the first and second floors.

TOURING TIPS Firehook Café inside the museum sells sandwiches, salads, snacks, sweets, coffee, and other beverages. The museum has also set up an outdoor barbecue stand with live music in warm weather. And the gift shop has some very nice merchandise for architecture and building enthusiasts.

IF YOU LIKE THIS Architecture lovers should add Frank Lloyd Wright's **Pope-Leighey House** tour in Alexandria to their plans (see page 187). The house-turned-museum offers regular tours April–December, daily, on the hour. Admission ranges from $7.50 to $15; free for children age 5 and under.

☺ National Children's Museum ★★★★

| PRESCHOOL ★★★★★ | GRADE SCHOOL ★★★★★ | TEENS ★★ |
| YOUNG ADULTS ★★ | OVER 30 ★★★★ | SENIORS ★ |

Location 1300 Pennsylvania Ave. NW, in the Ronald Reagan Building. **Nearest Metro stations** Smithsonian or Federal Triangle. **Contact** nationalchildrensmuseum.org. **Admission** $10.95. **Hours** Daily, 9 a.m.–4:30 p.m.

DESCRIPTION AND COMMENTS This sparkling new museum was built to inspire young children to embrace modern STEAM concepts—Science, Technology, Engineering, the Arts, and Mathematics. Blending hands-on high technology with the wonder of play, the museum is geared toward the interests of children ages 1–12. A dream motif is the theme behind the exhibits, especially the centerpiece called The Dream Machine—a 50-foot-high, three-story climbing structure with two slides. Amazon, which has its second headquarters in the region, helped fund *Data Science Alley,* an exhibit that demonstrates how virtual information is stored, collected, and used. There's a slime area sponsored by the children's television network Nickelodeon and a kid-controlled weather screen called Innovation Sandbox. Visitors can design cars and race them, as well as play in the beloved Bubble Room. The new museum has quiet rooms designed for children with sensory sensitivities and private rooms for breastfeeding moms.

TOURING TIPS The museum is directly above the Federal Triangle Metro station and has a café that serves coffee, drinks, and healthy snacks. The museum is located inside the Ronald Reagan Building, which also has a large food court.

IF YOU LIKE THIS This museum is located a few blocks from the **White House** (pages 183–184) and one block from the **National Museum of American History** (pages 159–160), which is also a kid-friendly museum. While not dedicated to younger kids, Washington has two other interactive science museums, the **National Building Museum** (page 153) and the **National Museum of Natural History** (pages 160–161).

National Cryptologic Museum ★★★½

| PRESCHOOL — | GRADE SCHOOL ★ | TEENS ★★ |
| YOUNG ADULTS ★★ | OVER 30 ★★★ | SENIORS ★★★ |

Location 8290 Colony Seven Rd., Annapolis Junction, MD, about 30 minutes north of Washington and east of Laurel, MD (MD 32 and Baltimore-Washington Parkway). **No Metro access. Contact** ☎ 301-688-5849, nsa.gov/about/cryptologic-heritage/museum. **Admission** Free. **Hours** Monday–Friday, 9 a.m.–4 p.m.; Saturday (1st and 3rd of the month), 10 a.m.–2 p.m.; closed federal holidays.

DESCRIPTION AND COMMENTS For visitors curious about the world of espionage and government surveillance, the ultra-hush-hush National Security Agency—often noted on cable news—operates this tiny museum dedicated to codes, ciphers, and spies in a former motel overlooking the Baltimore-Washington Parkway.

All the displays are static. They include such items as rare books dating from 1526, Civil War signal flags, a cipher believed to have belonged to Thomas Jefferson, KGB spy paraphernalia, and the notorious Enigma, a German cipher machine whose code was broken by the Poles and British during World War II. (*Spies,* a film on code breaking during World War II, tells the story continuously on a TV in a small theater in the museum.) There is an extensive library of codebooks and deciphered cables and some artifacts of the Navajo code talkers.

Highlights include the bugged Great Seal of the U.S. that hung in Spaso House, the U.S. ambassador's residence in Moscow (the microphone-equipped seal was uncovered in 1952). One room features spy devices used to guard against computer hackers. The adjoining open-air National Vigilance Park is more like a parking lot for two reconnaissance jets, a Vietnam-era Army RU-8D and a cold war–era Air Force C-130. Outside, you'll also get a glimpse of the huge NSA headquarters complex from MD 32. NSA is called "The Puzzle Palace" for its secretiveness and worldwide electronic eavesdropping capability. The agency's budget, by the way, is a secret.

TOURING TIPS You will need a car to get there, and they only offer group tours that require advance reservations. There are vending machines on site.

IF YOU LIKE THIS Don't miss the newly reconstructed **International Spy Museum** (pages 143–144) in L'Enfant Plaza.

National Gallery of Art ★★★★★

PRESCHOOL ★	GRADE SCHOOL ★★	TEENS ★★★
YOUNG ADULTS ★★★★★	OVER 30 ★★★★★	SENIORS ★★★★★

Location Constitution Ave. NW between Third and Ninth Sts., on the Mall. **Nearest Metro stations** Archives/Navy Memorial/Penn Quarter, Judiciary Square, or Smithsonian. **Contact** ☎ 202-737-4215, nga.gov. **Admission** Free. **Hours** Monday–Saturday, 10 a.m.–5 p.m.; Sunday, 11 a.m.–6 p.m.; closed January 1 and December 25.

DESCRIPTION AND COMMENTS This world-class collection is a must-see for everyone, even if you only have time for a brief visit. The National Gallery is a complex of buildings and gardens that burst with art in all forms. The West Building, designed by classicist John Russell Pope and clad in pink Tennessee marble, features European and American art from the 13th through the 19th centuries. The heart of the collection was donated—and the building largely constructed—by financier Andrew Mellon. This is where you find the heavy hitters: Leonardo, Rembrandt, Van Eyck, Vermeer, Raphael, Goya, Monet, Fra Lippo Lippi, El Greco, and David, just to name a few. Most of the museum's paintings are hung in many small rooms, instead of a few big ones, designed to complement the installations: hand-finished plaster walls in the Renaissance galleries, paneling in the Dutch galleries, etc. In a very classic way, it is filled with plants, benches, and a garden courtyard where classical concerts are often presented, most often on Sundays at 6:30 p.m.

Mellon's son, Paul, and daughter, Ailsa Bruce, continued this tradition by donating more than a thousand major pieces; they also financed the construction of I. M. Pei's East Building to house contemporary art. Outside, the popular building consists of unadorned vertical planes. Inside, it's bright, airy, and spacious—a series of triangles. Look for art by modern masters, such as Picasso, Matisse, Mondrian, Miró, Magritte, Warhol, Lichtenstein, and Rauschenberg. The exhibits change seasonally, and some exhibits require advance tickets. There are two soaring towers and a rooftop terrace with an Instagram-worthy giant blue rooster. The rooftop offers superb views of the U.S. Capitol and buildings along Pennsylvania Avenue.

The 6-acre National Gallery Sculpture Garden on the Mall side of the West Building holds works from the gallery's permanent collection. It's a favorite hangout for locals and visitors alike. In winter, the fountain is transformed into an ice rink. In the warmer months, the fountain becomes a gathering space for everyone wishing to cool off. From Memorial Day to Labor Day, there's free jazz on Friday evenings. The gleaming pyramids between the museum wings create a natural playground.

If you're looking for souvenirs, the Gallery Shops on the ground floor have irresistible art-oriented gifts, jewelry, scarves, books, games, toys, and prints and cards from the collection.

TOURING TIPS Free tours and gallery talks are offered throughout the day; check at the desk, on the website, or call ☎ 202-842-6247. Tours are available in more than a dozen foreign languages. Security is particularly tight here: No luggage, backpacks, or book bags allowed. No phone calls are allowed in the galleries. Occasionally, temporary exhibits are extremely popular and may require a free timed ticket. However, a number of tickets are set aside every day for distribution that day only.

Four cafés provide space to grab a bite, rest, and absorb the magnificent art that surrounds you here. The Concourse houses the Cascade Café, a cafeteria with a waterfall wall. The more elegant (and quiet) Garden Café near the West Building museum shop often has special menus to complement exhibits—Provençal fare for a Cézanne show, Catalan for Joan Miró, etc. The Terrace Café in the East Building offers soups, salads, and desserts. It's probably the quietest location among dining venues on the National Mall. The Pavilion Café is located in the Sculpture Garden and is open year-round with casual dining, wine, and beer. The Art Deco subway gate arching over the Pavilion Café is from the Paris Metro.

IF YOU LIKE THIS The fine art of the last 500 years by women is showcased at the much less hectic **National Museum of Women in the Arts** (pages 162–163). If you're seeking contemporary art created in the last two centuries, head to the **Hirshhorn Museum** (pages 142–143) across the Mall.

National Geographic Museum ★★★

PRESCHOOL ★★★	GRADE SCHOOL ★★★★	TEENS ★★★★
YOUNG ADULTS ★★★	OVER 30 ★★	SENIORS ★★

Location 1145 17th St. NW, 4 blocks north of the White House. **Nearest Metro stations** Farragut North, Dupont Circle, or Farragut West. **Contact** ☎ 202-857-7700, nationalgeographic.org. **Admission** $15 adults; $12 seniors 63+, military, and students with ID; $10 children ages 5–12. **Hours** Daily, 10 a.m.–6 p.m.; closed December 25.

DESCRIPTION AND COMMENTS Walking through these halls is something like flipping through a couple of *National Geographic* magazines. Located on the first floor of the National Geographic Society's headquarters, this small collection of exhibits showcases weather, geography, astronomy, biology, exploration, and space science. The goal is to spotlight researchers and provide a forum to express their transformative ideas through storytelling and educational programs. Temporary exhibits have covered the Queens of Egypt, the *Titanic,* and sea monsters. The society hosts Explorer Trivia Nights, educational lectures, concerts, films (both documentary and 3-D thrillers), and ethnic cultural events.

TOURING TIPS The admission fee is for the special exhibits. If you only want to browse the lobby exhibits (usually photography or interactive info) and the intriguing museum shop (which offers books, ethnic clothes and jewelry, travel gear, videos, maps, and magazines), you can enter for free. The 3-D theater has a $7 ticket, but the combined entry/movie ticket saves you a couple of bucks. The courtyard on M Street, a great spot for a brown-bag lunch, is filled with whimsical animal sculptures. Note that the museum sometimes closes early the night before holidays.

IF YOU LIKE THIS If you love nature and science, don't miss the **National Museum of Natural History** (pages 160–161).

National Museum of African American History and Culture
(a Smithsonian museum) ★★★★★

PRESCHOOL —	GRADE SCHOOL ★★	TEENS ★★
YOUNG ADULTS ★★★	OVER 30 ★★★	SENIORS ★★★

Location 1400 Constitution Ave. NW, on the Mall between 14th and 15th Sts. **Nearest Metro stations** Federal Triangle or Smithsonian. **Contact** ☎ 844-750-3012, nmaahc .si.edu. **Admission** Free with timed pass during peak season and on weekends. Same-day passes are released at 6:30 a.m. on Saturdays and Sundays. No timed passes needed on weekdays September–February. **Hours** Daily, 10 a.m.–5:30 p.m.; closed December 25; special hours on the day after Thanksgiving, December 26, and December 29.

DESCRIPTION AND COMMENTS The National Museum of African American History and Culture (NMAAHC), located on the National Mall to the west of the National Museum of American History, is adorned in bronze lattice, a design that is striking both for its color and three-tiered shape; it was inspired by a Yoruban crown worn by Ghanaian kings. The bronze ironworks encircling the three tiers symbolize work crafted by enslaved African Americans living in the American south.

Upon entering the eight-story building, you'll begin your visit in Heritage Hall, where you can check your coats and bags in the lockers (bring quarters). Next, take the escalator down to enter the History galleries, which transport visitors to the 1400s.

The tour begins with the dark story of the Trans-Atlantic Slave Trade, when Colonial-era ships transported millions of captured Africans to the Caribbean, South America, and North America to sell into slavery. Deeper inside, the exhibit opens into a multilevel atrium with depictions of incidents prior to, during, and after the Civil War. Here you'll see stirring objects like Nat Turner's Bible, Harriet Tubman's shawl, tiny iron shackles, and a cotton gin.

The next galleries depict President Lincoln's Emancipation Proclamation and the struggles of migration during the Reconstruction Era, then move to the perils of the Jim Crow era. Here you'll see stark representations, such as a segregated railroad car and a Louisiana penitentiary guard tower, demonstrating the American climate of discrimination. One of the most sorrowful is the small alcove containing the casket of Emmett Till, a young victim of racially motivated violence.

The exhibit also describes the results of the Plessy vs. Ferguson case, which declared education and other rights for African Americans would be "separate but equal," then shows examples like a drinking fountain marked COLORED.

The museum integrates the accomplishments of African Americans from 1968 and beyond through emotion-laden exhibits and interactives. The tradition of activism presents stories of groundbreaking leaders like the Tuskegee Airmen, Martin Luther King Jr., James Baldwin, and Malcolm X. Also featured are the contributions made by countless African Americans who served their country in every American war.

The upper floors feature stunning images and relics from African Americans in art, culture, food, sports, dance, and music. Don't miss the uplifting exhibit on African American sports heroes like Wilma Rudolph, Mohammed Ali, Michael Jordan, Dominique Dawes, and Serena and Venus Williams, to name a few. The important stance taken by the Olympians who expressed "black power" are represented with a standout statue.

Kids and teens particularly enjoy the *Musical Crossroads* exhibit, which focuses on the arts. Some highlights include Thomas Dorsey's piano and Marion Anderson's ensemble from the 1939 Concert on the Lincoln Memorial. You'll see costumes, guitars, and even George Clinton's Mothership. Other notable objects include Chuck Berry's red Cadillac and Ella Fitzgerald's black gown.

TOURING TIPS One of the best museum restaurants (although somewhat expensive) is **Sweet Home Cafe.** D.C. Top Chef Carla Hall created a menu of locally sourced, Southern-inspired dishes such as barbecue, Creole cuisine, Caribbean-style plates, and vegetarian meals. The gift shop has books and memorabilia, especially crafts that feature the dramatic architecture of the museum.

IF YOU LIKE THIS Visit the **National Museum of African Art** (see below), which is across the Mall, or the **Frederick Douglass National Historic Site** (pages 138–139) in Anacostia.

National Museum of African Art *(a Smithsonian museum)*
★★★½

PRESCHOOL ★	GRADE SCHOOL ★★	TEENS ★★
YOUNG ADULTS ★★★	OVER 30 ★★★½	SENIORS ★★★

Location Ninth St. and Independence Ave. SW, on the Mall. **Nearest Metro station** Smithsonian. **Contact** ☎ 202-633-4600, africa.si.edu. **Admission** Free. **Hours** Daily, 10 a.m.–5:30 p.m.; closed December 25.

DESCRIPTION AND COMMENTS This elegant subterranean museum is paired with the Sackler Gallery, a museum of Asian art, and separated by an aboveground garden. Inside is an extensive collection of African art in a wide range of media, including sculpture, masks, household and personal items, and religious objects. The museum also mounts special exhibitions. Intellectually, this museum transports museumgoers far away from the Mall. It's a good destination for older children, teens, and adults looking for some non-European cultural history and art, and it's a great alternative on hot or crowded days.

TOURING TIPS Ask at the information desk if there are any gallery tours scheduled. If you don't have to take the elevator, don't; artworks are all around the staircase. Don't miss the excellent museum shop, where you'll find textiles, jewelry, scarves and sashes, wood carvings, and books written by African authors. No food is available on site.

IF YOU LIKE THIS Washington has many world-class art museums. In addition to the **National Gallery of Art** (pages 155–156) and the **Hirshhorn Museum** (pages 142–143), the smaller **Phillips Collection** (page 172) is an outstanding independent museum featuring contemporary art. The **Freer Gallery of Art** (page 139) and the **Arthur M. Sackler Gallery** (page 131) are steps away from the Museum of African Art and worth visiting as well.

 National Museum of American History
(a Smithsonian museum) ★★★★★

| PRESCHOOL ★★★ | GRADE SCHOOL ★★★★ | TEENS ★★★★★ |
| YOUNG ADULTS ★★★★★ | OVER 30 ★★★★★ | SENIORS ★★★★★ |

Location 14th St. and Constitution Ave. NW, on the Mall. **Nearest Metro stations** Smithsonian or Federal Triangle. **Contact** ☎ 202-633-1000, americanhistory.si.edu. **Admission** Free. **Hours** Daily, 10 a.m.–5:30 p.m.; closed December 25.

DESCRIPTION AND COMMENTS This irresistibly eclectic museum—affectionately nicknamed "the nation's attic," catalogues the story of America. The entire collection tops 3 million items—and gives full due to such treasures as the original 30-by-42-foot Star-Spangled Banner, which, after an eight-year conservation, now has its own gallery on the second floor. Among the many notable artifacts rotated on display here are the desk on which Thomas Jefferson wrote the Declaration of Independence, the Greensboro lunch counter, Edison's light bulb from 1879, steam locomotives, printing presses, a Model T Ford, a pendulum three stories high that shows how the Earth rotates, a collection of ball gowns worn by First Ladies (including Michelle Obama and Melania Trump), a battle uniform worn by and letters by George Washington, a house in which five families lived over a period of two centuries, and a pair of Dorothy's ruby slippers. Just the collection of television objects and ephemera alone is stupefying: Mr. Rogers's sweater; Jerry Seinfeld's puffy shirt; the *60 Minutes* stopwatch; the Lone Ranger's mask; Jim Henson's original Oscar the Grouch and Kermit the Frog; and the real kitchen (pots, pans, and all) from Julia Child's Cambridge, Massachusetts, home, where she began her TV career. The Hall of Musical Instruments houses a Stradivarius quartet of ornamented instruments. There's a science lab on the first floor with experiments every half hour, a statue of George Washington as a Roman general, and a single Dumbo flying car. The spectacular dollhouse on the third floor, donated in 1951, had already had 50 years of care and furnishing. The array of fully rigged model ships on the first floor is a child-pleaser too. The Hall of Transportation in the museum's east wing features an expansive collection of cars, trains, trolleys, and motorcycles that will fascinate all ages.

The five-story-high atrium floods the museum with light, and thanks to the glass staircase and a panoramic window, you can see all the way through the museum from Constitution Avenue to the Mall and down to the Washington Monument. For a lot of people, this ranks as their favorite Mall museum. No wonder—it offers viewers a dizzying array of history, nostalgia, technology, and culture. And kids love it. It's a must-see for virtually all visitors.

TOURING TIPS Check at the information desk or peruse the website for a schedule of tours (usually daily at 10 a.m. and 1 p.m.), demonstrations, concerts, lectures, films, and other activities put on by the museum staff. A recent renovation established two new dining venues—The LeRoy Neiman Jazz Café on the first floor and Eat at America's Table Café on the lower level.

IF YOU LIKE THIS There is some overlap between the **National Museum of African American History and Culture** (pages 157–158) and this museum. Both have artifacts from the civil rights era. If the machinery is the stuff that fascinates you (or your kids), consider adding the **National Inventors Hall of Fame and Museum** in the United States Patent and Trademark Office in Alexandria, Virginia (invent.org/museum).

National Museum of Health and Medicine   ★★½

| PRESCHOOL — | GRADE SCHOOL ★★ | TEENS ★★★ |
| YOUNG ADULTS ★★★ | OVER 30 ★★★ | SENIORS ★★★ |

Location 2500 Linden Ln., Silver Spring, MD. **Nearest Metro station** Silver Spring (15-minute walk). **Contact** ☎ 301-319-3300, medicalmuseum.mil. **Admission** Free. **Hours** Daily, 10 a.m.–5:30 p.m.; closed December 25.

DESCRIPTION AND COMMENTS Ever since TV became fascinated with forensic medicine, this museum—which dates back to the Civil War, though it's in a modern building—figured out the way to a kid's heart is through his, um, heart. Excellent exhibits on the human body make this museum a worthwhile destination. Although there are still plenty of bottled human organs, skeletons, and graphic illustrations of the effects of disfiguring diseases, the emphasis is on science education. Exhibits on Civil War medicine and an extensive microscope collection (including huge electron microscopes) will probably have more appeal to physicians, scientists, and other health professionals (unless you're addicted to forensic-thriller TV or slasher films).

TOURING TIPS No food is available on site. Tours are offered to groups only, but perhaps you can tag along. You'll need a car and your identification to access this museum.

IF YOU LIKE THIS Visit the **National Institutes of Health** Visitor Center (nih.gov /about-nih/visitor-information), with its Nobel Laureate Exhibit Hall, in Bethesda, Maryland.

kids National Museum of Natural History
☺ *(a Smithsonian museum)*   ★★★★★

| PRESCHOOL ★★★★ | GRADE SCHOOL ★★★★★ | TEENS ★★★★★ |
| YOUNG ADULTS ★★★★★ | OVER 30 ★★★★★ | SENIORS ★★★★★ |

Location Tenth St. NW and Constitution Ave., on the Mall. **Nearest Metro stations** Smithsonian, Archives/Navy Memorial/Penn Quarter, or Federal Triangle. **Contact** ☎ 202-633-1000, naturalhistory.si.edu. **Admission** Free; butterfly pavilion admission $7.50 adults, $7 age 60+, $6.50 ages 2–12. **Hours** Daily, 10 a.m.–5:30 p.m.; open until 7:30 p.m. during the summer months and around selected holidays; closed December 25.

DESCRIPTION AND COMMENTS Distinguished by its golden dome and the towering bull elephant in the rotunda, the Museum of Natural History is a Washington landmark, and another of the Mall's most popular attractions. Visitors of all ages and tastes will find fascinating things to see here, from a mummified cat to a Neanderthal's skull. Long halls are filled with display cases of animal bones and fossils.

The new David Koch Hall of Fossils dives deep into the Earth's history by displaying 700 fossils, including an expansive collection of dinosaur bones. The most popular features are the aggressively posed T. Rex and more cuddly Triceratops. The exhibit covers 3.7 million years with a focus on climate change and the history of extinction on Earth. Kids love touch-friendly sections such as the interactive *Fossil Basecamp.*

The Janet Annenberg Hooker Hall of Geology, Gems, and Minerals is home, most famously, to the supposedly cursed 45.52-carat Hope Diamond, and to a blue diamond that may have inspired the movie *Titanic*'s fictional "Heart of the Ocean" gem. The exhibit features meteorites, emeralds, a 23,000-carat topaz, crystals, a walk-through mine, a re-creation of a cave, and a plate tectonics gallery showing how the Earth's surface shifts.

A stunning collection of taxidermy is a highlight at the Kenneth Behring Family Hall of Mammals. The 274 items displayed include mammals from every corner of the world, mostly in action poses and often interacting with each other as they would in the wild. Don't miss the short film on the evolution of the mammal family tree.

The museum's unofficial mascot is the 45-foot replica of a North Atlantic right whale hanging overhead, a scale model of a real whale named Phoenix. If you're looking for live creatures, check out the 1,500-gallon aquarium with a living coral reef and the Insect Zoo (some museums have shark feedings; here, it's tarantulas). Special exhibits are located on the ground level (Constitution Avenue entrance).

TOURING TIPS Check the website for highlight and exhibit tours throughout the week. On Tuesdays the live-butterfly pavilion is free. The museum's website has a handy guide to busier or quieter times; see how that matches your schedule. Two cafés are on site.

IF YOU LIKE THIS The **National Geographic Museum** (pages 156–157) rotates exhibits on various nature and science phenomena. For younger kids, visit the new **National Children's Museum** (page 154).

National Museum of the American Indian
(a Smithsonian museum) ★★★½

PRESCHOOL ★½	GRADE SCHOOL ★★	TEENS ★★
YOUNG ADULTS ★★★	OVER 30 ★★★	SENIORS ★★★

Location Fourth St. and Independence Ave. SW, on the Mall. **Nearest Metro stations** Federal Center or L'Enfant Plaza. **Contact** ☎ 202-633-1000, americanindian.si.edu. **Admission** Free. **Hours** Daily, 10 a.m.–5:30 p.m.; closed December 25.

DESCRIPTION AND COMMENTS This Smithsonian museum is an undulating four-story landmark, and clearly the Mall's first 21st-century museum design, in that it refers outside to what it holds inside. Architecturally, it honors traditional methods of worship and natural conservation as well as showcases American Indian arts and traditional crafts. It sits on a 4.25-acre site with natural rock formations and native plants set in a forest, wetlands, meadowlands, and croplands. Here, the term *American Indian* means much more than those of the United States; it also includes indigenous tribes from Canada, Mexico, and Central and South America (though they're less heavily represented).

The circular Lelawi Theater on the fourth level provides an overview of the American Indian experience through a 13-minute film. Exhibits change periodically and use artifacts and images to tell the stories of different tribes, including the *Algonquian People of the Chesapeake Region.* The *Americans* exhibit demonstrates how American history and culture have been influenced by American Indians. The museum shop is alluring, stocked with silver and turquoise (not knockoffs, the real thing), wood carvings, feather masks, fine pottery and glass, and ivory and stone carvings.

TOURING TIPS The museum's Mitsitam Café, an upscale cafeteria featuring regional American dishes from salmon and tacos to venison and bison, is one of the best around the Mall, so at lunchtime it's filled with federal workers as well as tourists.

IF YOU LIKE THIS The **National Museum of American History** (pages 159–160) offers a cultural overview of Latino History and Culture with artifacts from indigenous people of North, South, and Central America.

National Museum of the Marine Corps ★★★★

PRESCHOOL —	GRADE SCHOOL ★★	TEENS ★★★
YOUNG ADULTS ★★★★	OVER 30 ★★★★	SENIORS ★★★★

Location 18900 Jefferson Davis Hwy., Triangle, VA. **Nearest Metro station** Franconia/Springfield, then take a cab or Uber; another option is the Amtrak train from Union Station to Quantico, VA. **Contact** ☎ 877-653-1775, usmcmuseum.com. **Admission** Free. **Hours** Daily, 9 a.m.–5 p.m.; closed December 25.

DESCRIPTION AND COMMENTS Though it has been open only since 2006, the National Museum of the Marine Corps in Virginia has quickly become a top destination for visitors. The museum educates and engages people with its immersive, modern exhibits on Marine Corps history. The 135-acre site near Quantico has a breathtaking atrium, with airplanes suspended from the ceiling. Visitors can imagine themselves signing up to enlist, and then proceed through various galleries, featuring the American Revolution, World Wars I and II, the Korean and Vietnam Wars, and more. New galleries are set to open in phases through 2022. Plan to spend the day, take a docent-led tour, and see the *We, the Marines* film in the Medal of Honor Theater. The grounds are a peaceful place for meditation. This inspiring museum is a must-see for military-history buffs and service members and their families.

TOURING TIPS Try the museum's popular dining venues, Devil Dog Diner and Tun Tavern. There's a nice playground for kids near the parking lot and a beautiful Memorial Park to picnic in. Wheelchairs are available at no cost. Free docent-led tours are based on availability. The museum store has a wide array of Marine-themed merchandise.

IF YOU LIKE THIS Check out the **African American Civil War Museum** (afroamcivilwar.org) and the **Udvar-Hazy National Air and Space Museum** (pages 175–176). The new **National Museum of the U.S. Army** is in development at Fort Belvoir. For information, see thenmusa.org.

National Museum of Women in the Arts ★★★½

PRESCHOOL ★	GRADE SCHOOL ★★	TEENS ★★★
YOUNG ADULTS ★★★	OVER 30 ★★★★	SENIORS ★★★★

Location 1250 New York Ave. NW. **Nearest Metro station** Metro Center or McPherson Square. **Contact** ☎ 202-783-5000 or 800-222-7270, nmwa.org. **Admission** $10 adults, $8 seniors age 65 and up and students, free for visitors age 18 and under and Blue Star Families; admission to the Great Hall, Mezzanine, and Long Gallery is free.

Hours Monday–Saturday, 10 a.m.–5 p.m.; Sunday, noon–5 p.m.; closed January 1, Thanksgiving, and December 25.

DESCRIPTION AND COMMENTS This groundbreaking museum, the world's most important collection of art by women, has a permanent collection of more than 4,000 paintings and sculptures by women from the 16th century to the present: Georgia O'Keeffe, Mary Cassatt, Frida Kahlo, and Helen Frankenthaler, to name a few. From the outside, it looks like any other office building along crowded New York Avenue. But inside the former Masonic Grand Lodge are striking architectural features, such as a crystal chandelier, marble floors in the main hall and mezzanine, and the grand staircase. The second-floor balcony hosts temporary exhibits; the third floor is where you'll find the permanent collection. The annex showcases sculpture and contemporary works by lesser-known female artists. This beautiful museum is only a little off the beaten path, but it tends to be less crowded than most Washington, D.C., art museums, which is a nice benefit for visitors.

TOURING TIPS Admission is $10 adults, $8 students and seniors; free the first Sunday of the month. The Mezzanine Café is open for lunch Monday–Friday, 11 a.m.–2 p.m.

IF YOU LIKE THIS **The Phillips Collection** (page 172) showcases several female artists, including Georgia O'Keeffe and Betty Lane. The **National Museum of African Art** (pages 158–159) often focuses on female artists.

National 9/11 Pentagon Memorial ★★★★

| PRESCHOOL ★ | GRADE SCHOOL ★★½ | | TEENS ★★★ |
| YOUNG ADULTS ★★★★ | OVER 30 ★★★★ | SENIORS ★★★★ |

Location Near the south parking area of the Pentagon in Arlington, VA. **Nearest Metro station** Pentagon. **Contact** pentagonmemorial.org. **Admission** Free. **Hours** Open 24 hours. *Note:* The memorial will be closed for renovation through May 2020.

DESCRIPTION AND COMMENTS This intentionally low-key memorial to those who were killed on 9/11 is designed to encourage visitors to meditate on the enormity of the attack and of the human toll. As you approach from the plaza, you step across the Zero Line, inscribed "September 11, 2001 9:37 a.m." The border was cut from the original limestone walls and still shows scorch marks from the fire that followed the impact. There are 184 benches, one for each of those killed when Flight 777, traveling at a speed of 550 mph, struck the building. Under each bench, which resembles a jet wing, is a small pool; during the day they reflect sunlight and at night are lit from beneath the water. Each bench has been oriented so that if you read the name and you're looking at the sky, he or she was actually on the airplane; if the viewpoint is the Pentagon, the victim was in the building. (There is a slab with all the names and years of birth, which is also a locator for benches.) There is a point-of-impact marker, and an "age wall" rises along an arc and reflects the ages of the victims, ranging from 3-year-old Dana Falkenberg, who was in a day care center, to 71-year-old John D. Yamnicky. Although this is obviously an emotionally loaded site that may have even deeper meaning for anyone who lost family or friends, its symbolism is subtle enough that young children should not be disturbed.

TOURING TIPS Paved walkways allow for wheelchair accessibility. There are no metal detectors or security checkpoints to pass through, as you are not allowed to enter the Pentagon itself; however, in addition to the usual prohibitions on alcohol, etc., visitors may not carry firearms, fireworks, or political or commercial brochures or posters. You may not take photographs of the Pentagon itself. Restrooms are open daily, 7 a.m.–10 p.m. Like the Korean War Veterans Memorial, this is even more affecting after dark. There is a downloadable audio tour on the website, or call ☎ 202-741-1004 when you enter for a guide to points of interest. Some renovations are planned, check the website for closures.

IF YOU LIKE THIS Visit nearby **Arlington National Cemetery** (pages 128–131), where countless American heroes are buried and memorialized.

National Portrait Gallery–Smithsonian American Art Museum *(two Smithsonian museums)* ★★★★★

| PRESCHOOL ★ | GRADE SCHOOL ★★ | TEENS ★★½ |
| YOUNG ADULTS ★★★★ | OVER 30 ★★★★★ | SENIORS ★★★★★ |

Location Eighth and F Sts. NW. **Nearest Metro stations** Gallery Place/Chinatown or Archives/Navy Memorial/Penn Quarter. **Contact** ☎ 202-633-1000 americanart.si.edu. and npg.si.edu. **Admission** Free. **Hours** Daily, 11:30 a.m.–7 p.m.; closed December 25.

DESCRIPTION AND COMMENTS This is another of Washington's world-class stops—two of them, in fact. The National Portrait Gallery and Smithsonian American Art Museum are housed in one of Washington's great buildings: the 1836 Patent Office, which in Pierre L'Enfant's plan for the city marks the central point between the White House and Capitol building. The structure has been graced with the awe-inspiring Kogod Courtyard, which is covered by a glass ceiling and has a water walk running through it.

The building was nearly demolished in 1953 until preservationists prevailed, and now it's the city's most popular meeting place. This is where D.C. residents stood to celebrate when their professional hockey team, the Washington Capitals, won the Stanley Cup. These museums stay open late year-round to welcome the crowds who enjoy the nightlife in Penn Quarter.

Both museums house a combination of permanent and shifting exhibitions. Among the must-sees are the Presidential portraits, including the most recent additions, paintings of President and Michelle Obama. Among the fascinating portraits in the Presidents' Hall are the Gilbert Stuart portrait of Washington and an impressionistic painting of John F. Kennedy.

On the American art side, you'll find contemporary installations such as the model of the Statue of Liberty and the stunning *The Throne of the Third Heaven of the Nations' Millennium General Assembly,* a huge folk-art piece made of found materials, scavenged furniture, and chewing gum wrappers by handyman James Hampton; it was discovered in his rooms after his death. Often experimental artists are working in-house and sometimes involve visitors in their creative work.

While there, consider all the events that have taken place inside these hallowed walls. At one time, the same building housed the Declaration of Independence and Ben Franklin's printing press. It was also the site of several presidential inaugural balls—not to mention serving as a Union Army hospital during the Civil War, where volunteer nurse Walt Whitman tended the wounded and dying and wrote letters and poems for them.

TOURING TIPS Highlights tours are free and available at various times during the day; check the website. There is sometimes entertainment in the courtyard—in addition to the sight of barefoot kids playing in the water, that is. The shops are elegant and imaginative. The Courtyard Café has light fare and light alcohol as well.

IF YOU LIKE THIS Do not miss the Smithsonian American Art Museum's second building, **The Renwick Gallery** (page 173), located across the street from the White House. This recently remodeled museum features some of the most popular exhibits in D.C. history.

  National Postal Museum *(a Smithsonian museum)* ★★★

PRESCHOOL ★★	GRADE SCHOOL ★★★	TEENS ★★
YOUNG ADULTS ★★	OVER 30 ★★½	SENIORS ★★½

Location Washington City Post Office building, 2 Massachusetts Ave. NE, adjoining Union Station. **Nearest Metro stations** Union Station or Capitol. **Contact** ☎ 202-633-5555, postalmuseum.si.edu. **Admission** Free. **Hours** Daily, 10 a.m.–5:30 p.m.; closed December 25.

DESCRIPTION AND COMMENTS It's much more interesting than it sounds, even if you're not one of America's 20 million stamp collectors. Plus, it's officially the largest philatelic museum in the world, and its exhibits point up the social, historical, and technological impact of the U.S. postal system. The museum celebrates the beauty of stamps and how they represent significant American events, cultures, the natural world, and notable people. It is a family-friendly museum with interactive displays, and it tends to be less crowded than the other Smithsonian museums. Kids love the real airplanes hanging from the ceiling in the atrium (going back to the 1911 biplane) and the 1851 mail coach, plus hands-on fun like the chance to sort mail on a train and track a letter from Kansas to Nairobi. Exhibits are built around rotating themes that focus on the history of mail service, how the mail is moved, the social importance of letters, and the beauty and lore of stamps. Thirteen of the rarest and most valuable oddities in philatelic history, including the coveted Inverted Jenny (an airplane) stamp made in 1918, are on display. Serious collectors can call in advance for appointments to see any stamp in the museum's world-class collection or to use the extensive library.

TOURING TIPS Ask at the information desk about docent-led drop-in tours, usually held at 11 a.m. and 1 p.m. No food is available on site, but Union Station is just next door. The "Old Post Office," as it's known, is still operating— seven days a week!—and the lobby has an old-fashioned elegance worth a peek, even if you don't need a stamp.

IF YOU LIKE THIS The **National Archives** (page 152) contains American artifacts and documents that tell the story of American history in a similar way.

National World War II Memorial ★★½

PRESCHOOL ★	GRADE SCHOOL ★★	TEENS ★★
YOUNG ADULTS ★★★	OVER 30 ★★★★	SENIORS ★★★★★

Location At 17th St. NW on the Mall, between the Washington Monument and the Lincoln Memorial. **Nearest Metro station** Smithsonian. **Contact** wwiimemorial.com and nps.gov/nwwm. **Admission** Free. **Hours** Open 24 hours; rangers on site daily, except December 25. *Note:* The monument may be closed during July 4th celebrations.

DESCRIPTION AND COMMENTS The "greatest generation"—the 16 million Americans who served in uniform during World War II—gets its due for its contributions in winning the most devastating war in human history (50 million people were killed). Two 43-foot arches, a 17-foot pillar for each state and territory, and 4,000 gold stars honor the more than 400,000 soldiers who died in the conflict. The assemblies of white granite surround a large pool, fountains, and a piazza located in a spectacular setting. However moving to some, the overall effect is cold and oddly stilted, even militaristic (and not in an appropriate way); so, your reaction to the monument will be strongly influenced not only by your interest in military history or any family participation in the war (or wars) but also by your reaction to the atmosphere.

TOURING TIPS This memorial is spectacular at night when the fountain is active and illuminated. The location in the center of the National Mall offers the best views of the Lincoln Memorial, Washington Monument, and even the U.S. Capitol. Clean, modern, and air-conditioned restrooms—a scarce commodity on the Mall—are located behind the visitor center on the "Pacific" side of the memorial.

IF YOU LIKE THIS The **Vietnam Veterans Memorial** (page 182) and the **Korean War Veterans Memorial** (page 146) are both nearby and far more approachable. In time, the memorial to General and President Dwight D. Eisenhower will be a short walk away.

THE NATIONAL ZOO is one of my favorite D.C. spots. I love the orangutans, who climb on the O-Line, a suspended cable track high above visitors' heads; and the seals, who look so cool even on the hottest summer day. Oh, and the elephants of course. . . . You won't want to miss Zoo Lights, a magical festival of lights in December. It's a place that never fails to inspire me.

—Julie Langsdorf, best-selling author of
White Elephant and practically a lifelong D.C.-area resident

kids!
☺ National Zoo *(a Smithsonian museum)* ★★★★★

| PRESCHOOL ★★★★★ | GRADE SCHOOL ★★★★★ | TEENS ★★★★ |
| YOUNG ADULTS ★★★★ | OVER 30 ★★★★ | SENIORS ★★★★ |

Location 3001 Connecticut Ave. NW. **Nearest Metro stations** Cleveland Park or Woodley Park/Zoo/Adams Morgan. **Contact** ☎ 202-633-4888, nationalzoo.si.edu. **Admission** Free. **Hours** April–October: Grounds open 8 a.m.–7 p.m. (last entrance at 6), buildings open 9 a.m.–6 p.m.; October–March: Grounds open 8 a.m.–5 p.m., buildings open 9 a.m.–4 p.m.; closed December 25.

DESCRIPTION AND COMMENTS This expansive zoo strives to showcase the animals' natural environments so that many roam in large enclosures instead of pacing in cages. Two main paths link the many buildings and exhibits: Olmsted Walk, which passes all the animal houses, and the steeper Valley Trail, which includes all the aquatic exhibits. They add up to about 2 miles of trail. The zoo's nonlinear layout and lack of sight lines make a map invaluable; pick one up at the Education Building near the

National Zoological Park

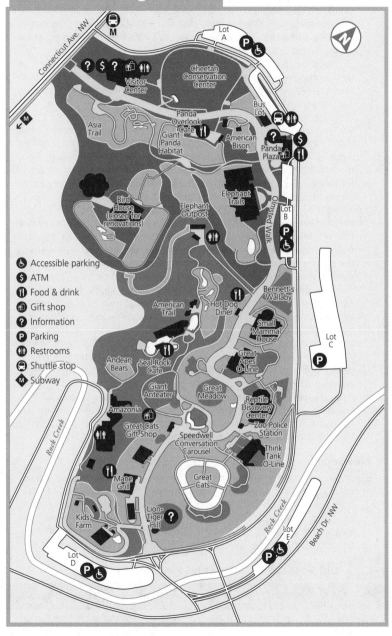

Connecticut Ave. NW

Lot A

Visitor Center

Cheetah Conservation Center

Bus Lot

Panda Overlook Cafe

Asia Trail

Giant Panda Habitat

American Bison

Panda Plaza

Olmsted Walk

Elephant Trails

Lot B

Bird House (closed for renovations)

Elephant Outpost

Bennett's Wallaby

American Trail

Hot Dog Diner

Small Mammal House

Lot C

Great Apes O-Line

Andean Bears

Seal Rock Cafe

Giant Anteater

Great Meadow

Reptile Discovery Center

Amazonia

Zoo Police Station

Great Cats Gift Shop

Speedwell Conversation Carousel

Think Tank O-Line

Mane Grill

Great Cats

Lion-Tiger Hill

Kids' Farm

Lot D

Lot E

Beach Dr. NW

Rock Creek

Legend

- 🦽 Accessible parking
- 💲 ATM
- 🍴 Food & drink
- 🏬 Gift shop
- ❓ Information
- 🅿 Parking
- 🚻 Restrooms
- 🚌 Shuttle stop
- Ⓜ Subway

entrance. The most popular exhibits include the Asian elephant house; the great apes; a collection of rare tigers; the cheetahs; and the giant pandas, Tian Tian, Mei Xiang, and their cub Bei Bei in their 12,000-square-foot habitat, complete with Chinese-style mist and rocky landscapes. The panda habitat is part of the Asia Trail, also stocked with sloth bears, red pandas, otters, fishing cats, and the endangered clouded leopards.

The American Trail showcases dozens of American species, many of them endangered, including sea lions and seals, gray wolves, otters, beavers, ravens, pelicans, and, of course, an American bald eagle. Kids love watching the sea lions cavorting in their swimming pools.

Think Tank attempts to answer the question "Can animals think?" by studying problem-solving ability, brain size, and language. Amazonia is a 15,000-square-foot rain forest habitat. If you're lucky—usually just before lunch—you might catch the orangutans barreling across their own private tramway in the air above Olmsted Walk. In summer the zoo offers live performances at their visitor center theater. Check the website for special events like ZooFiesta, Boo at the Zoo, and ZooLights.

TOURING TIPS Access to the zoo has been funneled to three points—Connecticut Avenue, Harvard Street, and the bus parking area. Despite the fact that one Metro station is called Woodley Park/National Zoo, it's downhill from the zoo entrance; take the Metro to Cleveland Park and walk down to the zoo for your visit, then take the easy way down to the Woodley Park station when you're done. Plan to visit either early or later, because animals are least active in the middle of the day. Many sections of the paths winding through the zoo's 163 acres are steep. If it is rainy, most of the indoor exhibits can be found along Olmsted Walk. Feedings, viewings, and demonstrations occur throughout the day at the cheetah, elephant, seal, and sea lion exhibits; check at the Education Building for times. Mane Grill, Sbarro, Auntie Anne's & Carvel, and various food trucks provide on-site dining options. The zoo rotates frequent closures for renovation and repairs, so check the website before you go.

IF YOU LIKE THIS The **National Museum of Natural History** (pages 160–161) has an infinite collection of animals, and although most are stuffed, you can see live tarantulas being fed, cavort with butterflies in the Butterfly Pavilion, and examine some other noteworthy insects there.

Newseum

DESCRIPTION AND COMMENTS When this groundbreaking museum dedicated to the First Amendment closes in late 2019, the founder, The Freedom Forum, will continue its quest to find a new home for the stunning collection of artifacts. The iconic building on Pennsylvania Avenue was sold to Johns Hopkins University in 2019. Check newseum.org for information on future plans for the museum.

 Old Post Office Tower and Pavilion ★★½

| PRESCHOOL ★★★ | GRADE SCHOOL ★★★★ | TEENS ★★★★ |
| YOUNG ADULTS ★★★ | OVER 30 ★★★ | SENIORS ★★★ |

Location 12th St. and Pennsylvania Ave. NW. **Nearest Metro stations** Federal Triangle or Archives/Navy Memorial/Penn Quarter. **Contact** ☎ 202-606-8691, oldpostofficedc .com or nps.gov/opot. **Admission** Free. **Hours** Daily, 9 a.m.–4:30 p.m.

DESCRIPTION AND COMMENTS This fine old building, a Pennsylvania Avenue landmark once incomprehensibly slated for demolition, was redeveloped by President Donald Trump and his family (prior to him becoming President) as Trump International Hotel, a luxury hotel complex. Fortunately, the agreement with the National Park Service ensures that the 315-foot clock tower remains open to the public. It offers a spectacular view of Washington, and through large plate glass windows, not tiny peepholes like those at the Washington Monument.

TOURING TIPS The National Park Service rangers on duty in the tower are a great source of advice about D.C. touring. Ask one to show you the lay of the land from the observation deck. Also, the tower houses the official U.S. Bells of Congress, a gift from Britain on the bicentennial of the Revolutionary War. (Now that's good manners.) The bells are rung on Thursdays (hence the early closing) and for some commemorative occasions.

IF YOU LIKE THIS Walk across Pennsylvania Avenue and up 15th Street NW to the **W Hotel** and try to get a drink or snack on the rooftop POV lounge; your might even get a better view.

Old Town Alexandria ★★★★

PRESCHOOL ★★	GRADE SCHOOL ★★★	TEENS ★★★
YOUNG ADULTS ★★★★★	OVER 30 ★★★★★	SENIORS ★★★★★

Location 8 miles south of Washington in Virginia. **Nearest Metro station** King Street. **Contact** ☎ 800-388-9119 or 703-838-5005 (Alexandria Visitor Center), visitalexandria va.com. **Admission** Some historic sites charge about $5 for adults; discount Key to the City pass available. **Hours** Historic houses, shops, and the Torpedo Factory Art Center generally open by 10 a.m. and remain open through the afternoon, but many have seasonal hours; check individual websites. Note that many of these attractions may be closed on Mondays.

DESCRIPTION AND COMMENTS This is really a walking tour of a partially restored Colonial port town on the Potomac River, featuring 18th-century buildings on cobblestone streets existing side by side with trendy shops, bars and restaurants, parks, and a huge art center.

As you exit the King Street Metro station, either board the free Old Town Trolley, which circulates between the station and the waterfront, or walk along King Street for a pleasant 25-minute stroll toward the river. The closer visitor center is at the **Lyceum** (201 S. Washington St., ☎ 703-746-4994), where two exhibition galleries and a museum of the area's history are featured; from King Street, turn right onto Washington Street and walk a block. There's a small museum featuring prints, documents, photographs, silver, furniture, and Civil War memorabilia. Farther down King on the left is **Ramsay House,** across from City Hall and the town square (221 King St., ☎ 703-838-5005). Built in 1724 for city founder William Ramsay and now Alexandria's official visitor center, it's open daily except Thanksgiving, December 24, and January 2. Ramsay House is the best starting point for a walking tour of Old Town Alexandria, where you can pick up brochures, walking tours, and a $15 Key to the City pass that cuts your total admission to nine local attractions by two-thirds, and includes discounts at restaurants and shops.

Alexandria claims both George Washington and Robert E. Lee as native sons, so history buffs have a lot to see. Topping the list are several period

Old Town Alexandria

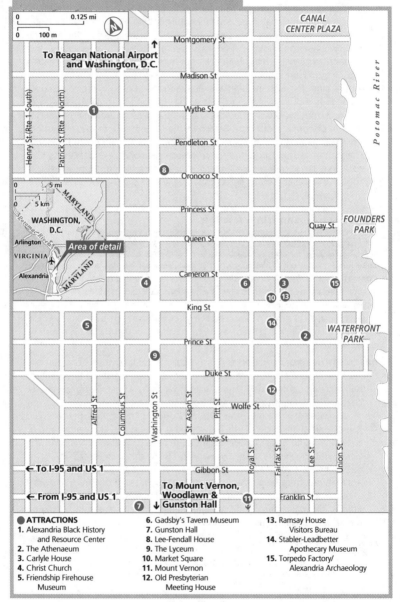

0   0.125 mi
0   100 m

CANAL CENTER PLAZA

Potomac River

To Reagan National Airport and Washington, D.C.

Montgomery St

Madison St

Wythe St

Pendleton St

Oronoco St

Princess St

Queen St

Quay St

FOUNDERS PARK

Cameron St

King St

WATERFRONT PARK

Prince St

Duke St

Wolfe St

Wilkes St

Gibbon St

Franklin St

Henry St (Rte 1-South)

Patrick St (Rte 1 North)

Alfred St

Columbus St

Washington St

St. Asaph St

Pitt St

Royal St

Fairfax St

Lee St

Union St

0   5 mi
0   5 km

MARYLAND

WASHINGTON, D.C.

Arlington

VIRGINIA

Alexandria

MARYLAND

Area of detail

←To I-95 and US 1

←From I-95 and US 1

To Mount Vernon, Woodlawn & Gunston Hall

● **ATTRACTIONS**
1. Alexandria Black History and Resource Center
2. The Athenaeum
3. Carlyle House
4. Christ Church
5. Friendship Firehouse Museum
6. Gadsby's Tavern Museum
7. Gunston Hall
8. Lee-Fendall House
9. The Lyceum
10. Market Square
11. Mount Vernon
12. Old Presbyterian Meeting House
13. Ramsay House Visitors Bureau
14. Stabler-Leadbetter Apothecary Museum
15. Torpedo Factory/ Alexandria Archaeology

revival houses that rival those in Georgetown, including the 1753 Georgian Paladian mansion **Carlyle House,** a living history museum at 121 North Fairfax St. (☎ 703-549-2997, nvrpa.org/park/carlyle_house_historic_park), where Washington not only slept but was also a frequent dinner guest and relation by marriage. Several times a year, re-enactors participate in events based on details from Washington's diaries, among other sources. Washington celebrated his birthday at **Gadsby's Tavern Museum** (134 N. Royal St., ☎ 703-746-4242), where you can dine in Colonial splendor; and he attended services at **Christ Church** (118 N. Washington St., ☎ 703-549-1450). The **Lee-Fendall House** (614 Oronoco St., ☎ 703-548-1789), built by a cousin of Revolutionary General and Virginia Governor Henry "Light Horse Harry" Lee in 1785, remained in Lee family hands until 1902; it has been restored to period glory. ("Light Horse" was Robert E. Lee's father.) The newly restored four-story **Stabler-Leadbeater Apothecary Museum** (105–107 S. Fairfax St., ☎ 703-746-3852), where receipts show Martha Washington and James Monroe both purchased items, is also the site where in 1859 Lieutenant J. E. B. Stuart, then at the U.S. Army, handed Colonel Robert E. Lee—then also an officer in the national force—his orders to quell John Brown's insurrection at Harper's Ferry. The **Alexandria Black History Museum** (902 Wythe St., ☎ 703-746-4356) highlights the contributions of Alexandria's African American residents. All of the above are included in the Key to the City pass.

Less historic but incredibly popular is the **Torpedo Factory Art Center** (torpedofactory.org) at the foot of King Street. It features more than 150 painters, printmakers, sculptors, and other artists and craftspeople, and visitors can watch artists at work in their studios housed in the former munitions factory. A couple of blocks from the King Street Metro at 101 Callahan St. is the ziggurat-like **George Washington National Masonic Memorial** (☎ 703-683-2007, gwmemorial.org). For $18 you can browse two floors of exhibits featuring Washington and Masonic memorabilia and take a guided tour, given daily at 9:30 and 11 a.m., and 1, 2:30, and 4 p.m.; children 12 and under admitted for free. Don't miss the view from the 333-foot tower and observation deck.

TOURING TIPS Old Town Alexandria makes itself welcoming to tourists by running a free trolley service between the King Street Metro along King Street to the waterfront, bringing you within walking distance of almost everything. If you drive to Alexandria, you can try parking in a two-hour metered space, putting in a little change, and going to a visitor center to pick up a pass that lets you park free for 24 hours; but you'll likely have to use a garage.

IF YOU LIKE THIS Read the profile on **Mount Vernon** (page 150), though you will likely need at least two days to cover all this.

The Phillips Collection ★★★★★

PRESCHOOL —	GRADE SCHOOL ★	TEENS ★★
YOUNG ADULTS ★★★★	OVER 30 ★★★★½	SENIORS ★★★★

Location 1600 21st St. NW. **Nearest Metro station** Dupont Circle. **Contact** ☎ 202-387-2151, phillipscollection.org. **Admission** Tuesday–Friday, free; Saturday and Sunday, $10 adults, $8 seniors and college students with ID; visitors under age 18 admitted free. Special exhibition tickets $12/$10 daily. **Hours** Tuesday, Wednesday, Friday, and

Saturday, 10 a.m.–5 p.m.; Sunday, noon–6:30 p.m.; Thursday, 10 a.m.–8:30 p.m.; closed January 1, July 4, Thanksgiving, and December 24 and 25.

DESCRIPTION AND COMMENTS Founded by Duncan Phillips, grandson of the founder of the Jones and Laughlin Steel Company, this was the first museum dedicated to modern art in the United States, and the complex still includes the family's former mansion, as well as an airy, well-lit addition. The collection, which now includes more than 5,000 works, is too large for everything to be on display at once, so the art is constantly rotated, although what is probably its most famous painting, Renoir's *Luncheon of the Boating Party,* is a staple. Expect to see works by Monet, Picasso, Miró, Renoir, and Van Gogh, among other modern masters; there is a large room that was specifically designed by Phillips and Mark Rothko to house some of the artist's signature large color works. The large and ornate Music Room is as spectacular as the art hanging on its walls. Although it isn't free, this museum is easily as important a stop for art lovers as the Hirshhorn and the National Gallery of Art.

TOURING TIPS There are frequent classical concerts Sundays at 4 p.m. ($45 adults, $20 students). The café is unusually nice; open Tuesday–Saturday, 10 a.m.–4 p.m., and Sunday, noon–5:30 p.m. Although admission to the permanent collection is free during the week, a donation is always welcome.

IF YOU LIKE THIS Visit the **National Museum of Women in the Arts** (pages 162–163) to see a collection of lesser-known but brilliant artists. Head to the **Hirshhorn Museum and Sculpture Garden** (pages 142–143) or the East Wing of the **National Gallery of Art** (pages 155–156) for other contemporary masterpieces.

President Lincoln's Cottage ★★★★★

| PRESCHOOL ★ | GRADE SCHOOL ★★★ | TEENS ★★★ |
| YOUNG ADULTS ★★★★ | OVER 30 ★★★★★ | SENIORS ★★★★★ |

Location Lincoln Dr. NW and Upshur St. NW. **No Metro access. Contact** ☎ 202-829-0436, lincolncottage.org. **Admission** $15 adults, $5 ages 6–12. **Hours** Daily, visitor center open 9:30 a.m.–4:30 p.m.; closed January 1, Thanksgiving, and December 25.

DESCRIPTION AND COMMENTS This Gothic Revival home—called a cottage and fairly simple, but with 34 rooms—served five chief executives, from James Buchanan to Chester A. Arthur, as a summer retreat; but the length of time Lincoln spent here (from June to November each year from 1862 to 1864), and the fact that several crucial historical events happened here, including the drafting of the Emancipation Proclamation, have indelibly linked it to the Civil War leader. The campus was the original Retired Soldiers' Home, so the mural in the visitor center across the driveway shows both the president and his son Tad engaging the veterans. The visitor center also has an orientation video and a four-room exhibition center with interactive maps, anecdotes (the president once barely escaped assassination riding from the White House to the cottage, and a bullet hole in his stovepipe hat attests to it), and signed copies of the Emancipation Proclamation and the 13th Amendment outlawing slavery.

In the cottage itself, guides provide part of the narration; dramatic readings and theatrical lighting provide the rest. (An elevator makes most of the cottage accessible.)

TOURING TIPS Guided tours of the cottage are offered daily 10 a.m.–3 p.m. on the hour. Limited food available on site. Of the several Lincoln-centric sites (Ford's Theatre, the Lincoln Memorial, Museum of American History), this might be the last on the list, but only because of its limited accessibility.

IF YOU LIKE THIS Spend a few extra minutes in **Rock Creek Cemetery** just north of the main gate, where many cabinet members, congressmen, Supreme Court justices, and presidential relations (Henry Adams, Alice Roosevelt Longworth, etc.) are buried. Its most famous monument is the statue and grove dedicated to Adams and his wife, Clover, with the hooded figure by Saint-Gaudens often called "Grief" and landscape setting by famed architect Stanford White. **St. Paul's Church** in the cemetery, built in 1712, is the only surviving Colonial church in Washington; its 18-inch brick walls and stained glass windows have survived many trials.

The Renwick Gallery ★★★★★

PRESCHOOL ★	GRADE SCHOOL ★★★	TEENS ★★★
YOUNG ADULTS ★★★★	OVER 30 ★★★★★	SENIORS ★★★★★

Location Pennsylvania Avenue at 17th Street NW. **Nearest Metro stations** Farragut West or Farragut North. **Contact** ☎ 202-633-7970, americanart.si.edu. **Admission** Free. **Hours** Daily, 10 a.m.–5:30 p.m.; closed December 25.

DESCRIPTION AND COMMENTS A branch of the Smithsonian American Art Museum, the gallery sits across the street from the White House. It contains uncommon art exhibits such as *Wonder* and *Burning Man*—shows that have transformed the historic mansion into wildly popular social media experiences. The Renwick focuses installations on contemporary craft and decorative arts, such as a room wallpapered in bugs or a metal dragon on wheels.

TOURING TIPS This is an easy museum to see in an hour. The Renwick offers a Highlights Tour that is free (check the website for specific dates and times), as well as gallery talks with curators and art experts. Most kids will enjoy the art here.

IF YOU LIKE THIS The Renwick is a branch of the **Smithsonian American Art Museum** (pages 164–165), which has the same kind of whimsical installations by American artists. Head south on the Mall to see the **Hirshhorn Museum** (pages 142–143) or the East Wing of the **National Gallery of Art** (pages 155–156), with its contemporary masterpieces.

Smithsonian Institution Building (aka the Castle) ★★★

PRESCHOOL —	GRADE SCHOOL ★★	TEENS ★★
YOUNG ADULTS ★★★	OVER 30 ★★★★	SENIORS ★★★★

Location 1000 Jefferson Dr. SW, on the Mall. **Nearest Metro station** Smithsonian. **Contact** ☎ 202-633-1000, si.edu. **Admission** Free. **Hours** Daily, 8:30 a.m.–5:30 p.m.; closed December 25.

DESCRIPTION AND COMMENTS This redbrick building—you can't miss it—contains limited exhibits and is its own showpiece. Known as the Castle for obvious architectural reasons, it is the original Smithsonian museum, and was designed by James Renwick, who also designed St. Patrick's Cathedral in New York (and the nearby Renwick Gallery). It now serves as an information center that will help you save time and reduce the frustration of visiting the Smithsonian's large and perplexing museum complex. The restored Children's Room is literally a child's garden of delights. Among the many interactive exhibits is a map that lights up the location of each of the museums on the Mall, as well as other popular D.C. sights, when you press the corresponding button.

TOURING TIPS There is a convenient cafeteria on site and it's a nice place to get your bearings before you begin exploring. Don't forget to pay your respects to the museum's founder, James Smithson, near the north entrance; his crypt is not fancy, but he deserves it.

IF YOU LIKE THIS The **U.S. Botanic Garden** (page 176) down the Mall, is a delight for all ages. The **White House Visitor Center** (page 184) is another destination that offers a valuable overview of a D.C. landmark.

Society of the Cincinnati Museum at Anderson House
★★★

PRESCHOOL ★	GRADE SCHOOL ★★	TEENS ★★
YOUNG ADULTS ★★	OVER 30 ★★★★	SENIORS ★★★★

Location 2118 Massachusetts Ave. NW. **Nearest Metro station** Dupont Circle. **Contact** ☎ 202-785-2040, societyofthecincinnati.org. **Admission** Free. **Hours** Tuesday–Saturday, 10 a.m.–4 p.m.; Sunday, noon–4 p.m.; closed federal holidays.

DESCRIPTION AND COMMENTS This 50-room Florentine-style mansion–cum–Revolutionary War museum on Embassy Row is a real stunner that few visitors ever see. Built in 1906 for diplomat Larz Anderson (at a cost of at least $20 million today), it's a reflection of fabulous turn-of-the-century taste and wealth. But it has even more historical value: Anderson was a member of the Society of the Cincinnati, which was cofounded in 1783 by George Washington and whose members are descendants of French and American officers who served in the Revolutionary Army. Anderson not only collected Revolutionary War artifacts but also lined the walls with tapestries and paintings by Gilbert Stuart, John Trumbull, and so on. After his death, his widow donated the mansion to the society. Today the building serves the society as both headquarters and museum. (See "The Best Tours in Town," starting on page 118, for more on the exhibits.)

TOURING TIPS A little eye candy: This is the heart of what was once called "Millionaire's Row," now called Embassy Row, and the **Indonesian Embassy** at 2020 Massachusetts Avenue belonged to Evalyn Walsh McLean, the last private owner of the Hope Diamond. Take the 15-minute tour; it might be brief, but this could be the most impressive mansion you've ever seen; email socialmedia@embassyofindonesia.org for a reservation.

IF YOU LIKE THIS The **Woodrow Wilson House** (page 185) is nearby and focuses on the former president's life after the White House. He lived in this town house with his wife, and it's filled with the many gifts and inventions he collected from dignitaries during his lifetime.

Tudor Place ★★★

PRESCHOOL ★½	GRADE SCHOOL ★★	TEENS ★★½
YOUNG ADULTS ★★★	OVER 30 ★★★	SENIORS ★★★½

Location 1644 31st St. NW. **No Metro access. Contact** ☎ 202-965-0400, tudorplace .org. **Admission** $10 adults; $8 seniors age 62+, military, and college students with ID;

$3 students ages 5–17; garden admission only, $3. **Hours** Tuesday–Saturday, 10 a.m.–4 p.m.; Sunday, noon–4 p.m.; closed the month of January, Easter, July 4, Thanksgiving, and December 24–25.

DESCRIPTION AND COMMENTS Martha Custis Peter, Martha Washington's granddaughter, and her husband, Thomas Peter, began construction on this lovely stucco-faced neoclassical mansion in 1806 with the $8,000 she inherited from the first president. It was designed by William Thornton, who also designed the U.S. Capitol, and its circular domed portico is unique. Like nearby Dumbarton House, Tudor Place had a clear view of the burning of the town in 1814. Andrew Jackson visited here on the anniversary of the Battle of New Orleans, and Robert E. Lee, whose wife was Martha Custis's niece, often slept here. Among the items, which constitute the greatest concentration of Washingtoniana outside Mount Vernon, are an affectionate note from George Washington to Martha that was found in a secret drawer of her desk, a miniature painting of George on ivory, swords, and antique toys. The grounds are lovely. (Here's a funny bit of trivia: The Peter children were patriotically named America, Britannia Wellington, George Washington, and Columbia.)

TOURING TIPS Guided tours on the hour Tuesday–Saturday, 10 a.m.–3 p.m., and Sunday on the hour, noon–3 p.m. Tours are not recommended for children under age 6. No food is available on site. The gardens are open daily, 10 a.m.–4 p.m.; you cannot enter the house except just before each tour to buy your tickets, but you can pick up a free garden tour map and walk about.

IF YOU LIKE THIS The George Washington family has a number of historic homes to visit. Of course, the most famous is **Mount Vernon** (page 150), but the imposing landmark called Arlington House in **Arlington National Cemetery** (pages 128–131) was owned by his wife's family and has a fine collection of furnishings from the period preceding the Civil War.

 Udvar-Hazy National Air and Space Museum
(a Smithsonian museum) ★★★★★

| PRESCHOOL ★★★★ | GRADE SCHOOL ★★★★★ | TEENS ★★★★★ |
| YOUNG ADULTS ★★★★★ | OVER 30 ★★★★★ | SENIORS ★★★★ |

Location 14390 Air and Space Museum Pkwy., Chantilly, VA. **Nearest Metro station** Silver Line to Wiehle-Reston station, then transfer to Fairfax Connector Bus No. 983. **Contact** ☎ 703-572-4118, nasm.si.edu. **Admission** Free; $15 parking fee before 4 p.m. **Hours** September–March: daily, 10 a.m.–5:30 p.m.; April–Labor Day: daily, 10 a.m.–7:30 p.m.; closed December 25. *Note:* There is no shuttle service between the museums.

DESCRIPTION AND COMMENTS The National Air and Space Museum's other facility, the Steven F. Udvar-Hazy Center outside Dulles International Airport, houses more than 80 aircraft and dozens of space artifacts, including the Space Shuttle *Discovery,* a Lockheed SR-71 Blackbird, and the *Gemini VII* space capsule, as well as its own flight simulators and IMAX theater. Many people prefer this branch of the Air and Space Museum, thanks to its mind-blowing collection of legendary and modern flying machines, and it's especially worthwhile to see while the Air and Space Museum on the National Mall is under renovation. The facility boasts two hangars full of aircraft, including the original Concorde, the F4U Corsair,

P-40 Warhawk, Focke-Wulf Fw 190, and the infamous *Enola Gay,* used to drop the atomic bomb on Hiroshima during World War II. There is ample space to peruse the thousands of displayed relics, from planes and jets to spacecraft. It's a fun place for kids to stretch their legs, and the museum hosts regular family days with interactive exhibits and opportunities to talk to aviation experts.

TOURING TIPS The facility offers free docent-led tours, and for those who prefer to explore on their own, audio tours are available in multiple languages. The museum has an IMAX theater and an observation tower that offers 360-degree views of the area; it's an exciting place to watch airplanes take off and land at nearby Dulles Airport. Be prepared to go through security and walk great distances here. No strollers are allowed. The museum contains a McDonald's & McCafe.

IF YOU LIKE THIS The outstanding **National Museum of the Marine Corps** (page 162), in suburban Northern Virginia's Quantico, showcases aircraft used in wars and peace beginning in World War I.

 Union Station ★★★

| PRESCHOOL ★ | GRADE SCHOOL ★★ | TEENS ★★★ |
| YOUNG ADULTS ★★★★ | OVER 30 ★★★★ | SENIORS ★★★★ |

Location Massachusetts Ave. and North Capitol St. NE. **Nearest Metro station** Union Station. **Contact** ☎ 202-289-1908, unionstationdc.com. **Admission** Free. **Hours** Always open; shops open Monday–Saturday, 10 a.m.–9 p.m.; Sunday, noon–6 p.m.; restaurant times vary.

DESCRIPTION AND COMMENTS This Beaux-Arts palace must have made a suitably capital impression in its time, and it still does, especially The Main Hall, with its 90-foot barrel-vaulted ceiling. Union Station is a popular meeting place, a food court, a shopping center, and a functional train station. Kiosks located at the front of the building offer tickets to attractions and sightseeing buses. The building houses multiple transportation lines, including Amtrak's Northeast Corridor line and the MARC Train, a Maryland line that runs from Baltimore to D.C. with a stop at Baltimore Washington International Airport (BWI). The Virginia Railway Express (VRE) offers passengers round-trip service from Union Station to Franconia/Springfield, Manassas, and Fredericksburg, Virginia. For more details, see page 90. The Union Station Metro on the Red Line is directly beside the building. Several clothing stores appeal to commuters, and shops selling souvenirs draw visitors. The restaurants are mostly coffee shops, bakeries, and fast-casual options, plus Thunder Grill, a traditional restaurant. There is also an international currency exchange, a post office, and multiple pickup stands for sightseeing companies, as well as rental-car companies on site.

IF YOU LIKE THIS The **National Museum of American History** (pages 159–160) has an exhibit called *America On the Move* that explores the history of the railroad in America. The centerpiece is a century-old locomotive and several artifacts used by conductors. The **National Postal Museum** (page 165) is directly adjacent to Union Station and has exhibits on the railroad's role in distributing mail. The **B&O Railroad Museum** (borail.org) in Baltimore, Maryland, is another Smithsonian museum that houses exhibits on the huge impact this historic railroad had on westward expansion in America.

U.S. Botanic Garden   ★★★

PRESCHOOL ★	GRADE SCHOOL ★★	TEENS ★★
YOUNG ADULTS ★★★	OVER 30 ★★★	SENIORS ★★★★

Location 100 Maryland Ave. SW (on the Mall near the U.S. Capitol). **Nearest Metro station** Federal Center SW. **Contact** ☎ 202-225-8333, usbg.gov. **Admission** Free. **Hours** Conservatory: daily, 10 a.m.–5 p.m.; garden: daily, 7:30 a.m.–5 p.m.

DESCRIPTION AND COMMENTS This permanent collection of tropical, subtropical, and desert plants, housed in a stunning 38,000-square-foot greenhouse, is completely unlike any other attraction on the Mall. The Conservatory, a building that reflects the grand manner of Victorian architecture (even though it was constructed in the 1930s), houses a living museum on the Mall. The central jungle resembles an abandoned plantation in a tropical rain forest under a dome that rises to 93 feet. Other sections display orchids, ferns, cacti, and other types of plants in naturalistic settings. Its outdoor portion is Frederic Bartholdi Park (open sunrise–sunset), located across Independence Avenue from the Conservatory and named for the designer of the Statue of Liberty. The park features displays of bulbs, annuals, perennials, sustainable plants, and more. The focal point is the 15-ton, 30-foot-tall cast-iron Bartholdi Fountain, originally exhibited at the 1876 Centennial Exhibition in Philadelphia.

TOURING TIPS Skip it on a sweltering summer day; however, it's a balmy respite after a cold walk on the National Mall. The garden offers daily workshops, lectures, cooking demonstrations, Bartholdi Park tours, and even yoga. Check the website to see what's going on.

IF YOU LIKE THIS The **Enid A. Haupt Garden,** on Independence Avenue near the Smithsonian Castle, is worth a visit year-round. **Dumbarton Oaks** (pages 135–136) in Georgetown is known for its splendid gardens, especially during spring and summer. The **U.S. National Arboretum** (page 180) is an American treasure, with its incredible Bonsai Museum and stunning azalea garden.

U.S. Capitol Visitor Center ★★★★★

PRESCHOOL ★	GRADE SCHOOL ★★★	TEENS ★★★
YOUNG ADULTS ★★★★	OVER 30 ★★★★★	SENIORS ★★★★★

Location The visitors entrance is at the end of the National Mall at the East Front Plaza on First St. NE. **Nearest Metro stations** Capitol South or Union Station. **Contact** ☎ 202-226-8000, visitthecapitol.gov. **Admission** Free, but tickets required. **Hours** Monday–Saturday, 8:30 a.m.–4:30 p.m.; closed January 1, Inauguration Day, Thanksgiving, and December 25.

DESCRIPTION AND COMMENTS The Capitol's Visitor Center has a glorious skylight view of the Capitol dome; the addition has made space for the many statues and artifacts that have been in storage. It also shows films on the history of the building. Here's where you sign up for a tour, if you haven't done so in advance: tours.visitthecapitol.gov. The public tour takes visitors through a small part of the Capitol (the Rotunda, Statuary Hall, and the Crypt) and is a worthwhile and interesting learning experience for all ages.

You can't walk in off the street and tour the *main* Capitol building without a pass or participating in a tour. Same-day passes are available at the public walk-up station near the information desk, but that can mean a long wait. One sure way to reserve a space is to request a ticket from one of your senators or representatives in advance online. If you want to see Congress in session, or either of the galleries even when nothing is happening, you will need a gallery pass, but again, you'll have to obtain one at the office of one of your Congress members. (International visitors should go to the House and Senate appointment desks upstairs in the visitor center.)

The statue atop the dome is *Freedom,* who holds a sword in her right hand and a laurel wreath of victory in the left. Her shield bears 13 stripes, and the helmet, encircled with stars, is adorned with an eagle's head, feathers, and talons. Just under 20 feet tall, she rises 300 feet above the East Front Plaza. If a white light surrounds her, the House is in session, and if a red light is shining, the Senate is meeting. Two lights are suitably bicameral.

TOURING TIPS The visitor center, which houses a cafeteria, gift shop, restrooms, and exhibit spaces, is underground at the East Front Plaza. Beyond the standard tour, The Capitol also offers tours called the Halls of the Senate, Freedom Fighters, Stories in the Old Senate Chamber, This Day in History, as well as family programs. See the website for information on these options. As the Capitol is on constant security alert, prohibited items include knives, pointed objects, pepper spray, duffel bags, backpacks, aerosol cans, and all beverages and food.

IF YOU LIKE THIS The **White House Visitor Center** (pages 184–185) has a similar introductory museum with a few educational films about presidential history and interesting relics from various presidential administrations.

U.S. Department of State Diplomatic Reception Rooms ★★★★

PRESCHOOL —	GRADE SCHOOL —	TEENS ★★★
YOUNG ADULTS ★★★★	OVER 30 ★★★★	SENIORS ★★★★

Location 2201 C St. NW. Nearest Metro station Foggy Bottom/GWU. Contact ☎ 202-647-3241, 202-736-4474 (TDD), receptiontours.state.gov. Admission Free, but reservations required. Hours Tours are given Monday–Friday at 9:30 a.m., 10:30 a.m., and 2:45 p.m. by advance reservation only; not recommended for children under age 12.

DESCRIPTION AND COMMENTS While the State Department goes about its important work in a building with architecture best described as "early airport," the interiors on the eighth floor are something else entirely: A seriously fabulous collection of 18th- and early-19th-century fine and decorative arts fills stunning rooms that are used daily to receive visiting heads of state and foreign dignitaries. This is a tour for almost anyone: antiques and fine arts lovers, history buffs, and just casual visitors. It's also a sight that the overwhelming majority of D.C. tourists miss. First-time visitors should make the effort to get reservations well in advance of their trip. (See "The Best Tours in Town" on page 118 for more information.)

TOURING TIPS Reservations are accepted up to 90 days before your visit, and you should certainly try to get them at least a month in advance.

IF YOU LIKE THIS Make advance reservations to visit the **White House** (pages 183–184) or drop in for a tour of **The Society of the Cincinnati** (page 174).

U.S. Department of the Treasury ★★★★

PRESCHOOL ★½	GRADE SCHOOL ★★½	TEENS ★★★
YOUNG ADULTS ★★★★	OVER 30 ★★★★★	SENIORS ★★★★

Location Alongside the White House at the corner of 15th St. NW and Pennsylvania Ave. **Nearest Metro stations** McPherson Square, Farragut Square, or Federal Triangle. **Contact** treasury.gov/services/tours-and-library/tours-of-the-historic-treasury-building. **Admission** Free, but reservation required. **Hours** Tours Saturday only at 9, 9:45, 10:30, and 11:15 a.m. (except some holidays).

DESCRIPTION AND COMMENTS Do *not* confuse this with the Bureau of Engraving: This is a much more imposing place. After an elaborate renovation, this Gilded Age beauty has been carried back to its glory days but given all the modern electrical and insulation services it had long needed. The renovation exposed a three-story cast iron ceiling dome with gilded trim, which had been obscured by a bank of elevators. Among the highlights of the tour are the Andrew Johnson Room, which was where Johnson ran the nation for six weeks after Lincoln's assassination to allow Mary Todd Lincoln time to move out (the black hangings are gone, but a portrait of the dead president remains); the two-story Cash Room with its three enormous chandeliers and seven types of marble (it was originally a bank—Lincoln was among those who used it—and also served as the reception site for Grant's inaugural); the Salmon P. Chase suite, which has two fabulous allegorical murals of "Treasury" and "Justice"; and diplomatic reception rooms.

TOURING TIPS Reservations can only be made through congressional offices. If you get passes, be on time; you will *not* be able to join another tour if you are late. No strollers or backpacks are allowed into the building.

IF YOU LIKE THIS The **Bureau of Engraving and Printing** (pages 132–133) is where the money is made! You can sign up for a tour by visiting the building for a timed ticket. The **U.S. Supreme Court** (page 181) is another imposing historical building with a walk-in museum that explains the history of the highest court in the land.

U.S. Holocaust Memorial Museum ★★★★★

| PRESCHOOL — | GRADE SCHOOL ★★ | TEENS ★★★ |
| YOUNG ADULTS ★★★½ | OVER 30 ★★★★½ | SENIORS ★★★★★ |

Location 100 Raoul Wallenberg Place SW (15th St.), near the Mall between the Washington Monument and the Bureau of Engraving and Printing. **Nearest Metro station** Smithsonian. **Contact** ☎ 202-488-0400, ushmm.org. **Admission** Free; timed tickets for permanent exhibit March–August. **Hours** Daily, 10 a.m.–5:30 p.m.; closed December 25 and Yom Kippur. **Special comments** For mature audiences.

DESCRIPTION AND COMMENTS As its designers intended, this $168 million museum is forbidding and grim—and it delivers a stern message about the evils of racial persecution. It also packs an emotional punch that may not fit some folks' vacation plans. Technologically and emotionally, it's a stunning experience: audiovisual displays, advanced computer technology, and a model of a Nazi death camp recreate one of the darkest periods in human history. But that's not all: As part of the museum experience, visitors are cast as victims of Nazi brutality. Visitors receive an identity card of a real Holocaust victim matched to their gender and age—a demographic doppelgänger. Diagonal walls in the exhibition areas create a disorienting effect. Ghostly shapes pass overhead on glass-bottomed walkways, suggesting Nazi prison guards patrolling a camp. Every moment spent inside the museum is orchestrated to impart the horror of Nazi persecution. In fact, the primary, and essential, difference between this museum and the Holocaust Museum in New York is that in Manhattan, the mood is "We will survive." This says, "We will never forget."

According to Holocaust Museum officials, the main permanent exhibit is inappropriate for children under age 11—and we agree. In fact, almost everyone can pinpoint the spot where their throat begins to feel tight. However, a special exhibit on the museum's first floor, "Daniel's Story: Remember the Children," is designed for visitors ages 8 and older. It gives a child's perspective on the Holocaust, but without the shocking graphics of the permanent exhibit, and serves as a sort of kid's parking lot while the adults continue.

While many exhibits focus on Jewish life prior to the Holocaust and the political and military events surrounding World War II, the most disturbing displays are graphic depictions of Nazi atrocities. Large TV screens scattered throughout the exhibits present still and motion pictures of Nazi leaders, storm troopers rounding up victims, and life inside Jewish ghettos. Some of the TV screens are located behind concrete barriers to prevent younger visitors from seeing them. They show executions, medical experiments on Jewish prisoners, and suicide victims. It's not an easy tour, but the U.S. Holocaust Memorial Museum is one of the most powerful experiences in Washington and an astounding example of how visionary architecture can magnify that power. Just don't try to squeeze this one into a multistop itinerary—it will leave you emotionally drained; however, there are shortcuts and softened children's exhibits.

TOURING TIPS During the busiest months (generally March–August), the Holocaust Museum employs a same-day, time-ticket system to eliminate long lines at its permanent exhibits; no tickets are required for the special exhibitions. While the ticket office opens at 10 a.m., plan on getting in line no later than 9 a.m. A limited number of advance reservation tickets (with a $1 fee per ticket) are available at ushmm.org/visit or by calling ☎ 877-808-7466. Tours for the visually or hearing impaired can be arranged in advance. The museum annex on Raoul Wallenberg Place has a small café that offers vegetarian and some prepackaged and certified kosher fare.

IF YOU LIKE THIS The **National Museum of African American History and Culture** (pages 157–158) showcases the diaspora of the African American experience from slavery, to reconstruction, to Jim Crow laws, to mass incarceration. It has a similar power and resonance and should not be missed. The Jewish Historical Society of Greater Washington will open the **Capital Jewish Museum** (on 1319 F St. NW near the FBI Building) in 2021 to show the political and social changes experienced by the Jewish communities in the Washington, D.C. area.

U.S. National Arboretum ★★★

PRESCHOOL ★	GRADE SCHOOL ★★	TEENS ★★
YOUNG ADULTS ★★	OVER 30 ★★★	SENIORS ★★★

Location 3501 New York Ave. NE. **No Metro access. Contact** ☎ 202-245-4523, usna .usda.gov. **Admission** Free. **Hours** Grounds open Friday–Monday, 8 a.m.–5 p.m.; closed December 25; visitor center open 8 a.m.–4:30 p.m. The National Bonsai and Penjing Museum is open 10 a.m.–4 p.m.

DESCRIPTION AND COMMENTS With 9 miles of roads and more than 3 miles of walking paths over 446 acres, the U.S. National Arboretum offers visitors an oasis of quiet and beauty for a drive or a stroll. Even people without green thumbs will marvel at the bonsai collection, whose dwarf trees are more like sculptures than plants. One specimen, a Japanese white pine, is 350 years old. When the National Mall is overcrowded with tourists on the hunt for pictures of cherry blossom trees, the arboretum is a quiet and less-crowded spot to commune with trees covered in pink blossoms. Later in the spring, fields of azaleas are in bloom. Flowering dogwood and mountain laurel bloom well into May. Late July and August feature blooming aquatic plants. The world-class bonsai collection is a treat all year. Folks with limited time who aren't gardening enthusiasts, however, shouldn't spend their touring hours on a visit.

TOURING TIPS The grounds are huge. You'll need a bike or car to see the whole thing. You can concentrate your tour around the visitor center and the National Bonsai Museum. Group tours, called Windshield Tours and Walking Tours, are available through the Friends of the National Arboretum on weekdays.

IF YOU LIKE THIS The city has many scenic gardens, and transformations occur among the flora and fauna during every season. Find two sumptuous landscapes with seasonal gardens in Georgetown—**Tudor Place** (pages 174–175) and **Dumbarton Oaks** (pages 135–136). The **U.S. Botanic Garden** (pages 176–177), next to the U.S. Capitol, is open year-round with some plantings that change seasonally. **Kenilworth Park and Aquatic Gardens** (pages 145–146) is about a mile from the National Arboretum.

 ## U.S. Supreme Court ★★★★

PRESCHOOL —	GRADE SCHOOL ★	TEENS ★★
YOUNG ADULTS ★★★	OVER 30 ★★★★	SENIORS ★★★★

Location 1 First St. NE, across from the east front of the U.S. Capitol. **Nearest Metro stations** Union Station or Capitol South. **Contact** ☎ 202-479-3000, supremecourt .gov. **Admission** Free. **Hours** Monday–Friday, 9 a.m.–4:30 p.m.; closed weekends and federal holidays.

DESCRIPTION AND COMMENTS This magnificent faux Greek temple is where the nine-member Supreme Court makes final interpretations of the U.S. Constitution and laws passed by Congress. On the Lower Level, visitors can take a self-guided tour that includes courtroom lectures and a film that explains the workings of the Supreme Court in more detail, and if the court is not in session, you can take a peek inside the majestic courtroom.

To see the court in session, look for oral arguments to be held Mondays, Tuesdays, and Wednesdays in two-week intervals from October through April. Check the website supremecourt.gov under "Today at the Court" for specific hearings.

TOURING TIPS Security here is no-nonsense: visitors pass through *two* X-ray machines before entering the courtroom. Small children are not allowed in the courtroom during oral arguments. The cafeteria on the ground level is one of the least expensive government eateries; it's open to the public 7:30 a.m.–4 p.m.

IF YOU LIKE THIS Visit the **U.S. Capitol Visitor Center** (pages 177–178) and the **White House Visitor Center** (pages 184–185) to learn about the other two branches of government.

Vietnam Veterans Memorial ★★★★

| PRESCHOOL ★ | GRADE SCHOOL ★★ | TEENS ★★ |
| YOUNG ADULTS ★★★ | OVER 30 ★★★★ | SENIORS ★★★★ |

Location On the west end of the Mall near the Lincoln Memorial. **Nearest Metro station** Foggy Bottom/GWU. **Contact** ☎ 202-426-6841, nps.gov/vive. **Admission** Free. **Hours** Open 24 hours; staffed daily, 9:30 a.m.–10 p.m., except on December 25.

DESCRIPTION AND COMMENTS "The Wall," as it is known, is a black, V-shaped rift in the earth, nearly 494 feet long and ranging from 8 inches tall at its outer edges to 10 feet tall at its center. The design competition for the memorial, which was open to the public, was won by Maya Lin, then a 21-year-old in her third year at Yale. Both her concept and her inexperience were the subject of great controversy, though its quality is now almost universally recognized; nevertheless, to placate those veterans and their families who thought it too severe and abstract, an additional sculpture depicting three soldiers was also commissioned. The Wall was dedicated on Veterans Day, November 13, 1982. Fredrick Hart's *Three Servicemen* sculpture was dedicated two years later, also on Veterans Day. Tucked to one side is a tribute to the women who served in Vietnam, sculpted by Glenna Goodacre and dedicated on Veterans Day in 1993.

TOURING TIPS At both ends of the Wall, visitors will find books that list the inscribed names and panel numbers to help them locate an inscription. No food is available on site. At night this memorial is especially moving, as people light matches to search for names inscribed on the wall.

IF YOU LIKE THIS Especially after dark, cross the lawn to the **Korean War Veterans Memorial** (page 146).

Washington Monument ★★★★

| PRESCHOOL ★★ | GRADE SCHOOL ★★★★ | TEENS ★★★★ |
| YOUNG ADULTS ★★★★ | OVER 30 ★★★ | SENIORS ★★★ |

Location On the Mall between 15th and 17th Sts. NW. **Nearest Metro station** Smithsonian. **Contact** ☎ 202-233-3520, nps.gov/wamo. **Admission** Free; timed tickets required. **Hours** Daily, 9 a.m.–5 p.m.

DESCRIPTION AND COMMENTS The obelisk commemorating the country's first president can be seen from nearly every downtown vantage point. This famous landmark's observation area is 555 feet up, and D.C.'s absence of other tall buildings (by law) guarantees a glorious, unobstructed view of Washington. Ride the elevator to the observation area at the top; the windows offer unparalleled, panoramic views of the National Mall. On a clear day, you can see the Ellipse and the White House, the Jefferson Memorial and the Tidal Basin, into the Virginia suburbs, and the entire length of the Reflecting Pool leading from the World War II Memorial to the Lincoln Memorial. If it's raining, visibility is greatly affected. If you can't score tickets, the outlook from the Old Post Office Tower is nearly as fine. Even if you don't have a ticket to ride the elevator up, it's impressive just to stand at the foot of the stones and look up.

TOURING TIPS Order advance tickets at recreation.gov or by calling ☎ 877-444-6777. Same-day, free tickets are also available daily on a first-come, first-served basis, beginning at 8:30 a.m. at the Washington Monument Lodge (on 15th Street between Madison Drive NW and Jefferson Drive SW).

Rangers are on hand to answer questions and offer tours 9:30 a.m.–5 p.m. Security limitations on what can be brought are strict and extensive. The monument and grounds may be closed during thunderstorms, periods of sustained high wind, or security alerts. Like any elevator, the one here occasionally malfunctions. Not recommended for those afraid of heights.

IF YOU LIKE THIS See the profile of the **Old Post Office** (pages 168–169). The **Washington National Cathedral**'s Tower Climb Tour offers breathtaking views but requires climbing 333 steps to the top (page below).

Washington National Cathedral ★★★★★

PRESCHOOL ★	GRADE SCHOOL ★★	TEENS ★★★★
YOUNG ADULTS ★★★★★	OVER 30 ★★★★★	SENIORS ★★★★★

Location Massachusetts and Wisconsin Avenues NW. **Nearest Metro station** The Woodley Park/Zoo/Adams Morgan station is about a half-hour walk. **Contact** ☎ 202-537-6200 for guided-tour information, nationalcathedral.org. **Admission** $12 adults; $8 children ages 5–17, seniors, and members of the military; admission is free on Sundays for those who visit to worship or pray. **Hours** Highlights tours are included with general admission. They operate Monday–Saturday at 10:15 a.m., 11 a.m., 1 p.m., 2 p.m., and 3 p.m.; and on Sundays as available.

DESCRIPTION AND COMMENTS This massive 102-year-old Gothic cathedral, formally called the Cathedral Church of Saint Peter and Saint Paul, is the official seat of the Presiding Bishop of the Episcopal Church in the United States (and of the Bishop of the Episcopal Diocese of Washington). There are 233 stained glass windows (including the great rose windows in the south transept, displaying scenes from the Book of Revelation, and in the west transept, showing the Creation); a 53-bell carillon (each bell, including the 12-toner, is carved with a Bible verse); a 10,250-pipe organ; nine chapels (many with fine murals or mosaics); dozens of wrought-iron gates; hundreds of elaborate carvings; and scores of gargoyles—including Darth Vader, devils, golfers, and caricatures of the famous and the humble. There's even a piece of moon rock, brought back by Neil Armstrong and Buzz Aldrin aboard the *Apollo 11*, embedded in a glass bubble of what is called the Space Window. It's 0.1 mile from the nave to the high altar; the ceiling is 100 feet high, the central tower more than 300. Don't miss the Bishop's Garden, designed by Frederick Law Olmsted and modeled on a medieval walled garden, or the Pilgrim Observation Gallery and a view of Washington from the highest vantage point in the city.

TOURING TIPS Guided highlights tours are offered daily. The Tour and Tea and behind-the-scenes tours are fabulous; see details under the "The Best Tours in Town" on page 118. There's a Tower Climb up 333 steps to the Central Tower, where you'll have intimate views of the gargoyles. You can also visit the grave of Woodrow Wilson, the only president buried here. The Cathedral isn't well served by public transportation, but walking there takes you through safe, pleasant neighborhoods that are home to Washington's elite: it's about a half-hour stroll up Cathedral Avenue from the Woodley Park–Zoo/Adams Morgan Metro.

IF YOU LIKE THIS The **Basilica of the National Shrine of the Immaculate Conception** (pages 131–132), which has been visited by Pope Francis, Pope Benedict XVI, and Saint Teresa of Calcutta (Mother Teresa), is the Catholic Church's most important D.C. landmark.

White House ★★★½

PRESCHOOL ★	GRADE SCHOOL ★★★	TEENS ★★★★
YOUNG ADULTS ★★★★	OVER 30 ★★★★★	SENIORS ★★★★

Location 1600 Pennsylvania Ave. NW. **Nearest Metro stations** Federal Triangle, Farragut North, or McPherson Square. **Contact** ☎ 202-456-7041 or 202-456-2121 (TDD), whitehouse.gov. **Admission** Free, but reservations required. **Hours** Tours are scheduled Tuesday–Thursday, 7:30–11:30 a.m.; Friday–Saturday, 7:30 a.m.–1:30 p.m. (excluding federal holidays).

DESCRIPTION AND COMMENTS Though this is the Executive Mansion, home to the First Family, you have only a random chance of seeing any member thereof unless you luck into a news event or photo op. This 30-minute tour passes through serious security measures, then enters the East Wing lobby. The tour passes by the Library and the Vermeil Room, with iconic portraits of Jackie Kennedy and Lady Bird Johnson. As you proceed, you'll see the presidential china collection and a glimpse of the Rose Garden. Next, it's up the stairs to the East Room, where famous visitors come to entertain the presidents and their families. The Green Room, the Blue Room, and the Red Room have all hosted important historical events, which your guide will likely share. The last room is the State Dining Room with its unforgettable portrait of President Lincoln, the only one in this room. The tour ends in the North Portico, through the Grand Foyer, and then out. It's hard to dispute the emotional pull of the presidential residence or its sumptuous beauty, but if you're on a first-time visit to Washington and on a limited schedule, consider visiting the White House on another trip, preferably in the fall or winter.

TOURING TIPS Requests for tour passes must be submitted through your member of Congress and are accepted at least three weeks and up to six months (a much better idea) in advance; start early because tours include only 20 people at a time, and slots are filled on a first-come basis. (International visitors should contact their embassies about passes.) White House tours may be subject to last-minute cancellation. All visitors should call the 24-hour Visitors Office information line at ☎ 202-456-7041 before arriving. Also read the list of prohibited items on the website. No food is available on site. While you're making advance reservations, check to see if your trip might coincide with a White House garden tour; that would give you another chance to get into the grounds.

IF YOU LIKE THIS Without advance planning, you will be unable to enter the White House, but you can tour the **White House Visitor Center,** just a few blocks away (see the description below). They have fascinating artifacts from various administrations and an excellent gift shop.

White House Visitor Center ★★★★

PRESCHOOL ★★	GRADE SCHOOL ★★★	TEENS ★★★★
YOUNG ADULTS ★★★★	OVER 30 ★★★★	SENIORS ★★★★

Location 1450 Pennsylvania Ave. NW. at President's Park. **Nearest Metro stations** Federal Triangle, Farragut North, or McPherson Square. **Contact** ☎ 202-208-1631, nps .gov/whho. **Admission** Free. **Hours** Daily, 7:30 a.m.–4 p.m.; closed January 1, Thanksgiving, and December 25.

DESCRIPTION AND COMMENTS This relatively new National Park facility has an excellent collection of White House artifacts, from President Lincoln's Telegraph Key to an adorable letter from an 8-year-old to President Nixon reminding him to eat his vegetables. Speaking of vegetables, they have a fun exhibit on what presidents and first ladies liked to eat, and you can relax for a few minutes in the theater to watch looping videos of the first families' lives in the White House over the decades. Instagrammers will want to pose in front of the White House mural. Along with viewing impressive objects owned by different administrations, you can also look inside the real White House using an interactive touch screen.

TOURING TIPS Even if you don't intend on visiting the White House, this small museum offers a first-class Washington, D.C., experience. You'll leave feeling well versed in the history of the house and the people who have lived there.

IF YOU LIKE THIS The **U.S. Supreme Court** (page 181) has a small but excellent museum on the lower level, which you can visit anytime. **Madame Tussauds DC** (pages 148–149) is a fun place to get your picture taken with the U.S. presidents, from George Washington to Donald Trump.

Woodrow Wilson House ★★★★

| PRESCHOOL ★ | GRADE SCHOOL ★★ | TEENS ★★★ |
| YOUNG ADULTS ★★★ | OVER 30 ★★★★ | SENIORS ★★★★ |

Location 2340 S St. NW. **Nearest Metro station** Dupont Circle. **Contact** ☎ 202-387-4062, woodrowwilsonhouse.org. **Admission** $10 adults, $8 seniors 62+, $5 students, children under age 12 admitted for free. **Hours** Wednesday–Saturday, 10 a.m.–4 p.m.; Tuesday and Sunday, noon–4 p.m.; closed all of January, Mondays, and major holidays.

DESCRIPTION AND COMMENTS After Woodrow Wilson left office in 1921, he became the only former president to retire in Washington, D.C., and he did so in this house. The guided tour takes you through the many elegant rooms that remain as they did when the president and his wife, Edith, lived there. Nearly every item in this handsome Georgian Revival town house is original, so visitors get an accurate picture of aristocratic life in the 1920s. On the tour you'll see Wilson's library (his books, however, went to the Library of Congress after his death), his bedroom (he so admired Lincoln's 7-foot-long bed that he had one made for himself), his old movie projector, and beautiful furnishings. Among other curiosities are his medicine chest; rollout bed, like a cruise ship deck chair; electric "shock box" designed to treat his paralyzed muscles (he never fully recovered from a serious stroke); graphoscope (an antique movie projector); kangaroo-fur coat; six-piece Tiffany desk set; and a mosaic of St. Peter given to him by Pope Benedict XV. The basement kitchen is virtually unchanged from Wilson's day, with original items, such as an ornate wooden icebox and a coal-and gas–fired stove. Peek inside the pantry, still stocked with items from the 1920s, such as Kellogg's Corn Flakes.

TOURING TIPS Tours are offered on the hour. The house has its era's worth of stairs, including a steep, narrow back staircase. Although there is an elevator (which is the upside of Wilson's invalidism), some areas are not accessible; call for details. No food is available on site. The gift shop has some unusual items. There is also a gallery that mounts special exhibitions, some surprisingly attractive, such as a collection of Presidential china.

IF YOU LIKE THIS See the profile of the **Heurich House Museum** (pages 141–142) or **Tudor Place** (pages 174–175).

MARYLAND SUBURBS

MARYLAND'S HISTORICAL ATTRACTIONS are famous, and both Annapolis and Baltimore are easy day trips (see pages 188–191), but some attractions of special interest are a little less centrally located.

C&O CANAL NATIONAL HISTORICAL PARK This is the most beloved and popular attraction in the Maryland suburbs of Washington, D.C., and for good reason. This national park features a towpath formerly used by mules to pull canal boats up and down the Potomac River. The path runs alongside this historical canal that was first envisioned by George Washington to transport coal from the mountains of Maryland into the thriving port of Georgetown. Construction on the canal dates back to the 19th and early 20th centuries. Visitors can learn the complicated story of the C&O Canal and then walk out to **Olmsted Island** in the middle of the Potomac River to see **Great Falls**, a series of 20-foot cascades falling a total of 76 feet in less than 1 mile (you can also view the falls from Virginia's Great Falls Park in McLean). Admission is $15 per car or $7 for each pedestrian. For more information, visit nps.gov/choh.

SIX FLAGS AMERICA Located in Bowie, Six Flags America (sixflags.com /america) is the biggest amusement park nearby, with more than 100 attractions and thrill rides and a water park to boot. It's accessible by public transportation: take the Blue Line Metro to Largo Town Center, and then take the C22 bus to the park (10–15 minutes). Among its attractions are a huge wave pool; the Bonzai Pipelines water slide (riders drop through a trapdoor and are whisked down 250 feet at up to 40 mph); and 10 roller coasters, including the spinning Ragin' Cajun, the superhero twins (the supertall Superman: Ride of Steel and the Batwing "flying coaster"), the old-school wooden coaster the Wild One, and the seven-story Bourbon Street Fireball. Operating hours are seasonal, but it's usually closed on Mondays. Tickets are about $70 at the park, but you can save about 40% by buying online; parking is $25.

GLEN ECHO PARK An amusement park of an older, simpler time, Glen Echo Park (glenechopark.org) lies just inside the Beltway in the Palisades area of Bethesda. The historic complex offers a children's theater with both live and marionette shows; a fine 1921 carousel ($1.25 per ride); a small viewing tower; and the Discovery Creek children's recreational area, which has trees for climbing, some live animals, nature trails, and more. The Art Deco Spanish Ballroom hosts contra and folk dances on weekends. Glen Echo is also home to several artist studios (photography, glassblowing, pottery) and galleries and offers arts and crafts classes. There are sometimes ranger-led park tours. Admission to the park is free, although the theaters and dances have fees. The park is open daily, 6 a.m.–1 a.m. (the next day), but the individual attractions have varying hours. The **Clara Barton National Historic Site** (nps.gov/clba), the home and original office of the founder of the American Red Cross, is across the parking lot. A massive two-story stone and yellow wood building, it's an architectural curiosity: The famously frugal Barton covered the ceilings (appropriately) with bandage muslin rather than the then-expensive plaster; cupboards are filled with needles and thread; and there is a stained glass window in the sitting room with two large red crosses. Guided tours are available Fridays and Saturdays, 1–4 p.m., on the hour.

BROOKSIDE GARDENS Near Wheaton, Brookside Gardens offers some of the region's best landscapes. The conservatory houses tropical plants and features an annual butterfly experience called Wings of Fancy. The outdoor gardens have miles of walking paths (all lit up for Christmas), through woods and dales, and each distinct area has a theme and is decorated with stone bridges, Japanese statues, and bubbling fountains. Admission is free. For more information, visit montgomeryparks.org /parks-and-trails/brookside-gardens.

VIRGINIA SUBURBS

NOT SURPRISINGLY, THE NORTHERN VIRGINIA SUBURBS are filled with historical sites, many that would be of special interest to families or veterans.

FORT WARD MUSEUM & HISTORIC SITE Just off I-395 South on West Braddock Road, **Fort Ward** (fortward.org) is a well-preserved Civil War fort and living-history museum with frequent reenactments and exhibits portraying Washington and Alexandria in wartime.

WOODLAWN PLANTATION Often overlooked in the Mount Vernon hoopla, in spite of its close connections (and collections, some of which came from Mount Vernon), is **Woodlawn Plantation** (9000 Richmond Highway/US 1, Alexandria; woodlawnpopeleighey.org). Constructed in 1800–05 for Major Lawrence Lewis, George Washington's nephew and social secretary, and his wife, Nelly Custis Lewis, Martha Washington's granddaughter, the estate is only about 3 miles from Mount Vernon. The Lewises were married at Mount Vernon on Washington's last birthday, in 1799, and he gave them 2,000 acres from the Mount Vernon estate on which to build a home (and engaged the architect of the U.S. Capitol to design it). The Palladian mansion, with a two-story central block and one-and-a-half-story wings, was sheathed in brick baked by slaves on the plantation grounds. The Lewises and Nelly's brother were Washington's executors, and there is plenty of Washingtoniana here, as well as a bedroom that was furnished for a visit from the Marquis de Lafayette in 1824.

A second major attraction at Woodlawn is the **Pope-Leighey House** (woodlawnpopeleighey.org), an intact Frank Lloyd Wright Usonian home, built in 1940 and moved from Falls Church to Woodlawn when highway construction threatened its preservation. Tiny but impressive, it is complete with all the furniture Wright designed for it and is constructed entirely of cypress, brick, glass, and concrete.

MY FAVORITE OFF-THE-BEATEN-TRACK DESTINATION is Frank Lloyd Wright's **Pope-Leighey House** in Alexandria. I've been several times and will return again because each time I learn something new from the friendly, informed tour guides.

—Bill O'Sullivan, senior managing editor at *Washingtonian*

OATLANDS HISTORIC HOUSE AND GARDENS If you head toward the big Leesburg Outlet Malls and the historical town of Leesburg, stop by **Oatlands Historic House and Gardens** (20850 Oatlands Plantation Road, Leesburg; oatlands.org). This 1798 wheat plantation features a stuccoed-brick Federal mansion with an octagonal family room, half-octagonal interior stairs at either end, and a grand portico (the mansion is closed to the public January through March). Sunday afternoon tea is a popular treat. Open daily, April–December, except Thanksgiving and December 24 and 25.

KING'S DOMINION Finally, if you have thrill-seekers in the party, **King's Dominion** (kingsdominion.com), a 400-acre amusement park with 12 roller coasters (several highly rated among adrenaline freaks), is about 75 miles south of Washington on I-95. If the Drop Tower, with its 305-foot, 72-mph fall doesn't shut the kids up, nothing will.

DAY-TRIPPING

IF YOU'VE GOT THE TIME, or if your visit to Washington is a repeat trip, consider exploring the region farther outside the city. With mountains to the west and the Chesapeake Bay to the east, there's plenty to see. Furthermore, a look at something that's not made of marble or granite can be a welcome relief to eyes wearied by the constant onslaught of Washington edifices and office buildings.

In addition to the day or even overnight trip destinations below, wine lovers should note that both Maryland and Virginia have thriving wine industries, Virginia in particular, and quite a few of the wineries are an easy and picturesque drive away on Loudoun County's rambling country roads. To see some of the possible tour routes—this might be a good time to hire a driver and make a party of it—and tasting room hours, go to virginiawine.org or marylandwine.com.

Annapolis, Maryland

Maryland's capital for more than 300 years, Annapolis is more than a quaint little town on the Chesapeake Bay: it's one of the biggest yachting centers in the United States. Often called the sailing capital of the country, it welcomes tens of thousands of boats a year—and it's also a favorite weekend retreat for Washingtonians. Acres and acres of sailboats fill the marinas, and you can watch a steady stream of these vessels parade by City Dock during the sailing season, April–late fall. If you want to try it yourself, you can take a harbor cruise aboard the two-masted schooner **Woodwind** (☎ 410-263-7837, schoonerwoodwind. com). You'll see oyster and crab boats that work the bay, in addition to pleasure boats, cruise ships, and old sailing ships. Annapolis is home to the **U.S. Naval Academy** (John Paul Jones is buried in the huge century-old chapel) and the even older fine-arts college of **St. John's,** whose domed 1742 McDowell Hall was admired by Thomas Jefferson. Both schools are nice places to stroll to take in their rich histories.

The center of town, known as **State Circle,** is where you'll find the **Maryland State House,** the oldest U.S. state capitol still operating in the nation. Stop in this impressive building to see the state chamber where George Washington resigned his commission as commander in chief of the Continental Army. Surrounding the State House are historic hotels dating back to Colonial times. From State Circle, walk down to the harbor, passing independent shops, restaurants, bars, and music clubs. Step into the **Banneker-Douglass Museum** (bdmuseum. maryland.gov), which documents the history of African Americans in Maryland. It includes a reproduction of the September 29, 1767, newspaper notice advertising a shipment of slaves including Kunta Kinte. The **Annapolis Maritime Museum** (amaritime.org), across the harbor bridge in Eastport, also operates tours of the Thomas Point Shoal Lighthouse at the mouth of the South River.

Annapolis is about a 1-hour drive from Washington on US 50; parking can be tough, but most of the time you can park at the Navy–Marine Corps Memorial Stadium and take a free shuttle to City Dock.

Baltimore, Maryland

Steamed crabs, H. L. Mencken, the Orioles baseball team (or the NFL Ravens), and the National Aquarium are just a few of the reasons Washingtonians trek north one hour on a regular basis to this industrial city on the Chesapeake Bay, affectionately known as Charm City.

Day-trippers can explore the **Inner Harbor,** a short walk away from the Orioles Park at Camden Yards, where you can sign up for a sightseeing tour or visit the **U.S.S. Constellation,** the 1854 sloop-of-war. The very fine **National Aquarium** (aqua.org) is a must-see. The aquatic museum features a tropical rain forest, towers of floating jellyfish, a dolphin sanctuary, and a sea mammal pavilion.

*un*official **TIP**
If you plan to see several of these attractions, look into purchasing a discounted Harbor Pass in advance (baltimore.org).

Kids will love the **Maryland Science Center** (mdsci.org), with its IMAX theater, and **Port Discovery Children's Museum** (portdiscovery.org). **Fort McHenry** (nps .gov/fomc) is the historic military base used during the War of 1812. Take a ranger tour to hear how Francis Scott Key wrote the national anthem from a ship anchored offshore. On the aquarium side of the harbor you'll find the old **Little Italy,** with its old-style family restaurants; **Heavy Seas Beer** (hsbeer.com) restaurant and brewery; and the **Star-Spangled Banner Flag House** (flaghouse.org), where the flag was stitched. The historic **Fells Point** neighborhood is the last place Edgar Allan Poe was seen before his mysterious death (he's buried in the Westminster Presbyterian Church graveyard). Also on the waterfront is the **MECU Pavilion,** site of summer concerts and a restaurant center; the **Power Plant Live!** (powerplantlive.com) entertainment complex; and a group of upscale restaurants. Avant-garde-art lovers should stop into the **American Visionary Art Museum** (avam.org) alongside the Maryland Science Center, and traditional-art lovers should check out **Baltimore Museum of Art** (artbma.org) uptown near the Johns Hopkins University campus. Renee's personal favorite is the historic **Mount Vernon** neighborhood, where you can walk up the 227 stone steps of the original Washington Monument and see elegant brownstones built in the 19th century. It's also the home of **Walters Art Museum** (the walters.org), a community gathering place with a collection of fine art spanning the ages and the world. Other Baltimore attractions near the Inner Harbor and Orioles Stadium include the **B&O Railroad Museum** (borail.org), the **Edgar Allan Poe House** (poeinbaltimore.org), and the **Babe Ruth Birthplace and Museum** (baberuthmuseum.org).

Frederick, Maryland

Frederick's well-preserved downtown has streets with homes and businesses dating back to the 18th century. The town began with early German and Dutch settlers, becoming a flourishing city of commerce around the Revolutionary War, a haven from bloody skirmishes during the Civil War, and an important stop on the Great Wagon Road for America's western expansion. The architecture is some of the best in the region, with beautifully preserved buildings from the 18th and 19th centuries, old churches with quirky steeples, and a city park filled with water lilies and trompe l'oeil designs on its stone walls. Drive along country roads dotted with covered bridges to visit **Catoctin Mountain Park** (nps.gov/cato), the **National Shrine Grotto of Our Lady of Lourdes** (nsgrotto.org), and the **National Shrine of Saint Elizabeth Ann Seton** (setonshrine.org). Stroll the town's historical streets, past upscale boutiques, antiques shops, and first-class dining, perhaps stopping to visit the haunting **National Museum of Civil War Medicine** (civilwarmed.org). Frederick was transformed into a hospital during the Civil War because of the many battles fought around the region, including Gettysburg and Antietam. Visitors might also enjoy touring Maryland's popular **Flying Dog Brewery** (flyingdog.com) and hiking on the **Appalachian Trail** to Chimney Rock. For more information, check visitfrederick.org.

Harpers Ferry National Historical Park

This restored 19th-century town, at the confluence of the Shenandoah and Potomac Rivers in West Virginia, offers visitors history and natural beauty in equal doses—one reason that hikers, bikers, kayakers, and tubers pack the parking lots. At the park's visitor center, you can see a film about radical abolitionist John Brown's 1859 raid on a U.S. armory here, an event that was a catalyst for the Civil War. Then you can tour a renovated blacksmith's shop, ready-made clothing store, and general store. The winding main road climbs past taverns and boutiques to a glorious hilltop view. A short hike to Jefferson Rock is rewarded with a spectacular mountain view of three states (Maryland, Virginia, and West Virginia), as well as the two rivers. Thomas Jefferson said the view was "worth a voyage across the Atlantic." Luckily, the trip by car from Washington is only about 90 minutes (don't miss the nearby village of Hillsborough or Breaux Vineyards), and this is one of the destinations accessible by MARC train. For more information, visit nps.gov/hafe.

Civil War Battlefields

From the number of battlefield sites, it would seem that the entire Civil War was fought in nearby Virginia, Maryland, and Pennsylvania—which is not all that far from the truth. Visitors with an interest in history and beautiful countryside can tour a number of Civil War sites within a day's drive of Washington. Several of the larger touring companies, such as Gray Line, offer bus excursions to some of these sites.

One of the closest Civil War museums is at **Fort Ward** (fortward .org), a 40-acre site just south of King Street and Interstate 395 in Alexandria, which is often staffed by volunteer reenactors. **Ball's Bluff** in Leesburg is one of Loudoun County's largest battlefields, with a 1-mile walking trail, interpretive signs, and a military cemetery.

Gettysburg, where the Union turned the tide against the South, is about 2 hours north of D.C. The **National Military Park** (nps.gov/gett) features a museum, a tower that gives sightseers an aerial view of the battlefield, and many acres of rolling countryside dotted with monuments, memorials, and stone fences. It's a popular tourist destination and worth the drive. In the summer, there are kid's programs that include learning marching formation and the discomforts of 19th-century soldiering.

The first battle of the Civil War took place at Bull Run near Manassas, on the fringe of today's Virginia suburbs. **Manassas National Battlefield Park** (nps.gov/mana) features a visitor center, a museum, and miles of trails on the picturesque grounds.

The Confederate victory set the stage for the next major battle, at Antietam, across the Potomac River in Maryland. **Antietam National Battlefield** (nps.gov/anti), near Sharpsburg, is the site of the bloodiest day of the Civil War: on September 17, 1862, there were 12,410 Union and 10,700 Confederate casualties in General Robert E. Lee's failed attempt to penetrate the North. The battlefield, about a 90-minute drive from Washington, is 15 miles west of Frederick, Maryland. Another lesser-known but worthwhile stop for Civil War buffs is the **Monocacy National Battlefield Center** (nps.gov/mono), also near Frederick, Maryland. This battle was said to have stopped the Confederate Army from entering Washington, D.C.

A number of later Union campaigns are commemorated at **Fredericksburg and Spotsylvania National Military Park** (nps.gov/frsp) in Virginia, halfway between Washington and Richmond. Included in the park are the battlefields of Fredericksburg, Chancellorsville, the Wilderness, and Spotsylvania. The park is about an hour's drive south of D.C.

WHAT'S NEW *in* WASHINGTON, D.C.?

THE CITY IS EXPECTING TO WELCOME some new landmark attractions in the coming years. Visit TheUnofficialGuides.com for updated information.

CHINESE AMERICAN MUSEUM Located next to the Jefferson Hotel, a 1907 Beaux Arts–style mansion will be the home of the new Chinese American Museum, with historical and contemporary artifacts and Chinese American art demonstrating the history of the Chinese residents who helped shape the city (chineseamericanmuseum.org).

NATIONAL LAW ENFORCEMENT MUSEUM This immersive new museum demonstrates the work of law enforcement in history and the modern age. Using interactive exhibits, the museum has a Decision-Making Training Simulator, allows you to try gathering forensic evidence at a crime scene, and shows how crime was handled when the American colonies were first populated. Located in Judiciary Square, the museum operates daily, 10 a.m.–6 p.m.; admission is $17–$21.95, and kids under 5 are admitted free (lawenforcementmuseum.org).

NATIONAL MUSEUM OF THE UNITED STATES ARMY A free museum that honors 240 years of American Army history with a comprehensive portrayal of U.S. Army traditions and the role military members played in the history of the country. Located in Fort Belvoir, Virginia, the museum has innovative exhibits like the Medal of Honor Experience, Army Theater, and Army Trail for visitors to explore. The three main galleries—Soldier Stories, Fighting for the Nation, and Army and Society—will each cover a period in the Army's history, beginning with the Revolutionary War and ending with the wars in Iraq and Afghanistan. More than 45,000 artifacts are part of this collection. The U.S. Army will own and operate the museum, while the Army Historical Foundation will manage the store, café, and special events (thenmusa.org).

PLANET WORD At a time when writing is often dashed off in a text or tweet, a new museum called Planet Word opens in the Historic Franklin School with a goal of engaging visitors with words. In 10 galleries, visitors will give speeches, sing songs, listen to poetry, explore the language of advertising, and enjoy jokes and puns. In the auditorium, visitors will hear poetry slams, book talks, and discussions about everything from "what is a lie?" and whether emojis are a language to how to construct your own language and whether animals have language. Includes a restaurant and gift shop (planetwordmuseum.org).

TALL SHIP *PROVIDENCE* Old Town Alexandria's newest waterfront attraction is *Providence*, a reproduction of the first ship to serve in the Continental Navy under the command of Captain John Paul Jones. The original *Providence* was renowned during the American Revolution for being a fast and lucky sailing ship. Daily tours run every 30 minutes, and on weekends, the 110-foot, 12-gun sloop also hosts themed voyages, like a craft beer cruise, family-friendly pirate cruises, sunset sails, and adult pirate cruises (tallshipprovidence.org).

HIDDEN GEMS *and* FREE THINGS *to* SEE *and* DO

ARTECHOUSE This new museum features the intersection between art and technology with interactive installations and stimulating concepts. Visitors should purchase tickets online ahead of arrival (dc.artechouse.com).

ART MUSEUM OF THE AMERICAS Located in the Organization of American States building near the White House, this small museum, with its enchanting tropical garden, is a perfect place to beat the heat or cold while touring the Mall. The museum has a collection featuring Latin American artists, with sculpture, drawings, and photographs (museum.oas.org).

BEN'S CHILI BOWL The original location in the U Street Corridor is the place to try Washington, D.C.'s most iconic dish, the Half-Smoke (beef/pork sausage on a soft white bun and smothered in chili and onions). The building also has a patriotic mural featuring African American heroes (benschilibowl.com).

DEA MUSEUM Located in Arlington, this museum showcases the US Drug Enforcement Agency's work, including their work combating historic opium dens, Colombian cartels, post-9/11 narco-terrorism, and D.C.'s 1970s-era head shops (deamuseum.org).

THE DEPARTMENT OF INTERIOR MUSEUM This government agency has a free museum that requires advance reservations. Take a tour of their stunning collection of Ansel Adams photographs featuring the national parks at the time of their founding. The exhibit is called *People, Land and Water.* Grab a bite or have some coffee in their cafeteria surrounded by impressive murals at the end of the tour (doi.gov/interiormuseum).

FORT DERUSSY The Civil War garrison located in Rock Creek Park is mostly swallowed up with trees and shrubs, but it was where Confederate soldiers attacked Fort Stevens to the west and Fort DeRussy's Union soldiers fought back by firing 100 rounds at the enemy to protect Washington, D.C. (nps.gov).

GRAVELLY POINT PARK This park is located along the George Washington Memorial Parkway in Arlington, Virginia, beside the grounds of Reagan National Airport. Take a picnic and watch as the jets fly directly over or by you (virginia.org).

HISTORIC CONGRESSIONAL CEMETERY Here you can cavort with the spirits of many of Washington's most notable residents, including bandleader John Philip Sousa, congressmen and senators, and FBI director J. Edgar Hoover. It was a place to honor the dead with formal processions starting from the U.S. Capitol. State funerals for First Lady Dolley Madison and Presidents John Quincy Adams, William Henry Harrison, and Zachary Taylor took place here (congressionalcemetery.org).

MANSION ON O STREET Built in 1896, this historic mansion is now a combination of hotel, gathering space, and museum filled with eclectic artifacts. It was the home of Rosa Parks, the civil rights icon, and countless celebrities have stayed there (omansion.com).

NATIONAL FIREARMS MUSEUM The museum, inside the offices of the National Rifle Association headquarters, has 15 galleries with more than 3,000 firearms used in American history. Some highlights include the rifles at the Jamestown Fort to gun factories in New England. Exhibits represent events such as the Western Front during World War I. The museum also catalogues 120 guns used in movies such as *No Country for Old Men, Dirty Harry,* and *Die Hard* and displays Annie Oakley's gun (nramuseum.org).

SMITHSONIAN ANACOSTIA COMMUNITY MUSEUM Located in Anacostia, this small branch of the Smithsonian looks at how Washington, D.C., has changed over the last century and the impact on development in the various neighborhoods (anacostia.si.edu).

THEODORE ROOSEVELT ISLAND This spit of land is operated by the National Park Service and honors President Theodore Roosevelt, who was the founder of the National Park System. He was a lover of nature and adventure, so this is a fitting memorial to him. The statues in the island's center contain an image of him and etchings of his most famous statements. It's an entertaining place for a hike, with views of the Potomac River waterfront, Georgetown, and a boardwalk over lush wetlands (nps.gov/this).

THE *TITANIC* MEMORIAL Take a walk from The Wharf (in the Southwest Waterfront neighborhood) to see this unique and stunning memorial funded and built by 25,000 American women to honor the men who died during the sinking of the massive ship in 1912. Women and children were evacuated first from the ship, which left the majority of all men onboard to die.

PART FIVE

DINING

The WASHINGTON CUISINE SCENE

THE WASHINGTON DINING SCENE is a reflection of our community diversity. Because the city is home to millions of international residents, and because residents have a taste for global gastronomy, diners have their pick of nearly every kind of cuisine.

In 2016 *Bon Appétit* ranked Washington, D.C., as the Restaurant City of the Year. In the 2019 rankings, D.C. claimed three of the country's 50 best restaurants. In the past, the city always had "great meals in big-box restaurants in the center of town," writes Andrew Knowlton of *Bon Appétit*. "But now D.C. has more than that: It finally has a ton of great neighborhood restaurants. . . . And what all these restaurants have in common is fearlessness."

Washington continues to rank at the top of Michelin's, Zagat's, and *People* magazine's lists of best food cities thanks to its ever-expanding restaurant scene with a multicultural flair. Many are helmed by women. **Maydan** was recognized as the second-best new restaurant in America in *Bon Appétit*'s "Hot Ten" in 2018. This much-admired eatery serves modern Middle Eastern cuisine and is owned by Rose Previte, a Lebanese American, who fires every dish in a blazing oven in the center of the restaurant. Another popular female chef is Marjorie Meek-Bradley, who won Eater.com 2018 Chef of the Year at her **St. Anselm** tavern. She reimagined menus found at traditional D.C. steakhouses to make room for vegetable-focused entrées.

unofficial **TIP**
The most reenergized areas in the city for dining, loosely defined, are the **Atlas District, Capitol Hill,** the **Northwest** area, **Penn Quarter,** and **U Street.**

Another notable trend is the expansion of fast-casual restaurants. Washington, D.C. was the incubator for **Sweetgreen,** the salad empire; **Cava,** featuring a taste of Greece in a bowl; and the international expansion of our own **Five Guys,** beloved for pick-your-own-toppings chargrilled burgers. D.C. was also the first location for the vegetarian fast-casual restaurant **Beefsteak,** debuted by local chef and renowned humanitarian José Andrés. The design-your-own-pizza bar **&Pizza** opened its first location on Capitol Hill. New concepts—including **Rasa,** a fast-casual gourmet Indian restaurant; **Flower Child,** with ultra-healthy vegetarian, vegan, and Paleo dishes; **Taco Bamba,** an authentic Mexican street food–style eatery with creative garnishes; **Poki DC,** featuring Hawaiian seafood options; **TaKorean,** with Korean-style tacos in multiple food markets, and **Buredo,** which serves giant sushi rolls in the shape of a burrito—are introduced all the time. According to Sam Oches of *QSR* magazine, which chronicles the movement, Washington is "a hotbed for Fast Casual 2.0."

Several fine dining restaurants offer tasting menus, where you can savor a parade of small plates in imaginative combinations, using technically demanding molecular gastronomy. For a unique but pricey experience, we recommend **Minibar, Rose's Luxury** (page 211), **Pineapple & Pearls, Masseria, Obelisk**, and **Kinship.**

D.C. has celebrated restaurants showcasing fusion menus combining two or more cultures, like the Nigerian–Jamaican blend served at **Kith/Kin** (page 204). You'll find other fusion menus at Smithsonian museums too. Iconic Southern American classics from across the nation appear at **Sweet Home Café** in the National Museum of African American History and Culture. The Smithsonian Museum of the American Indian's cafeteria, **Mitsitam Native Foods Cafe,** represents regional cuisine originating from indigenous tribes in the South, Central, and North Americas. Expect to find restaurants with lesser-known gastronomies too, like **Ambar**'s bountiful Balkan dishes, **Thip Khao**'s flavorful Laotian fare, and **Supra**'s feasts from the Republic of Georgia.

We'll also describe the best D.C. dining districts and our favorite restaurants found in each. Especially exciting are the D.C. chefs who are digging into their roots, tapping into their native homeland's recipes for Afghan, Algerian, Argentine, Belgian, Ethiopian, Filipino, Honduran, Israeli, Korean, Mediterranean, Nepalese, Peruvian, Sri Lankan, Thai, Turkish, Uzbek, and Yemeni, as well as the more familiar Chinese, French, Indian, and Italian. Several food markets have sprung up around the Washington area, although most of them are in the suburbs. For those who want to sample Latin American dishes, try the new **La Cosecha,** or to find a diverse collection of Vietnamese merchants, visit the historic **Eden Center** in Northern Virginia. If you can't find a brick-and-mortar restaurant that suits your fancy, feast on the area's diverse food truck fare.

 FOR YEARS, D.C.'S MOBILE FOOD TRUCK MENUS were limited to hot dogs, ice pops, and pretzels. But today you can find food trucks with a variety of cuisines sprinkled around popular gathering places. Look for food trucks at Farragut Square (17th and K Streets NW), L'Enfant Plaza, near the Foggy Bottom/GWU Metro station, at Eastern Market on Capitol Hill, alongside the Penn Quarter Farmers

Market, and on 14th and 17th Streets NW between the National Mall's memorials and monuments.

A WORD OF WARNING Washington is not known for bargains, outside of the fast-casual restaurants. Lines can be quite long for recently opened restaurants or those getting major press. Whenever possible, we recommend reservations, and for the restaurants that don't allow reservations, you may be able to reserve tables for large groups of typically eight or more. Lastly, consider using the reservation services on OpenTable.com or Resy.com; they make it easy to obtain and cancel restaurant reservations.

PRIME DINING NEIGHBORHOODS

ALONG WITH THE AWAKENING of the Washington palate, there has been a huge expansion of the city's dining map. Redevelopment and gentrification led to the growth of dining centers in suburban areas like **Ballston, Mosaic District, Tysons,** and **Clarendon** in Virginia, and **Downtown Bethesda, Pike & Rose, Silver Spring,** and **Wheaton** in Maryland. All have lured established and first-time restaurateurs to those mini-cities. For example, the restaurants in **Rockville Town Center** offer Indian–French fusion, Irish, Korean, Lebanese, Peruvian, Russian–Tajik, Spanish, Taiwanese, and Thai. Usually mixed in these suburban–urban communities, there's at least one brewpub, burger joint, frozen yogurt shop, and coffeehouse.

unofficial **TIP**
When you're looking for cost-effective ways to try an upscale restaurant, consider the lunch menu, where you can get many of the same dishes for significantly less money. Also, stop in for happy hour or for the early-bird menu, where you'll usually find discounted drinks and food. Another option is to visit during Washington, D.C.'s Restaurant Weeks in January and August.

While we have included some less conveniently located standouts in the restaurant profiles, we have predominantly focused our recommendations in areas that are easily accessible to visitors, especially via public transportation, and preferably around popular attractions where hunger may strike. Our profiles are organized by neighborhood, but if you would like to see a listing of restaurants by cuisine, check out the table on pages 202–203.

Each restaurant profile features a heading that allows you to quickly check out the restaurant's star rating, cuisine, and cost.

STAR RATING This rating encompasses the entire dining experience, not only the flavor and quality of the food but also presentation, service, and ambience. It also reflects the value for the expense. Five stars is the highest rating possible and connotes the best of everything. Four-star

continued on page 200

Washington, D.C., Dining

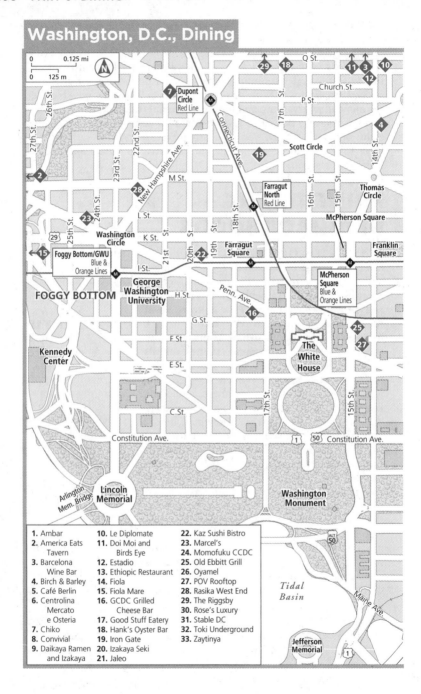

1. Ambar
2. America Eats Tavern
3. Barcelona Wine Bar
4. Birch & Barley
5. Café Berlin
6. Centrolina Mercato e Osteria
7. Chiko
8. Convivial
9. Daikaya Ramen and Izakaya
10. Le Diplomate
11. Doi Moi and Birds Eye
12. Estadio
13. Ethiopic Restaurant
14. Fiola
15. Fiola Mare
16. GCDC Grilled Cheese Bar
17. Good Stuff Eatery
18. Hank's Oyster Bar
19. Iron Gate
20. Izakaya Seki
21. Jaleo
22. Kaz Sushi Bistro
23. Marcel's
24. Momofuku CCDC
25. Old Ebbitt Grill
26. Oyamel
27. POV Rooftop
28. Rasika West End
29. Rose's Luxury
30. Rose's Luxury
31. Stable DC
32. Toki Underground
33. Zaytinya

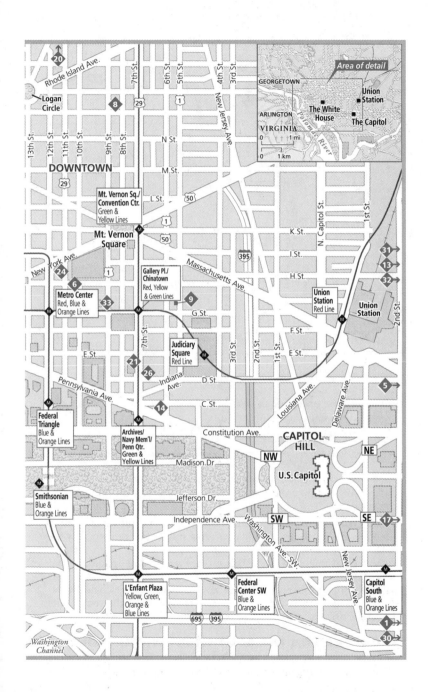

Area of detail

GEORGETOWN
Union Station
ARLINGTON
VIRGINIA
The White House
The Capitol
Potomac River

0   1 mi
0   1 km

20
Rhode Island Ave.
Logan Circle
8
29
7th St.
6th St.
5th St.
4th St.
3rd St.
1
New Jersey Ave.
13th St.
12th St.
11th St.
10th St.
9th St.
8th St.
N St.
M St.
29
DOWNTOWN
L St.
50

Mt. Vernon Sq./
Convention Ctr.
Green &
Yellow Lines
1
Mt. Vernon
Square
50

K St.
N. Capitol St.
1st St.

New York Ave.
24
1
6
33
Massachusetts Ave.
395
I St.
H St.
31
13
32

Metro Center
Red, Blue &
Orange Lines
Gallery Pl./
Chinatown
Red, Yellow
& Green Lines
9
Union
Station
Red Line
Union
Station
2nd St.

G St.
7th St.

F St.

Judiciary
Square
Red Line
3rd St.
2nd St.
1st St.
E St.

E St.
21
26
Indiana Ave.
D St.
5

Pennsylvania Ave.
14
C St.
Louisiana Ave.
Delaware Ave.

Federal
Triangle
Blue &
Orange Lines
Archives/
Navy Mem'l/
Penn Qtr.
Green &
Yellow Lines
Constitution Ave.
CAPITOL
HILL
NW
NE

Madison Dr.

Smithsonian
Blue &
Orange Lines
Jefferson Dr.
U.S. Capitol

Independence Ave.
SW
SE
17
Washington Ave. SW

L'Enfant Plaza
Yellow, Green,
Orange &
Blue Lines
Federal
Center SW
Blue &
Orange Lines
New Jersey Ave.
Capitol
South
Blue &
Orange Lines

695
395
1
30

Washington
Channel

Waterfront Dining

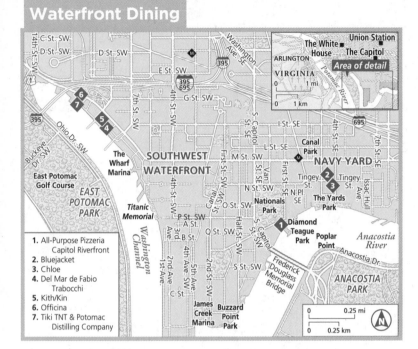

1. All-Purpose Pizzeria
   Capitol Riverfront
2. Bluejacket
3. Chloe
4. Del Mar de Fabio
   Trabocchi
5. Kith/Kin
6. Officina
7. Tiki TNT & Potomac
   Distilling Company

continued from page 197

restaurants are exceptional, and three-star restaurants are well above average. Two-star restaurants are good.

• Inexpensive $25 or less per person	• Moderate $26-$40 per person
• Expensive $41-$60 per person	• Very Expensive More than $60 per person

COST generally includes an appetizer (or dessert) and entrée with side dish; drinks and tip are excluded. Some restaurants serve only a fixed-cost meal.

IF YOU LIKE THIS This category at the end of each profile lists suggested alternatives—nearby restaurants featuring similar fare or owned by the same chef.

Note: Washington, D.C. restaurants are required to uphold the tenants of the Americans with Disabilities Act, and only in very rare cases will not provide accessibility for a person using a wheelchair. Unless we have noted otherwise, you can assume that all of the restaurants we profile are accessible.

THE WHARF ON THE SOUTHWEST WATERFRONT

OPEN SINCE 2017, the District Wharf has evolved to be one of the most popular destinations in the city. This development, which is set to

Upper Northwest Dining

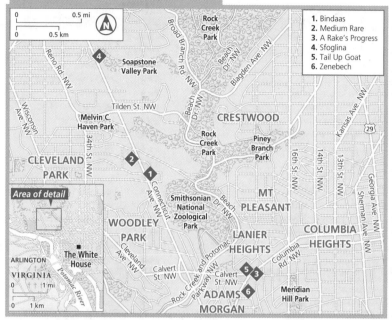

1. Bindaas
2. Medium Rare
3. A Rake's Progress
4. Sfoglina
5. Tail Up Goat
6. Zenebech

expand in 2021, is a community that is beloved by visitors and locals alike. Perched along The Wharf's mile-long boardwalk, nearly every restaurant features views of the Washington Channel.

At a variety of price points, you can have a luxurious dinner that will transport you to another part of the globe, like Spanish seafood at **Del Mar** (page 204), Asian-fusion cuisine at **Kaliwa,** and Afro–Caribbean fare at **Kith/Kin** (page 204). You can absorb the festive waterfront vibe at rum distillery **Tiki TNT** (page 206) or at **Cantina Bambina,** a casual eatery on the Transit Pier. If you want sophisticated Mexican, try **Mi Vida;** for Irish pub fare, there's **Kirwan's on The Wharf.** Specializing in Italian food, from deli sandwiches to homemade pastas, are **Officina** (page 205) and **Grazie Grazie.**

Don't miss visiting one of the neighborhood's rooftop cocktail bars: **Whiskey Charlie,** at the Canopy by Hilton Washington DC The Wharf hotel, is popular with a youthful bunch,

unofficial **TIP**

"My favorite area of Washington, D.C. is the newly built-up **Wharf.** The waterfront boasts incredible dining options, with Michelin-starred chef Nick Stefanelli opening his second restaurant, **Officina**; the incredible desserts at **Milk Bar** by Christina Tosi; and **Whiskey Charlie,** offering delicious bar bites and drinks with the best sunset views in the city.
—D.C. social media expert Nicole Sunderland, on Instagram @EatLiveTravelDrink and @NickiEatstheGlobe

continued on page 204

RESTAURANTS BY CUISINE

CUISINE/NAME	OVERALL RATING	PRICE
AMERICAN		
THE INN AT LITTLE WASHINGTON	★★★★★	Very Expensive
ROSE'S LUXURY	★★★★½	Very Expensive
CONVIVIAL	★★★★	Expensive
BIRCH & BARLEY	★★★½	Moderate-Expensive
IRON GATE	★★★½	Moderate
PATSY'S AMERICAN	★★★½	Moderate
POV ROOFTOP	★★★½	Moderate
A RAKE'S PROGRESS	★★★½	Expensive
THE RIGGSBY	★★★½	Moderate-Expensive
VERMILION	★★★½	Expensive
AMERICA EATS TAVERN	★★★	Moderate
GCDC GRILLED CHEESE BAR	★★★	Moderate
GOOD STUFF EATERY	★★★	Inexpensive
THE LIBERTY TAVERN	★★★	Inexpensive-Moderate
THE OLD ANGLER'S INN	★★★	Moderate-Expensive
OLD EBBITT GRILL	★★★	Moderate-Expensive
TED'S BULLETIN	★★½	Moderate
ASIAN FUSION		
MOMOFUKU CCDC	★★★½	Moderate
DOI MOI AND BIRDS EYE	★★★	Inexpensive
BALKAN		
AMBAR	★★★½	Inexpensive
BELGIAN		
MARCEL'S	★★★★	Very Expensive
CHINESE		
CHIKO	★★★	Inexpensive
Q BY PETER CHANG	★★★	Moderate-Expensive
TOKI UNDERGROUND	★★½	Inexpensive
ETHIOPIAN		
ETHIOPIC RESTAURANT	★★★	Inexpensive
ZENEBECH	★★★	Moderate
FRENCH		
MARCEL'S	★★★★	Very Expensive
LE DIPLOMATE	★★★½	Moderate
GASTROPUB		
BLUEJACKET	★★★★½	Moderate
OWEN'S ORDINARY	★★★	Moderate
GERMAN		
CAFÉ BERLIN	★★★	Moderate
GLOBAL		
ROSE'S LUXURY	★★★★½	Very Expensive
CHLOE	★★★★	Expensive
GREEK		
NOSTOS	★★★★	Moderate-Expensive

RESTAURANTS BY CUISINE *(continued)*

CUISINE/NAME	OVERALL RATING	PRICE
GREEK *(continued)*		
ZAYTINYA	★★★½	Moderate
HAWAIIAN		
TIKI TNT & POTOMAC DISTILLING COMPANY	★★★	Inexpensive
INDIAN		
BINDAAS	★★★	Inexpensive–Moderate
RASIKA WEST END	★★★	Expensive
ITALIAN		
FIOLA MARE	★★★★★	Italian Seafood
CENTROLINA MERCATO E OSTERIA	★★★★½	Expensive
OFFICINA	★★★★½	Moderate–Expensive
FIOLA	★★★★	Very Expensive
ALL-PURPOSE PIZZERIA CAPITOL RIVERFRONT	★★★½	Inexpensive–Moderate
SFOGLINA	★★★½	Moderate–Expensive
JAPANESE		
DAIKAYA RAMEN AND IZAKAYA	★★★★	Inexpensive–Moderate
IZAKAYA SEKI	★★★½	Moderate–Expensive
KAZ SUSHI BISTRO	★★★½	Moderate–Expensive
SUSHIKO	★★★½	Moderate–Expensive
TOKI UNDERGROUND	★★½	Inexpensive
KOREAN		
CHIKO	★★★	Inexpensive
MEDITERRANEAN		
TAIL UP GOAT	★★★½	Moderate
MEXICAN		
OYAMEL	★★★½	Moderate
MIDDLE EASTERN		
ZAYTINYA	★★★½	Moderate
NIGERIAN AND JAMAICAN		
KITH/KIN	★★★★½	Expensive
SEAFOOD		
FIOLA MARE	★★★★★	Very Expensive
CANTLER'S RIVERSIDE INN	★★★½	Moderate
HANK'S OYSTER BAR	★★½	Inexpensive–Moderate
SPANISH		
DEL MAR DE FABIO TRABOCCHI	★★★★★	Very Expensive
BARCELONA WINE BAR	★★★½	Moderate–Expensive
ESTADIO	★★★½	Inexpensive
JALEO	★★★½	Moderate
STEAK		
IRON GATE	★★★½	Moderate
MEDIUM RARE	★★★	Moderate
SWISS		
STABLE DC	★★½	Moderate–Expensive

continued from page 201

while **Waves,** in the InterContinental Washington D.C.–The Wharf, serves sophisticated types. Although they get especially busy in nice weather, be sure to visit, even if it's just for the views. In an area that is all about water, sample seafood sourced right at Maine Avenue's historic **Municipal Fish Market,** which first opened in 1805. Seafood is a specialty of the Southern-influenced **Hank's Oyster Bar,** as well as **Rappahannock Oyster Bar,** which sources bivalves from its oyster farm in the Tidewater of Virginia. For something quick, pick from **Shake Shack, Toastique,** and **Falafel Inc.** Finish up with a treat from **Milk Bar** or **Dolcezza Gelato,** or roast some marshmallows at **Camp Wharf,** a s'mores food truck on the waterfront.

Del Mar de Fabio Trabocchi ★★★★★

• **MODERN SPANISH** • **VERY EXPENSIVE**

791 Wharf St. SW; ☎ 202-525-1402; delmardc.com

Reservations Recommended. **Metro** Southwest Waterfront. **Wine selection** Very good. **Open** *Lunch:* Tuesday–Friday, 11:30 a.m.–2:30 p.m. *Dinner:* Sunday–Thursday, 5–10 p.m.; Friday–Saturday, 5:30–10:30 p.m. *Brunch:* Saturday–Sunday, 11:30 a.m.–3 p.m. *Sunset menu (available at bar only):* Tuesday–Sunday, 2:30–5 p.m. *Happy hour (available at bar only):* Monday–Thursday, 4–5:30 p.m.

THE PREMISE Dinner at Del Mar will be an evening to remember. The decor was inspired by the seaside villas on the Mediterranean's Costa de Sol, and the seductive restaurant showcases creatures of the sea spiced with the mesmerizing flavors of Spain. Each course is arranged artfully on intriguing dishware. Sky-high ceilings, with swanlike chandeliers, offer tantalizing views of the river. From this gorgeous perch overlooking the Potomac River, you'll be transformed from an ordinary diner to a serious VIP. *The Washington Post* ranked Del Mar the number one restaurant in the D.C. region in 2018.

THE PAYOFF Owners Fabio and Maria Trabocchi are the dazzling duo behind this restaurant. Maria is from the Spanish island of Mallorca and has infused her family traditions into the menu. Del Mar is acclaimed for the squid-ink paella, hand-carved *jamón Ibérico, gazpacho de melocotón* (peach gazpacho), and signature "sunset cocktails." Some dishes are prepared by your server table-side.

IF YOU LIKE THIS The Trabocchis have six restaurants in romantic settings, all of which receive critical acclaim. **Fiola Mare** (page 225), **Fiola** (page 219), and **Sfoglina** (page 238) are their Italian counterparts.

Kith/Kin ★★★★½ • **NIGERIAN AND JAMAICAN** • **EXPENSIVE**

801 Wharf St. SW; ☎ 202-878-8566; kithandkindc.com

Reservations Recommended for dinner. **Metro** Southwest Waterfront and L'Enfant Plaza. **Wine selection** Exceptional cocktail program. **Open** *Breakfast:* Monday–Friday, 6:30–10:30 a.m.; Saturday–Sunday, 6:30–11 a.m. *Lunch:* Daily, noon–2:30 p.m. *Dinner:* Sunday–Thursday, 5–10:30 p.m.; Friday–Saturday, 5–11 p.m. *Bar bites menu:* Daily, noon–11 p.m. *Lounge:* Sunday–Thursday, noon–midnight; Friday–Saturday, noon–1 a.m.

THE PREMISE Executive Chef Kwame Onwuachi blended his heritage—Nigerian, Jamaican, Creole—to create a medley of unforgettable dishes at his Michelin-starred Kith/Kin, which serves as the InterContinental Washington D.C.-The Wharf's primary restaurant. Winner of a James Beard Rising Star Award, Onwuachi calls his cooking "comfort soul food," but around dinnertime, the dishes are elevated to unusual heights as a result of the chef's mastery of spices, sauces, and inspired ingredients. Enjoy the camaraderie you'll share with your fellow diners as you experience these new flavors and preparations. Dining at Kith/Kin also provides a front-row seat to the action on The Wharf's boardwalk.

THE PAYOFF It will be hard to find any traditional American dishes on this dinner menu. Onwuachi struts his Caribbean traditions, like jerk chicken; deconstructed goat roti with dal poori; curried goat; and *jollof* rice. Sample Nigerian delicacies like *egusi* monkfish accompanied by *fufu* and toasted melon seeds. The whole fried snapper will thrill and amaze adventurous eaters. With the head on, the tangy skin tastes far better than you could ever imagine. Vegetarians and veggie lovers, don't miss the Brussels or the Mushroom Forest with charred eggplant dip.

IF YOU LIKE THIS Another exceptional dining experience at The Wharf can be found a block away at **Kaliwa,** a southeast Asian restaurant known for its fiery entrées and jaw-dropping decor. Chef Cathal and Meshelle Armstrong have adapted the best flavors of Korea, the Philippines, and Thailand using locally sourced ingredients to create this unique menu.

Officina ★★★★½ • ITALIAN • MODERATE-EXPENSIVE
1120 Maine Ave. SW; ☎ 202-747-5222; officinadc.com

Reservations Not needed except on weekends. **Metro** Southwest Waterfront. **Wine selection** Exceptional beverage program. **Open** *Mercato:* Sunday–Wednesday, 10 a.m.–7 p.m.; Thursday–Saturday, 10 a.m.–8 p.m. *Café:* Monday–Friday, 10 a.m.–10 p.m.; Saturday–Sunday, 10 a.m.–11 p.m. *Trattoria:* Monday–Friday, 5–10 p.m.; Saturday–Sunday, 11 a.m.–10 p.m. *Salotto:* Daily, 5–10 p.m. *Terrazza:* Monday–Wednesday, 5–10 p.m.; Thursday–Friday, 5–11 p.m.; Saturday, noon–midnight; Sunday, noon–10 p.m.

THE PREMISE This bright and modern three-story restaurant also functions as an Italian market and rooftop bar, and it has become a favorite gathering place at The Wharf. The cozy and playful rooftop bar often attracts the D.C. glitterati—whether they're sports stars, TV personalities, musicians, or influencers. The Wharf has many outstanding eateries, but what sets Officina (pronounced oh-fee-she-nah) apart is the enthusiastic staff; they're the essence of hospitality and friendliness. On the ground floor, the Mercato sells handmade cheeses, pastries, and bread to go. On the second level, the Trattoria has golden banquettes and serves a collection of authentic Italian dishes. The Salotto is a refined *amaro* library where you can sample a collection of Italian liqueurs and coffees. In fair weather, don't miss having cocktails and appetizers on the Terrazza, taking in a bird's-eye view of the Municipal Fish Market and the Potomac River.

THE PAYOFF Michelin-starred chef Nicholas Stefanelli has already drawn raves from Washington's diners, including former First Lady Michelle Obama, who's a regular at his restaurant **Masseria** near Union Market. Officina has relaxed spaces with accessible dishes, some for sharing and some to guard with your lives. Focus on the classics, like the mushroom risotto, cone-shaped rice fritter with veal ragù, crisp calamari in saffron and chilies, and clam linguine.

IF YOU LIKE THIS For additional rooftop viewing at The Wharf, check out **Waves,** a sophisticated nightclub–style bar at the InterContinental.

Tiki TNT & Potomac Distilling Company ★★★
● **HAWAIIAN** ● **INEXPENSIVE**
1130 Maine Ave. SW; ☎ 202-900-4786; tikitnt.com

Reservations Not accepted. *Metro* Southwest Waterfront and L'Enfant Plaza. *Wine selection* Exceptional cocktail program from in-house distillery. *Open* Monday–Friday, 3 p.m.–last call 1 a.m.; Saturday, 11 a.m.–last call 1 a.m.; Sunday, 11 a.m.–last call 11:30 p.m. *Brunch:* Saturday–Sunday, 11 a.m.–3 p.m. *Happy hour:* Monday–Friday, 3–6:30 p.m. *Late-night food menu:* Daily, 11 p.m.–last call. *Distillery:* Tuesday–Saturday, 10 a.m.–5 p.m.

THE PREMISE Todd Thrasher is D.C.'s most award-winning bartender. He also distills **Thrasher's Rum,** which is served in cocktails alongside the restaurant's traditional Hawaiian dishes. The chill atmosphere benefits from picturesque views of the waterfront as well as the **Municipal Fish Market.** There are multiple bars, and the tiki theme is carried over into the decorative glasses and classic rock music. Tiki TNT offers a Boozy Brunch on Sundays with bottomless mimosas, pitchers of daiquiris, and frozen spiced-rum-and-Coke drinks. After Dark Parties are held following a show at The Wharf's music venues, like **The Anthem.** You can't miss this place—just look for the smokestack lettered with THRASHER'S RUM and MAKE RUM NOT WAR.

THE PAYOFF The snacks here are conducive to drinking, of course. The restaurant has small, medium, and large plates for individuals or group sharing. For diners new to Hawaiian, try the Spam Musubi, layered sushi bites made with the salty canned meat. Tiki Tots (tater tots) are accompanied by fruit salsa, cheese, and spices. For a heartier choice, try the Pumba Platter with pulled pork and slaw. Recommended cocktails: Missionary's Downfall, with Thrasher's White Rum, peach, mint, lime, and pineapple—like the tropics in a glass; Thrasher's signature Frozen Rum in Coke; and The Grog—Thrasher's Spiced Rum, verbena tea, lemon juice, and soda water.

IF YOU LIKE THIS At the other end of the boardwalk, at the Canopy by Hilton hotel, is **Whiskey Charlie,** one of the "top" rooftop bars in Washington, D.C., thanks to its views. With both indoor and outdoor lounges, it features a collection of small plates, wines by the glass, and local craft beer. Lovers of Cuban cuisine should check out **Cuba Libre** in Penn Quarter and the new **Casta's Rum Bar** in the West End section of Georgetown; they're great places for rum lovers as well.

CAPITOL RIVERFRONT AND NAVY YARD

THE AREA BETWEEN the Washington Navy Yard and Nationals Park is flourishing. Perhaps because it's a rather new development, the neighborhood goes by an assortment of labels, such as Capitol Riverfront, Yards Park, and Navy Yard—the latter because of its proximity to the Navy Yard Metro station. The area was home to Washington's earliest brewery and now houses its finest brewery, **Bluejacket** (next page). Other popular eateries include **Osteria Morini,** an upscale Italian restaurant beside the river; **Bonchon,** a spicy Korean chicken place; **Nando's**

Peri-Peri Chicken, serving legendary chicken grilled with Portuguese and African spices; **Shake Shack,** focused on affordable burgers and milkshakes; and the Mexican-influenced, art-adorned **Él Bebe. District Winery** is a fabulous place for date night, thanks to the tasting room's sweeping views of the Anacostia River. On Saturdays June–October, several of D.C.'s most popular eateries are represented at the **Smorgasburg** outdoor food market.

All-Purpose Pizzeria Capitol Riverfront ★★★½
• **ITALIAN** • **INEXPENSIVE-MODERATE**

79 Potomac Ave. SE; ☎ 202-629-1894; allpurposedc.com

Reservations Recommended. **Metro** Navy Yard/Ballpark. **Wine selection** Good, also beer and spirits. **Open** *Dinner:* Monday-Thursday, 4-10 p.m.; Friday, 4-11 p.m.; Saturday, 11 a.m.-11 p.m.; Sunday, 11 a.m.-10 p.m. *Happy hour:* Monday-Friday, 4-7 p.m.

THE PREMISE Located across the street from Nationals Park and a few blocks from Audi Field (home of the D.C. United major league soccer team), All-Purpose is just what it says: a place that serves everyone's needs. With a seasonal rooftop bar and views of the Anacostia River from its big windows, the space itself is a draw. But what really matters is how great the pizza is. It's so good, in fact, *The Washington Post* food critic declared it one of his top restaurants. Be aware that it's especially popular on game days, and the noise inside can be deafening. Another reason for its shining reviews may be that you can bring your own wine bottle for a $20 corkage fee.

THE PAYOFF This Italian American restaurant is a destination spot featuring traditional Italian favorites with a modern edge. They fry risotto into savory arancini balls, and the crust on the deck-oven-baked pizza is always the perfect combination of crisp and chewy. Innovative toppings are another draw. Notable pies are the clam-smoked-bacon Handsome Dan and the Bazooka Joe with Parm fonduta, roasted sweet corn, 'nduja sausage, cilantro crema, and spring onions.

IF YOU LIKE THIS The original location of **All-Purpose** is in the Shaw neighborhood, near the Convention Center. Its sister restaurants are **The Red Hen** and **Boundary Stone.**

Bluejacket ★★★★½ • **GASTROPUB** • **MODERATE**

300 Tingey St. SE; ☎ 202-524-4862; bluejacketdc.com

Reservations Accepted. **Metro** Eastern Market or Navy Yard/Ballpark. **Wine selection** Beer only. **Open** Monday-Thursday, 11 a.m.-1 a.m.; Friday-Saturday, 11 a.m.-2 a.m.; Sunday, 11 a.m.-1 a.m. *Lunch:* Monday-Saturday, 11 a.m.-4:30 p.m.; Saturday, 10 a.m.-4:30 p.m. *Brunch:* Sunday, 11 a.m.-3 p.m. *Dinner:* Sunday-Monday, 4:30-10 p.m.; Tuesday-Thursday, 4:30-11 p.m.; Friday-Saturday, 4:30 p.m.-midnight.

THE PREMISE Bluejacket is the landmark eatery and bar in Navy Yard and is the second establishment opened by Neighborhood Restaurant Group and Greg Engert, Washington's most influential beer director (their first was Birch & Barley). Bluejacket's brewery and restaurant are located inside what had been a munitions manufacturing complex built in 1919. The brewery occupies 5,600 square feet over three levels. The restaurant, known as the Arsenal, seats 200 people.

THE PAYOFF Many come here for the beer, but the kitchen turns out memorable offerings as well, most that pair nicely with beer, of course. It offers 20 Bluejacket beers and 5 Bluejacket cask ales on tap. Serving imaginative pub food, like loaded potato nachos and pan-seared pierogi, is what the kitchen does best. But dinner is a little more formal, with plates of seafood, short ribs, and bratwurst sausages. The brunch is very popular, a combination of New American—think blue crab avocado toast, pretzel bread, and smoked salmon and cream cheese with pickled onions—and international dishes, like the Middle Eastern falafel burger and Israeli baked egg *shakshuka* (my favorite).

IF YOU LIKE THIS Engert has two other beer-centric restaurants: **Birch & Barley/ChurchKey** (page 228) in Logan Circle and **Owen's Ordinary** (page 239) in North Bethesda, Maryland. Other fun beverage-oriented spots in Navy Yard are **The Big Stick,** a sports bar featuring Polish fare, and **Ana at District Winery,** with a dedicated tasting room and airy patio with scenic views of the Anacostia River.

Chloe ★★★★ • GLOBAL • EXPENSIVE

1331 Fourth St. SE; ☎ 202-313-7007; restaurantchloe.com

Reservations Recommended. **Metro** Navy Yard/Ballpark. **Wine selection** Good. **Open** *Dinner:* Monday–Thursday, 5–10 p.m.; Friday, 5–11 p.m.; Saturday, 4–11 p.m.; Sunday, 4–9 p.m. *Happy hour:* Monday–Friday, 4–7 p.m. *Brunch:* Saturday, 11 a.m.–2 p.m.; Sunday, 11 a.m.–4 p.m.

THE PREMISE Named for the Greek goddess of agriculture, this is chef Haidar Karoum's first restaurant, but he's been cooking in Washington's best kitchens for decades. Trained by the renowned Michel Richard and Nora Pouillon, among other prestigious chefs, Karoum was recognized as Chef of the Year in 2014 by the Restaurant Association Metropolitan Washington. In 2019 Chloe was included on the Michelin Guide's Bib Gourmand list. Karoum is adept at preparing dishes in a variety of cuisines, including Vietnamese, Thai, Indian, Japanese, French, and Lebanese, his native heritage. He says his menu consists of dishes he likes, and the critics are raving.

THE PAYOFF Probably the most iconic image is the whole fish flanked with salsa *verde*, but he also puts out a stellar Vietnamese chicken with chili-lime sauce. The oysters with crème fraîche and horseradish are acclaimed, along with cobia crudo, a Vietnamese-influenced bowl of raw slices of this delicate white fish marinated in lime, Thai chilies, and fish sauce. For a hearty appetite, consider the Bavarian white sausage with spaetzle, and we recommend you finish with the Meyer lemon tart with blueberry compote when available.

IF YOU LIKE THIS Down the street in Barracks Row, **Rose's Luxury** (page 211) won Best Restaurant of the Year from *Bon Appétit* in 2014. You will find the same imaginative global fare crafted in a charming converted town house. No reservations except for large parties.

CAPITOL HILL AND BARRACKS ROW

OVER THE DECADES, Capitol Hill's most venerable restaurant is the long-running political annex **The Monocle,** whose classic mid-Atlantic steak-and-seafood menu remains as dignified as its reputation for discretion (notable members of the Republican party are known to frequent this vintage dining room). Among other popular power stops are **Charlie Palmer Steak,** the Louisiana lovers' **Johnny's Half Shell,** and **Art & Soul** inside the Liaison Washington Capitol Hill hotel with a view of the Capitol. Hang out with the Hill interns at **Tortilla Coast, Capitol Lounge,** or the **Hawk 'n' Dove.**

Spike Mendelsohn, one of D.C.'s *Top Chef* celebrities, has a trio of hot spots in the 300 block of Pennsylvania Avenue Southeast—an inexpensive retro burger-and-shake shop called **Good Stuff Eatery** (page 210); **We, the Pizza,** serving slices with abundant topping options; and, most recently, **Santa Rosa Taqueria,** a casual Latin American eatery.

When it comes to breakfast, check out **The Market Lunch** inside Eastern Market, well known for its blueberry pancakes and shrimp and grits (it's packed on weekends), and **Ted's Bulletin** (page 245), which features a decadent menu with homemade Pop-Tarts–like tarts and alcohol-laced milkshakes.

 BARRACKS ROW ON CAPITOL HILL was the first commercial center in Washington, D.C., dating back to 1799. When the Navy Yard was built on the banks of the Anacostia River, it was the Marine Corps' first base, established to protect the Capitol. In the late 18th century, the neighborhood had markets and restaurants specializing in oysters. On nearby streets, you'll see some of the original homes that escaped the fires during the Battle of 1812.

Capitol Hill expands into **Barracks Row,** a stretch on Eighth Street SE between Pennsylvania Avenue and the **Washington Navy Yard.** In the center of the neighborhood, you'll find the Marine Commandant's impressive quarters and town houses where some US Marines reside. Among the many restaurant choices are **Ambar** (Serbian and Croatian fare with all-you-can-eat specials; see below) and **Belga Café** (mussels plus classic Belgian). For casual but full-service fare, try **Cava Mezze, Medium Rare** (page 237), **CHIKO** (page 228), and the festive **Tortuga Caribbean Bar & Grille.**

Ambar ★★★½ • BALKAN • INEXPENSIVE
523 Eighth St. SE; ☎ 202-813-3039; ambarrestaurant.com

Reservations Recommended. **Metro** Eastern Market. **Wine selection** Good. **Open** *Lunch:* Monday–Friday, 11 a.m.–2:30 p.m. *Dinner:* Monday–Thursday, 4–10 p.m.; Friday, 4–11 p.m.; Saturday, 4:30–11 p.m.; Sunday, 4:30–10 p.m. *Brunch:* Saturday–Sunday, 10 a.m.–3:30 p.m. *Happy hour:* Monday–Friday, 4–7 p.m.

THE PREMISE This Serbian tapas joint serves dishes ranging from stuffed cabbage to Weiner schnitzel. The restaurant describes itself as the meeting of southeastern Europe and southeast D.C. The two-story restaurant's upper level is long and sleek, with wood accents that echo the name: *ambar* are barnlike corncribs of Serbia.

THE PAYOFF The wide-ranging menu echoes the many countries that meet in central Europe, including Greece, Turkey, Hungary, Austria, and a touch of France: kebabs, flatbreads, grilled calamari, hummus, mussels, grilled duck breast, veal stew, veal and vegetable soup, burgers, Parmesan-crusted sirloin, asparagus topped with a quail egg, and Brussels sprouts with bacon. Dishes may be small, but they are meticulously presented. The $49-per-person all-you-can-eat dinner and the $39 all-you-can-eat brunch options are a round-the-world voyage for the whole table if you're really hungry.

IF YOU LIKE THIS There is a second location in Ballston, and the neighborhood also has a Russian–Uzbek restaurant called **RusUz.**

Café Berlin ★★★ • GERMAN • MODERATE
322 Massachusetts Ave. NE; ☎ 202-543-7656; cafeberlin-dc.com

Reservations Accepted. **Metro** Union Station. **Wine selection** limited. **Open** *Lunch:* Monday–Friday, 11:30 a.m.–3 p.m. *Dinner:* Monday–Thursday, 3–10 p.m.; Friday, 3–11 p.m.; Saturday, 11:30 a.m.–11 p.m.; Sunday, 2–10 p.m. *Brunch:* Sunday, 11 a.m.–2 p.m.

THE PREMISE German restaurants aren't plentiful in Washington, D.C., so this is a standout. Located in a small row house just steps from the Capitol, this white-tablecloth establishment remains friendly and unfussy. Diners of German heritage swear the kitchen turns out authentically Deutsche fare, and the restaurant has been part of the neighborhood for more than 20 years. Expect hefty portions of quintessential dishes, and in good weather, head out to the Munich-style beer garden for a stein and soft pretzel, two to an order. The beer garden offers a regular rotation of German beers and ciders.

THE PAYOFF The menu is notable for the spaetzle, a crowd favorite, and the five traditional German sausages in the Wurstfeast. The Weiner schnitzel and sauerkraut also receive rave reviews. There are several small plates perfect for sharing, like the charcuterie boards and *kartoffel pfannkuchen* (potato pancakes). Brunch offers egg dishes as well as a traditional German breakfast of cold cuts, cheese, and pretzel rolls.

IF YOU LIKE THIS Down the street at Barracks Row is **The Brig Secret Beer Garden,** a German-style beer garden that is open year-round and welcomes your pup. Another festive German outpost is the **Biergarten Haus** on H Street Northeast. **Café Mozart** in Penn Quarter is an old-school German café and deli, with live oompah music.

Good Stuff Eatery ★★★ • AMERICAN DINER • INEXPENSIVE
303 Pennsylvania Ave. SE; ☎ 202-543-8222; goodstuffeatery.com

Reservations Recommended. **Metro** Capitol South or Eastern Market. **Wine selection** Very good. **Open** Daily, 11 a.m.–10 p.m.

THE PREMISE This was the first and most modest kitchen from *Top Chef* Spike Mendelsohn and his family, though since the founding of this original outpost, he now serves his handcrafted burgers, hand-cut fries, and hand-spun milkshakes as far as Saudi Arabia. The Mendelsohn family is serious about sourcing local, humanely raised and handled meats.

THE PAYOFF This is a manageable menu, where the burgers come topped with various cheeses, eggs, mushrooms, bacon, tomatoes, and so on. The burgers may be old-fashioned, but that old mustard-and-ketchup condiment bar now offers sriracha, mango, Old Bay, and chipotle mayo sauces to slather on your burger or dip your fries in. There are a few tributes: the version with applewood bacon, Roquefort cheese, horseradish mayo, and onion marmalade is called the Prez Obama, and the free-range turkey burger with caramelized onions and Swiss cheese on whole wheat honors Michelle Obama. There is also a cheese-stuffed portobello version; an Asian-flavored one with pickled daikon and Thai basil; and the option to go bunless and have any burger lettuce-wrapped instead. And it's really a bargain: even the double is only $9.95.

IF YOU LIKE THIS Good Stuff has other locations in Georgetown and Crystal City, Virginia. Located in Barracks Row, **Ted's Bulletin** (page 245) is a cheerful diner that also offers burgers, sandwiches, and boozy milkshakes. It's also somewhat more expensive. Vegetarians should sample the cauliflower steak with chimichurri sauce.

Rose's Luxury ★★★★½ • GLOBAL AMERICAN • VERY EXPENSIVE
717 Eighth St. SE; ☎ 202-580-8889; rosesluxury.com

Reservations Recommended. Same-day tables and advance reservations (for groups of 6–12) are booked exclusively online. **Metro** Eastern Market. **Wine selection** Good. **Open** Monday–Saturday, 5–10 p.m.; closed Sundays.

THE PREMISE Named the Best American Restaurant by *Bon Appétit* in 2014, Rose's Luxury began its life with 2-hour-plus lines that went around the block. Although the crowds have slowed down, there is still a line waiting at the door most nights (a portion of the tables are set aside for same-day and group reservations; see website for details). Chef Aaron Silverman, who grew up in suburban Maryland, worked for acclaimed chefs like David Chang and George Mendes before opening his own restaurant, which he named after his grandmother. The place is beloved for its clever dishes presented in unique crockery, and the narrow town house has a rustic look and an outdoor patio. The service is impeccable, warm, and welcoming, and the staff is deeply knowledgeable about the menu.

THE PAYOFF Rose's has mastered contemporary yet whimsical American fare, and it's hard to predict what will be on the menu, which is seasonally driven. Silverman is full of surprises, yet there are a few regular dishes to look for—lychee salad with pork sausage, habañero, and peanuts, and hand-shaped farfalle with honey and pecorino cheese. Other memorable dishes are the Tandoori-ish Chicken, and do save room for dessert.

IF YOU LIKE THIS If you're looking for an inventive, unforgettable dining experience, try to reserve a seating at Silverman's **Pineapple & Pearls,** with its playful nine-course ($325 per person) and five-course ($150 per person) tasting menus. It received five stars from *The Washington Post* critic, who rarely gives such honors.

H STREET CORRIDOR AND NOMA

WHILE THE H STREET NORTHEAST neighborhood is still more of a music-and-nightlife playground, it has recently expanded the number of good and quite varied restaurant options. East of Union Station, you can access H Street via the DC Streetcar. One of the first to open was

unofficial **TIP**
The bright-red **DC Streetcar** is a 2.2-mile line that runs along H Street from Union Station to Benning Road and, at this writing, is free to ride. The streetcar has eight stations on both sides of the street.

Granville Moore's, a Belgian gastropub whose mussels and *frites* helped owner/chef Teddy Folkman beat Bobby Flay in a throw down. Like other neighborhood dives, **Toki Underground** (next page) is hugely popular, especially with nightlife types, and is largely responsible for the ramen craze in Washington. Its broader-minded (Cambodian to Taiwanese) sibling, **Maketto,** is equally popular and slightly more expensive.

Enthusiasm for vegetarian fare is growing in D.C., and this neighborhood has some of its best. **Fare Well** and **Fancy Radish** cater to vegetarians and vegans but remain popular among all residents. **Ethiopic** (see below), at the west end of Fourth Street Northwest, is one of the top Ethiopian kitchens in the city and is appreciated for its rainbow of sautéed and spiced veggies and legumes. Nearby, **Sidamo Coffee and Tea** features Ethiopian-style beverages with bright floral tones, harvested from the country's wild arabica trees. **Sticky Rice** packs in fans of Pan-Asian, with rice and noodle bowls, some catering to vegan and gluten-free diners.

For a quick meal, check out **Farmbird,** a fast-casual restaurant that focuses on tender chicken with rice, and French baguettes with varied toppings and sauces. **Ben's Chili Bowl** is a Washington institution; the chili fries and half-smokes are served at the counter downstairs, while the upscale rooftop dining area features Southern-meets-Caribbean fare. **Thamee** is a hot newcomer.

Drinking is a popular sport in the H Street Corridor/Shaw neighborhood. Beer lovers, head to the **Biergarten Haus** for brats and brews on the heated patio or deck. The **H Street Country Club** has been around awhile and has three inviting floors to explore. Check out the taco-and-tequila minigolf, Skee-Ball, and shaded rooftop bar.

Ethiopic Restaurant ★★★ • ETHIOPIAN • INEXPENSIVE

401 H St. NE; ☎ 202-675-2066; ethiopicrestaurant.com

Reservations Suggested. **Metro** Not Metro accessible. **Wine selection** Good. **Open** Tuesday–Thursday, 5–10 p.m.; Friday–Sunday, noon–10 p.m.; closed Mondays.

THE PREMISE There are a lot of similar Ethiopian restaurants in this area, but perhaps none as charming or photo-friendly. With exposed brick, Federal-style windows, and calligraphy-covered columns, this is an upscale introduction to the varied cuisine you eat with your fingers (they'll provide a fork if you prefer). The ingredients are clearly high quality. Some sidewalk seating is available.

THE PAYOFF The menu will be generally familiar to fans of Ethiopian fare, but this one has attitude—that is, the kind of heat Ethiopians themselves go for. *Doro wat,* the chicken leg/hard-boiled egg dish that is the unofficial national dish, can be ordered mild or spicy; the *tibs* (boneless leg of lamb) is marinated until tender; and there is also a curried lamb, not just a sauced one, and chickpeas done as a spicy dumpling. The crunchy fried croaker is a treat, found in plentiful supply in the Chesapeake Bay, and there are plenty of veggie/vegan options. The injera is authentically teff-based.

IF YOU LIKE THIS Try **Zenebech** in Adams Morgan. A family-owned restaurant that some consider the best in town, it features a wide variety of traditional dishes with solicitous service.

Stable DC ★★½ • SWISS • MODERATE–EXPENSIVE
1324 H St. NE; ☎ 202-733-4604; stabledc.com

Reservations Recommended. **Metro** Union Station, plus streetcar. **Wine selection** Focused on absinthe, schnapps, and digestives. **Open** *Dinner:* Tuesday–Thursday, 5:30–10 p.m.; Friday–Saturday, 5:30–10:30 p.m. *Brunch:* Saturday–Sunday, 10:30 a.m.–2:30 p.m.

THE PREMISE Step into the rustic Stable DC, and you'll be transported to a cozy Alpine chalet in the hills of Gruyères. The owners feature authentic Swiss dishes using imported ingredients, especially cheeses from their homeland. Located on the patio in the rear of the restaurant is the Absinthe Bar, a setup that employs the traditional method of preparation—ice water dribbled over a sugar cube into a shot of absinthe—used for centuries. The owners are both internationally acclaimed chefs, and their enthusiasm for bringing this homey food to the American palate is demonstrated in the personal and friendly service.

THE PAYOFF The menu features cheese, and lots of it, served in a variety of ways, but most notably the traditional Swiss cheese fondue. A minimum of two diners are required to share this bubbling pot of deliciousness. For groups of four, opt for the raclette experience, which is popular among the après-ski set back in Switzerland. Raclette allows each guest to cook their own slices of pungent cheese, and then drip the melty molten mess onto salted boiled potatoes. Other standouts include the Veal Zurich Style paired with potato *rösti* and mushrooms, as well as *landjäger*, smoked Swiss salami with pickles and pearl onions.

IF YOU LIKE THIS **Café Berlin** (page 210) on Capitol Hill focuses on Swiss German dishes. **Café Mozart,** a Viennese restaurant in Penn Quarter, combines a deli/market and cozy bistro. Down the street from Stable is **Le Grenier,** which is heavier on French favorites but offers a similar rustic charm.

Toki Underground ★★½ • JAPANESE/CHINESE • INEXPENSIVE
1234 H St. NE; ☎ 202-388-3086; tokiunderground.com

Reservations Not accepted. **Metro** Union Station (15-minute walk). **Wine selection** Focused on sake and Asian beer. **Open** *Lunch:* Monday–Saturday, 11:30 a.m.–2:30 p.m. *Dinner:* Monday–Thursday, 5–10 p.m.; Friday–Saturday, 5 p.m.–midnight; closed Sundays. *Note:* This restaurant is not wheelchair accessible.

THE PREMISE The restaurant was D.C.'s first introduction to ramen and remains a favorite hot spot for its youthful vibe and crowded countertop eating: the "decor" consists of wind-up Taiwanese action figures, Japanese anime, paper lanterns in faux trees, graffiti-like swirls of paint, an antique pinball machine, and skateboards in all directions. Recognized with a Michelin Bib Gourmand designation in 2019, the menu is limited but close to perfection. Because all of the traffic is walk-up (in both senses—it's on the second floor) and it only seats about two dozen (on stools), the dinner line sometimes starts at 5, and the wait can be substantial.

THE PAYOFF It's a short menu—mostly dumplings (fried, pan-fried, or steamed) and bowls of ramen, along with a few specials (Korean-flavored barbecue) and pumped-up American desserts, such as snickerdoodles with pepper flakes or chocolate chip cookies with red miso icing. (The chef was born in Taipei but raised in Tokyo and then nearby Woodbridge, Virginia. He occasionally teaches a Cambodian cooking class.) Except for the vegetarian version, the ramen recipes all start with a 24-hour-simmered porky broth. Toki Underground has a good sake list, interesting Asian beers, and cocktails.

IF YOU LIKE THIS **Daikaya** (page 218), located in Penn Quarter, is another of Washington, D.C.'s best ramen joints. The lower level has ramen only, and the upper level features *izakaya* fare. **Jinya Ramen Bar,** a California chain, has multiple locations in the area, including 14th Street, North Bethesda, and Fairfax.

NATIONAL MALL AND THE WHITE HOUSE

THIS NEIGHBORHOOD IS OBVIOUSLY ON THE RADAR of the majority of visitors. Most want to see the White House and explore the monuments and memorials. For decades, this was a restaurant desert, but today nearly every corner of Washington has established a diverse profusion of restaurants, from fast food and tourist-friendly food courts to fast-casual, full-service casual, and fine-dining options.

The luxury hotels in particular offer some of D.C.'s best settings. We recommend **Café du Parc** and the **Round Robin Bar** in the Willard InterContinental Hotel; **POV Rooftop** (page 216) in the W Hotel; the Sofitel's **Opaline Bar & Brasserie**; The Hay-Adams's **Lafayette** and legendary **Off the Record** bar; and the St. Regis's lovely **Alhambra** and **St. Regis Bar.**

High-quality casual options include **District Taco, GCDC Grilled Cheese Bar** (next page), **Buredo, La Betty, Astro Doughnuts & Fried Chicken, &Pizza, Five Guys, Pret A Manger,** and **Fuel Pizza & Wings.**

 FOOD COURTS NEAR THE WHITE HOUSE: The Reagan Building Food Court Eatery is a pleasant escape from the heat or cold. On the Concourse Level are **Market to Market, Timgad Café,** and **Panera Bread.** On the Lower Level, you'll find well-liked vendors such as **California Tortilla** and **Quick Pita.** Stop there for breakfast, lunch, or early dinner Monday–Friday, 7 a.m.–7 p.m.; Saturday, 11 a.m.–6 p.m.; and Sunday (March 1–August 31 only), noon–5 p.m.; closed on major holidays. **Eat at National Place** has a food hall located inside the National Press Building, a block east of Metro Center station; pick up a hearty burger at **Five Guys** or a pizza at **A Slice of Italy Pizzeria,** or try **TaKorean Korean Taco Grill** for something out of the ordinary.

For elevated and memorable dining experiences, we think highly of **Lincoln, Founding Farmers, MXDC Cocina Mexicana, Georgia Brown's, The Bombay Club, Alta Strada, The Dabney, The Oval Room,** and **Old**

Ebbitt Grill (see below). If you're a music fan, see who's playing at **The Hamilton,** a centrally located restaurant and nightclub with gorgeous decor serving lunch, dinner, brunch, sushi, and late-night munchies.

GCDC Grilled Cheese Bar ★★★ • AMERICAN • MODERATE
1730 Pennsylvania Ave. NW; ☎ 202-393-4232; grilledcheesedc.com

Reservations Not necessary. **Metro** Farragut North or McPherson Square. **Wine selection** Limited. **Open** Saturday, 11 a.m.–6 p.m.; closed Sundays. *Lunch:* Monday–Friday, 11 a.m.–3 p.m. *Dinner:* Monday–Friday, 4–9 p.m. *Happy hour:* Monday–Friday, 4–6:30 p.m.

THE PREMISE What started as a fast-casual restaurant quickly expanded into a larger space with longer hours thanks to the popularity of its grilled cheese sandwiches and macaroni-and-cheese concoctions. The service is still relatively fast, and prices are reasonable. The location is just steps from the White House and the Renwick Gallery, and it attracts office workers as well as tourists, so expect to wait during the lunch rush. The sandwiches and sides are all prepared to order, with ingredients sourced by local vendors, and the menu has expanded to include gourmet cheese and meat boards, as well as craft cocktails. It's a welcoming escape after a busy day of touring.

THE PAYOFF The restaurant is famous for its spicy tomato soup and signature ooey-gooey grilled cheese sandwiches. Customize your sandwich or noodles with sauces, veggies, cheeses, and choice of bread (including gluten-free). The Loaded Tots and Poutine Tots (potato bites with brown gravy) garner rave reviews. In the evenings, the menu expands into shareable plates of restaurant favorites, as well as soups and salads. Local craft beers are on tap, along with luscious cocktails like the White House Sour and Watermelon Mojito.

IF YOU LIKE THIS **White House Deli** is nearby, serving American favorites during breakfast and lunch, but it's closed for dinner and on Sundays. Just a few blocks away on I Street, **Wicked Waffle** features made-to-order waffles with a variety of toppings, as well as soups and salads. **Bub and Pop's** is a family-owned Annapolis institution that opened its second location near Dupont Circle. It's revered for unique, handcrafted hoagies/submarine sandwiches accompanied by gourmet pickles.

Old Ebbitt Grill ★★★ • AMERICAN • MODERATE–EXPENSIVE
675 15th St. NW; ☎ 202-347-4800; ebbitt.com

Reservations Recommended. **Metro** Metro Center or McPherson Square. **Wine selection** Good. **Open** *Brunch:* Saturday–Sunday, 8:30 a.m.–4 p.m. *Breakfast:* Monday–Friday, 7:30–11 a.m. *Lunch:* Monday–Friday, 11 a.m.–5 p.m. *Dinner:* Monday–Friday, 5 p.m.–midnight; Saturday–Sunday, 4 p.m.–midnight. *Late night:* Daily, midnight–1 a.m.

THE PREMISE The Old Ebbitt Grill is a Washington landmark. The original, opened nearby in 1856, has a list of presidential patrons to equal any in Washington. It doesn't get a lot of food-trend buzz, but it doesn't need it. The mahogany main bar, white-linen-and-wood dining room, and classic oyster bar (around back off the atrium) are almost always humming with lawyers, lobbyists, politicos, and tourists. Don't miss the antique marble staircase or the carved-glass partitions showing the White House, Capitol, and Treasury buildings. All four bars have art and decor worth exploring. If you're planning to come around Cherry Blossom Festival, Fourth of July, inauguration, or other busy times, make reservations far in advance. It's a perfect place to dine when visiting the President's Park to view the National Christmas Tree.

THE PAYOFF The restaurant is part of the local Clyde's group, which is known for stellar service, consistency, and quality. The menu runs an all-American gamut but is heavy on local seafood, including Maryland crab cakes, blue crab linguine, Chesapeake Bay catfish, and Maryland Day Boat scallops. Clyde's burger is an institution. The oyster bar is lovely, and its oyster-centric wine list is first-rate. Even the late-night menu is lively, with Clyde's Chili and Oyster Stew.

IF YOU LIKE THIS The raw bar happy hours are another Clyde's tradition, and remarkable: half price every day 3–6 p.m. and after 11 p.m., and that includes the lobster and shrimp as well as shellfish. No doubt that deal has something to do with the restaurant's selling 20,000 oysters a week. **Clyde's Georgetown, Tower Oaks Lodge, Reston,** and **Gallery Place** locations also have extensive late-night options, and Gallery Place has oyster happy hours as well.

POV Rooftop ★★★½ • MODERN AMERICAN • MODERATE
515 15th St. NW; ☎ 202-661-2437; povrooftop.com

Reservations Online reservations only. **Metro** Farragut North or McPherson Square. **Wine selection** Very good. **Open** Sunday–Thursday, 11 a.m.–midnight; Friday–Saturday, 11 a.m.–2 a.m.

THE PREMISE I hate to write about my favorite places in D.C., but because you're my dear readers, I will share this insider intel. POV is a hotel bar where you'll enjoy unmatched views of the city. Located on the rooftop of the W Hotel, a block from the White House and the Renwick Gallery, POV functions as a scenic lunchtime or cocktail hour stop. Enjoy a sunset at one of its small tables, and prepare to swoon. From here, you'll have a panoramic view of the National Mall, Washington Monument, Jefferson Memorial, and even the top of the White House (no zoom lenses allowed). In summer, cool breezes blow from that height; in winter, they heat up the place. No one under age 21 is allowed in after 7 p.m., so if you're with teens, go for lunch or early dinner. It's not an appropriate restaurant for younger children.

THE PAYOFF POV's cocktail menu is named for D.C. trivia, and the bar snack plates are small but tasty, particularly the grilled artichoke dip. The restaurant serves up a robust POV Burger with double-beef patties, along with a lobster grilled cheese, Maryland crab cakes, and a vegetarian Impossible Burger.

IF YOU LIKE THIS **Crimson View** inside the Pod DC hotel is a new rooftop restaurant getting rave reviews. It's located across from the Chinatown/Penn Quarter Metro station, with vistas of D.C.'s colorful China Gate. **Top of the Gate** is a new rooftop bar at The Watergate Hotel that has a sublime view of the Potomac River and Virginia, although it's rather pricey. In winter, Top of the Gate erects clear-tented igloos with heaters, so you can enjoy these stellar views year-round. The Wharf has several rooftop outposts with sweeping views of the Potomac River—try **Waves, Officina** (page 205), or **Whiskey Charlie.**

PENN QUARTER, CHINATOWN, AND CONVENTION CENTER

PENN QUARTER IS A MIX of condo dwellers, tourists, business types, pretheater diners, and post-sports/concert drinkers. These restaurants are clustered around the Capital One Arena and around the neighborhood known as Chinatown (which has few Chinese restaurants, as most have decamped to the suburbs). The restaurants here are convenient to the National Mall and the Washington Convention Center.

unofficial **TIP**
The huge CityCenterDC has brought in New York stars Daniel Boulud (**DBGB**) and David Chang (**Momofuku/Milk Bar,** page 220); a (franchise) version of Miami's **Joe's Stone Crab**; and **Centrolina** (see below), an Italian market/café from Amy Brandwein.

Among the best restaurants in Penn Quarter are **China Chilcano, Jaleo** (page 220), **Oyamel** (page 221), and **Zaytinya** (page 221)—all under the watchful eye of Catalonian superchef José Andrés. All are family-friendly, especially during the day. **The Partisan** is the sandwich/charcuterie/café adjunct to Red Apron butcher shop. Other highly regarded, mostly casual options include **Baby Wale, Capitol City Brewing Company, City Tap House, Cuba Libre, Daikaya Ramen and Izakaya** (page 218), **Fiola** (page 218), **The Smith, Succotash,** and **Unconventional Diner.** Some of the best pizza in town is served at **All-Purpose Pizza** in what is now called the Shaw area (its Navy Yard location is profiled on page 207). For more upscale options, try **Brasserie Beck, Convivial** (page 218), and **RPM Italian.**

The area's popular chain restaurants include **Fogo de Chão Brazilian Steakhouse, Nando's Peri-Peri Chicken,** and **Rosa Mexicano.** When you want a quick pause from sightseeing, check out **Corner Bakery Cafe, District Taco, Luke's Lobster,** and **Potbelly Sandwich Shop.** In search of your favorite hot beverages? We recommend **Café Mozart, The Courtyard Café** at the National Portrait Gallery, and **Teaism.**

Among the more family-friendly, something-for-everyone eateries is **Hill Country Barbecue Market,** with Texan treats and live bands playing "rock and twang." Also popular with groups and those seeking generous portions is **Carmine's Italian Restaurant.** When they say family-style, they mean it; expect to take home leftovers for your hotel fridge.

Centrolina Mercato e Osteria ★★★★½ • ITALIAN • EXPENSIVE
974 Palmer Alley NW; ☎ 202-898-2426; centrolinadc.com

Reservations Recommended. **Metro** Penn Quarter or McPherson Square. **Wine selection** Very good. **Open** *Brunch:* Sunday, 11 a.m.–2:30 p.m. *Lunch:* Monday–Saturday, 11:30 a.m.–2:30 p.m. *Dinner:* Sunday–Thursday, 5–10 p.m.; Friday–Saturday, 5–10:30 p.m.

THE PREMISE Step into chef Amy Brandwein's gourmet Italian market, then find a seat at one of the cozy tables with views of the buzzy CityCenterDC complex, known for its sophisticated dining and shopping. Each plate comes out elegantly prepared and surprising in its near-complete perfection. Brandwein is known for reinventing Italian classics, and in 2018, *The Washington Post* ranked Centrolina one of the top three restaurants in D.C. The wine list focuses on Virginia wines, and the cocktail menu is imaginative and Italian-influenced.

THE PAYOFF Begin your day with the homemade granola or buckwheat pancakes with peanut butter and jelly, or stop in for pasta at lunch. Dinner is slightly more formal but maintains its friendly atmosphere while feeling posh. Highlights from the small menu include the arugula salad with its divine lemon vinaigrette and fresh grated Parmigiano. For pasta lovers who enjoy trying something new, the Stracci comes with homemade whole-wheat pasta and suckling pig ragù. The Grigliata takes advantage of the fresh seafood market, incorporating both shellfish and fresh fish to make a sultry seafood stew. At lunch, order the Burrata with fresh cherries and basil. Finish up your meal with anything created by the restaurant's brilliant pastry chef, Caitlin Dysart.

IF YOU LIKE THIS CityCenterDC has other exceptional restaurants (albeit on the expensive side) helmed by award-winning chefs, such as **DBGB Kitchen & Bar,** a French bistro by Daniel Boulud. **Estuary,** by Bryan and Michael Voltaggio, is located inside the Conrad Hotel and features dishes created by two *Top Chef* winners from Maryland who like to showcase ingredients from the Chesapeake Bay. Chef Edward Lee's menu at **Succotash** blends traditional Southern cuisine with Asian-influenced recipes.

Convivial ★★★★ • MODERN AMERICAN • EXPENSIVE

801 O St. NW; ☎ 202-525-2870; convivialdc.com

Reservations Recommended. **Metro** Mount Vernon Square. **Wine selection** Very good. **Open** *Lunch:* Monday–Friday, 11:30 a.m.–4:30 p.m.; Saturday–Sunday, 10:30 a.m.–2:30 p.m. *Dinner:* Sunday–Monday, 5–9 p.m.; Tuesday–Thursday, 5–10 p.m.; Friday–Saturday, 5–10:30 p.m. *Happy hour:* Sunday, 2:30–9 p.m.; Monday 5–9 p.m.; Tuesday–Thursday, 5–7 p.m. and 9–10 p.m.; Friday 5–7 p.m.; Saturday 2:30–7 p.m.

THE PREMISE This light-filled dining room with rustic wooden tables is unfussy and welcoming. Chef/owner Cedric Maupillier strolls through the dining room, welcoming diners (you'll often see members of Congress there) and making sure everyone is comfortable no matter what their status. Convivial has one of the best happy hours in town, where you can try nearly every dish for a substantial discount. The details and imaginative combinations are what make this a favorite of *Washington Post* food critic Tom Sietsema and of this author, who chose to spend her birthday there.

THE PAYOFF Blending French and American cuisine for inspiration, Maupillier plays with the dishes of his homeland in innovative ways. Don't miss the crispy fries made from chickpeas and served with harissa aioli, and the Poulet Rouge for two with all the fixin's. Ask about the five-course tasting menu with wine pairings.

IF YOU LIKE THIS Maupillier opened his first restaurant, **Mintwood Place,** in Adams Morgan, where it famously attracted President Barack Obama during his first term. It's also where local chefs hang out on their days off. The Mintwood menu is heavier on French cuisine, and the decor is pure bistro.

Daikaya Ramen and Izakaya ★★★★ • JAPANESE
• INEXPENSIVE–MODERATE

705 Sixth St. NW; ☎ 202-589-1600; daikaya.com

Reservations Not accepted downstairs; recommended upstairs. **Metro** Gallery Place/Chinatown or Dupont Circle. **Wine selection** Very good. **Open** *Ramen bar:*

Sunday–Thursday, 11 a.m.–10 p.m.; Friday–Saturday, 11 a.m.–11 p.m. Izakaya: *Brunch:* Sunday, 11 a.m.–3 p.m. *Lunch:* Monday–Friday, 11:30 a.m.–2 p.m. *Dinner:* Sunday–Thursday, 5–10 p.m.; Friday–Saturday, 5–11 p.m. *Happy hour:* Monday–Friday, 5–7 p.m.

THE PREMISE If you're looking for an authentic Japanese experience, check out Daikaya. The ramen bar on the ground level gets its shipment of noodles from Sapporo, Japan (you may see some drying on a rack). Upstairs is the *izakaya,* or Japanese pub, which turns out small plates. Two of Washington's true food stars are partners in this double-decker establishment—chef Daisuke Utagawa, whose Sushiko was among Washington's first great Japanese restaurants, and chef Katsuya Fukushima, who worked for years at José Andrés's groundbreaking Minibar. The decor helps transport you to a sake bar or ramen shop you might find in the alleyways of Kyoto.

THE PAYOFF Downstairs is the no-reservations ramen bar, where you can see the noodles boiling and the long-simmered broths (chicken, pork, beef, or vegan) prepared. Upstairs in the *izakaya,* nibbles include grilled eggplant, ginger-spiked turkey wings, grilled avocado, pork-stuffed rice balls, and an assortment of skewers.

IF YOU LIKE THIS You may not be able to get both cooking styles in one spot, but **Izakaya Seki** (page 233) is near the U Street/African American Civil War Memorial/Cardozo Metro, and for ramen, try **Bantam King** in Chinatown or **Toki Underground** (page 213) in the Atlas District.

Fiola ★★★★ • ITALIAN • VERY EXPENSIVE
601 Pennsylvania Ave. NW; ☎ 202-525-1402; fioladc.com

Reservations Highly recommended. **Metro** Archives/Navy Memorial/Penn Quarter or Gallery Place/Chinatown. **Wine selection** Very good. **Open** *Dinner:* Monday–Thursday, 5–9 p.m.; Friday–Saturday, 5–9:30 p.m.

THE PREMISE Though he's worked all over the world, Fabio Trabocchi is considered a hometown chef in Washington. Fiola is one of the area's best Italian restaurants (along with his others, such as Sfoglina, page 238), and it has a volume level you can actually converse over. The decor is like a Frank Lloyd Wright concoction—part rustic with leather banquettes and massive cut-glass chandeliers. The menu follows suit with a house-made spaghetti with sea urchin, mussels, and scallops that's elegant and intoxicating.

THE PAYOFF Think big and assured: lobster-stuffed ravioli in a gingery sauce; carpaccio and tartare ("Italian sushi"); tortellini stuffed with lamb belly and served with sweetbreads and fennel confit; roast veal rib eye sauced with sweetbreads and osso buco; and prosciutto-wrapped veal chop. The selection of caviar is the best in town. For a special occasion, spring for one of the tasting menus: the $220-per-person Fabio Grand Tasting Menu (add $180 for wine pairings), the Liguria Grand Tasting Menu for $155 (add $125 for wine pairings), or the five-course tasting menu for $125.

IF YOU LIKE THIS The Trabocchis put their infinite talents into fine Italian cooking and sumptuous, inspiring decor, but they also ensure that every diner feels like a treasured guest. Their restaurant empire includes **Del Mar** at The Wharf (page 204); **Fiola Mare** at Georgetown's Washington Harbour (page 225); and three locations of **Sfoglina** in Rosslyn, Penn Quarter, and Van Ness (page 238).

Jaleo ★★★½ • SPANISH • MODERATE
480 Seventh St. NW; ☎ 202-628-7949; jaleo.com

Reservations Recommended, although walk-ins are given full respect. **Metro** Archives/ Navy Memorial/Penn Quarter. **Wine selection** Good. **Open** Sunday, 10 a.m.–10 p.m.; Monday, 11 a.m.–10 p.m.; Tuesday–Thursday, 11 a.m.–11 p.m.; Friday, 11 a.m.–midnight; Saturday, 10 a.m.–midnight.

THE PREMISE This fine tapas restaurant with several locations in the D.C. area from chef José Andrés is a lot like Andrés himself: simultaneously faithful and irreverent. (The cocktail and wine menus come on an iPad, just for a start.) A renovation replaced the downtown restaurant's signature John Singer Sargent mural of a gypsy tango with a painting of *Footloose*-like dancing feet (and a Foosball table), chicken fritters are served in a Cinderella–meets–Michael Jordan glass sneaker, and gazpacho is served as a sauce from which tomatoes and bread emerge like the rocks of a Zen garden. The Crystal City, Virginia, branch, on the other hand, has a much more aristocratic feel, with its gold-stenciled purple wallpaper and Joan Miró–like swirls. Though the menus are similar, small distinctions reflect the locations and patrons: Downtown has a pretheater menu, Downtown and Bethesda have a three-course express lunch menu, and Crystal City's Sunday brunch is all-you-can-eat family-style paella.

THE PAYOFF Tapas change frequently, but among recent choices are grilled sausages over white beans, named for the late senator and fan Daniel Patrick Moynihan; oysters gin and tonic; a sort of sea urchin crostini; five types of paella, including a porcini–veggie version, a squid ink *fideuà,* and a soupy lobster risotto; rabbit confit with apricot puree; grilled quail; black-footed *ibérico* pork sliders; four-cheese grilled sandwiches with honey; "wrinkled" potatoes with red and green mojo sauces; and the crispy-thin *pan con tomate* that is closer to flatbread than crostini. They may not be called charcuterie and cheese boards, but varieties of fine *ibérico* hams, sausages, and cheeses are a strong presence, both as stars and supporting characters. Nevertheless, vegetarians could spend a whole day here. Daily specials and particularly seasonal rarities are extremely good bets.

IF YOU LIKE THIS If you like the idea of duck, achiote-roasted pork, or beef-tongue tacos, head to **El Centro D.F.,** with locations on 14th Street and in Georgetown. **Barcelona Wine Bar** (page 227), in the U Street Corridor, has an extensive selection of tapas.

Momofuku CCDC ★★★½ • ASIAN FUSION • MODERATE
1090 I St. NW; ☎ 202-602-1832; ccdc.momofuku.com

Reservations Recommended. **Metro** McPherson Square or Penn Quarter. **Wine selection** Good. **Open** *Lunch:* Monday–Friday, 11:30 a.m.–3 p.m. *Dinner:* Sunday–Wednesday, 5–10 p.m.; Thursday–Saturday, 5–11 p.m. *Brunch:* Sunday, 11 a.m.–3 p.m. (last seating at 2:30 p.m.) *Happy hour:* Monday–Friday, 5–7 p.m.

THE PREMISE Vintage rock music and attentive service help maintain the high-energy atmosphere at David Chang's D.C. outpost of Momofuku in the stylish CityCenterDC complex. It might be hard to converse here, but you won't mind—you'll be concentrating on the multifaceted zestiness of the ramen, *bao* buns, banh mi, dumplings, and tangy vegetable salads. The space is modern, with communal-style tables and floor-to-ceiling windows overlooking an urban park (individual tables are available for small parties). The restaurant is attached to Milk Bar, a bakery (with a second location in The Wharf) that features sugary confections; it's the perfect way to conclude a very satisfying meal.

THE PAYOFF Returning to his native Maryland after three years at The Progress in San Francisco, chef Tae Strain incorporates regional ingredients into his Asian-fusion dishes. His family-style meals—the chicken with grilled lemons and the steak *ssäm*—are perfect for groups. Try the spicy cucumbers for starters, along with the shrimp-and-pork dumplings, and don't miss the Crack Pie for dessert.

IF YOU LIKE THIS **Spoken English,** inside the lobby of the Line DC hotel in Adams Morgan, is a small boutique restaurant by D.C. chef Erik Bruner-Yang. The two communal tables limit the guest list, but it's worth trying to score a table for the shareable whole duck with all the fixin's. If you're looking for outstanding ramen, try **Daikaya** in Penn Quarter (page 218).

Oyamel ★★★½ • MEXICAN • MODERATE
401 Seventh St. NW; ☎ 202-628-1005; oyamel.com

Reservations Accepted. **Metro** Archives/Navy Memorial/Penn Quarter or Gallery Place/Chinatown. **Wine selection** Good. **Open** *Brunch:* Saturday-Sunday, 11 a.m.-2:30 p.m. *Dinner:* Sunday-Wednesday, 11 a.m.-midnight; Thursday-Saturday, 11 a.m.-2 a.m.

THE PREMISE *Oyamel* refers to a kind of tree that is the destination of monarch butterflies that annually migrate to Mexico, hence the fabulous mobile of a butterfly flurry (look for the Day of the Dead butterfly, representing the day when the monarchs generally arrive in Mexico). While Oyamel accepts reservations, it holds aside plenty of tables for walk-ins. It is particularly popular with kids for its salsa and chips (free), tangy guacamole made table-side, and fries in mole.

THE PAYOFF Focusing on Mexican street food, the menu features standout dishes like hanger steak and eggs with refried beans and salsa *verde* on a house-made corn tortilla; local pork spareribs; tacos served in fresh corn tortillas filled with pork belly, chilies, and pineapple; confit of suckling pig; turkey leg confit blanketed with an almost Middle Eastern pecan, almond, and sesame mole; and belly chicharróns. Vegetarians and vegans have plenty of options, including seasonal veggie mole; plantain and squash fritters stuffed with black beans; and a sort of Swiss chard, hazelnut, and dried-fruit pilaf. In addition to good wine, beer, and tequila lists, Oyamel serves a mean margarita. The lunch special includes two appetizers and a taco (or one appetizer and a sweet) for $20—in this case, the little bites range from spicy cactus paddles to mahi-mahi ceviche with avocado and olives.

IF YOU LIKE THIS While each has a different take on small plates, the Mediterranean **Zaytinya** (see below), Spanish **Jaleo** (previous page), and Chinese-Peruvian **China Chilcano** are all within eyeshot.

Zaytinya ★★★½ • GREEK/MIDDLE EASTERN • MODERATE
701 Ninth St. NW; ☎ 202-638-0800; zaytinya.com

Reservations Available. **Metro** Gallery Place/Chinatown or Metro Center. **Wine selection** Very good. **Open** Sunday-Monday, 11:30 a.m.-10 p.m.; Tuesday-Thursday, 11:30 a.m.-11 p.m.; Friday-Saturday, 11:30 a.m.-midnight.

THE PREMISE　Not Middle Eastern in the usual sense, or in its looks, Zaytinya—which means "olive oil" in Turkish—is specifically Eastern Mediterranean. This is a showpiece: a big, high, and airy minimalist room—white and angular with a soaring atrium-style ceiling; cut-through shelving walls stocked with lit candles; a long (and very busy) bar; half-hidden dining nooks and niches; a fireplace; and a mezzanine overlooking the Manhattan-style table in the center of the main dining room. It's loud, it's lively, and it's delicious. After all, it's another José Andrés production.

THE PAYOFF　The endless hot-from-the-oven pita, as inflated as a balloon, is to most pita bread as a soufflé is to scrambled eggs. And you don't have to choose just one of the half-dozen dips—you can order a combo. The menu changes frequently, but among indicative dishes are lamb mini-meatballs with cinnamon oil and dried fruit; potato-crusted snails; prawns in smoked tomato sauce; giant favas with tomatoes and red onions; traditional pressed mullet caviar; squid and octopus in a variety of treatments; braised lamb shanks; imported Turkish pastrami; Feta-and-tomato-stuffed quail; crab cakes with shaved fennel; flaming cheese; fried eggplant; veal cheeks with chanterelle puree; grilled pork and orange-rind sausage; braised rabbit with lentils; and fried mussels with pistachios. For vegetarians and vegans, this is a throwback Garden of Eden, with dozens of options.

IF YOU LIKE THIS　Appearing on multiple best-of restaurant lists in 2018, **Maydan** offers Middle Eastern delicacies grilled to perfection. If you're looking for casual but festive, try **Mama Ayesha's,** near the Woodley Park Metro, whose owner cooked for the Syrian Embassy.

FOGGY BOTTOM

WEST OF THE WHITE HOUSE IS FOGGY BOTTOM. Though it's not a major restaurant area in itself, there are enough eateries to supply folks from the State Department, the World Bank, George Washington University, and the Kennedy Center. **Kaz Sushi Bistro** (see below) is popular for visitors, as is **Founding Farmers,** featuring heartland fare and a breakfast hefty enough to fill you for a day of sightseeing. **Ris** offers seasonally driven American fare from acclaimed local chef Ris Lacoste. **Bindaas,** with a second location in Cleveland Park (page 236), serves contemporary versions of Indian street food.

The perfect preshow meal can be found at the subdued and sophisticated **Roof Terrace Restaurant** atop the Kennedy Center. For the ultimate fine French dining, book a table at **Marcel's** (next page). For dramatic ambience, consider **Kingbird** in The Watergate Hotel; it specializes in Mediterranean cuisine and craft cocktails.

For lunch, look to **District Commons** for flatbreads, soups, and salads. Fast-casual faves catering to college students and office workers include **GRK Fresh Greek** and **Beefsteak,** the place to eat your veggies. Find quick and personalized burgers at **Burger Tap & Shake.** Stop for buttery baked goods at **Paul,** a Parisian bakery with soups and salads.

Kaz Sushi Bistro ★★★½ • JAPANESE • MODERATE–EXPENSIVE
1915 I St. NW; ☎ 202-530-5500; kazsushibistro.com

Reservations Recommended. **Metro** Farragut West or Farragut North. **Wine selection** Fair. **Open** Closed Sundays. *Lunch:* Monday–Friday, 11:30 a.m.–2 p.m. *Dinner:* Monday–Saturday, 5:30–10 p.m. *Note:* This restaurant is not wheelchair accessible.

THE PREMISE Chef/owner Kaz Okochi earned many of his fans while working at **Sushiko** (page 241), where he created many of what he calls his original small dishes, both cold and hot. The quality of the more traditional sushi is first-rate, of course, but you can get good sushi in a number of places; instead, order the eight-course Tasting Omakase, the chef's choice ($90–$120), or a plate-at-a-time tasting menu. Although the dining room is calm and attractive, with a mini–fountain wall in front, it's more fun to sit at the smallish sushi bar in the rear. The restaurant has impressive lunch specials in the form of lavish bento boxes.

THE PAYOFF Though he doesn't advertise his hot dishes as *izakaya* fare, Kaz (who prefers to go by his first name) offers a variety of meat-and-veggie dishes that extend beyond the usual sushi-bar fare: sake-poached scallops, lobster salad, glazed and grilled baby octopus, spicy broiled green mussels, foie gras infused with plum wine, Japanese-style duck confit in miso, or torched salmon. When fugu, the famous blowfish, is in season, Kaz (one of the few sushi chefs in Washington certified to handle the potentially lethal fish) makes traditional multicourse fugu meals (about $150). Look for the Okonomi Yaki, a customized Japanese pancake, and Green Tea–Tequila Ice Cream for dessert.

IF YOU LIKE THIS Other Japanese restaurants in the Foggy Bottom neighborhood are **Toryumon Japanese House,** serving steaming bowls of ramen, sushi, and *bao* buns, and a new fast-casual option, **Kin's Sushi,** with sushi rolls named for American presidents.

Marcel's ★★★★ • FRENCH-BELGIAN • VERY EXPENSIVE
2401 Pennsylvania Ave. NW; ☎ 202-296-1166; marcelsdc.com

Reservations Highly recommended. **Metro** Foggy Bottom/GWU. **Wine selection** Very good. **Open** *Dinner:* Monday–Thursday, 4:30–10 p.m.; Friday–Saturday, 4:30–11 p.m.; Sunday, 4:30–9:30 p.m.

THE PREMISE This cool ultralounge-look retreat is a showplace for unapologetically classic French fare with a Belgian accent. The long marble bar exudes sleek elegance, and the partially exposed (and elevated) kitchen is not as intrusive as elsewhere. Chef/owner Robert Wiedmaier gets bigger and more Belgian all the time, turning out confits, root vegetables (including the various endives, of course), artichokes, and flavorful but not heavy sausages. But there is an element of playfulness—like matching pan-seared salmon with black-eyed peas and bacon. Wiedmaier has several restaurants, but this was the first, and most consider it his best. Another draw is the three-course pretheater menu for $68 per person (beverages, gratuity, and tax not included) 4:30–6:30 p.m. You can have two courses early, take the restaurant's complimentary limo to the Kennedy Center for a show, and then return in the limo for dessert. Other prix fixe menus range from $70 for the four-course vegetarian menu to $170 for seven courses, but the entire table does not have to participate. And no worries—all dishes can be ordered à la carte as well.

THE PAYOFF The boudin *blanc* is a signature dish and not to be missed, and so are game dishes in season, such as a sort of venison Wellington with loin and foie gras wrapped in phyllo with black trumpet mushrooms, pheasant and foie gras tortellini with chanterelles, or roulade of rabbit stuffed with sausage over caramelized cabbage. Seafood fans, look for pesto-marinated sardines bruschetta, squid-ink tagliatelle with escargots and crispy sweetbreads, cold-smoked cod with blood orange and paprika croutons, and seared scallops with butternut squash and applewood bacon hash.

IF YOU LIKE THIS In Old Town Alexandria's Kimpton Lorien Hotel, Wiedmaier's **Brabo** has a menu of similar swagger.

GEORGETOWN AND WEST END

THE SPELLBINDING **Fiola Mare** (next page) in Washington Harbour has river views as impressive as its food. **Sequoia,** which is also part of the Harbour development, has similar views and is less expensive. In between is **Farmers Fishers Bakers,** an offshoot of **Founding Farmers** in Foggy Bottom, which emphasizes seasonal and sustainable surf, turf, tacos, pizza, and "farmers market brunch" on weekends.

With a canal and footpath view above the river, chef Johnny Spero's **Reverie** is a fine dining restaurant with a variety of price points. Reverie earns four-star reviews for its creative starters and craft cocktails. **Chez Billy Sud** is a calmly handsome Southern French bistro that ranks in the *Washingtonian*'s top 100 restaurants every year. **Pizzeria Paradiso** in Georgetown has gourmet pies and a *birreria*—a cellar full of brews. **Leopold's Kafe** is a European-style cafeteria serving sweet and savory pastries.

Cafe Milano's Italian food is a little big on price but even bigger on famous face–watching. Keep an eye out for the glitterati, if you can get in. Every list of special-event romantic dining spots includes **1789,** a lovely and surprisingly quiet Federal town house with an intimate bar and fireplaces (but no wheelchair access). **Martin's Tavern,** where you can see the booth where then-Senator John F. Kennedy proposed to Jacqueline Bouvier, has been championing comfort food for more than 80 years and offers its substantial brunch every day. **Clyde's,** on M Street, is the chain's original location and remains a family favorite. **Il Canale** is an Italian restaurant cooking up brick-oven pizza in a cozy dining room. For dessert, stop in **Ladurée,** a posh new bakery with stellar macarons.

Up the Wisconsin Avenue hill toward Glover Park are **Cafe Divan,** serving Turkish cuisine, and the classic French **Bistrot Lepic & Wine Bar,** in a pretty two-story town house.

The fine dining scene in the West End caters to the expense-account set and well-heeled visitors. The neighborhood has a surplus of luxury hotels, each with its own fine dining venues. **Blue Duck Tavern** is a farm-to-table stunner with handcrafted furnishings inside the Park Hyatt; the sumptuous high tea is a standout. The Westin's rustic but high-end **Boveda** bills itself as a Latin speakeasy.

Rasika West End (page 226) is a Washington, D.C., foodie haven, with its modern and sophisticated take on Indian cuisine. The sleek Japanese/Peruvian **Nobu Washington D.C.** is a luxurious escape with a fashionable bar. **The Caucus Room Brasserie** has been a staple in the West End neighborhood for years; the menu is focused on steak and seafood. For heaping goblets of coffee and light French fare, visit **Le Pain Quotidien.** If you're in the mood for brunch, check out **Bread & Chocolate.**

America Eats Tavern ★★★ • CLASSIC AMERICAN • MODERATE

3139 M St. NW; ☎ 202-450-6862; americaeatstavern.com

Reservations Suggested. **Metro** Foggy Bottom/GWU. **Wine selection** House. **Open** *Lunch:* Friday-Sunday, 10 a.m.–4 p.m. *Dinner:* Sunday-Monday, 4-10 p.m.; Tuesday-Thursday, 4-11 p.m.; Friday-Saturday, 4 p.m.–midnight. *Social hour:* Monday-Friday, 5-7 p.m.

THE PREMISE This innovative restaurant grew from chef José Andrés's love for his adoptive nation. In coordination with the National Archives, Andrés collected recipes that stretch across American history and made them his own. The menu notes where the dish is from and what year it represents. You'll find iconic dishes like hush puppies from New Orleans, sloppy joe sliders from Iowa, vermicelli mac and cheese from Philadelphia, and cheese grits from Wisconsin. The decor is nostalgic Americana. If you're out touring the area, pop in for social hour. America Eats hosts live music every Wednesday night and has an expansive patio for outdoor dining.

THE PAYOFF The menu takes many of its recipes from the heartland, but you'll have options from sea to shining sea as well. For the East Coast experience, Andrés offers lobster rolls and Chesapeake crab cakes. Try the Low Country Hopping John or a grilled pimento cheese sandwich from the South. Andrés has focused recently on barbecue, with versions from St. Louis to Kansas to Amish Country in Pennsylvania (glazed chicken with house sauce and creamy coleslaw). He's a master with vegetables as well, so don't miss the parsnips and carrots or the cauliflower casserole. Find room for dessert, or share a warm chocolate cookie pie with vanilla ice cream and macerated berries (recipe courtesy of Andrés's daughter).

IF YOU LIKE THIS Andrés's restaurants are some of the most prized in D.C. His original tapas at **Jaleo** (page 220) are still some of the best in town. Everyone adores his Greek meze at **Zaytinya** (page 221), and **Oyamel** (page 221) in Penn Quarter was the first to feature authentic Mexican dishes beyond tacos and burritos.

Fiola Mare ★★★★★ • ITALIAN SEAFOOD • VERY EXPENSIVE

3050 K St. NW; ☎ 202-525-1402; fiolamaredc.com

Reservations Strongly recommended. **Metro** Foggy Bottom/GWU. **Wine selection** Very good. **Open** *Lunch:* Tuesday-Friday, 11:30 a.m.-2:30 p.m. *Dinner:* Sunday, 5-10 p.m.; Monday-Thursday, 5-10 p.m.; Friday-Saturday, 5-10:30 p.m. *Brunch:* Saturday, 11:30 a.m.-2:30 p.m.; Sunday, 11 a.m.-2:30 p.m. *Happy hour:* Monday-Friday, 4-7 p.m. and Sunday-Thursday, 9-10 p.m.

THE PREMISE This is a $5 million blockbuster, both visually and culinarily. The huge walls of glass and natty nautical stripes make it look like a yacht from some angles and a gigantic fish tank from others. The main bar has a fabulous view of the river where the sun sets behind historic Key Bridge, which extends from Georgetown to Arlington. Though it passes as a special occasion spot (and is seriously large), it's busy enough at all times to suggest advance planning.

THE PAYOFF Co-owner Fabio Trabocchi's father is from the Marches region of Italy, along the coast east of Tuscany, and *fiola* means something like "faithful one" or "sweetheart." Seafood runs from raw (crudo, tartare, carpaccio, sashimi) to seared skate wing to olive oil–poached sea bream with mussels and clams to whole fish carved table-side to mixed grills. And it's not scant fare: if Ariel had ever eaten "under the sea"—lobster, branzino, sea urchin, langoustines, scallops, mussels, *and* foie gras and *maitake* mushrooms—she would never have been able to rise to the surface. Fortunately, there is a Maria Menu with healthier options here as well. A few signature dishes from Fiola have been carried over, such as the lobster ravioli and Wagyu beef (not everyone's a pescatarian), but they're almost concessions to mixed parties.

IF YOU LIKE THIS The beautiful **Bistrot Lepic & Wine Bar** is another swanky fine dining experience in Georgetown. Expand your Trabocchi experiences by dining at **Del Mar** (page 204) at The Wharf or **Sfoglina** (page 238) in the Van Ness neighborhood.

Rasika West End ★★★ • INDIAN • EXPENSIVE

1190 New Hampshire Ave. NW; ☎ 202-466-2500; rasikarestaurant.com/westend

Reservations Recommended. **Metro** Foggy Bottom/GWU and Dupont Circle. **Wine selection** Good. **Open** *Lunch:* Monday–Friday, 11:30 a.m.-2:30 p.m. *Dinner:* Sunday, 5-10 p.m.; Monday–Thursday, 5:30-10:30 p.m.; Friday–Saturday, 5-11 p.m. *Brunch:* Sunday, 11 a.m.-2:30 p.m.

THE PREMISE Chef Vikram Sunderam has taken the concept of Indian fare to new heights and has established Rasika West End as one of Washington's best restaurants. In 2015 Sunderam won the James Beard Foundation's Best Chef Mid-Atlantic Award and elevated the common perception of Indian food from buffet fare to a fine dining experience. The variety of seating areas—a lounge, tables near the exposed kitchen, a communal table, and smaller private areas—and the rich spice colors (cinnabar red, paprika, saffron gold, and twinkling glass) give a nod to this modern Indian restaurant's eclectic take on classic ingredients.

THE PAYOFF The menu is divided into *tawa* (griddle) dishes; *sigri* (barbecue) dishes, more like sautéed or stir-fried; and entrées, which include the curries, tandoori dishes, and stews (plus superb breads, savories, and sides). These go beyond the usual offerings to include venison chop, duck, lamb with red chilies or caramelized onions and tomatoes, and Indonesian-hot lobster *peri-peri.* Vegetarian options, which can be ordered in half portions as side dishes, are very good, especially the baby eggplant sauté, mushrooms with peas and cashews, okra with dry mango powder, and cauliflower and green peas with ginger and cumin. Even the chutneys are fresh (in both senses): eggplant ginger, tomato–golden raisin, and the more familiar mango.

IF YOU LIKE THIS **Rasika** in Penn Quarter has a similar menu. The same owner operates Farragut Square's elegant **Bombay Club**—a favorite hangout for

D.C. power brokers. It was known as one of Bill Clinton's favorite restaurants while he was president.

DUPONT CIRCLE AND LOGAN CIRCLE

DUPONT CIRCLE WAS ONCE KNOWN as the best restaurant neighborhood in D.C., but in the last decade, the U Street Corridor stole its thunder. Today, Dupont Circle has plenty of fast-casual restaurants and a few very high-end places like **Komi,** Johnny Monis's fixed-price Greek feast, and his equally praised Northern Thai **Little Serow**—also with a tasting menu only. For a special night out under the stars, consider **Iron Gate** (page 231), a romantic restaurant where guests can dine alfresco year-round on a twinkly patio; the still impressive **Obelisk,** with its rustic Italian multicourse tasting menu; and the special-occasion Japanese bistro found at **Sushi Taro.** The neighborhood's trendsetting **Pizza Paradiso** was the first "gourmet" pizzeria in town and is still a local favorite.

Hank's Oyster Bar (page 230) has four locations, including Dupont Circle, where the menu focuses on New England favorites like lobster rolls and clam chowder, as well as mid-Atlantic classics. **Anju** is a new Korean gastropub wowing critics. **Ankara** is a cheerful place for lunch and happy hour on the patio; it's a fun spot for people-watching. Try its *pide* (Turkish pizza) and kebabs. **The Palm** remains a bipartisan hangout, where politicos, CEOs, and media folks go for a premier cut of steaks and the whole Maine lobster. **The Riggsby** (page 231), inside the Carlyle Hotel, is a stylish fine dining restaurant with intimate leather booths. Dupont Circle has an array of high-quality fast-casual restaurants, such as **Beefsteak, BGR The Burger Joint, Bibibop Asian Grill, Bub and Pop's** handcrafted sandwiches, **CHIKO** (page 228), **Philz Coffee, Surfside, Sweetgreen, Tiki Taco, Yafa Grille,** and **Zorba's Café.**

Just a few blocks east is Logan Circle, which serves the growing nightlife district at P and 14th Streets. Among the top names there are **Estadio** (page 230); the stylish gastropub **Birch & Barley/ChurchKey** (page 228); **The Pig,** a pork-centric eatery; **Barcelona Wine Bar** (see below); **Le Diplomate** (page 229); **Pearl Dive Oyster Palace;** and **Slipstream,** a coffee and cocktail bar. Pizza connoisseurs will rejoice in the attentive preparation and gourmet ingredients found at the Tuscan-influenced **Ghibellina** and the rustic-chic **Etto.** Both are lauded for their wine lists, charcuterie, and cocktails.

Barcelona Wine Bar ★★★½ • SPANISH • MODERATE-EXPENSIVE

1622 14th St. NW; ☎ 202-588-5500; barcelonawinebar.com

Reservations Recommended. **Metro** Dupont Circle and U Street Cardozo. **Wine selection** Very good. **Open** *Dinner:* Monday–Wednesday, 4 p.m.–late; Thursday–Friday, 2 p.m.–late; Saturday–Sunday, 3 p.m.–late. *Brunch:* Saturday–Sunday, noon–3 p.m.

THE PREMISE This is the place for groups to emulate the brilliant Spanish and South American habit of drinking wine and sampling small plates late into the night. It's a favorite among millennials but welcomes anyone who loves Latin American and Spanish delicacies. In good weather, enjoy the rustic patio with pretty street views. The massive floor-to-ceiling windows bring the outside in throughout the year, and the long marble bar is a fun place to watch bartenders mix up fruity sangria.

THE PAYOFF This restaurant features traditional Spanish dishes and tapas like Serrano ham and duck eggs over fried potatoes; spiced beef empanadas; and *parrillada,* an overflowing plate of gaucho sausage, New York strip steak, grilled chicken, and pork chops (for two or more to share). Most notable are the taste and gorgeous presentation of its signature paella dishes. The menu changes by season, but save room for dessert if churros with fudge sauce are on the menu.

IF YOU LIKE THIS Two other Barcelona Wine Bar locations are in the area—one in Reston, Virginia, and one in Cathedral Heights (Northwest D.C.). You will find another superb Spanish experience at **Jaleo** (page 220), a collection of restaurants in D.C. and Maryland owned by chef José Andrés featuring Spanish tapas, as well as **Toro Toro,** a Latin American restaurant near the White House with a rowdy happy-hour crowd and romantic decor.

Birch & Barley ★★★½
• **MODERN AMERICAN** • **MODERATE-EXPENSIVE**
1337 14th St. NW; ☎ 202-567-2576; birchandbarley.com

Reservations Recommended. **Metro** Dupont Circle, Mount Vernon Square, or Shaw/Howard University. **Wine selection** Good. **Open** Closed Mondays. *Dinner:* Sunday, 5:30–9 p.m.; Tuesday–Thursday, 5:30–10 p.m.; Friday–Saturday, 5:30–11 p.m. *Brunch:* Sunday, 11 a.m.–3 p.m.; Saturday, 11:30 a.m.–3 p.m.

THE PREMISE This is the first of its kind, and a decade later it remains one of the city's best gastropubs, with a beer list that tops 555 (with correctly designed glassware to match). The display of copper draft lines behind the bar is nicknamed the pipe organ, and the historic digs attract beer aficionados who enjoy rubbing shoulders with like-minded enthusiasts. The more informal upstairs bar, ChurchKey, has a younger, clubbier, and louder crowd. The menu is shorter, but the beer list is the same.

THE PAYOFF Beer Director Greg Engert of the Neighborhood Restaurant Group is passionate about craft beer; *Food & Wine* has named him as a top beer sommelier. He's put together a daunting selection of craft beers, and chef Bill Williamson's beer-centric food is the perfect accompaniment. Some of the winners here are the fresh pretzels, flatbreads, and pasta. Also worth a try: house-brined corned beef hash, house-made charcuterie, fried chicken and waffles, rabbit ragout, and a brat burger with beer-braised kraut. Brunch features two cocktails for $12, bottomless coffee or tea, fresh oysters, and avocado toast with poached eggs in a bed of tangy yogurt.

IF YOU LIKE THIS If you're more into wine than beer, check out nearby **Cork,** which offers dozens of wines by the glass and a mix of small and shareable midsize plates. **Bluejacket** (page 207), Birch & Barley's sister brewery in Navy Yard, is packed seven days a week, especially around Nationals games.

CHIKO ★★★ • KOREAN/CHINESE • INEXPENSIVE
2029 P St. NW; ☎ 202-331-3040; chikodc.com

Reservations First come, first served, except for the Kitchen Counter. **Metro** Dupont Circle. **Wine selection** None. **Open** Sunday–Thursday, 11 a.m.–10 p.m.; Saturday–Sunday, 11 a.m.–11 p.m. *Note:* This restaurant is not wheelchair accessible.

THE PREMISE Three of D.C.'s most innovative chefs—Scott Drewno, Danny Lee, and Drew Kim—created The Fried Rice Collective. From this was born CHIKO, which blends traditional Chinese and Korean flavors for a fancy fast-casual restaurant with an optional tasting menu. The four-seat Kitchen Counter experience at 6 or 8:30 p.m. is $55 per person (excluding tax, tip, and beverages) and gives you a memorable view of the cooks in action as well as a taste of the celebrated menu, which includes snacks, bowls, and a solo dessert called Sesame Custard. Check out the CHIKO After Dark series, where guest chefs prepare a themed menu in the kitchen. Try to make a reservation (though walk-ins are welcome) for the 9:30 p.m. show.

THE PAYOFF There's a lot to love on this menu, with the pork and kimchi pot stickers getting raves. Enjoy dipping the diced shrimp into the fiery Korean XO sauce. The chef serves ingredients from D.C.'s beloved Wagshal's deli to create Wagshal's Chopped Brisket with soy-brined soft egg, rice, and *furikake* butter. The Half-A-Cado Salad is refreshing, and the Smashed Salmon with mushrooms and peas is a tasty bowl of health. It's easy to go vegan, gluten-free, and vegetarian here.

IF YOU LIKE THIS **CHIKO** has other locations—inside Nationals Park and on Capitol Hill. **Bibibop** is a fast-casual Korean restaurant with fresh, healthy ingredients at a low price point.

Le Diplomate ★★★½ • FRENCH • MODERATE
1601 14th St. NW; ☎ 202-332-3333; lediplomatedc.com

Reservations Recommended. **Metro** Dupont Circle; U Street/African American Civil War Memorial/Cardozo or Shaw/Howard University. **Wine selection** Good. **Open** *Lunch:* Friday, noon–4 p.m. *Midday:* Saturday–Sunday, 3–5 p.m. *Dinner:* Sunday–Thursday, 5–11 p.m.; Friday–Saturday, 5 p.m.–midnight. *Brunch:* Saturday–Sunday, 9:30 a.m.–3 p.m. *Happy hour:* Monday–Friday, 4–6 p.m.

THE PREMISE Stephen Starr, the José Andrés of Philadelphia, owns Italian, German, and even Cuban and Japanese restaurants, and he knows the value of atmosphere. The decor here reportedly topped $6 million, with "authentic" nicotine stains on the ceiling, lipstick-red banquettes, silvered mirrors, a bread bakery display, floors that look as if they've been tangoed on, and conservatory windows on the garden-room roof. Predictably, it became a local foodie rave and a very hot spot with notable patrons like Ivanka Trump and Taylor Swift. It's also as loud as a real French market.

THE PAYOFF Foie gras "parfait" layered with chicken liver; crispy duck à l'orange; mushroom tart in fine pastry; steak *frites*; escargots; tartare; beef Bourguignonne; lamb shank with couscous; and duck confit, with the richness cut by kumquats and kale. In addition to the shellfish appetizer, such as oysters and lobster halves, look for live scallops, king crab legs, and beef tongue carpaccio. Brunch is an event, with sandwiches, salads, hors d'oeuvres, and egg dishes. Le Diplomate also offers its version of a blue plate special, only a little fancier: lobster risotto, cassoulet, bouillabaisse, and even prime rib on Saturday.

IF YOU LIKE THIS Also in the neighborhood, **B Too** is a contemporary bistro serving Belgian fare, notably the classics cooked on an aromatic charcoal grill. Stop in for breakfast, lunch, brunch, or dinner to sample its creative Belgian waffles. **Bistro Cacao** on Capitol Hill is within eyeshot of Union Station and has outdoor seating; it's a favorite of Hill staffers and a few bosses as well.

Estadio ★★★½ • SPANISH • INEXPENSIVE

1540 14th St. NW; ☎ 202-319-1404; estadio-dc.com

Reservations Available only for parties of 6 or more. **Metro** U Street/African American Civil War Memorial/Cardozo or Dupont Circle. **Wine selection** Very good. **Open** *Lunch:* Friday, 11:30 a.m.-2 p.m. *Dinner:* Sunday, 5-9 p.m.; Monday-Thursday, 5-10 p.m.; Friday-Saturday, 5-11 p.m. *Brunch:* Saturday-Sunday, 11 a.m.-2 p.m.

THE PREMISE It might seem like just another tapas bar in a neighborhood crammed with small plates, but Logan Circle's Estadio remains a prime choice and makes *Washingtonian* magazine's Very Best list every year. The look is Moorish with patterned tiles, wrought iron, stone, heavy wood, and a touch of steel; food might be plated on wood boards or even slate.

THE PAYOFF The open-faced *montaditos* are not your grandmother's tea sandwiches, with toppings such as lump crab with jalapeños, *escalivada*-style vegetables, and smoked salmon with yogurt and honey. The two-sided kind include pork belly with *shishito* peppers, blood sausage, and grilled vegetables. Grab a toothpick and nosh on chorizo, Manchego (among a dozen or so cheeses), anchovies, or artichokes. Or go big with pork loin, halibut *romesco,* spicy grilled chicken, mussels, and Galician-style scallops with trumpet mushrooms. The sherry and Madeira lists are unusually extensive and are mixed into some delectable cocktails.

IF YOU LIKE THIS Estadio's sibling restaurant is the Southeast Asian **Doi Moi** (page 232). Pork-aholics should check out **The Pig,** a nose-to-tail restaurant down the street.

Hank's Oyster Bar ★★½ • SEAFOOD • INEXPENSIVE-MODERATE

1624 Q St. NW; ☎ 202-462-4265; hanksdc.com

Reservations Not accepted. **Metro** Dupont Circle; Eastern Market or Capitol Hill South; King Street (Old Town); or Southwest Waterfront (The Wharf). **Wine selection** Good. **Open** Sunday, 11 a.m.-1 a.m.; Monday-Thursday, 11:30 a.m.-1 a.m.; Friday, 11:30 a.m.-2 a.m.; Saturday, 11 a.m.-2 a.m. *Happy hour:* Monday-Friday, 3-7 p.m.

THE PREMISE Jamie Leeds is an upscale New American chef who turned to her roots (Hank was her father) with a series of New England–style fish houses (she calls it urban beach food). Though the menus are similar, each has its own twist and decor, but all with a cool pun on fish-warehouse chic. At the Capitol Hill branch, she has hooked into the signature cocktail bar-within-a-bar trend (with a nice local beer and wine selection). Leeds has also partnered with a prime Virginia oyster farm for her own brand, and she uses the empty shells to restore the beds.

THE PAYOFF Even with the influx of lobster rolls, those at Hank's are deservedly popular. Other staples include crab cakes, fried Ipswich clams, popcorn shrimp, and calamari. Entrées generally include grilled seafood, lobster, or shrimp and grits; plenty of raw, fried, steamed, or grilled seafood; and her signature Meat & Two's, daily specials that range from molasses-braised short ribs to oven-roasted or fried chicken to grilled duck breast or chops.

IF YOU LIKE THIS **Johnny's Half Shell,** in Adams Morgan, is another seafood restaurant owned by a celebrated female chef. Chef Ann Cashion is cooking up New Orleans gumbo, crab cakes, poached scallops, and vintage treats like spoon bread and shrimp cocktail. **Hank's** has other locations at Capitol Hill, The Wharf, and Old Town Alexandria.

Iron Gate ★★★½ • MODERN AMERICAN/STEAK • MODERATE

1734 N St. NW; ☎ 202-524-5202; irongaterestaurantdc.com

Reservations Recommended. **Metro** Farragut North or Dupont Circle. **Wine selection** Good. **Open** *Lunch:* Tuesday–Friday, 11:30 a.m.–2 p.m. *Dinner:* Sunday, 5:30–9 p.m.; Monday–Thursday, 5:30–10 p.m.; Friday–Saturday, 5:30–11 p.m. *Brunch:* Saturday–Sunday, 11 a.m.–2 p.m.

THE PREMISE This has been among the city's most picturesque spots for years—built from an old stable, half hidden down a lantern-lit alley, and with some of the most alluring fireplaces in town. This eclectic tavern highlights Southern Italian and Greek flavors, including Sardinian and Sicilian; chef Tony Chittum is a native of the Eastern Shore, but his wife is Greek. Long a proponent of local sourcing, Chittum turns regional seafood and game on rotisseries and in a wood-burning grill and oven.

THE PAYOFF The menus change with the seasons, so in summer, expect to see local seafood and vegetables beside meats and cheeses from local farms. Popular items include the deviled duck eggs and the Pikilia Platter, with fried lamb meatballs, pepper dips, and Feta. Don't miss the summer squash arancini or the chilled tomato-melon soup when it's on the menu. Iron Gate is one of the few D.C. restaurants that boasts a few ghosts.

IF YOU LIKE THIS If you're looking for other exceptional dining experiences in the neighborhood, check out the supper-club vibe at **The Riggsby** (see below) or the historic and cozy **Tabard Inn.**

The Riggsby ★★★½
• TRADITIONAL AMERICAN • MODERATE-EXPENSIVE

1731 New Hampshire Ave. NW; ☎ 202-787-1500; theriggsby.com

Reservations Recommended. **Metro** Dupont Circle. **Wine selection** Good. **Open** *Breakfast:* Monday–Friday, 7–10:30 a.m.; Saturday–Sunday, 8–10:30 a.m. *Lunch:* Daily, 11:30 a.m.–3 p.m. *Dinner:* Daily, 5–10:30 p.m. *Brunch:* Saturday-Sunday, 11 a.m.–3 p.m. *Cocktail party:* Daily, 4–7 p.m.

THE PREMISE Located inside the Carlyle Hotel and nicknamed a supper club, The Riggsby's retro vibe harks back to the Brat Pack era. At this white-tablecloth restaurant, you'll find nostalgic American favorites like wedge salads, rack of lamb, and brownie sundaes. Keep your eyes open for celebrities; they come for the solicitous yet discreet service and reliably good menu.

THE PAYOFF Chef Michael Schlow is a James Beard Award winner who often selects hotels for the sites of his restaurants. Although breakfast, lunch, and dinner are served here, supper is its bread and butter, so to speak. First-course standouts are the Stracciatella (a salad of peaches and prosciutto di Parma) and the mountainous Tableside Wedge. The raw bar is well stocked with local oysters and the Colossal Shrimp Cocktail. The Original Roast Chicken, served with broccoli rabe and roasted potatoes, is a winner, as is The Schlow Burger, topped with Cheddar, horseradish sauce, and crispy onions.

IF YOU LIKE THIS Chef Schlow has other superb restaurants in the area, including **Alta Strada** in Fairfax, **Casolare** in Glover Park, and **Tico** on 14th

Street. His fast-casual restaurant in Bethesda called **Prima** offers bowls of traditional Italian ingredients.

U STREET CORRIDOR

THE U STREET CORRIDOR continues to blossom and expand its selection of superb restaurants. Along the blocks of U Street Northwest between about 10th and 14th Streets, and 14th Street from U Street down toward P, you'll find D.C.'s literary Washington cafés: **Café Saint-Ex,** named for *The Little Prince* author Antoine de Saint-Exupéry; **Bar Pilar,** named for Ernest Hemingway's boat; the Belgian pub **Marvin,** named for local soul star Marvin Gaye; and the flagship location of **Busboys and Poets,** a bookstore, café, and poetry lounge named for poet Langston Hughes, who was working as a busboy at the Wardman Park Hotel when he began writing.

There are fine Ethiopian restaurants in this neighborhood, too, most notably **Dukem** and **Shebelle.**

Located beside D.C.'s hipster spots is the legendary **Ben's Chili Bowl,** which since 1958 has been dishing out chili half-smokes (half pork and half beef smoked sausage on a bun, topped with mustard, onions, and chili) to stars and presidents alike. The **Florida Avenue Grill** is known as "the oldest soul-food restaurant in the world"—and at 75-plus, it might well be.

Higher-end restaurants are part of the landscape as well—**Compass Rose, Izakaya Seki** (next page), the affordable **Doi Moi** (see below), and the aforementioned **Maydan,** which *Bon Appétit* named as the second-best new restaurant in America in 2018.

Doi Moi and Birds Eye ★★★ • ASIAN FUSION • INEXPENSIVE
1800 14th St. NW; ☎ 202-733-5131; doimoidc.com

Reservations Recommended. **Metro** U Street/African American Civil War Memorial/Cardozo. **Wine selection** Very good. **Open** Sunday, 2:30–9 p.m.; Monday–Thursday, 2:30–10 p.m.; Friday–Saturday, 2:30–11 p.m. *Birds Eye:* Monday–Friday, 8 a.m.–2:30 p.m.; Saturday–Sunday, 8 a.m.–3 p.m.

THE PREMISE This celebration of Southeast Asian street food mixes noodles, skewers (really fresh head-on shrimp), dumplings, curries of a refreshingly broad flavor spectrum, and family-style platters of roast chicken, ribs, or chargrilled whole fish. This is a playful and also deft kitchen: noodles sometimes turn into origami. Don't underestimate the spice ratings here. Doi Moi opened a fast-casual coffee bar and eatery within the restaurant, called Birds Eye, that serves Southeast Asian–inspired breakfast and lunch fare, including smoothie bowls, sandwiches for breakfast and lunch, spicy vegetable salads, and Vietnamese coffee and tea drinks (think pour-overs sweetened with rich coconut milk).

THE PAYOFF Street food may have inspired the venue, but the upscale wine and beer lists are American benefits. (The wacky-sweet drink desserts are true cultural fusions.) The restaurant also has an extremely lengthy vegan/veggie and gluten-free menu, with its own mild-spicy range. Except for the family dishes, however, some plates may seem small. Birds Eye has pushed this restaurant to new heights, with some seriously Instagrammable dishes such as passion fruit–coconut chia seed pudding, five-layer Indonesian coffee cake, and the Doi Nut with a crème brûlée filling. Don't miss the banana blossom salad or the pork belly sandwich with lemongrass.

IF YOU LIKE THIS Check out **Sakerum,** an interesting fusion of Asian with Latin American on 14th Street. In Adams Morgan, **Spoken English** won a Michelin Bib Gourmand for its *tachinomiya*-style Asian street food and sake collection.

Izakaya Seki ★★★½ • JAPANESE • MODERATE–EXPENSIVE

1117 V St. NW; no phone; sekidc.com

Reservations Accepted only for parties of 5–8. **Metro** U Street/African American Civil War Memorial/Cardozo or Shaw/Howard University. **Wine selection** Good. **Open** Tuesday–Sunday, 5–10 p.m.; closed Mondays.

THE PREMISE If you want authenticity in Japanese dining, you'll find it at the restaurant of father–daughter team Hiroshi and Cizuka Seki. Located inside a row house, the *izakaya* (basically the Japanese version of a neighborhood pub) offers a menu much like what you find in mom-and-pop shops all over Japan. Watch as chef Hiroshi puts together a stunning sashimi platter, or feast on cold soba noodles or snappy cucumbers in miso-cured barley.

THE PAYOFF Not only is the sushi super fresh, but it's also offered in inventive ways: oversize scallops, flown in daily, are glazed with soy and miso in the broiler and finished with an egg-creamy sauce, while slow-braised pork belly yields broth that's recycled to bathe udon noodles. Grilled yellowtail jaw is a classic, but heartier are the Korean-flavored short ribs and the skewered grilled pork belly.

IF YOU LIKE THIS Try **Daikaya** in Penn Quarter (page 218).

 WASHINGTON CHEFS LIKE TO CONCOCT BURGERS with their individual spin. Notable burgers can be found at **Mintwood Place** in Adams Morgan, with its wood-grilled, dry-aged bacon cheeseburger. Try to get your hands around the triple-decker patty with cheese and more bacon at **Lucky Buns,** also in Adams Morgan. Go upscale at **Reverie** in Georgetown, where acclaimed local chef Johnny Spero makes his burgers from dry-aged rib eye and adds pickled Asian toppings. **Duke's Grocery,** in Dupont Circle, Woodley Park, and Foggy Bottom, serves a burger on a brioche bun with homemade sweet chili sauce, Gouda, and charred onions. See more burger recommendations on page 249.

ADAMS MORGAN AND COLUMBIA HEIGHTS

ADAMS MORGAN IS CENTERED at 18th Street and Columbia Road and has traditionally been the home of recent immigrants from Latin American and African countries. The neighborhood has experienced some gentrification but remains a popular nightlife spot with a robust selection of late-night eats and eclectic restaurants with global cuisines.

The recent opening of the swanky **Line DC** hotel has added notable dining venues to the neighborhood, including **Brothers and Sisters,**

Spoken English, and **A Rake's Progress** (see below), all of which are standouts. This historic church-turned-hotel is where some of D.C.'s best chefs cook under one roof.

Several restaurants are situated inside row houses on 18th Street, and their exteriors are painted in a kaleidoscope of colors with iconic murals, like a witty version of Henri de Toulouse-Lautrec and a voluptuous redhead on the exterior of **Madam's Organ,** a long-established blues club. **Roofers Union** is a popular cocktail bar with outstanding views from its rooftop. **Jack Rose Dining Saloon** has more than 2,000 bottles of scotches, bourbons, and whiskeys and is known for its pioneering handcrafted cocktails in D.C.

There are multiple places to grab a quick bite, like **Amsterdam Falafelshop,** a Middle Eastern fast-casual joint with a choice of 20 toppings. Stand in line for freshly made South American pastries at the window of **Julia's Empanadas. Tryst** is a welcoming coffee shop with occasional live music performances. If you love Japanese-style seafood, stop in **Donburi DC** for a bowl of sticky rice with seafood and pickled vegetables. **Lucky Buns** serves the neighborhood's most notable burger.

For a sit-down restaurant with sass, try **Tail Up Goat** (next page), with a focus on Mediterranean cuisine. **Zenebech** (next page) is an established Ethiopian restaurant that many say is the best among many outstanding options. Afghan cuisine is an unexpected delight, and you can find it at **Lapis** Afghan bistro or **Mama Ayesha's,** a Washington institution nearly as venerable as Ben's Chili Bowl. Mama Ayesha's was opened back in 1960 by a longtime embassy cook and chef and still serves traditional meze, kebabs, and stuffed veggies Mama's way. For fine French, **Mintwood Place** is noteworthy, as is **Perry's,** a longtime staple of Adams Morgan that remains trendy for its drag brunch and rooftop dining.

A Rake's Progress ★★★½
• **MID-ATLANTIC AMERICAN** • EXPENSIVE
1770 Euclid St. NW; ☎ 202-588-0525; thelinehotel.com/dc

Reservations Recommended. **Metro** Woodley Park/Zoo or Columbia Heights. **Wine selection** Good. **Open** Closed Monday-Tuesday. *Dinner:* Sunday, 5–9 p.m.; Wednesday-Thursday, 6–10 p.m.; Friday-Saturday, 6–11 p.m. *Brunch:* Sunday, 11 a.m.–3 p.m. *Note:* This restaurant is not wheelchair accessible.

THE PREMISE This stunning restaurant resides on the upper level of the Line DC hotel, which was formerly a historic church. Owned by locavore Spike Gjerde, a James Beard Award winner, the restaurant is focused on showcasing locally sourced mid-Atlantic ingredients in an elegant way. The cathedral-like ceiling opens to the lower level, and the sound can be quite deafening when crowded. The restaurant's name comes from a series of paintings by William Hogarth. The paintings inspired a 1935 ballet, an opera, and a British comedy film. President Barack Obama and former First Lady Michelle Obama were the restaurant's first customers.

THE PAYOFF Gjerde plays with the bounty he finds in the farms and hills of Maryland and the inlets of the Chesapeake Bay. The menu features fish and shellfish, such as oysters and blue crab, while local mills provide the ingredients for the johnnycake with tomato jam. The generous salads are fit for two or more to share, as is the ember-grilled bone-in rib eye, served family style with Parker House rolls and seasonal vegetables. Although the menu varies by season, keep an eye out for the country ham, crab cake, spit-roasted pork loin with buttered grits, and watermelon mimosas.

IF YOU LIKE THIS The Line DC hotel is a communal gathering space where local chefs have come together in a variety of dining venues. **A Rake's Bar** features cocktails made from locally distilled spirits and craft beer and cider from local breweries, while **Brothers and Sisters** is the place for small plates like avocado toast, pastas, and an elegant selection of desserts served with Chinese teas.

Tail Up Goat ★★★½ • MEDITERRANEAN • MODERATE
1813 Adams Mill Rd. NW; ☎ 202-986-9600; tailupgoat.com

Reservations Recommended. Metro Woodley Park/Zoo or Columbia Heights. Wine selection Good. Open *Dinner:* Monday–Thursday, 5:30–10 p.m.; Friday–Sunday, 5–10 p.m. *Brunch:* Sunday, 11 a.m.–1 p.m. *Note:* This restaurant is not wheelchair accessible.

THE PREMISE The ebullient restaurant is named for the free-range goats that roam the hills of the US Virgin Islands, where owner Jill Tyler grew up. She and her business partners Jon Sybert (Jill's husband) and Bill Jensen founded this stylish, understated restaurant decorated with a mix of bistro furniture, a tiled open kitchen, and an industrial-rustic feel. The service has a sense of humor sharp enough to match its ingredients. The menu changes with the season, even daily. Put your trust in this team to feed you a groundbreaking meal.

THE PAYOFF Plates of meats, seafood, and pasta are influenced by their locally sourced ingredients. Look for pork prepared in unusual ways with whimsical ingredients. Don't miss the signature lamb ribs in date and molasses jus, or the house-made breads with seaweed butter and fermented carrots. A family-style tasting meal for six to eight people costs $90 per person (excluding tax, gratuity, and beverages).

IF YOU LIKE THIS The team who created Tail Up Goat are veterans of the foodie paradises **Komi** and **Little Serow,** both near Dupont Circle, where you can experience the same caliber of quality, imaginative hospitality, and dining chops.

Zenebech ★★★ • ETHIOPIAN • MODERATE
2420 18th St. NW; ☎ 202-667-4700; zenebechdc.com

Reservations Suggested. Metro Woodley Park/Zoo. Wine selection None. Open Monday–Wednesday, 5–11 p.m.; Thursday–Sunday, 11 a.m.–11 p.m.

THE PREMISE This family-owned restaurant began in 1993 as an injera bakery (traditional Ethiopian bread used to scoop from communal plates). Catering to the large population of Ethiopians who live in D.C., it evolved to a full-service restaurant when it opened in Adams Morgan in 2017. Vibrant Ethiopian art adorns the bright, comfortable restaurant, which serves a steady stream of takeout orders, as the wooden tables inside the restaurant are small. It consistently gets positive reviews from local food critics.

THE PAYOFF The menu is more expansive and the preparations not as spicy as at some Ethiopian outposts in D.C. If you want to try a variety of dishes, consider ordering the Vegetarian Combo with split peas, red lentils, collard greens, cabbage, and chickpea stew (*shiro*). Another good option is the Mehaberawi, a combination of four meat dishes and four veggie dishes. For something spicy, consider the Goden Tibs, beef ribs with jalapeños and tomatoes. The *sambusas,* fried pastry with fillings, are a must.

IF YOU LIKE THIS **Ethiopic** (page 212) in Shaw, near the H Street Corridor, is another highly regarded Ethiopian restaurant with more emphasis on heat. If you want to taste slightly different preparations, consider **Keren Restaurant and Coffee Shop,** which has an Eritrean menu. (Eritrea is a neighbor of Ethiopia that gained its independence in 1993. The country's cooking was influenced by its Italian colonists.)

UPPER NORTHWEST: WOODLEY PARK, CLEVELAND PARK, AND VAN NESS

THESE METRO NEIGHBORHOODS bookend the National Zoo and are located along Connecticut Avenue Northwest. Cleveland Park is a well-to-do neighborhood with historic homes and tree-lined streets. A few restaurants and shops—including two excellent Indian restaurants, **Indique** and **Bindaas** (see below)—are clustered around the Metro station. Other dining spots worth noting include **Medium Rare** (next page), which offers a $23 prix fixe menu of salad, steak, and *frites* with fresh crusty bread; and **Spices Asian Restaurant,** putting out Pan-Asian comfort food. With the family in tow, you can't beat the Tex-Mex fast-casual **California Tortilla. 2Amys Neapolitan Pizzeria** has served D.C.'s favorite brick-oven pizza for three decades.

Van Ness is adjacent to the University of the District of Columbia and has a few noteworthy restaurants, including **Sfoglina** (page 238), a sophisticated Italian eatery; and **Buck's Fishing & Camping,** with an emphasis on seasonal American fare. For something quick and tasty, stop at **Bread Furst Bakery** for bold-flavored salads, soups, and sandwiches.

At the Woodley Park end is **Open City,** a diner with breakfast all day and a sweeping view down Connecticut Avenue. **Afghan Grill** is a must for the adventurous eater; expect excellent service and don't miss the appetizer sampler here. The original branch of Washington's first Middle Eastern outpost, **Lebanese Taverna,** is in Woodley Park. **Duke's Counter,** located between Cleveland Park and Woodley Park, is a new gastropub catering to diners who are seeking a satisfying meal and a hearty selection of craft beer.

Bindaas ★★★ • INDIAN STREET FOOD • INEXPENSIVE–MODERATE

3309 Connecticut Ave. NW, Cleveland Park; ☎ 202-244-6550; bindaasdc.com

Reservations Recommended. Metro Cleveland Park. Wine selection Good. Open Dinner: Sunday, 4–9 p.m.; Monday–Thursday, 5–10 p.m.; Friday, 5–11 p.m.; Saturday, 4–11 p.m. Brunch: Saturday–Sunday, 11 a.m.–4 p.m.

THE PREMISE This hip restaurant stands out for its menu of Indian street food and cocktails. The casual but sophisticated vibe works well with the variety of fabulous finger food, small plates, and *golgappa*. Bollywood movies play in the background beside colorful spice jars. The robust menu stretches from Mumbai to Goa to Kerala.

THE PAYOFF Start with a salad or snack, or *chaat*. Probably the most famous dish is the *golgappa*, which is hollow unleavened bread that is fried and stuffed with avocado, sweet yogurt, and tamarind chutney. Other recommendations include bhel poori, a puffed-rice salad with mango, mint, and cilantro; and naan, traditional Indian bread with Bindaas's clever additions, such as stuffing the bread with bacon, Cheddar, and chili. Another favorite is *uttapam,* rice pancakes with tomatoes, sweet corn, and mushrooms.

IF YOU LIKE THIS **Bindaas** has a second location in Foggy Bottom. Other Indian food of note also comes from D.C.'s entrepreneur Ashok Bajaj, including **Rasika West End** (page 226) and his **Bombay Club,** just steps from the White House. The upscale **Indique** is located in the Cleveland Park area as well.

Medium Rare ★★★ • STEAK • MODERATE

3500 Connecticut Ave. NW, Cleveland Park; ☎ 202-237-1432; mediumrarerestaurant.com

Reservations Recommended. **Metro** Cleveland Park. **Wine selection** Good. **Open** *Dinner:* Monday–Thursday, 5–10 p.m.; Friday–Saturday, 5–11 p.m. *Brunch:* Saturday–Sunday, 10:30 a.m.–2:30 p.m.

THE PREMISE This restaurant remains popular in the city because you know exactly what you're getting and exactly what it will cost. For dinner, there is a fixed-price menu, with few substitutions, for $23.95 per person. The medley of courses includes any second helpings you want. The simplicity helps make this a favorite standby for the steak-and-potato lovers and hungry teens.

THE PAYOFF The meal begins with rustic crusty French bread, followed by a mixed green salad. Then comes the main course: sliced culotte steak with irresistible hand-cut fries—use the buttery, tangy secret sauce if you like. The menu expands for brunch, and the prix fixe menu of $27.99 per person is served with bottomless Bloody Marys, mimosas, and screwdrivers, along with its hot, crusty sliced bread, followed by egg and steak options. The restaurant has scrumptious desserts, if you have room. The house specialty is the hot fudge sundae, but Grandma's apple pie à la mode and the six-layer carrot cake are also winners.

IF YOU LIKE THIS Medium Rare has other locations—in Arlington, Bethesda, and Navy Yard's Eighth Street Barracks Row. **Annie's Paramount Steak & Seafood House** in Dupont Circle was recognized in 2018 with a James Beard Award called America's Classics. If you want to splurge, treat yourself to a 38-ounce prime Porterhouse steak at **Bourbon Steak,** at the Four Seasons Hotel in Georgetown. The politicos' favorite is **Charlie Palmer Steak,** on Capitol Hill, which includes Chesapeake Bay oysters and crab cakes on the menu.

Sfoglina ★★★½ • ITALIAN • MODERATE-EXPENSIVE

4445 Connecticut Ave. NW, Van Ness; ☎ 202-244-7995; sfoglinadc.com

Reservations Recommended. **Metro** Van Ness. **Wine selection** Very good. **Open** Monday, 5–10 p.m.; Tuesday–Thursday, 11:30 a.m.–10 p.m.; Friday–Saturday, 11:30 a.m.–10:30 p.m.; Sunday, 11:30 a.m.–9 p.m. *Brunch:* Saturday–Sunday, 11:30 a.m.–3 p.m. *Happy hour:* Monday, 5–7 p.m.; Tuesday–Friday, 3–7 p.m.

THE PREMISE Sfoglina is a new addition to Maria and Fabio Trabocchis' acclaimed restaurant empire—they also own Fiola (page 219), Fiola Mare (page 225), and Del Mar (page 204). This time, their focus is on homemade pastas inspired by those Italian mamas who took the time to roll out fresh dough. This is not a loud, hearty red-sauce joint but rather has a hushed atmosphere appropriate for revering the splendor that arrives on every plate. The stylish dining room at this location looks like a Valentine's Day combination of red and white, with teardrop light fixtures that create a flattering glow. How can you not fall in love here?

THE PAYOFF The menu includes nibbles, seafood, salads, vegetables, and desserts, but pasta is the true star. Handmade noodles are delicate and infused with fresh and seasonal ingredients. Especially distinguished are the mushroom and pecorino cheese featured in the Soft Polenta Cacio e Pepe; the Fisherman's Style Octopus; and the carbonara-style shells with pancetta, escarole, and a soft egg.

IF YOU LIKE THIS Sfoglina has two other locations: Rosslyn and downtown on New York Avenue. You can find comparable expertly made pasta at **Obelisk** in Dupont Circle.

unofficial **TIP**
The **Bethesda Crab House** is a traditional grab-your-mallet steamer shop; if your family's never been to one, it could be a fun night.

MARYLAND SUBURBS

Bethesda and Chevy Chase

The Woodmont Triangle area of Bethesda has a lot of restaurants, and a few are excellent. Generally, **Q by Peter Chang** (page 240), Yannick Cam's **Bistro Provence**, a branch of **Jaleo** (page 220), **Raku** (a fusion of Japanese, Thai, and Chinese), **Black's Bar & Kitchen** (pricey seafood), and **Woodmont Grill** (American classics) are reliably first-rate. The elegant **Passage to India, Mussel Bar & Grille** (Belgian mussels and *frites*), **Mon Ami Gabi** (French bistro), and **Olazzo** (red-sauce Italian) have lasted awhile and continue to do brisk business.

unofficial **TIP**
The **Bethesda location of Tastee Diner,** one of three left (along with Silver Spring and Laurel), is an original Jerry O'Mahony dining car, dating from 1935. It's open 24/7, except December 25, and has hosted plenty of politicians and celebrities—even Julia Child.

Chevy Chase has some worthwhile options around the Friendship Heights Metro at the intersection of Wisconsin and Western Avenues Northwest (actually the Montgomery County/D.C. border). **Sushiko** (page 241) and its sister **Kobo** are among the best 50 restaurants in D.C. An ode to Pittsburgh, **Blue 44** serves as a local gathering place. **The Capital Grille** is an upscale steakhouse with a posh, clublike atmosphere. Groups enjoy the festive ambience and hearty portions at **Maggiano's Little Italy.**

North Bethesda is a new hot spot for diners, thanks to the addition to the Pike & Rose development. This compact area has several popular restaurants, including **Jinya Ramen Bar** (Japanese ramen and street food); **City Perch Kitchen + Bar** (a Southern-influenced menu with a delightful patio); **Nada** (stellar modern Mexican); and **Julii** (a fine French restaurant that's part of the mighty **Cava** chain). A personal favorite is **Owen's Ordinary** (see below), a gastropub specializing in Maryland craft beers, headed by D.C. craft beer legend Greg Engert.

Outside of the urban communities that run north of Washington, D.C.—Chevy Chase, Bethesda, and Rockville—are a few destination-style restaurants known for their iconic D.C. history: **The Old Angler's Inn** (see below) and **The Irish Inn at Glen Echo**.

The Old Angler's Inn ★★★ • CLASSIC
AMERICAN • MODERATE-EXPENSIVE
10801 MacArthur Blvd.; Potomac, MD; ☎ 301-365-2425; oldanglersinn.com

Reservations Recommended. **Metro** Not Metro Accessible. **Wine selection** Very good. **Open** *Breakfast:* Saturday–Sunday, 9–11 a.m. *Brunch:* Sunday, 11:30 a.m.–2:30 p.m. *Lunch:* Tuesday–Sunday, 11:30 a.m.–2:30 p.m. *Dinner:* Monday–Saturday, 5:30–9:30 p.m.; Sunday, 5:30–9 p.m. *Happy hour:* Monday–Thursday, 4:30–6:30 p.m.

THE PREMISE Located on a gorgeous stretch of Maryland country roads, The Old Angler's Inn's lifespan began in 1860, when the restaurant was founded as a stop on the C&O Canal and was patronized by local fisherman. Fast-forward to today, and rustic has been replaced with white-tablecloth seating by a roaring stone fireplace. The formal-ish dining room serves its modern American fare on traditional fine china, while the stone patio functions as a beer garden with fire pits. On weekends, live music on the patio attracts hikers visiting Great Falls on the C&O Canal.

THE PAYOFF The menu in the dining room focuses on classic American comfort food, like rack of lamb, steak *frites*, and crab cakes. Outside in the beer garden, order the bratwurst with peppers and onions or the fish sandwich. At lunch, the warm ahi tuna Niçoise salad tastes fresh and is made with real anchovies. Vegetarians will love the spiced lentil veggie burger with yogurt-cucumber sauce.

IF YOU LIKE THIS Other notable destination restaurants with fine dining include **L'Auberge Chez François,** located on the Virginia side of the Potomac River. It's consistently voted the city's most romantic restaurant. In Georgetown, the legendary **1789 Restaurant** earns superlative reviews for its provincial menu and Federal-style dining room. **Gadsby's Tavern** in Old Town Alexandria dates back to Colonial times and was a favorite hangout of America's founding fathers, including George Washington, Thomas Jefferson, and James Madison. **The Restaurant at Patowmack Farm** in Lovettsville, Virginia, has a world-class culinary team behind its artful tasting menus created from foraged and locally sourced ingredients.

Owen's Ordinary ★★★ • GASTROPUB • MODERATE
11920 Trade St. N, Bethesda, MD; ☎ 301-245-1226; owensordinarymd.com

Reservations Recommended. **Metro** White Flint. **Wine selection** Known for craft beer. **Open** *Lunch:* Wednesday–Friday, 11 a.m.–3 p.m. *Dinner:* Monday–Tuesday, 4–10 p.m.;

Wednesday–Sunday, 5–10 p.m. Limited menu: Wednesday–Sunday, 3–5 p.m. *Brunch:* Saturday–Sunday, 11 a.m.–3 p.m. *Happy hour:* Monday–Friday, 4–6 p.m. *Late-night menu:* Daily, 10 p.m.–close.

THE PREMISE Located in the Pike & Rose development in North Bethesda, this is the fourth craft beer eatery from beer expert Greg Engert. This time, the menu focuses on Maryland-brewed beers. With an outdoor garden, stylish bar, and restaurant filled with rustic tables, the tavern is a warm and welcoming gastropub and a fine place to watch sports in a communal environment.

THE PAYOFF Beer aficionados will enjoy sampling a flight of beers with bar bites like shrimp sliders, fried oysters, and Bavarian soft pretzels. The charcuterie plates may be customized, and the mushroom and kale flatbread and the spicy Italian sausage and peppers flatbread are notable. Most beers are brewed somewhere in the state of Maryland and feature different categories like Tart & Funky, Hop, Roast, and Fruit & Spice.

IF YOU LIKE THIS Engert was the first to bring locally brewed beer to the area at **ChurchKey** and then **Bluejacket** (page 207). Other restaurants in the Pike & Rose development are **Nada,** authentic Mexican small plates, and **Summer House Santa Monica,** with a California beach vibe and a superb happy hour.

Q by Peter Chang ★★★ • MODERN SZECHUAN CHINESE
• MODERATE-EXPENSIVE
4500 East–West Hwy., Bethesda, MD; ☎ 240-800-3722; qbypeterchang.com

Reservations Recommended. **Metro** Bethesda. **Wine selection** Good. **Open** *Lunch:* Monday–Thursday, 11 a.m.–3 p.m. *Dinner:* Monday–Thursday, 5–9:30 p.m. *Lunch and dinner:* Friday–Saturday, 11 a.m.–10:30 p.m.; Sunday, 11 a.m.–9 p.m. *Dim sum brunch:* Saturday–Sunday, 11 a.m.–3 p.m.

THE PREMISE There are many, many people who are members of the Peter Chang fan club. The chef worked at the Chinese Embassy for years, until he moved to Northern Virginia and began cooking at local restaurants. Specializing in Chinese Szechuan, the flavorful, fiery cuisine of southwestern China, Chang opened his eponymous restaurants in the D.C. area, beginning with Arlington, Virginia, and then Rockville, Maryland. Building on the success of his cafés, the chef and his family expanded their dynasty to include the fine dining restaurant Q By Peter Chang in downtown Bethesda. Q is Chang's flagship and largest restaurant with 8,000 square feet of modern Chinese design.

THE PAYOFF The jaunty restaurant has an expansive menu, but many come for his brunch dim sum sampler. A few of his dishes contain his famous "hot and numbing" sauces, but Q focuses on making his Cantonese renditions delicate, like the deconstructed Peking duck; braised tofu with scallion puree and prawns; chili prawns; and stir-fried eggplant slices that look like fries. Don't miss his famous steam-filled scallion pancakes, beloved by all Chang followers.

IF YOU LIKE THIS Chang's original restaurants, **Peter Chang** in Arlington and Rockville, are better known for big plates of stir-fries with exotic elements like lotus root. **Mama Chang,** which opened in Fairfax in 2019, received accolades from all D.C. reviewers.; this is where he cooks his mother's traditional recipes.

Sushiko ★★★½ • JAPANESE • MODERATE-EXPENSIVE

5455 Wisconsin Ave., Chevy Chase, MD; ☎ 301-961-1644;
sushikorestaurants.com

Reservations Recommended. **Metro** Friendship Heights. **Wine selection** Very good.
Open *Lunch:* Daily, noon–3 p.m. *Dinner:* Sunday–Thursday, 5:30–10 p.m.; Friday–
Saturday, 5:30–10:30 p.m. *Happy hour:* Daily, 5:30–7:30 p.m.

THE PREMISE Thanks to its unusual seasonal dishes, Sushiko attracts a broad, generally knowledgeable, and fairly affluent crowd of sushi lovers. The original location opened in 1976, making it D.C.'s oldest sushi bar. The kitchen and sushi bar offer both traditional and improvisational fare based on market availability and seasonal factors. Each dish arrives on a bespoke plate to emphasize color, texture, and shape. The minimalist interior is both elegant and inviting.

THE PAYOFF You'll find first-quality sushi and *sashimi,* as well as seasonal small dishes in which Executive Chef Piter Tjan often combines fish (both cooked and raw) with seaweed, wild greens, grains, herbs, caviar, and sometimes unexpected American touches. If you want to see what he can do, order one of the *omakase* menus: you'll be full but not stuffed. Spring for real wasabi; you'll never go back to the canned stuff. The menu has a choice of sakes, and the wine list may come as a pleasant surprise—Creative Director Daisuke Utagawa was in the forefront of pairing wines, particularly Bordeaux, with seafood.

IF YOU LIKE THIS The world-famous **Nobu,** a combination of Peruvian and Japanese dishes in Washington's West End, offers an impressive *omakase* tasting menu ($120–$150 for two).

National Harbor

While National Harbor primarily serves the convention crowd, it has ramped up its seasonal attractions, such as the ICE! Christmas extravaganzas and regular food-and-wine festivals. The Harbor also encompasses an 80-store outlet mall and the spectacular MGM resort, with its shops, upscale dining, and flashy casino. The vast number of restaurants here **feature some of Washington's most acclaimed chefs, such as José Andrés's Fish** and **Voltaggio Brothers Steak House.** The Gaylord resort alone has a half-dozen restaurants, including the **Old Hickory Steakhouse** and eateries serving burgers, crab cakes, pizza, and pub fare. Fine dining/standalone restaurants offer views of the waterfront like **Fiorella Italian Kitchen & Pizzeria, Rosa Mexicano, McCormick & Schmick's, Sauciety** at the Westin, **Grace's Mandarin,** and **Redstone American Grill.** Other noteworthy dining options include the New Southern cuisine at **Succotash,** happy hangout **The Walrus Oyster & Ale House,** New York chophouse **Bond 45,** and Jersey Shore import **McLoone's Pier House.**

Silver Spring

Two of the neighborhood's most promising new spots are curiously opposite in flavor: the lounge-y, eclectic nose-to-tail **Urban Butcher** and **All Set,** a mostly Nantucket-themed (and priced) seafood restaurant and bar. Among other favorites within walking distance of the Metro are

McGinty's Public House and Cubano's; several Ethiopian restaurants, including Abol, Abyssinia, Addis Ababa, Beteseb, Lucy, and Meleket; Mandalay, one of the few Burmese kitchens in the region; and the classic Crisfield Seafood, known for its crab cakes. Additionally, in and around The Fillmore and AFI Silver Theatre, there are a number of family options—some franchise but many mom-and-pop.

Wheaton

Although it's not a major tourist spot, Wheaton has a remarkable spread within easy distance of the Metro. For starters, consider Nava Thai, Ruan Thai, and Thai Taste by Kob; noodle shops Mi La Cay, Pho Hiep Hoa, and Ren's Ramen; and the Salvadoran Los Chorros, plus Irish and Scottish pubs and even one of the area's longest-running kosher delis, Max's. The dim sum at Hollywood East Cafe is very popular, as is the roast poultry at the Chinese Full Key and Paul Kee (not a typo; they're not related). Almost all of these are both budget- and family-friendly.

VIRGINIA SUBURBS

Old Town Alexandria

Old Town Alexandria may be known to tourists mostly for its historic buildings, but it is also home to several inviting restaurants, in particular Virtue Feed & Grain, the long-running Bilbo Baggins, and Southern nostalgic Majestic. The best French restaurant in town is Bastille.

Belgian fave Robert Wiedmaier of Marcel's, et al., has a high-end spot adjoining the Kimpton Lorien Hotel called Brabo. Gadsby's Tavern is a nostalgic Colonial-era museum serving Colonial-period food (George Washington had his birthday there), while Magnolia's on King is a haute New Southern showcase. The long-running Fish Market Restaurant & Raw Bar features Chesapeake Bay seafood in a renovated warehouse by Old Town's harbor area. If you're in the mood for noodles, prepare to slurp up some *mixian*, the Chinese rice and pork noodle soup, at Yunnan by Potomac.

unofficial TIP
Think you know hot dogs? You can have organic beef, chicken, veggie, Reuben-style, Coney Island–style, Fenway Park–style, Chicago-style, Saigon-style, even Peking duck-style—among others—at Haute Dogs and Fries.

Old Town has pubs and taverns in abundance. Be sure to check the menus on the sidewalk when possible; many charge tourist-trap prices. The best view probably goes to the savvy chain Chart House, a glass-enclosed family favorite at the end of a pier.

Vermilion ★★★½ • MODERN AMERICAN • EXPENSIVE

1120 King St., Old Town Alexandria, VA; ☎ 703-684-9669; vermilionrestaurant.com

Reservations Recommended. Metro King Street. Wine selection Very good. Open Lunch: Monday, Wednesday, and Friday, 11:30 a.m.–3 p.m. Dinner: Monday–Thursday, 5:30–10 p.m.; Friday–Saturday, 5:30–11 p.m.; Sunday, 5–9 p.m. Brunch: Saturday–Sunday, 10:30 a.m.–2:30 p.m.

THE PREMISE A graduate of the Culinary Institute of America, chef Thomas Cardarelli cooked in critically acclaimed New York restaurants before taking over Vermilion. His menu reflects the bounty he relentlessly sources from mid-Atlantic farms, ranches, and fishermen. As *the* place to celebrate a special occasion in Alexandria, Vermilion is nearly always packed, and a recent refresh has even elevated its status. Expect a memorable experience at this fine-dining restaurant located in the heart of Old Town.

THE PAYOFF There's no skimping here. Prepare to be wowed by the generous basket of freshly baked breads—focaccia, sourdough, and Parker House rolls served with house-made butter. The menu changes with the seasons, but keep an eye out for the rib eye cap, eggplant puree, fried soft-shell crab, or house-made cavatelli. The Chef's Tasting Menu is five courses for $72 per person, $99 with wine pairings.

IF YOU LIKE THIS Located in a gorgeous natural setting in Falls Church, Virginia, is the elegant **2941.** Also in Alexandria is **Bastille,** a quaint French brasserie with dishes that would charm Julia Child.

Tysons Corner

The neighborhood has traditionally been a destination for transient shoppers but has developed a much better food scene since the installation of a Metro station. Today, Tysons Corner has a solid lineup of options for tourists, but the area remains challenging to navigate for pedestrians. Visitors with cars can more easily access the upscale and family-friendly restaurants located here. The Tysons Galleria mall, across from Tysons Corner mall, has 300 stores and restaurants inside or along the perimeter, including a food hall. The area has become a haven for steak lovers, thanks to the recent openings of **The Capital Grille, Earls, Eddie V's, Fogo de Chão, Morton's, Randy's,** and **Ruth's Chris.** Along Leesburg Pike (VA 7) are first-rate, family-owned places: **Clarity** for imaginative American, **Nostos** for Greek (see below), **Patsy's American** (page 244), **Sapphire** for Indian, and **Shamshiry** for Persian.

Nostos ★★★★ • GREEK • MODERATE-EXPENSIVE

8100 Boone Blvd. (intersection of Aline Avenue and Leesburg Pike), Vienna, VA; ☎ 703-760-0690; nostosrestaurant.com

Reservations Strongly recommended. **Metro** Tysons Corner. **Wine selection** Very good. **Open** *Lunch:* Tuesday–Friday, 11:30 a.m.–2:30 p.m. *Dinner:* Monday–Saturday, 5–10 p.m.; closed Sundays.

THE PREMISE This cozy family-owned restaurant transports diners to the islands of Greece—Santorini, Crete, Rhodes—with its serene white and blue decor. The stucco walls contain black-and-white images of long-ago movie stars who spent glamorous times in Greece. The menu features traditional Greek dishes approached in new ways. On special occasions, the restaurant offers a five-course tasting menu with Greek wines for $100—the restaurant carries more than 50 Greek wines from every region of the country.

THE PAYOFF You can order meze plates to enjoy a sampling of Greek dips, and don't miss the exceptionally good grilled octopus with a fava bean puree. The Greek cheese platter and cod bites are also a worthy start to your meal. Entrées consist of lightly prepared fresh fish; customary favorites like moussaka, in which zucchini, eggplant, and potato are layered with spiced beef; *kakavia,* a tomato-based seafood stew with potatoes and crusty bread; and *biftekakia,* Greek-style meatballs with tzatziki.

IF YOU LIKE THIS Located in Penn Quarter, **Zaytinya** (page 221) is a Greek restaurant with an abundant menu and festive atmosphere. **Cava** is modern Greek cuisine and has several locations, including Barracks Row near Capitol Hill. Both are owned by well-respected chefs.

Patsy's American ★★★½ • AMERICAN • MODERATE

8051 Leesburg Pike, Vienna, VA; ☎ 703-552-5100; patsysamerican.com

Reservations Recommended. **Metro** Tysons Corner. **Wine selection** Good. **Open** Daily, 11 a.m.–2 a.m.

THE PREMISE This family-owned restaurant is an outpost of the Great American Restaurants group, which operates a variety of restaurants throughout the Northern Virginia and Maryland suburbs. The building resembles an old-fashioned train station with high ceilings that allow natural light to stream in, while the open kitchen and colorful murals on the walls give the place a festive atmosphere. One mural depicts a carnival, while the other is a collection of well-known characters from real life and movies. The back bar caters to sports fans and late-night dining. This is a great place to go when you arrive late in the evening from travel and want a hearty meal and/or drinks.

THE PAYOFF The menu is heavy on classic American fare and features seafood towers with oysters, shrimp, lobster, mussels, and clams. Patsy's is known for excellent crab cakes, hand-cut fries, and a nice selection of fresh salads. They also have sandwiches, burgers, and some of the best desserts in town.

IF YOU LIKE THIS Also located in the Tysons area is **Earls,** which has superb steaks, seafood, and sushi. Great American Restaurants also operates **Randy's Prime Seafood and Steaks,** in the same building as Patsy's, and **Coastal Flats** in Tysons Corner Center, which features a menu punctuated with Southern American dishes.

Ballston

As a neighborhood populated by a number of government agencies, nonprofits, and college students (both full time and commuting), Ballston is starting to move beyond casual dining by adding more-upscale spots, including offshoots of downtown establishments. **SER** (Simple, Easy, Real) gets rave reviews for its Spanish tapas and global wine list. Robert Wiedmaier's **Mussel Bar & Grille** has more than mussels and *frites*, including raw-bar specials, brick-oven pizza, and grilled entrées. **RusUz** is one of the few Eastern European (Russian-Uzbek) kitchens in the area, offering caviar-filled puffs, more than a baker's dozen of piroshki, authentic stroganoff and chicken Kiev, pilaf, and cabbage rolls—all startlingly inexpensive. **Rustico** is focused on beers that pair easily with grilled poultry and meat, as well as burgers. **Big Buns Damn Good Burger Co.**'s name tells you pretty much what you need to know. **Grand Cru Wine Bar and Bistro** is also just what it sounds like, except that the menu might be a little more polished than you'd expect. There's also another outpost of homegrown **Cava,** a casual restaurant with contemporary Greek food. But the most efficient way to sample food from some of D.C.'s best chefs is at **Ballston Quarter.** In this indoor/outdoor marketplace are 24 restaurants and vendors, including diminutive versions of D.C.'s classics **Ice Cream Jubilee, Ted's Bulletin** (see below), and **True Food Kitchen.** Offshoots of Himitsu (**Hot Lola's**) and Timber Pizza Co. (**Turu's**) serve up tempting tastes, including slices and hot chicken.

Ted's Bulletin ★★½ • AMERICAN DINER • MODERATE

4238 Wilson Blvd., #1130, Arlington, VA; ☎ 703-848-7580; tedsbulletin.com

Reservations Recommended. **Metro** Ballston/MU. **Wine selection** Very good. **Open** Sunday-Thursday, 7 a.m.-10 p.m.

THE PREMISE Ted's Bulletin arrived about a decade ago. A favorite of the millennial set and teens, the upscale diner serves photogenic food, including its famous homemade version of Pop-Tarts. The atmosphere is welcoming, often noisy, and very family-friendly, and the classic dishes are mostly decadent but usually delicious. Diners rave about the Boozy Shakes. Breakfast is served all day.

THE PAYOFF Most of the dishes are very hearty and some noteworthy, like the corned beef and potato hash, candied bacon, and soups made from scratch. They do offer a few lighter entrées, but treat yourself to the classics—Brick Chicken, meat loaf, burgers, or the House Pastrami sandwich.

IF YOU LIKE THIS Ted's Bulletin has five other locations: 14th Street; the original location in Capitol Hill; Gaithersburg, Maryland; and two in Virginia: the Mosaic District in Fairfax and Reston. For other great brunch-style restaurants, check out **The Diner** in Adams Morgan, serving breakfast all day but with healthier options, such as veggie omelets and a tofu scramble. **The Commissary** in Dupont Circle has the best bagels, plus California-influenced breakfasts like an egg-white sandwich with avocado, sprouts, and tomato.

Clarendon

Clarendon is one of Northern Virginia's hottest dining districts, thanks to the influx of single millennials who make their home here. The neighborhood eateries of note include **The Liberty Tavern** (see below) and its casual sidekick, **Lyon Hall**; the surprisingly inventive **Green Pig Bistro**; a branch of the popular **Cava Mezze**; the deservedly adored Balkan **Ambar** and the swanky bar **Baba,** both operated by the same group. The music-minded **Galaxy Hut** has 28 taps of craft beer and casual munchies. **Mala Tang,** specializing in Sichuan street food, is especially welcome on a chilly night. Clarendon is home to the D.C.-area's pioneer in the Vietnamese cultural boom: **Four Sisters Grill.**

The Liberty Tavern ★★★
• MODERN AMERICAN • INEXPENSIVE-MODERATE

3195 Wilson Blvd., Arlington, VA; ☎ 703-465-9360; thelibertytavern.com

Reservations Recommended. **Metro** Clarendon. **Wine selection** Good. **Open** *Lunch:* Monday-Friday, 11:30 a.m.-2:30 p.m. *Dinner:* Daily, 5-10 p.m. *Brunch:* Saturday-Sunday, 9 a.m.-3 p.m. *Happy hour:* Daily, 3-7 p.m. *Late-night pizza:* Daily, 10 p.m.-midnight.

THE PREMISE This lovingly restored historical building with exposed brick, a fabulous staircase, and a carved Masonic symbol over the door became one of the neighborhood's central hangouts when Clarendon began the gentrification process from its roots as an ethnic enclave. The restaurant uses high-quality, artisanal, and sustainable ingredients (including farmhouse cheeses) and has two wood-burning ovens, one for pizza and the other for everything else. Saturday and Sunday brunch is all you can eat for $24.

THE PAYOFF The menu isn't overtly unusual but is unusually deft: charred octopus with bottarga and preserved lemon; homemade semolina *mafalde* pasta with chicken sausage and broccoli rabe; spring vegetable gnocchi; and stellar Red Pie pizza, which you can personalize with toppings. The Monday special is pickle-brined fried chicken with two sides and a biscuit for $18—and the chicken is also on the extensive brunch menu.

IF YOU LIKE THIS Liberty Tavern has an offshoot brasserie, **Lyon Hall,** just down the street; it has a slightly heavier German tone, with more of the pâtés, sausages, schnitzel, and cassoulet. The frankfurter made from short ribs is a local fave.

Crystal City/National Place

Crystal City is the new home of Amazon HQ2. Amazon selected the location for several reasons. One is because it's a subway stop from Reagan National Airport, which makes for quick flight arrivals and departures. Another is that Crystal City has plenty of hotels and a fairly extensive retail/restaurant strip. There are plenty of chain/franchise offerings, such as **McCormick & Schmick's, Ruth's Chris Steak House, Legal Sea Foods,** and **Ted's Montana Grill.** When looking for local favorites, choose the family owned-and-operated fine dining Italian restaurant **Portofino. Skydome** is a revolving rooftop restaurant in the DoubleTree hotel. Among the less-expensive local bets are **Bar Louie; Freddie's Beach Bar; Good Stuff Eatery** (page 210); **Neramitra Thai; Kabob Palace; Epic Smokehouse; We, The Pizza;** and **Bob & Edith's Diner,** serving breakfast 24/7. Crystal City was home to one of the first Ethiopian/Eritrean café clusters outside of the District, and it still has a few, including the excellent **Enjera.** For something sweet, head to **The Stand** for its quirky doughnuts.

TWO DINING DESTINATIONS WORTH A DRIVE

Cantler's Riverside Inn   ★★★½
• **CHESAPEAKE BAY SEAFOOD** • **MODERATE**
458 Forest Beach Road, Annapolis, MD; ☎ 410-757-1311; cantlers.com

Reservations Recommended for groups. **Metro** Not Metro accessible. **Wine selection** None. **Open** Sunday–Thursday, 11 a.m.–10 p.m.; Friday–Saturday, 11 a.m.–11 p.m. *Note:* This restaurant is accessible, but the space between the tables is very tight.

THE PREMISE Located just outside of Annapolis, this iconic Maryland restaurant has been in business for nearly four decades. Opened as a port where Chesapeake Bay watermen would unload the catch of the day, Cantler's became the place for boaters to stop by and enjoy a Maryland blue crab feast. Local watermen still bring in bushels of crabs and fresh rockfish and oysters every day, especially in the summer. Rustic picnic tables have a view of the peaceful inlet called Mill Creek. Expect to wait awhile in the summer; the line moves, but try to go early for lunch or dinner.

THE PAYOFF You'll find classics such as Maryland crab soup, which is tomato-based with veggies and shredded crabmeat; cream of crab soup; butter-broiled lump crab cake (with very little filler); mussels and clams from Prince Edward Island; jumbo peel-and-eat shrimp; and crab cake sandwiches. All the seafood comes with Maryland's famous Old Bay spices, butter, and Cantler's signature sauces. Be prepared to get your hands dirty!

IF YOU LIKE THIS You can get a similar menu in rustic digs at **Bethesda Crab House,** but expect to pay a lot more. Or visit the **Municipal Fish Market** at The Wharf in D.C.

The Inn at Little Washington ★★★★★
• **MODERN AMERICAN** • **VERY EXPENSIVE**

Middle and Main Streets, Washington, VA; ☎ 540-675-3800; theinnatlittlewashington.com

Reservations Required (accepted up to a year in advance; $100-per-person deposit). **Metro** Not Metro accessible. **Wine selection** Excellent. **Open** *Dinner:* Wednesday-Monday (visit website for seating times).

THE PREMISE For more than 40 years, this culinary legend—it has been profiled in *The New Yorker* and selected by *Travel & Leisure* as the second-finest hotel in the United States and the eighth-finest in the world—has been Washington's most famous distant dining destination. Chef Patrick O'Connell makes magic in gourmet (and gourmand) circles all over the country. But it is without a doubt a special-occasion intention: the prix fixe menu is $248 per person, before wine and gratuity (which should be generous because of the layers of service), although holiday menus may vary. The two Kitchen Tables flank the huge fireplace and seat up to six apiece. A seat at one will set you back more than double, but consider that you are paying for some of the most meticulous and labor-intensive cooking in the country. And although the dinner is purportedly four courses, there are plenty of extras along the way. If you really want a superb vegetarian experience, this is your chance. Incidentally, the exquisite mansion is worth wandering about, as is the garden, where you will get a glimpse into the bustling kitchen.

THE PAYOFF O'Connell's strength is a sense of balance: dishes are never overly fussy, and local produce is emphasized (he was among the first to credit sources), which guarantees freshness and inventiveness. The menu changes continually, but some of the standards include lamb carpaccio with Caesar salad ice cream; blackened heart of Wagyu rib eye with grilled romaine and bone marrow custard; and the Tin of Sin, Imperial-grade caviar with Chesapeake blue crab. Everyone remembers his or her first passion here—whether it's homemade white-chocolate ice cream with bitter-chocolate sauce or an array of perfect dime-size biscuits with country ham—and for some Washingtonians, driving down to the *other* Washington becomes an addiction, a compulsion.

IF YOU LIKE THIS **Minibar, Pineapple & Pearls, Métier,** and **Komi,** though different in approach, would be the top D.C. foodie destinations. In the meantime, O'Connell is generous with his recipes, often posting them on the website or mailing out newsletters.

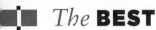

The BEST

Note: **The following lists** are in alphabetical order and not by rank.

Best Bars for Hard Cider and Beer

- **Anxo Cidery**   NoMa
- **Atlas Brew Works**   Ivy City near the National Arboretum
- **Bluejacket**   Navy Yard
- **Board Room DC**   Dupont Circle
- **Capitol Cider House**   Petworth near President Lincoln's Cottage
- **ChurchKey**   Logan Circle
- **Columbia Room**   Penn Quarter
- **Dacha Beer Garden**   Navy Yard, NoMa
- **District Winery**   Navy Yard
- **Jack Rose Dining Saloon**   Georgetown
- **Owen's Ordinary**   North Bethesda
- **The Sovereign**   Georgetown
- **Tortuga Caribbean Bar & Grille**   Capitol Hill
- **Union Pub**   Capitol Hill
- **Wunder Garten**   NoMa

Best Breakfast

- **A Baked Joint**   Convention Center
- **Bayou Bakery, Coffee Bar & Eatery**   Capitol Hill; Arlington, VA
- **Bread & Chocolate**   Foggy Bottom; Chevy Chase, MD
- **Busboys and Poets**   Multiple locations
- **Call Your Mother: A Jew-ish Deli**   Columbia Heights
- **The Diner**   Adams Morgan
- **Kramerbooks & Afterwords Café**   Dupont Circle
- **Little Red Fox**   Tenleytown
- **Open City**   Woodley Park
- **Red Apron**   Penn Quarter
- **Slipstream**   Logan Circle
- **Ted's Bulletin**   Multiple locations, including Capitol Hill
- **Unconventional Diner**   Penn Quarter
- **Uptowner Cafe**   Foggy Bottom
- **Wicked Waffle**   White House

Best Brunches

- **Agora**   Dupont Circle
- **Ambar**   Capitol Hill
- **Ana at District Winery**   The Wharf
- **Bastille Brasserie & Bar**   Alexandria, VA
- **Belga Café**   Barracks Row

- **Birch & Barley** Logan Circle
- **Bistro Cacao** Capitol Hill
- **Blue Duck Tavern** West End
- **Bombay Club** White House
- **Busboys and Poets** Multiple locations
- **Le Diplomate** Logan Circle
- **Espita Mezcaleria** Shaw
- **First Watch** Fairfax, VA
- **Founding Farmers** Georgetown
- **Four Seasons Hotel** Georgetown
- **Garden Café** National Gallery of Art Penn Quarter
- **The Liberty Tavern** Arlington, VA
- **Old Ebbitt Grill** Downtown
- **Perry's Drag Brunch** Adams Morgan
- **Ted's Bulletin** Multiple locations
- **Tryst** Adams Morgan
- **Tupelo Honey** Arlington, VA

Best Burgers

- **The Avenue** Chevy Chase
- **Bobby's Burger Palace** Multiple locations
- **Burger Tap & Shake** Foggy Bottom
- **Capital Burger** Convention Center
- **Le Diplomate** Logan Circle
- **Duke's Grocery** Dupont Circle, Foggy Bottom
- **Five Guys** Multiple locations
- **Good Stuff Eatery** Multiple locations
- **The Lounge at Bourbon Steak** Georgetown
- **Lucky Buns** Adams Morgan
- **A Rake's Bar** Adams Morgan
- **Red Apron** Penn Quarter
- **Reverie** Georgetown
- **The Salt Line** Navy Yard
- **Shake Shack** Multiple locations
- **Unconventional Diner** Penn Quarter

Best Chains (* designates local)

- **Busboys and Poets*** 6 locations, including U Street Corridor, Brookland, and Hyattsville, MD
- **Carmine's Italian Restaurant** Penn Quarter
- **Cava Mezze*** Capitol Hill; Clarendon; Rockville, MD
- **Clyde's*** 8 locations, including Georgetown; Chevy Chase and Rockville, MD; and Willow Creek Farm in Virginia

Best Chains (* *designates local*) *(continued)*

- **Corner Bakery** 13 locations, including White House; Penn Quarter; Bethesda, MD; and Tysons Corner, VA
- **Founding Farmers** Georgetown; Tysons Corner and Reston, VA
- **Jaleo*** Penn Quarter; Bethesda, MD; Crystal City, VA
- **Joe's Seafood, Prime Steak & Stone Crab** White House
- **Lebanese Taverna*** 5 full-service locations, including Adams Morgan; Baltimore, MD; and Arlington and Tysons Corner, VA
- **Maggiano's Little Italy** Chevy Chase, MD; Tysons Corner, VA; Springfield, VA
- **Shake Shack** Multiple locations, including Union Station and The Wharf
- **Tara Thai*** 7 locations in Maryland and Virginia
- **Ted's Bulletin*** Capitol Hill, U Street Corridor; Gaithersburg, MD; and Arlington, Fairfax, and Reston, VA
- **True Food Kitchen** Multiple locations, including Bethesda, Fairfax, and Reston, VA

Best Hotel Fine Dining

- **Alhambra** St. Regis Hotel White House
- **Bistro Bis** Kimpton George Hotel Capitol Hill
- **BLT Prime** Trump International Hotel White House
- **Blue Duck Tavern** Park Hyatt West End
- **Bourbon Steak** Four Seasons Hotel Georgetown
- **Brabo/Brabo Tasting Room** Kimpton Lorien Hotel & Spa Old Town Alexandria, VA
- **Café du Parc** Willard InterContinental White House
- **Empress Lounge and Muze** Mandarin Oriental Southwest Waterfront
- **Kingbird** The Watergate Hotel Foggy Bottom
- **Kith/Kin** InterContinental Washington D.C.–The Wharf The Wharf
- **Morrison-Clark Restaurant** Morrison-Clark Historic Inn & Restaurant Convention Center
- **Old Hickory Steakhouse** Gaylord Hotel National Harbor
- **Plume** The Jefferson Downtown
- **A Rake's Progress** The Line DC Adams Morgan
- **The Riggsby** Kimpton Carlyle Hotel Dupont Circle

Best International Food Markets

- **The Block** Annandale, VA
- **La Cosecha** NE Washington, D.C./Gallaudet Metro
- **Eastern Market** Capitol Hill
- **Eden Center** Falls Church, VA
- **Pike Kitchen** Rockville, MD
- **Quarter Market** Arlington, VA
- **The Spot** Rockville, MD; College Park, MD
- **Tastemakers** Brookland
- **Union Market** NE Washington, D.C./Gallaudet Metro
- **Urbanspace** Tysons Galleria in Tysons Corner, VA

Best Museum Restaurants

- **Hillwood Estate, Museum & Gardens** Merriweather Cafe
- **Hirshhorn Museum** Dolcezza Coffee & Gelato
- **International Spy Museum** Sandella's Flatbread Café and L'Enfant Plaza food court (both near the museum)
- **Museum of the Bible** Manna
- **National Gallery of Art, West Building** Garden Café
- **National Gallery of Art, East Building** Cascade Café
- **National Museum of African American History and Culture** Sweet Home Café
- **National Museum of American History** Eat at America's Table (best for families)
- **National Museum of the American Indian** Mitsitam Cafe
- **National Museum of Natural History** Atrium Café (best for kids)
- **National Museum of Women in the Arts** Mezzanine Café
- **The Phillips Collection** Tryst at The Phillips
- **U.S. Holocaust Memorial Museum** Museum Cafe (best for vegetarian, kosher)

Best Night-Out Activities

- **Board Room bar** Dupont Circle
- **Bobby McKey's Dueling Piano Bar** National Harbor
- **Booze and blowouts at Sip and Dry Bar** NoMa/Shaw
- **Cooking classes at Sur La Table** Alexandria, VA
- **Decades nightclub** Dupont Circle
- **Destination Wedding** U Street Corridor
- **Friday ARTnights at Capitol Hill Arts Workshop** Capitol Hill
- **Latin dancing at Cuba Libre** Penn Quarter
- **Paint and Sip at ArtJamz** Dupont Circle
- **Picnic and concert at Wolf Trap Concert Hall** Vienna, VA
- **Primrose Wine Bar** Brookland
- **Rock and Twang Karaoke at Hill Country Barbecue Market** Penn Quarter
- **Salsa classes at Cafe Citron** Dupont Circle
- **Wild Days rooftop bar at the Eaton Hotel** Penn Quarter
- **Wine tasting at Flight Wine Bar** Penn Quarter

Best Pizza

- **All-Purpose** Penn Quarter
- **&Pizza** Multiple locations
- **Comet Ping Pong** Northwest D.C.
- **Ella's** Penn Quarter
- **Etto** Logan Circle
- **Ghibellina** Logan Circle
- **Il Canale** Georgetown

Best Pizza *(continued)*

- **Pete's New Haven Style Apizza**   Friendship Heights
- **Pizzeria Paradiso**   Dupont Circle; Georgetown; Old Town Alexandria, VA
- **Potomac Pizza**   Chevy Chase, College Park, Potomac, Rockville (all MD)
- **7th Hill**   Capitol Hill (Eastern Market)
- **2Amys Neapolitan Pizzeria**   Northwest D.C.
- **We, the Pizza**   Capitol Hill; Crystal City, VA
- **Wiseguy Pizza**   Foggy Bottom, Navy Yard, Penn Quarter

Best Restaurants with a View *(Reservations Recommended)*

- **Brixton bar**   U Street
- **Del Mar**   The Wharf
- **DNV Rooftop Lounge at the Donovan Hotel**   Thomas Circle near Convention Center
- **Fiola Mare**   Georgetown
- **The Graham Georgetown Rooftop Bar in The Graham hotel**   Georgetown
- **Kith/Kin in the InterContinental**   Southwest Waterfront/The Wharf
- **The Lafayette at The Hay-Adams**   White House/National Mall
- **Mi Vida Restaurante**   The Wharf
- **Osteria Morini**   Navy Yard/Capitol Riverfront
- **Officina**   The Wharf
- **Roof Terrace Restaurant at The Kennedy Center**   Foggy Bottom
- **Sequoia**   Georgetown

Best Restaurants Worth a Drive

- **The Ashby Inn & Restaurant**   Paris, VA
- **L'Auberge Chez François/Jacques' Brasserie**   Great Falls, VA
- **Cantler's Riverside Inn (Maryland crabs)**   Annapolis, MD
- **Field & Main**   Marshall, VA
- **Harrimans Virginia Piedmont Grill at Salamander Resort & Spa**   Middleburg, VA
- **The Inn at Little Washington**   Washington, VA
- **The Old Angler's Inn**   Potomac, MD
- **The Restaurant at Patowmack Farm**   Lovettsville, VA
- **Volt**   Frederick, MD
- **Woodberry Kitchen**   Baltimore, MD

Most Romantic Restaurants

- **Barmini**   Penn Quarter
- **Blue Duck Tavern**   Foggy Bottom/West End
- **Bombay Club**   White House
- **Bourbon Steak**   Georgetown
- **Café du Parc**   White House
- **Chez Billy Sud**   Georgetown

- **Del Mar**   The Wharf
- **Fiola Mare**   Georgetown
- **Floriana**   Dupont Circle
- **The Inn at Little Washington**   Washington, VA
- **Iron Gate**   Dupont Circle
- **Marcel's**   Foggy Bottom
- **Métier**   Shaw
- **Plume**   Dupont Circle
- **Rasika**   Penn Quarter
- **The Riggsby**   Dupont Circle
- **1789**   Georgetown
- **Sfoglina**   Van Ness/UDC
- **Tabard Inn**   Dupont Circle
- **Taberna del Alabardero**   White House

Best Steaks

- **BLT Prime**   White House
- **Bobby Van's**   White House
- **Bourbon Steak**   Georgetown
- **The Capital Grille**   Penn Quarter; Chevy Chase, MD; Tysons Corner, VA
- **Charlie Palmer Steak**   Capitol Hill
- **Del Frisco's Double Eagle Steakhouse**   Penn Quarter
- **Fogo de Chão Brazilian Steakhouse**   Penn Quarter; Bethesda, MD; Tysons Corner, VA
- **Joe's Seafood, Prime Steak & Stone Crab**   White House
- **Mastro's Steakhouse**   Penn Quarter
- **Medium Rare**   Multiple locations
- **Morton's Steakhouse**   Multiple locations
- **The Palm**   Dupont Circle; Tysons Corner, VA
- **The Prime Rib**   Foggy Bottom
- **Rare**   White House
- **Urban Butcher**   Silver Spring, MD

Best Sushi

- **Donburi**   Dupont Circle
- **Izakaya Seki**   Mid City
- **Kaz Sushi Bistro**   Foggy Bottom
- **Kintaro**   Georgetown
- **Kotobuki**   Northwest D.C.
- **Himitsu**   Petworth
- **Nobu Washington D.C.**   West End
- **Sushi Hachi**   Capitol Hill
- **Sushiko**   Chevy Chase, MD

Best Sushi *(continued)*

- **Sushi Taro**   Dupont Circle
- **Yuzu**   Bethesda, MD

Best Sweetshops

- **Astro Doughnuts and Fried Chicken**   Penn Quarter
- **Baked and Wired**   Georgetown
- **Bayou Bakery**   Capitol Hill; Arlington, VA
- **Buttercream Bakeshop**   Convention Center
- **Captain Cookie & the Milk Man**   Foggy Bottom
- **District Doughnut**   Barracks Row
- **Dolcezza Gelato & Coffee**   Multiple locations
- **Georgetown Cupcake**   Georgetown; Bethesda, MD
- **Lulabelle's Sweet Shop**   Petworth
- **Milk Bar**   Logan Circle (flagship), Penn Quarter, The Wharf
- **Olivia Macaron**   Georgetown; Bethesda, MD; Tysons Corner, VA
- **Pitango Gelato**   Multiple locations
- **Thomas Sweet**   Georgetown

Washington, D.C.-Area's Best Fast-Casual Restaurants

RANK	FAST CASUAL	QUALITY RATING
1	**Cava Grill** Greek bowls and wraps with salad greens or rice	99
2	**&Pizza** Design your own pizza with wheat or white crust and a wide array of toppings.	98
3	**Beefsteak** Vegetarian bowls and soups with creative sauces and toppings	96
4	**District Taco** Custom-designed tacos for breakfast, lunch, and dinner	96
5	**Sweetgreen** Design your own salads.	96
6	**Good Stuff Eatery** *Top Chef*–designed burgers and unique milkshakes	95
7	**Shake Shack** Internationally acclaimed burgers, hot dogs, crinkly fries, and frozen custard	95
8	**Bibibop Asian Grill** Custom bowls of veggies, rice, meat, and Korean sauces with complimentary miso soup	95
9	**Rasa** Well-spiced, inventive Indian elements in a bowl	95
10	**Poke Papa** Hawaiian raw and marinated fish with flavorful toppings influenced by Korea and Thailand	94
11	**Call Your Mother** Wood-fired bagel sandwiches	94
12	**Arepa Zone** Meats and cheese folded into soft and crunchy arepas	93
13	**Wiseguy Pizza** New York–style slices and salads	92
14	**Falafel Inc.** Israeli-style fried chickpea patties in pita and bowls with choice of toppings	91
15	**Mi Cuba Cafe** Cuban sandwiches and specials	91
16	**Julia's Empanadas** Takeout-only crisp empanadas with a variety of fillings	90
17	**Farmbird** Chicken and tofu with farm-fresh sides	90

PART SIX

ENTERTAINMENT *and* NIGHTLIFE

WASHINGTON NIGHTLIFE:
More Than Lit-Up Monuments

WASHINGTON AFTER-HOURS consists of sporting events, theatre, breweries, concerts, and bars. One challenge for patrons of late-night activities is that Metrorail runs until 11:30 p.m. Monday–Thursday, until 1 a.m. Friday and Saturday, and until 11 p.m. Sunday. As a result, using public transport is limited, even for attending a sporting event, forcing people to use car services like taxis, Lyft, and Uber.

Washington is a hodgepodge of artists, federal workers, congressional employees, lawyers, interns, journalists, diplomats, recently arrived immigrants, CEOs, tech titans, and college students, and the fact that many of these groups overlap, and others evolve, means you can dabble in a variety of entertainment options.

unofficial **TIP**
Drinking and dining are major elements of night-life culture these days; check the "best" lists and neighborhood descriptions in Part Five: Dining as well.

Let's start with Washington's theatre scene. It's widely acknowledged within the theatrical community as excellent—and it's booming, both physically and intellectually. The city boasts what might be considered a trio of Shakespeare theatres, including one that evokes the Bard's own London Globe; numerous ethnic theatres (Hispanic, Jewish, Irish); and touring venues hosting the best of Broadway and London. In the past decade, the expansions of **Signature Theatre, Studio Theatre,** and the highly regarded **Arena Stage,** plus the **Music Center at Strathmore** and **AMP** in Bethesda, have increased the number of performances available to visitors. Two outdoor venues—**Wolf Trap** in suburban Virginia and **Merriweather Post Pavilion** in Columbia, Maryland—plus the **Clarice Smith Performing Arts Center** at the University of Maryland and other multispace performance sites have established Washington as one of the country's premiere arts centers.

To top it off, in September of 2019, the **John F. Kennedy Center for the Performing Arts** opened a new complex, called **The Reach,** that extends over the Potomac River. The modern complex adds three new performing-arts venues, including an open-air pavilion, as well as classrooms for what might be one of its most important legacies: the training of arts management. Also, a pedestrian bridge enables guests to access the Kennedy Center from either the Georgetown waterfront or the Lincoln Memorial without having to dodge traffic.

unofficial **TIP**
If you are considering taking a (free) tour of the Kennedy Center, wait until later in the afternoon; stick around for the (also free) Millennium Stage show and take in the rooftop view.

THE BIG-TICKET VENUES

WASHINGTON BOASTS more than a dozen major theatrical venues—not even counting the Kennedy Center's eight venues separately—and a wealth of smaller residential and repertory companies, university theaters, and small special-interest venues for itinerant troupes. Washington's "big six" are the places to see national touring companies, classical musicians, and celebrity productions: The Kennedy Center, Harman Center for the Arts, the National Theatre, Ford's Theatre, Warner Theatre, and the Arena Stage.

Downtown Destinations

On any given night at the **Kennedy Center for the Performing Arts,** you might see the resident National Symphony Orchestra in the 2,500-seat **Concert Hall;** a straight drama or classic farce in the 1,200-seat **Eisenhower Theater;** and a Broadway musical, Kabuki spectacular, or big-name ballet company in the 2,300-seat **Opera House** (that is, when the Washington National Opera is not in residence). Speaking of, **Washington National Opera** is one of the world's most acclaimed opera companies, often playing to full houses (including their most enthusiastic fan, Supreme Court Justice Ruth Bader Ginsburg). Philip Johnson's steeply canted and gracious **Terrace Theater,** a gift from the nation of Japan, is an intimate venue of fewer than 500 seats, ideally suited for experimental or cult-interest productions, specialty concerts, and showcases. In the even smaller **Theater Lab,** designed to accommodate the avant-garde and cabaret, the semi-improv comedy whodunit *Shear Madness* has been in residence for more than three decades. The smallest venue, the **KC Jazz Club** (actually just the Terrace-level gallery, tricked out cabaret-style) is open only on weekends but hosts such first-rate groups as the Chick Corea Trio. The **Family Theater** on the lobby level is the setting for interpretations of favorite kids' books, folk music, all-ages pops concerts by the National Symphony Orchestra, and even educational plays.

Perhaps most remarkable, however, is the Kennedy Center's gift to music lovers: the free **Millennium Stage,** which provides national and top local acts in an indoor venue at 6 p.m. every day of the year, usually in the 630-foot-long Grand Foyer (which, as docents love to point out, could easily cradle the not-quite-555-foot Washington Monument, though it might bust out part of the ceiling), but occasionally in the Theater Lab. The **Renee Fleming VOICES** series offers a range of performances showcasing a diverse selection of talented vocal artists. The newish **Hip Hop Culture** program offers a home for this dynamic art form. The Kennedy Center's iconic waterfront building is located at Virginia and New Hampshire Avenues NW, next to the Watergate Complex; the closest subway station is Foggy Bottom, and the center operates a free shuttle from the station. For tickets and information, call ☎ 202-467-4600 or visit kennedy-center.org.

The other major downtown venues are in or near Penn Quarter and accessible by several Metro stations.

The critically acclaimed **Shakespeare Theatre Company** (STC) moved first from its beloved but cramped home at the **Folger Shakespeare Library** on Capitol Hill into the 450-seat **Lansburgh Theatre** on Seventh Street NW, which it still operates, and then migrated to **Sidney Harman Hall** around the corner on F Street (named for the philanthropist and public servant who donated generously for its construction and who, appropriately, was one of the founders of Harman Kardon audio company). Both theatres make up the **Harman Center for the Arts. Sidney Harman Hall** houses jazz, dance, film, and chamber music, as well as theatrical productions; the Lansburgh houses smaller touring shows or quirkier Shakespeare Company productions. Each season, STC produces four classic plays, three by

Shakespeare and at least one for families (in 2019 it was *Potted Potter*, a production based on the *Harry Potter* books). It also puts on another of Washington's very best freebies: the annual Shakespeare Free for All series in late August and early September. The Harman Center is across from the Capital One Arena and the Gallery Place/Chinatown Metro; the Lansburgh Theatre is just a minute closer to the Archives/Navy Memorial/Penn Quarter stop. For information call ☎ 202-547-1122 or 202-638-3863 or visit shakespearetheatre.org.

 ESPECIALLY IN TERMS OF ARTS AND HISTORY, the following are modern heroes of Washington. **David Rubenstein** donated $121 million in one year to support the National Gallery of Art's modernization, purchased a $22 million Magna Carta to display in the National Archives, and contributed $7.5 million to rehab the Washington Monument after it was damaged by an earthquake. **Donald W. Reynolds,** whose philanthropy spanned numerous states and foundations, gave essential donations to create what is now the twinned National Portrait

Gallery–Smithsonian American Art Museum; he also made possible the extensive visitor center and exhibit galleries that were added to Mount Vernon in 2006. Developer **Robert H. Smith** donated hugely to the University of Maryland (including the Clarice Smith Performing Arts Center, named for his wife), the auditorium at Mount Vernon, and the restoration of James Madison's Montpelier; he also served as chairman of the board of the National Gallery of Art during an era of expansion from 1993 to 2003. And Smith's partner and brother-in-law **Robert Kogod and his wife, Arlene,** were key to the creation of the beloved glass-covered canopy between the Portrait Gallery and American Art Museum, as well as the expansions of Signature Theatre, Arena Stage, and Shakespeare Theatre, among others. One of the main proponents of a "national theater" was **William Wilson Corcoran,** he of the Renwick Gallery and Corcoran Gallery (now closed) and numerous other Washington institutions. A successful tycoon at a young age, he contributed not only to area colleges and churches (and Oak Hill Cemetery) but also to the fund to rescue Mount Vernon from foreclosures and for firewood for the poor.

The National Theatre (☎ 202-628-6161, thenationaldc.com) got its name from its founders—some of the few early proud Washingtonians—who wanted the nation's capital to have a theatre rivaling those in other big cities. That was in 1835, a quarter-century before John T. Ford turned an abandoned Baptist church into an entertainment venue. The National has been in nearly continual operation ever since ("nearly" because it refused for four years in the late 1940s and early 1950s to integrate). On the night Lincoln was assassinated at Ford's Theatre, he had dropped off his young son Tad at a performance of *Aladdin and the Wonderful Lamp* at the National. The theatre also hosted the world debut of *West Side Story* in 1957. Today, the National hosts touring Broadway productions, famous performers in concert, magic shows, and pre-Broadway tryouts. It also offers free programs—Saturday-morning family shows and Community Stage Connections for communities with mobility issues or limited resources. The National is at 13th Street and Pennsylvania Avenue NW, near the Federal Triangle or Metro Center stations.

The Warner Theatre (☎ 202-783-4000, warnertheatredc.com), a 1922 silent-movie house and vaudeville venue, is a rococo delight. It is the home of one of Washington's most beloved traditions, the Washington Ballet's version of *The Nutcracker*. Back in the late 1970s, it was one of the best small-concert venues for popular music (the Rolling Stones played a surprise show here, and the reclusive Brian Wilson chose the Warner for his *Smile* and final *Pet Sounds* tours) or big-name comedians. Today, it's booked by the national powerhouse Live Nation with a variety of concerts, from vintage performers to family-friendly shows. The Warner is at 13th and E Streets NW, near

Federal Triangle or Metro Center. Look for the walk-of-fame auto-graphs on the sidewalk out front.

At Ford's Theatre (☎ 202-347-4833, fords.org), the balcony box in which Abraham Lincoln was shot remains draped in black (and spectrally inhabited, according to rumor). Take one of the daily tours conducted by the National Park Service to see the restored theater, and then tour the Lincoln-centric museum in the basement. They have arti-facts such as Lincoln's blood-spattered overcoat and the derringer that John Wilkes Booth used to shoot him. Along with a notable season of programming, Ford's holiday complement is its annual production of *A Christmas Carol,* which ranges from very traditional to extremely spooky. Located on 10th Street NW between E and F Streets, Ford's is near several subway stops on various lines.

It's not of the same size or profile, but the undiminished **Woolly Mammoth** (☎ 202-393-3939, woollymammoth.net) now has a 265-seat courtyard-style venue near the Lansburgh Theatre at Seventh and D Streets NW in the heart of Penn Quarter. It has won more than two dozen Helen Hayes Awards, many for premiering new works, and even hosts a few pay-what-you-can programs. The majestic **Historic Sixth and I Street (NW) Synagogue** (☎ 202-408-3100, sixthandi.org) offers programs featuring a wide array of authors—Ann Patchett, Bill Bryson, and Salman Rushdie—as well as celebrations for the Jewish holidays.

The newest theatre on the scene is the **World Stage Theater at the Museum of the Bible** (☎ 866-430-6682, museumofthebible.org /museum/world-stage). Adjacent to the National Mall at Federal Cen-ter SW Metro station, the 472-seat theatre is inspired by a sacred tabernacle of Moses's time and has cutting-edge acoustics and a com-fortable ambience. Here, you can see Broadway musicals with a reli-gious theme, as well as hear scripture readings and even see fashion shows. This season's feature was *Amazing Grace,* and the ticket includes two hours of touring the museum (adult tickets are $19.99 online and $24.95 at the door).

Neighborhood Theatres

Several of Washington's smaller, special-interest theaters are clustered around the revitalized U Street/Logan Circle neighborhood, a short walk from the Dupont Circle Metro. The most impor-tant is **Studio Theatre** (14th and P Sts. NW, ☎ 202-332-3300, studiotheatre.org), which fea-tures edgy contemporary theatre, modern clas-sics, and experimental plays. **Washington Improv Theater** (1835 14th St. NW, ☎ 202-204-7770, witdc.org) puts on spontaneous performances by their house ensemble. In the same location, **Constellation Theatre Company** (☎ 202-204-7741, constellationtheatre.org) focuses on provocative creativity with adaptations of important plays and musicals and features three interpre-tive shows per season.

*un**official** **TIP**
Dickens's *A Christmas Carol* is a Washington tradition in all sorts of ways: The Keegan Theatre produces *An Irish Carol,* a somewhat more adult version whose central character is not a money lender but a publican.

The **Keegan Theatre,** which specializes in American and Irish plays, has grown from a basement ensemble to having a permanent home at the 115-seat Church Street Theatre (1743 Church St. NW, ☎ 202-265-3767, keegantheatre.com) in Dupont Circle. In 2019 they performed *Legally Blond, Memphis,* and *An Irish Carol.* Among other niche-specific troupes are **Theater J** (☎ 202-777-3210, theaterj.org), a few blocks away at 16th and Q Streets NW, which offers underexplored works by Jewish playwrights; and the 45-year-old Spanish-language (with subtitles) **GALA Hispanic Theater** (☎ 202-234-7174, galatheatre. org) in the beautifully restored 270-seat Tivoli Theater at 14th Street NW and Park Road, two blocks north of the Columbia Heights Metro.

In the U Street Corridor is the revitalized **Lincoln Theatre** (1215 U St. NW, ☎ 202-888-0050, thelincolndc.com), across the street from the U Street/African American Civil War Memorial/Cardozo Metro. This 1922 beauty, once the heart of the Black Broadway neighborhood, now hosts a range of theatrical productions (including some pre-Broadway tryouts) and concerts; it's also a major venue for the annual Duke Ellington Jazz Festival in June.

 THE COTTON CLUB AND APOLLO THEATER may be more famous, but Washington's Black Broadway was in full bloom long before the Harlem Renaissance, and outlasted it by decades. The area around U Street had become an upscale black Victorian neighborhood even before the end of the Civil War, but starting in the early 20th century, a slew of black-owned nightclubs and restaurants drew not only an elegant crowd but also some of the greatest names in entertainment, particularly jazz. This included Louis Armstrong, Pearl Bailey (who is believed to have coined the term "jazz"), Cab Calloway, Duke Ellington (who grew up in the neighborhood and truly fell in love with the piano hanging around the Howard Theatre), Ella Fitzgerald, Billie Holiday, and Sarah Vaughan.

Though not directly accessible by Metro, the multistage **Atlas Performing Arts Center** (14th and H Sts. NE, ☎ 202-399-7993, atlasarts. org), a restored Deco movie theater, is an easy, free trolley ride away from Union Station. The Atlas acts as home base for Step Afrika!, Capital City Symphony, Joy of Motion Dance Theatre, Mosaic Theater Company of DC, and other community arts groups.

On the Waterfront

The biggest excitement in recent Washington theater circles was the reopening of the soaring and state-of-the-art **Arena Stage** (1101 Sixth St. SW, ☎ 202-554-9066, arenastage.org), formally known as the Arena Stage at the Mead Center for the American Theater. Founded 65 years ago as a haven for the preservation and encouragement of American theater, the Arena was already one of the country's most influential theaters before it emerged from the two-and-a-half-year, $135-million reconstruction as a towering, 200,000-square-foot glass-and-concrete vessel, the largest performing arts center in the region since the Kennedy Center. In fact, Arena, along with Nationals Park, has sparked a revitalization not only of the theatre scene but also of the entire Southwest sector, leading to The District Wharf.

The new arena, which is more than twice the size of the old, has three venues: the 510-seat **Kreeger Theater;** the 680-seat **Fichandler Stage,** which was the original Arena Stage and has been embedded in the new design; and the completely new, 200-seat **Kogod Cradle,** which is like a chambered nautilus, with a semicircular entrance ramp on the outside and a slat-sided "basket" of a stage within. Designed by Bing Thom, the complex includes bars and an upscale catered café; glass walls, wood columns, sloping floors, and long steel elbow bars; and a rock garden, lots of overhung walkways, and mysterious vistas. Arena Stage is only a couple of blocks from the Southwest Waterfront and L'Enfant Plaza Metro stops. This entire stretch of waterfront along the Washington Channel is the most dazzling in the city today.

Superb Suburbanites

As dominant as the downtown theatrical scene may seem, the suburbs on all sides of the District have more opportunities than we can list here. Check the "Guide to the Lively Arts" in *The Washington Post* Friday "Weekend" section or the free *City Paper,* for a full listing, but here are some of the most important.

A number of impressive performance venues are located in the Maryland suburbs, and most are accessible by subway. The **Clarice Smith Performing Arts Center** (☎ 301-405-2787, theclarice.umd.edu), on the College Park campus of the University of Maryland, offers almost as many venues as the Kennedy Center (and in several cases, even more cutting-edge acoustical and recording technology): the 1,100-seat Dekelboum Concert Hall, with its modern-Gothic arches and choral loft; the 180-seat Dance Theatre; the 650-seat proscenium Kay Theatre; the 300-seat Gildenhorn Recital Hall; the intimate 100-seat Cafritz Foundation Theatre; and the 200-seat black box–style Kogod Theatre. Smith Center offerings have ranged from Chinese opera and the Shanghai Traditional Orchestra to Phillip Glass—plus productions featuring the university's dance, music, theater, and voice departments.

Closer in, and Metro accessible via an underground pedestrian tunnel, is the **Round House Theatre** (☎ 240-644-1100, roundhousetheatre .org) on East-West Highway, near the Bethesda Metro station. Round House mounts a mix of family, experimental, classic, and premiere productions. Just a bit farther from the Bethesda Metro, an eight-minute walk at most, is one of the area's most important children's and family theaters, **Imagination Stage** (☎ 301-280-1660, imaginationstage.org), which began as a school for the performing arts but now has a two-stage complex, with rehearsal and classroom space.

And although they require cars (or friends), there are two other prominent venues in Montgomery County. The historic **Olney Theatre**

(☎ 301-924-3400, olneytheatre.org), on Route 108 in Olney, Maryland, started out in 1938 producing high-quality summer stock. Now open year-round, the Olney offers a variety of children's, classic, touring company, and musical productions, as well as free Shakespeare in the summer. **BlackRock Center for the Arts** (☎ 301-528-2260, blackrockcenter.org) in Germantown has three venues: a 210-seat main stage; a 130-seat dance theater; and an outdoor performance stage for theatrical productions, festivals, concerts, and outdoor family films. Artists booked there include Alvin Ailey II, the Baltimore Symphony Orchestra Chamber Players, Janis Ian, the Nighthawks, indie filmmakers, and storytellers.

The Virginia suburbs are equally star-studded. The fascinating **Synetic Theater** (☎ 866-811-4111, synetictheater.org), which calls itself "D.C.'s premier physical theater," rethinks fantastic and often supernatural stories—Shakespeare, Edgar Allan Poe, *Don Quixote, Phantom of the Opera, Treasure Island,* and *The Snow Queen*—as intensely visual dream works mixing ballet, modern dance, artscapes, multimedia, and mime. Its home stage is about a block from the Crystal City/National Place Metro.

Near the Pentagon City Metro is one of Washington's most successful companies, **Signature Theatre** (☎ 703-820-9771, sigtheatre.org), whose crystalline two-story center launched the redevelopment of the Shirlington Village of Arlington. Signature has sent several of its theatrical productions to Broadway and frequently brings in national names for locally mounted productions of both established and avant-garde theater and cabaret. Remarkably, every Signature production offers a limited number of reasonably priced tickets—$40, $25 for full-time students with an ID—and discounts are available for first responders, active military, and Five Star families and educators. Signature is also remarkable for devoting whole seasons to the work of a single playwright.

The Center for the Arts at George Mason University in Fairfax is not Metro accessible, but if you have access to a car, it also hosts opera, jazz, popular music, cabaret, symphony performances, Cirque du Soleil–type performances, and so on (cfa.gmu.edu).

unofficial **TIP**
The bottom line is, always ask if there's a way to boost your bottom line. What's to lose?

CUTTING CURTAIN COSTS

THOUGH MANY OF THESE professional productions can be pricey and often sell out, there are ways to trim the ticket tab for less-popular or longer-running shows. **Ticketplace,** operated by the Cultural Alliance of Greater Washington, sells half-price tickets online for some same-day shows and concerts (ticketplace.org or culturecapital.tix.com). There is a service charge, and all sales are final.

Gold Star (goldstar.com) is one of several online/social media sites that sends out notices of discount offers, not only to shows (many of them at major venues) but also to museums, cruises, clubs, and so on.

In addition, several venues, including the Kennedy Center and Arena Stage, offer discounts to special groups, typically students (and sometimes teachers), seniors, patrons with disabilities, military, Metro subway patrons, or those willing to stand or stand by. As noted above, Signature Theatre offers some discounted tickets to its new productions. Call the venue's box office and just say you're from out of town and don't really know all the ins and outs of ticket pricing; operators will do the best they can for you. Or check the website for opportunities.

In the meantime, don't overlook the myriad freebies available, particularly during good weather. In addition to the several mentioned above—the Shakespeare Theatre Company's Free for All series, the nightly Millennium Stage performances at the Kennedy Center, the National Theatre's Saturday mornings, and so on—several public sites frequently hold concerts of classical, jazz, pop, and folk music, and even some medieval consorts. Among them are the **Washington National Cathedral, National Gallery of Art,** and the **Library of Congress.** For information on these, plus the handful of smaller theaters and itinerant companies, check their websites, or read *The Washington Post Weekend Going Out Guide* on Friday or online.

> *unofficial* **TIP**
> Here's a little insider intel that only longtime residents know: The popular National Symphony Orchestra holiday concerts are always packed with patrons, but there are also full dress rehearsals that are a little easier to get into. The Memorial Day and Fourth of July rehearsals are the day before; the Labor Day rehearsal is usually in the afternoon a few hours before the performance.

If you are visiting in midsummer, check to see if the Smithsonian's **Folklife Festival** will be held on the Mall. Typically, the event runs for two weeks, around the last week of June until the first week of July (culminating around the Fourth of July fireworks display). Folklife focuses on a region of the United States and an international culture, complete with all-day live concerts, performances, and food demonstrations.

> *unofficial* **TIP**
> If you intend to book tickets for big shows, don't be confused by the name of the website; make sure you are dealing directly with the venue whenever possible, not being shuffled onto a secondhand or resale site that will cost more.

Several other warm-weather outdoor music venues are downtown, including **Woodrow Wilson Plaza,** at 13th and Pennsylvania Avenue NW, and **Freedom Plaza,** at 14th and Pennsylvania. The **National Mall** is the site of many festivals during the year in addition to the Folklife Festival, notably on Memorial Day, the Fourth of July, and Labor Day, when the National Symphony Orchestra and special guest celebrities offer family concerts. Wednesdays are entertainment nights on Georgetown's waterfront (make it a double-header—hit the Kennedy Center's Millennium Stage first and walk over).

A WASHINGTON TRADITION: LIVE LOCAL MUSIC

WASHINGTON IS A DRAW FOR MUSIC LOVERS of all types, from classical to college-radio rock, indie to outrageous, retro to roots, and from hole-in-the-wall to hip hop. Venues range from a few hundred to a few thousand to super-size sports arenas. D.C. has boasting rights to a number of breakout artists and trends over two centuries. John Phillip Sousa and Duke Ellington were both homegrown innovators, and so were soul agnostic Marvin Gaye, soulful singer Eva Cassidy, early femme-confessional pianist Tori Amos, and Dave Grohl of Nirvana and Foo Fighters, to name a very few. D.C. was the birthplace of Go-go, a form of African American music concocted by "godfather" Chuck Brown. The musical genre exploded onto the local scene during the 1980s and into the 1990s, before rap was popularized. Times have changed, and now the DMV (District, Maryland, and Virginia) claim hip-hop and rap stars such as Wale, Shy Glizzy, GoldLink, DJ Cool, and Fat Trel. And while there are obviously commercial interests involved in booking the midsize and larger sites in particular, a lot of the credit for the vital live music scene in the area belongs to the stubborn musicians and underground entrepreneurs who have established venues and support networks for themselves and one another.

 PATRIOTIC MUSIC: A D.C. SPECIALTY One of the merriest experiences during the summer is listening to the armed forces bands that play free concerts around the city. From about Memorial Day to Labor Day, ensembles from the four branches perform evening concerts Monday–Friday, generally starting at 8 p.m., before the west front of the Capitol (aoc.gov/news); select Tuesdays at 7:30 p.m. at the Navy Memorial (Seventh St. and Pennsylvania Ave. NW); Wednesday at Fort Myer in Rosslyn; and Friday (a little later, 8:30 p.m.) at the Marine Barracks on Capitol Hill. Sunday matinees at Constitution Hall are the largest events, featuring well-known entertainers in patriotic and martial, country, jazz, pop, and some classical music (usarmyband.com). You're welcome to bring a picnic to the outside performances, but as with all National Park Service concerts, including the NSO holiday concerts on the Mall, alcohol is not permitted.

The Larger Venues

As in many big cities, the downtown sports arenas do double duty as mega-rock concert venues, especially the 20,000-plus-seat **Capital One Area** downtown, home to the Washington Wizards NBA team and the Capitals NHL team. As it's an all-season indoor venue, and has more hookups for lights and tech, that's where the off-season and theatrically elaborate tours tend to stop: Lady Gaga, Jennifer Lopez, Paul McCartney, and those family-friendly and orchestral music/light show spectaculars (Trans-Siberian Orchestra, *Star Wars* in concert, Disney on Ice, and so on). Capital One Arena has its own entrance from the Gallery Place/Chinatown Metro.

Though only partially covered, the 42,000-seat **Nationals Park,** at the Navy Yard Metro, has hosted Billy Joel and Elton John, Dave

Matthews, Taylor Swift, and Bruce Springsteen. (Nats Park is also used for live simulcasts of the Washington Opera.)

The massive District Wharf development along the Southwest waterfront, a mix of retail, residential, and cultural sites, is home to **The Anthem** (☎ 202-888-0020, theanthemdc.com), which hosts world-class performers such as Elvis Costello, Billie Eilish, anthropologist Jane Goodall, RuPaul, and Kacey Musgraves. The Anthem also has the Marquee Bar, where you can take in views of the Potomac River with special drink prices before and after the show. The Anthem is comanaged by the 9:30 Club.

More progressive rock acts, which draw strong college and postgrad audiences, tend to be booked into college sports spaces, such as George Washington University's **Smith Center** or Georgetown's **Gaston Hall**. National acts with midsize audiences—revived rockers, R&B, gospel, soul, and folk—are often booked into the **DAR Constitution Hall** (dar.org/constitution-hall) alongside the Ellipse.

Outside the city are several of the area's largest venues, which are not so easily accessible but are regular summer commutes for Washingtonians. Perhaps the most sentimentally popular outdoor commercial venue, and the only one with any sort of Metro connection, is the most sophisticated of them: **Wolf Trap National Park** off Route 7 in Vienna, Virginia, which offers almost nightly entertainment—pop, country, jazz and R&B, MOR (middle-of-the-road) rock, and even ballet and Broadway musical tours—and picnicking under the stars during the summer at its **Filene Center** amphitheater. (It also operates a full-service restaurant.) During the winter season, Wolf Trap shifts to its small (220 seats) but acoustically great **Barns**—literally two rebuilt vintage barns—which book everything from Wolf Trap's own highly regarded opera company to the Beach Boys, American Ballet Theatre, Nas, Tony Bennett, and the National Symphony Orchestra accompanying movies like *E.T.* and *Star Wars.* On summer nights, the Metro operates a $5 round-trip shuttle service called The Fairfax Connector from the West Falls Church station to the Filene Center, but watch your watch: The return shuttle leaves either 20 minutes after the final curtain or no later than 10:30 p.m. Monday–Thursday, 11:30 p.m. Friday and Saturday, and 10 p.m. Sunday to ensure that riders don't miss the Metro.

The gorilla in the Beltway backyard is **Jiffy Lube Live** (livenation .com), just off I-66 outside Manassas, Virginia. It's a surprisingly attractive amphitheater with 10,000 covered seats and lawn seating for another 15,000 people (and parking lots and hillsides for tailgates and picnicking). Operated by Live Nation, the largest promoter in the country, it books the full range of big-ticket acts.

Merriweather Post Pavilion (merriweathermusic.com) in Columbia, Maryland, which also mixes under-cover and lawn seating, has the busiest pop-rock outdoor arena and mixes old-favorite rock and pop tours with younger-draw and cult acts. Keep in mind it is some distance from Washington and can only be reached by car. In addition to concerts, the venue hosts multiact, all-day festivals with a cornucopia of food trucks.

The 10,000-seat **Eagle Bank Arena** (eaglebankarena.com) at George Mason University in Fairfax tends to carry the big-name country concerts, as well as college-draw rock and pop. The adjoining GMU Center for the Arts, described on page 262, is a lovely midsize venue for classical and jazz music and drama.

Midsize Settings

Here we mean the smaller theaters and largest clubs, between 300 and 2,000 seats. One of the most impressive is the **Music Center at Strathmore Hall** (☎ 301-581-5100, strathmore.org) in North Bethesda, which, happily for tourists, has a dedicated pedestrian overpass from the Grosvenor/ Strathmore Metro station. A beautiful blond-wood space with comfortable chairs and first-rate acoustics, it seats 2,000, and books national classical and pop singers, visiting symphony orchestras, and folk and blues society shows. The original Strathmore Hall Mansion, a much more intimate affair, hosts tea-time concerts (harp, Japanese koto, violin) on Tuesdays and Wednesdays, as well as summertime concerts and family films on the lawn; it also has art galleries and crafts shows.

Strathmore's extension, **AMP** (☎ 301-581-5100, ampbystrathmore.com), is about a mile north in the Pike & Rose mixed-residential development near the White Flint Metro, and has seats for 240 plus 350 standing-room spaces. Most shows—and the variety is eccentric—are Thursday–Saturday. Its main advantage over its parent is freshly prepared (rather than café-style) fare from the ChurchKey group and a much more elaborate cocktail list.

In Silver Spring, a short stroll from the Silver Spring Metro, the 2,000-seat **Fillmore** (☎ 301-960-9999, fillmoresilverspring.com) actually holds 2,000 standing-room spaces and a handful of "premium" seats. It opened its doors with a sold-out Mary J. Blige concert, and has followed up with classic rock/reruns (Guns N' Roses, Slayer, Steve Winwood); reggae from Stephen Marley; dance-hall pop (Kelly Rowland and Carley Rae Jepsen); semi-indie songwriters (Sarah Bareilles and Gavin DeGraw); country hunks and punks (Chris Young and Kid Rock); tribute bands; and even the Psychedelic Furs and comic Andrew Dice Clay. The sound system is vast, showy, and bass-heavy. In terms of decor, the club also seems to want to cover all bases, mixing bordello red drapes, oversize pop art and cartoon graphics, vintage concert posters, chandeliers, and a few lighting effects.

The Hamilton (☎ 202-769-0122, thehamiltondc.com) downtown is actually a huge, sprawling restaurant with benefits (that is, a cozy concert hall on the lower level). It belongs to the local stalwart Clyde's chain, and the upstairs menu includes sushi, plus a full sweep of upscale appetizers and sandwiches, steaks, seafood, and pasta—all available fairly late. The Hamilton Live, as the downstairs music room is called, seats 300, with another 200 standing-room spaces. Bookings range from classic rock to up-and-coming iTunes, jazz, R&B, folk, blues, and country: Dr. John, Emmylou Harris, NRBQ, Leon Russell, Booker T., and the Tubes, plus the very occasional bluegrass act or comedian. It has also picked up on the tribute-band craze. You could eat upstairs and then go down for the music, but the Hamilton adheres to the new standard operating procedure: general admission/first come, first seated, and otherwise SRO. It's also all-ages, so depending on which artist you're seeing, the line may be even longer. If you're a fan of gospel brunches, this is one of the most expansive Sunday spreads around.

The Howard Theatre (☎ 202-803-2899, thehowardtheatre.com) has performances of notable, mostly African American, artists such as R&B crooner Elle Varner, local hero Dave Chappelle, and former Prince drummer, Sheila E. The Howard has a nightclub where you can dance to the beat of celebrity DJs, but you'll have to call to get the upcoming show information.

The **9:30** club (☎ 202-265-0930, 930.com), arguably the most important progressive music venue in the region, holds 1,200 ("seats" not being exactly the word) for an amazingly eclectic range of music: alt, country, top 40, hardcore, hip-hop, prog, reggae, semi-punk, and true rock. Consider a scrapbook that includes James Brown, Elvis Costello, the Damned, Bob Dylan, Five for Fighting, Fugazi, Joan Jett, Sergio Mendes, Liz Phair, Radiohead, Smashing Pumpkins, Squeeze, Richard Thompson, Justin Timberlake, Suzanne Vega, and Dwight Yoakam. (Before you go, be sure you know who's playing: The crowd that pays up for Ice-T isn't the same as the one for Marshall Crenshaw, They Might Be Giants, or Anthrax.) It's close to the U Street/African-American Civil War Memorial/Cardozo Metro, but being an old building, it has limited wheelchair access.

The **Birchmere** (☎ 703-549-7500, birchmere.com) in Alexandria, the premiere site for country, bluegrass, new-alt, and ethnic folk acts, holds about 500 (with a smaller roadhouse-style second stage). This is a serious eclectic venue and easily the biggest for acoustic, alternative, bluegrass, and country acts, such as hometown heroine Mary Chapin Carpenter, Rosanne Cash, Lyle Lovett, Marty Stuart, Jerry Jeff Walker, Shawn Colvin, Jeffery Osborne, k.d. lang, Patty Loveless, Little River Band, Don McLean, and Suzanne Vega. The bad news—it's not anywhere near the Metro, and although it is a table-service restaurant, all seating is first come, closest in. If you go, go early and expect to stand in line. (But don't worry—it's a bit of a tailgate atmosphere.)

Black Cat (☎ 202-667-4490, blackcatdc .com) in U Street Corridor was another early breakthrough on the music scene and is still a main attraction, booking

unofficial **TIP**
The 9:30 is one of an increasing number of area clubs that believes in seating democracy—that is, general admission SRO—so it's first come, first stand (with very few exceptions); you might find an odd ledge to lean on, and there are a few stools around the mezzanine.

unofficial **TIP**
Another thing to know about the Washington nightlife scene is that an increasing number of these venues are cash-only, which eliminates some underage freeloading (at best) and greatly increases the bartending speed. Make sure you know the policies at any club before you head out.

a mix of hot regional and early-national alternative rock, funky-punk, post-punk, Brit-pop, indie rock, and revivals, from Arcade Fire, Death Cab for Cutie, Kings of Leon, the White Stripes, and Hank Williams III to the Damned, Foo Fighters, Fleshtones, and Zombies. The main stage can hold about 1,000 fans; the smaller back room holds only about 150, so that goes to up-and-coming bands and (mostly) DJs. In keeping with the neighborhood playground style, the main-floor bar has pinball and pool tables. This is not a swank joint, but it's not scuzzy, either. If you can make it to the box office, you'll save the ticket fee; it's all cash-only with two ATMs on site. Get there early for a concert—the check-in system is fairly slow because Black Cat is an all-ages club, so IDs are closely scrutinized and 21-and-over hands have to be stamped for alcohol consumption.

The **State Theatre** (☎ 703-237-0300, thestatetheatre.com), a renovated Art Deco movie house in Falls Church that is a 10-minute walk from the East Falls Church Metro, books rock, blues, reggae, Cajun R&B, jam, alt-country, folk, and indie bands, not to mention cult heroes and one-hit-wonders. Cases in point: Asleep at the Wheel, Hanson, Leon Russell, the Smithereens, Toots and the Maytals, Johnny Winter, Wu-Tang Clan, and the odd burlesque show. It holds about 215 upstairs but has cocktail tables and standing room on the ground floor.

Another eclectic music club in Virginia, **Jammin' Java** (☎ 703-255-1566, jamminjava.com) is locally owned (by three musician brothers); open seven days a week; and books rock, country, folk, blues, punk, cult favorites, open mic nights, and even daytime children's entertainers. The club's drawbacks include seating (there are a few advance-reservation tables, but otherwise it might be folding chairs or standing); a surprisingly loud volume level (consider that the owners are music producers); and no Metro access.

Gypsy Sally's (☎ 202-333-7700, gypsysallys.com), a 300-seat-plus venue almost hidden along the Georgetown waterfront, books what its owners describe as "Americana," including alt-country, blues, and bluegrass. The adjoining Vinyl Lounge is a lovely throwback where the decor is Summer of Love, and the music really is on vinyl. Now one of the last live music spots in this once after-dark destination, Gypsy Sally's pays homage to those now-shuttered Georgetown stages such as the Bayou, the Cellar Door, and Desperado's. Google them sometime.

Specialty Clubs: Blues, Jazz, Irish

Jazz has a long history in Washington, and the grandest old jazz club of Washington, in terms of big-name bookings and length of uninterrupted service, is **Blues Alley** (☎ 202-337-4141, bluesalley.com) in Georgetown. The venue has hosted the biggest names in jazz and (more rarely) R&B or soul for 45 years, like Melba Moore, Charlie Byrd, Dizzy Gillespie, David Benoit, Poncho Sanchez, and every member of the Marsalis family—sometimes together. The menu is more or less New Orleans–style, with entrées named for stars (Sarah Vaughan's filet mignon, Tony

Bennett's shrimp and artichoke hearts). It's an old Georgetown town house, so it's not the most luxurious environment—there is little elbow room, and wheelchair access is limited—and since table and bar seating are first come, first served, show up early.

Bethesda Blues and Jazz Supper Club (☎ 240-330-4500, bethesda bluesjazz.com) is located in another refitted Art Deco cinema, with dinner tables right up to the apron (except when the front area is cleared for dancing), features live entertainment nightly. The management uses "jazz and blues" in the broadest terms: doo-wop, harmonic, horns, jazz orchestra, Latin, lounge, New Orleans beat, piano trios, swing, tango, zydeco, occasionally classic country and bluegrass, a little funk, and top-flight tributes to big-band, pop, rock, and soul artists. Recent artists include Peabo Bryson and Betty Wright. It's an easy walk from the Bethesda Metro and is wheelchair-friendly as well.

Washington's equivalent of the Lincoln Center Jazz Orchestra, the **Smithsonian Jazz Masterworks Orchestra,** calls the National Museum of American History home; the ensemble plays infrequently but has the advantage of access to original transcriptions and even recordings of classic performances.

The Old Naval Hospital on Capitol Hill near the Eastern Market Metro has been renovated as the **Hill Center** (☎ 202-549-4172, hill centerdc.org), a home for art, cultural nonprofits, and music, especially zydeco and jazz. The **Carlyle Club** (☎ 703-548-8899, thecarlyleclub .com) at the edge of Old Town Alexandria is an elegant throwback, a 1930s-style supper club with retro cocktails and, again, a Creole-inflected menu. The venue features mostly tribute bands. For R&B and blues, check out the venerable (and authentically worn) **New Vegas Lounge** (☎ 202-483-3971, newvegasloungedc.com), just off the 14th and P Street strip near Logan Circle.

Irish bars, real or otherwise, do a flourishing business in Washington, with the help of a resident community of performers. Among the Metro-accessible pubs with live music at least a couple of times a week—and preferably at least one fireplace—are the Dubliner on Capitol Hill, its nearby semi–sibling rival Kelly's Irish Times, Ri Ra Irish Pub in Georgetown, and the theatrically "authentic" Fado Irish Pub near the old Chinatown/Gallery Place entrance.

The Dubliner (☎ 202-737-3773, dublinerdc.com), across from Union Station, is not the oldest Irish bar in town (though it is more than 40 years old), but it has become the clan leader: it's centrally located, politically connected, and has provided the training ground for founders of a half dozen other bars, including Kelly's. It's also one of the few places in Washington to offer live music seven nights a week. Fittingly, the Dubliner also has one of the most colorful histories, filled with romantic intrigue, boom-and-bust bank troubles, and riotous St. Patrick's week parties. The Dubliner is filled with antiques, such as the 1810 hand-carved walnut bar in the back room. The front bar is louder and livelier. The snug is a discreet, heads-together hideaway in the finest tradition, and the parlor is where the tweeds gather.

In warm weather, there's patio seating. Be sure to have at least one Guinness on draft: The Dubliner pours an estimated quarter-million pints a year, making it the largest purveyor of Guinness in the country.

Drop by **Kelly's Irish Times** (☎ 202-543-5433, kellysirishtimesdc .com) for a breather and the *Finnegan's Wake* crazy-quilt of literary pretense, political conversation, and interns' raves downstairs. **Ri Ra** (☎ 202-751-2111, rira.com/Georgetown) in Georgetown has "late-night" Irish bands (that is, 9:30 or later) on weekends. **Fado Irish Pub** (☎ 202-789-0066, fadoirishpub.com) is decorated with classic Irish antiques, if you don't mind the cost. Despite its name, and a sophisticated take on Irish fare, **Flanagan's Harp and Fiddle** (☎ 301-951-0115, flanagansharpandfiddle.com) in Bethesda is a neighborhood bar with a lineup that includes not just Irish and folk but a wide range of blues, jazz, pop, and rock acts. In Old Town Alexandria, **Murphy's** (☎ 703-548-1717, murphyspub.com) on King Street has nightly entertainment.

Washington is full of jokes—but the only full-time comedy spot is the **DC Improv** (☎ 202-296-7008, dcimprov.com) below Dupont Circle near the Farragut North Metro. Another D.C. institution is the **Capitol Steps** (capsteps.com), a group of former and current Hill staffers who roast politicos by rewriting familiar songs with punishing, though not too pointed, lyrics. The Steps are a popular tourist attraction and perform Friday and Saturday nights at the Ronald Reagan Building and International Trade Center at 13th Street and Pennsylvania Avenue NW (Federal Triangle).

Comedy fans should also check out the DC Comedy Showcase at **Comedy Club DC** (☎ 202-594-6245, comedyclubdc.com). The club, which gets its bookings from the DC Improv team, hosts local talent and nationally touring comedians. Occasionally the club attracts the same big names you'll find on Netflix, HBO, and Comedy Central. **Underground Comedy** (undergroundcomedydc.com) in Dupont Circle is a smaller venue, where you can see rising comics, many of whom have gone on to stardom. In addition to 60 performances a month, the Underground hosts 8 free shows a week, so it's a fun place to drop in for a drink to see Washington's up-and-coming comedians.

unofficial **TIP**
After the music stops, when the crowd is searching for a cure for the "Drunchies" (drunk food munchies), D.C. night owls can find theirs at **Duccini's, Italian Kitchen on U,** and **Jumbo Pizza**. The pies are as good as the people-watching. Alternatives to pizza include the iconic **Amsterdam Falafelshop** or **Ben's Chili Bowl.**

NIGHTLIFE NEIGHBORHOODS: CLUBS, BARS, LIVE MUSIC, AND DANCING

D.C.'S NIGHTCLUBS COME IN AS MANY FLAVORS as their patrons: dance halls, salsa bars, specialty bars, sports bars, billiard bars, espresso bars, and gay bars. A nightclub renaissance has revitalized whole neighborhoods, a shift that has been particularly visible in areas that once were nearly deserted after rush hour, or at least after cocktail hour.

U Street Corridor: Show Your Pride

The U Street Corridor, centered on 14th and U Streets NW, is a lively restaurant and socializing center. Along with sophisticated bars and dining, people come to enjoy underground DJs and modern music at **U Street Music Hall** (☎ 202-588-1889, ustreetmusichall.com) and the **Black Cat** (pages 267–268), as well as hipster fare at **DC9** (☎ 202-483-5000, dc9.club) and the **Velvet Lounge** (☎ 202-462-3213, velvetloungedc.com). The historic **9:30 Club** (page 267) on U Street still reigns as the top place to see legendary and rising bands. All of these venues are clustered around the U Street/African American Civil War Memorial Metro station.

unofficial **TIP**
The District's Capital Pride Alliance Celebration is one of the most festive events of the year. Usually held in late May to early June, Capital Pride involves a huge parade and festival. However, the LGBTQ community has many places to celebrate throughout the year.

The trendy area is also a popular hangout for Washington's LGBTQ community. There are many gay-friendly clubs, but at the corner of 9th and U, you'll find **Nellie's Sports Bar** (☎ 202-332-6355, nelliessportsbar.com), which may not have been the first gay sports bar in the area, but it's the most fun, with Tuesday drag bingo, Wednesday "smart-ass trivia," weekend back-slapping football on the TVs, and a rooftop bar to boot.

The **Saloon** at 12th and U is famous for its rules: no standing, no TVs, no stool hogging—in other words, you're there to enjoy a drink and conversation with your neighbor. No martinis either. What makes it special is that The Saloon is actually a nonprofit that donates its proceeds to fund schools in poor communities. And at the far end of the strip, past 16th Street, is **Chi-Cha Lounge** (☎ 202-906-9417, chichadc.com), with a hookah menu and South American snacks.

Atlas District: Bring Your "H" Game

The Atlas District, a three-block stretch of H Street NE centered around the **Atlas Performing Arts Center,** is without question the quirkiest entertainment district in the Washington area. Bars, dance halls, and restaurants all juggle DJs and games: mini-golf, tabletop shuffleboard, bocce, Skee-Ball, karaoke, dress-up, and even the irregular burlesque.

Some of the more irresistible attractions are clustered between 11th and 15th Streets NE (just to get you going). Starting at the 11th Street end, there's **Little Miss Whiskey's Golden Dollar** (littlemisswhiskeys .com), which looks like a bit of fine New Orleans decadence (if Annie Oakley had run the bar), complete with wrought-iron benches, a courtyard fountain, and DJs ranging from yacht rock to 1980s alternative.

Between 13th and 14th is **H Street Country Club** (☎ 202-399-4722, hstcountryclub.com), which boasts a two-level, nine-hole adults-only mini-golf course—with miniature D.C. landmarks, including the Lincoln Theatre, a gauntlet of lobbyists, and a graveyard full of zombie presidents among the traps—plus Skee-Ball, shuffleboard, and, logically for H Street, Mexican food. Up from that is the **Rock & Roll Hotel** (rockandrollhoteldc.com), a one-time funeral home renovated not as a real overnighter but as a midsize (capacity 400) 18-and-older rock venue with VIP suites, pool tables upstairs, and a huge rooftop deck. This is another gamesters' hangout: To stay in the Friday night spelling bee, you have to down a brew or a shot between rounds, which is one reason the upper reaches are 21-and-up.

And then there's **Biergarten Haus** (☎ 202-388-4053, biergarten haus.com), which can make space for 300 mug-huggers and pig-roast pickers in the (obviously) beer garden at long wooden tables amid the odd strolling accordion players and tuba bands. On Tuesdays, trivia begins at 8 p.m. The rest of the place looks like an Alpine lodge, more or less.

Adams Morgan: The Big Mixer

It's reasonably calm by day—when you can easily see the building-side murals that are one of its hallmarks—but by night, Adams Morgan is a combination carnival midway and meet-market madhouse, and there's no way tourists, or even locals, can hit more than a few of its popular lounges in one visit. (Weekends after midnight, you'd be lucky to find room to move, even down the middle of the street.) And the fact that it's one of the city's older row-house neighborhoods makes it charming to look at, but many of its establishments have accessibility issues. (And some of those that are "officially" accessible have some pretty minimal bathroom facilities.)

Most of the hot spots lie along 18th Street NW between Kalorama and Columbia Roads, and on Columbia Road itself. Just stick your head into a few of them—the trendier, lounge-life nightclubs with white sofas, pastel drinks, and DJs; the truculently retro beer bars and dives; and the live-music and dance venues—and pick your spot.

The grandmother of all Adams Morgan music clubs is **Madam's Organ** (☎ 202-667-5370, madamsorgan.com), which has three floors plus a rooftop tiki bar and live music (blues, jazz, R&B, bluegrass) every night, and a famously, um, pulchritudinous eponymous mural, in whose honor all redheads pay only half price for selected drinks.

Other notables include **Columbia Station** (☎ 202-462-6040, columbiastationdc.com), with live jazz and blues; **Songbyrd Café** (☎ 202-450-2917, songbyrddc.com), featuring retro music activities (make your own recordings here); and **Club Timehri** (☎ 202-518-2626, clubtimehri.com), specializing in reggae, soca, and other eclectic sounds. See new-on-the-scene comedians at **Comedy Club DC** (page 270) and **Capital Laughs** (capitallaughs.com).

Long a center of Washington's Central American and South American communities, Adams Morgan also has some of the area's nicer Latin jazz and samba joints, including **Bossa Bistro** (☎ 202-667-0088, bossadc .com) and **Habana Village** (☎ 202-975-1927, habanavillage.com).

If you're more in the mood for American comfort food, **Duplex Diner** (☎ 202-265-7828, duplexdiner.com) is a fun place to nosh on tater tots and enjoy 1980s dance music.

DRINKS, ANYONE?

WASHINGTON WAS IN THE FOREFRONT of the cocktail craze, ever since groundbreaking mixologist Todd Thrasher opened his **PX** "speakeasy" in Old Town Alexandria over a decade ago, followed by the nearby **TNT.** His new project opened in The Wharf: Potomac Distilling Company, a distillery with four types of Thrasher's Rum, and the neighboring waterfront bar, Tiki TNT, with a perfect view of the historic Maine Avenue Fish Market. Also at The Wharf, Whiskey Charlie, is a rooftop bar with reimagined cocktails, such as the signature M2—pisco, mango, citrus, mint, and syrup—and a wide array of wines by the glass and large format tankards. Several other bars in in the heart of U Street Corridor are dedicated to the making of original and authentic cocktails, notably the speakeasy-style **Gibson**, Bar Pilar's (try the bacon bloody Mary), and Brixton, a multistory bar with a third-floor rooftop beer garden that offers a sweeping view of the Washington Monument.

Join the staffers on Capitol Hill at Hank's Oyster Bar for house-made sodas and esoteric brews; Sonoma Restaurant and Wine Bar, an urban bar that serves the politicos who love wine; **Wisdom** for gin craft cocktails; and Union Pub for the cheapest happy hour in town. Denson Liquor Bar in Penn Quarter is a subterranean bar with New Orleans–inspired cocktails like Sazeracs, Negronis, and Hemingway daiquiris.

Craft whiskey is fashionable as well, especially in Adams Morgan, where the three-story, Art Deco–style **Jack Rose Dining Saloon** boasts a running tally of more than a thousand bottles of whisk(e)y on the wall, and **Smoke and Barrel,** a barbecue house, provides similar bourbon (and scotch and rye) benefits. **Black Whiskey** in Logan Circle has dozens of small-batch whiskies and a cool meat-carving station, while **Barrel** (nicknamed Rum-DMV) on Capitol Hill offers close to 100. And the Georgetown outpost of the **Ri Ra** Irish pub chain offers not flights but "duels" of rare whiskies costing up to $180.

Clear liquor fans should not worry: **MXDC** has a tequila menu of more than 100 brands, and you'll find about the same number of vodkas at the **Russia House** (favorite hangout of the Washington Capitals's star Alex Ovechkin) or the D.C. branch of New York's **Mari Vanna,** another Russian outpost. They're located at either end of Dupont Circle (which means you'll see a lot of hockey imports hanging out as well).

Washington now has a handful of small craft distilleries producing a variety of whiskies, gin, and vodka, which is only appropriate, as the capital lays (perhaps exaggerated) claim to some classic cocktails: the rickey, first made in the 1880s at Shoomaker's Bar on E Street NW as a morning tonic for lobbyist "Colonel" Joe Rickey (and now the official drink of the District), and the mint julep, which was popularized at the Round Robin Bar around the corner in the Willard Hotel—which, coincidentally, is said to be where the word "lobbyist" originated.

Penn Quarter: D.C.'s Capital of Merriment

Because Capital One Arena is at the heart of the neighborhood, Penn Quarter has a collection of amiable sports bars, and you don't have to be a hometowner to find your people. Washington has a diverse population, and alumni of various colleges converge at different bars to watch their teams during important matchups.

Penn Quarter has also picked up on the Atlas District game-night trend. At the bi-level **Iron Horse Tap Room** (☎ 202-347-7665, iron horsedc.com), the steeds referred to are not locomotives but vintage motorcycles, several of which hang about the place. It's not a biker bar except in name, however; upstairs it's lounge-a-lot territory, and downstairs are Skee-Ball machines, shuffleboard tables, and a plentiful supply of TVs, 20 beers on tap, and as many bourbons. Iron Horse shares ownership with the even more games-away-from-the-game **Rocket Bar** (☎ 202-628-7665, rocketbardc.com), at Seventh and G Streets, which sports a subterranean vibe with 17 TVs.

The neighborhood is famous for its forward-thinking cocktail culture. Every restaurant here is vying for the most Instagrammable creation. But for reliably tasty tropical rum drinks and free salsa lessons, **Cuba Libre Restaurant** (☎ 202-408-1600, cubalibrerestaurant .com) is the place to go. **SAX Dinner Theater and Lounge** (☎ 202-737-0101, saxwdc.com) is a cabaret-style club featuring acrobats, circus performers, and clever craft cocktails.

Dirty Habit (☎ 202-449-7095, dirtyhabitdc.com), inside the historic Hotel Monaco, offers edgy cocktails and small globally inspired tapas. For a more divey experience, visit **b DC** (☎ 202-808-8720, burgers beerbourbon.com/dc-penn-quarter), a gastropub known for its burgers. **Flight Wine Bar** (☎ 202-864-6445, flightdc.com) is notable for its wine menu and food pairings. If you love to nibble while you drink, **The Partisan** (☎ 202-524-5322, thepartisandc.com) is a meat-centric bar affiliated with D.C.'s venerable Red Apron Butcher. **Denson Liquor Bar** (☎ 202-499-5018, densondc.com), a subterranean spirits-bar, has lots of "drunchies" and a notable Cubano sandwich.

 WHILE IT'S NEARLY IMPOSSIBLE TO GET A RESERVATION (or afford) **barmini by Jose Andres,** this is D.C.'s most buzzy place to experience the craft cocktail craze at new levels. At this futuristic and exclusive escape, you'll see those out for a special occasion, CEOs on an expense account, and celebrities hobnobbing.

For beer-o-philes, **City Tap Kitchen & Craft** (☎ 202-733-5333, city tap.com) hauls in craft beers from around the country, while **Capitol City Brewing Company** (☎ 202-628-2222, capcitybrew.com) and **District Chophouse & Brewery** (☎ 202-347-3434, districtchophouse .com) brew their own.

Dupont Circle and Logan Circle:
Where Everybody Knows Your Name

These neighborhoods remain mostly residential and thus have fewer nighttime haunts than the other areas in this chapter. Still, they have a collection of cozy hangouts, some with late-night dining and rooftop bars to keep you entertained. Several of these are located inside hotels, like the Embassy Row's **Station Kitchen** and **The Quill** at the Jefferson. Rub elbows with local millennials at **Duke's Grocery** (☎202-733-5623, dukesgrocery .com), a gastropub with excellent cocktails and craft beer. **Heist** (☎ 202-688-0098, heistdc.com) is a chic lounge with dancing and champagne specials. **Lucky Bar** (☎ 202-331-3733, luckybardc.com) attracts the D.C. interns who like to dance, but the most exciting place to party in Dupont Circle is the 15,000-square-foot nightclub **Decades** (☎ 202-853-3498, decadesdc.com), with four floors of music and decor from different eras—the 1980s, 1990s, 2000s, and current day. Another favorite is **J. R.'s Bar and Grill** (☎ 202-328-0090, jrsbar-dc.com), an institution that offers impressive drink specials and Family Feud-style trivia.

Georgetown: The Sophisticated Salon

Georgetown has a few first-rate draws for night owls. See all-American music at **Gypsy Sally's** (page 268). If you prefer an international vibe, **L2 Lounge** (☎ 202-965-2001, l2lounge.com) attracts an eclectic crowd and sometimes has flamenco dancing. **Blues Alley** (page 268) is one of D.C.'s oldest nightclubs, and the best place to see jazz and blues headliners up close and personal. Sing along with the piano man (and woman) at **Georgetown Piano Bar** (☎ 202-827-3236, georgetownpianobar.com).

PART SEVEN

SHOPPING

WITH ITS VAST NUMBER OF TOURIST ATTRACTIONS, it's hard to believe that Washington also has visitors for whom museums are not the main draw. But it's true—many people come here simply to shop. These folks enjoy sifting through merchandise at the haute boutiques, eclectic bodegas, consignment shops, and super-stocked shoe stores. They peruse little grocers packed with international spices. They come to lay claim to original art and designer clothes. In fact, nowadays, many people plan their vacations around the shopping, not the other way around.

As a result of Washington's high median household income, the city has some of the most exclusive shops in the nation. In addition, the increasingly diverse population demands more international offerings from their stores. This means Washington's visitors will find a very wide variety of products and shopping experiences during their visit.

On some weekend afternoons, and especially around the holidays, roads leading to the shopping centers are as congested as commuter routes during rush hour. The stretch of I-95 south of Washington around the **Potomac Mills** factory outlet complex in Dale City—the largest tourist draw in the state of Virginia—is often backed up to a crawl in both directions. **Arundel Mills,** from the same folks who brought you Potomac Mills, bookends the metropolitan area on the north side of I-95. The **Tanger Outlets** at National Harbor; **Clarksburg Premium Outlets** off I-270 in Clarksburg, Maryland, just south of Frederick; and the **Leesburg Corner Premium Outlets** on Route 7, around 27 miles west of Tysons Corner, all offer a budget-boggling spread of well-known, and in some cases exclusive, retailers.

But shoppers aren't relegated to suburban malls. Oh, no. They can shop to their heart's content at the many mixed-use developments in downtown Washington too. Consider the uber-fashionable **CityCenterDC,** just a block from the convention center. Visitors make their way to CityCenterDC to stop for ice cream, and then peek their heads into Hermès, David Yurman, and Burberry.

The trendsetting streets of Georgetown are also essential. Dozens of big-name retailers have stores on Wisconsin Avenue NW and M Street NW. Some fashion-forward websites, known for their strong online presence, have opened brick-and-mortar versions where you can try on clothes and accessories (Rent the Runway, Warby Parker, Reformation) or sample the latest technology (Apple, Amazon, and Microsoft).

Maybe you're the shopper craving the pioneer spirit of new designers and vintage finds. If so, there are a number of neighborhoods where the stylistas are more daring. The U Street Corridor has a line of shops that cater to particular customers who work in the arts or attend Howard, Georgetown, and American Universities. The curated pieces sold here guarantee you won't see yourself coming and going.

Outside of town, Old Town Alexandria, Frederick, and Leesburg have always attracted spirited shopkeepers, and even if you don't buy anything, it's fun to window-shop there.

As Washington continues to attract young professionals to the workforce, they've livened up the city's dress code. Where once the suit-and-tie crowd ruled, now countless offices have changed "casual day" to every day. Even the most traditional of workplaces, like law firms and lobbyist offices, accept standard attire mixed with edgy accessories. To see what Washington's most fashionable are wearing, check out the fashionablybroke.com, aliciatenise.com, refinery29.com, districtofchic .com, and dcfashionfool.com (of course, we can't all rock those clothes, but it's fun to get ideas). These urban dwellers embrace trends and add playful accessories, such as designer bags, jewelry, and scarves. Some outfits you'll see in restaurants and on the street may have been inspired by D.C.'s famous television characters—Selina Meyer from *Veep*, Olivia Pope from *Scandal*, and Emily Rhodes from *Designated Survivor*. Tourists, however, should not worry too much about fashion; instead, focus on comfortable shoes and dress for the ever-changing weather.

▌ MALL SHOPPING

SERIOUS BUYERS AND BARGAIN HUNTERS will have to decide up front if they are going to bring a car, rent one, use a ride service like Uber or Lyft, or stick to using public transportation. Although we have recommended against driving in Washington, if one of the big outlet malls is a major part of your itinerary, that would be one reason to override us.

But unless you really plan to load up—and if so, you'll have to budget a lot of time as well as money—there are a few malls within the District of Columbia itself and in the surrounding suburbs that you can reach by public transportation (Tysons I and II, Pentagon City, Friendship Heights). And in addition to the formal malls, Washington has a growing number of neighborhoods with intriguing boutiques and stores, often the same neighborhoods that have trendy restaurant and entertainment options, so you can really make a day, or night, of it.

SUPERMALLS AND OUTLETS

WHILE THERE ARE PLENTY OF PRICEY SHOPPING VENUES, the region also has a surprising number of discount stores. For every socialite flashing an Hermès Birkin bag or CEO tugging at his Armani suitcoat, there are savvy shoppers quietly gloating over their discounted Kate Spade dress or their Jack Spade tie. After all, the reason to buy good-quality items is that they last a long time, so why not buy leather goods from one season back, when you're going to use them for 10 years? And if you only want something for a year or so, then a quirky boutique or discount stores such as TJ Maxx and Marshalls are definitely the way to go.

Just 45 minutes south of Washington, off I-95 in Dale City, Virginia, is **Potomac Mills Mall** (simon.com/mall/potomac-mills), one of the world's largest outlet malls, with more than 225 shops covering 1.6 million square feet of retail delirium and 22 anchor tenants. Potomac Mills draws more visitors each year than any other Virginia tourist attraction—about 24 million shoppers, maneuvering feverishly into 8,000 parking spaces. It's nearly impossible to hit all of the stores, which include Bloomingdale's, Burlington Coat Factory, Coach, H&M, BCBG, Nordstrom Rack, Banana Republic, Pandora, Bose, Armani Exchange, Levi's, Movado, True Religion, Timberland, Nike, Saks Fifth Avenue OFF 5TH, Last Call from Neiman Marcus, the Disney Store, and Brooks Brothers. It also has an 18-screen AMC multiplex with a 3-D IMAX screen, a Bobby's Burger Palace from celebrity chef Bobby Flay, a Cheesecake Factory, and a dozen other noshing options. IKEA, which was the mall's original anchor, is across the street.

Northeast of Washington, at the intersection of Baltimore-Washington Parkway and MD 100 near BWI Airport (about 2 miles east of I-95), is Potomac Mills' sibling, **Arundel Mills** (simon.com/mall/arundel-mills) in Hanover, Maryland. More than a million square feet of name brands echo the Virginia complex, but Arundel Mills trumps them with entertainment options, including a 24-theater multiplex (with XD) that looks like an Egyptian pyramid, a Medieval Times restaurant/theater that looks like an 11th-century castle, and a Bass Pro Shops Outdoor World. And then there's the attached casino, Maryland Live!, open 24 hours a day with nine restaurants, including branches of local raves, the Prime Rib and Philips Seafood Express. Oh, and there's a Dave & Buster's Sports Café with billiards, arcade games, and shuffleboard.

To the west of town, perhaps 30-45 minutes past the various Tysons Corner malls (see page 280) at the intersection of VA 7 and the Leesburg Bypass, is the **Leesburg Corner Premium Outlets** (premiumoutlets .com), with many designer names, like Michael Kors, Calvin Klein, Kate Spade New York, Nautica, and True Religion. There's also a branch of Restoration Hardware, Williams-Sonoma, and Le Creuset.

Tanger Outlets (tangeroutlet.com/nationalharbor) has opened an 80-store shopping center in the National Harbor development, which is across the Potomac River from the District in Maryland and about 8 miles south of the White House. It features Adidas, Elle Tahari, Converse, H&M, Tommy Hilfiger, Brooks Brothers, Calvin Klein, Oakley Vault, J.Crew, Steve Madden, and Coach.

Clarksburg Premium Outlets (premiumoutlets.com/outlet/clarks burg) is on I-270 on the way to Frederick, Maryland. You'll find high-end international brands like AllSaints, Clarins, Ermenegildo Zegna, Salvatore Ferragamo, Superdry, and UGG, to name a few.

CITY MALLS

THERE ARE A FEW MALLS within the District limits. **Georgetown Park** (georgetownpark.com), which anchors the intersection of M Street and Wisconsin Avenue, is the most extravagant in appearance, featuring a lush Victorian design that fronts for some popular retailers, including Anthropologie, TJ Maxx, H&M, and J.Crew. Hu's Wear is quintessentially Georgetown, with its two-story showroom filled with the highest of the high-end fashion lines. Across the street is a shoe fashionista's dream, Hu's Shoes. Georgetown Park is also home to a large entertainment complex, Pinstripes, which has 14 bowling alleys, six bocce courts, a bistro, and a wine cellar. It still fronts the original Clyde's of Georgetown. (In any case, you cannot go hungry in Georgetown; nearly every space that isn't a shop is a restaurant.)

 A MAJOR WASHINGTON LANDMARK, **Union Station** (union stationdc.com) has been partly reborn as a shopping center. Functioning primarily as a transportation hub—it's an Amtrak station and has its own subway stop—the historic train station is contained in a grand Beaux Arts building with two stories of shops. You'll find familiar names, including H&M, Comfort Shoes (a great place to find comfortable shoes for sightseeing), The Body Shop, Ann Taylor, Blue Mercury, L'Occitane, MAC Cosmetics, UNIQLO, as well as purveyors of ties, jewelry, souvenirs, and accessories. In addition to a large and quite varied food court, Union Station has several restaurants, including a Ladurée, Legal Sea Bar, Magnolia Bakery, Johnny Rockets (burgers and fries), and Shake Shack (famous for its milkshakes).

There is also a 500,000-square-foot big-box shopping complex at 14th and Irving Streets NW in Columbia Heights, called **DCUSA** (shop dcusa.com) that houses a Target, Bed Bath & Beyond, DSW, Best Buy, Petco, and Marshalls. The Columbia Heights Metro and a parking garage are also part of this complex. If you're in town because your child is going to college in Washington or just got an internship, this might be a good one-stop spot for you.

unofficial **TIP**
Though both Mazza Gallerie and the Chevy Chase Pavilion shopping malls are (just) within the District boundaries, and with easy Metro access, they are really part of the larger border-crossing shopping district in Chevy Chase; see the description in "Great Neighborhoods," page 285.

SUBURBAN MALLS

WASHINGTON'S MAJOR SUBURBAN MALLS are probably similar to what you have back home, though perhaps a little bigger. Some are accessible by subway, including the multimall Tysons Corner area, just west of the Beltway, thanks to the opening of the Silver Line at the Tysons Metro station.

Westfield Montgomery Mall (westfield.com/montgomery) does not have subway access, but for serious shoppers, it's only a 10-minute cab ride from the Grosvenor/Strathmore Metro station; or on weekdays you can catch a Ride-On bus at the White Flint Metro or Grosvenor/Strathmore. Westfield Montgomery Mall is anchored by Nordstrom and Macy's and includes Apple, Vera Bradley, J.Crew, J. Jill, Sephora, Under Armour, Bonobos, ECCO, Kiehl's, Lily Pulitzer, Stuart Weitzman, Madewell, Tesla, Liljenquist & Beckstead jewelers, Zara, and Vineyard Vines. It also has a large food court, a Cheesecake Factory, and the luxurious ArcLight Cinema.

Westfield Wheaton Mall (westfield.com/wheaton), just one block from the Wheaton Metro stop, features JCPenney, Macy's, H&M, Dick's Sporting Goods, DSW, Giant grocery store, Costco, and Target, as well as a food court and a six-screen multiplex.

One of the area's most sumptuous malls is **The Fashion Centre at Pentagon City** (simon.com/mall/fashion-centre-at-pentagon-city) in Arlington, Virginia. It's a beautiful conservatory-style building filled with 170 primarily high-end retailers (it belongs to the same folks as Potomac Mills and Arundel Mills): Macy's, Cole Haan, Hugo Boss, Kate Spade, Nordstrom, Coach, Swarovski, Apple, Sephora, A|X Armani Exchange, Michael Kors, and Microsoft. The Fashion Centre also leads (through the parking garage) to a second fairly extensive shopping and (mostly) restaurant complex called **Pentagon Row** (for listings, go to pentagonrow.com). At the other end, the Fashion Centre connects to the Ritz-Carlton Hotel, where you can have an elegant meal or high tea in the lounge. The Pentagon City Metro stop, on the Blue Line, has a tunnel with direct access to Pentagon City mall.

The **Tysons Corner** neighborhood, just west of the Beltway, is a city with its own Metro station. Centered on the intersection of Chain Bridge Road/VA 123 and Leesburg Pike/VA 7, between the towns of Vienna and McLean, Tysons is actually a sort of Siamese twin supermall, with the original **Tysons Corner Center** (tysonscornercenter.com) hosting the slightly more predictable list of stores, and **Tysons Galleria** (tysonsgalleria.com) having a few more ritzy shops. Between the two, Tysons is estimated to serve some 60,000 shoppers daily at more than 400 shops, including Nordstrom, Lord & Taylor, Louis Vuitton, Nespresso, Anthropologie, Peloton, Prada, Tory Burch, Bloomingdale's, Crate & Barrel, Versace, Burberry, Chanel, Neiman Marcus, Gucci, Bottega Veneta, Macy's, Cartier, Coach, Ermenegildo Zegna, and much more. A big attraction for kids is the American Girl store. There are dozens of sit-down restaurants of various flavors, especially the big-name steak chains such as Morton's, along the corridor, not to mention the snack shops and food courts. In fact, the "food court" at the Galleria is Urban Space (a modern cafeteria), and the Galleria adjoins the Ritz-Carlton Hotel.

There is actually a third shopping section in Tysons Corner, seriously upscale, known as the **Shops at Fairfax Square** (fairfaxsquare .com), a sort of mini-mall of super-label shops, including Tiffany & Co., Miele, and an Elizabeth Arden Red Door Spa that you can hit after working out at the Equinox Fitness Center.

FLEA MARKETS

WASHINGTON IS NOT A GREAT FLEA MARKET TOWN in the way that New York City is, but the most well-established one is Sunday's **Georgetown Flea Market** (georgetownfleamarket.com), in the parking lot of Hardy Middle School on Wisconsin Avenue between 34th and 35th Streets NW. It's manned by vendors of vintage jewelry, rugs, sterling, flatware, architectural remnants, and occasionally political memorabilia.

The Sunday Flea Market at Eastern Market (easternmarket.net), on Seventh Street SE, is subway accessible. It's a two-block street festival that's just a few steps from the Eastern Market Metro station. You'll find art, antiques, and collectibles from around the globe.

MUSEUM SHOPS

IF YOU'RE SEEKING the sort of souvenirs you take home for the family, you can combine your sightseeing with your shopping. Some of Washington's greatest finds are in its museum gift shops. A museum's orientation is a good guide to its shop's merchandise: prints, art-design ties, greeting cards, and art books fill the **National Gallery of Art** shop; model airplanes and other toys of flight are on sale at the **Air and Space Museum,** and so on. The largest Smithsonian shops are at the **Museum of American History,** which sells toys, clothing, and musical instruments. The new location for the **International Spy Museum** stocks video and CD copies of old spy TV shows and themes, pens disguised as lipsticks, handcuff bracelets, and an Eye-in-the-Sky 360-degree Wi-Fi camera. The **Museum of African American History and Culture** stocks Gullah spices, sweetgrass baskets from the Low Country, and jewelry capturing the unique design of the bronze lattice exterior. There aren't many souvenirs at **Madame Tussauds,** but you can take selfies with the wax celebrities.

Several museum shops are overlooked by tourists. The best are at the **National Building Museum,** which sells design-related books, jewelry, architecturally inspired greeting cards, and gadgets; the **National Museum of the American Indian,** with its turquoise and silver jewelry, pottery, hand carvings, and Navajo rugs; the **National Museum of Women in the Arts,** with Frida Kahlo dolls and Rosie the Riveter bookends; the **National Museum of African Art,** a bazaar filled with colorful cloth, Ethiopian crosses, and wooden ceremonial instruments, such as hand drums and tambourines; the **Hirshhorn Museum,** with its selection of gifts for the photography enthusiast, imaginative jewelry, and home decor; the **Arthur M. Sackler Gallery,** with cases full of brass Buddhas, Chinese lacquerware, jade and jasper jewelry, feng shui kits, and porcelain; the **Renwick Gallery,** which stocks contemporary crafts such as handblown glass and colorful scarves; the **Folger Shakespeare Library,** with its Shakespeare-lovers' treasure trove (everyone needs a Shakespeare magnetic poetry kit); and the **John F. Kennedy Center for the Performing Arts,** which sells opera glasses and other gifts for Jackie and John lovers (such as costume jewelry inspired by the late former first lady).

The **Hillwood Estate Museum** has jewelry and ornaments inspired by Marjorie Merriweather Post's famous collection of Fabergé eggs and Russian porcelains. The expanded shop at **Mount Vernon** offers reproductions of Martha's cookbook, George's key to the Bastille, as well as period china and silver patterns. The **Daughters of the American Revolution Museum** shop sells Americana-themed memorabilia, such as patriotic ring trays, mugs, flags, and quilts. The shop at the **National Geographic Museum** offers clothing, toys, and accessories from around the globe. The store on the grounds of **Washington National Cathedral** features stone gargoyles, prayer books, rose-window silk scarves, statues of religious icons, and rosaries. The **Bible Museum** gift shop sells Bible-inspired memorabilia, including Christmas ornaments, Hanukkah menorahs, Israeli oil candles, and kids' religious books. Lincoln fans should stop in **Ford's Theatre** for books and T-shirts emblazoned with his memorable countenance. The **National Portrait Gallery** sells art-inspired textiles and merchandise with a presidential theme.

A visit in late April may mean you'll catch the **Smithsonian Craft Show** at the National Building Museum. This weekend event features such treasures as basketry, decorative fabric, glass, leather, and wearable art. Another excellent shopping opportunity comes during early November: at the annual **Museum Shop Holiday Market,** held at the Mansion at Strathmore, shoppers will find (for an entry fee of $10) merchandise from all the private museums, such as Hillwood, The Phillips Collection, and the International Spy Museum, under one convenient roof.

GREAT NEIGHBORHOODS
for WINDOW-SHOPPING

GEORGETOWN

GEORGETOWN HAS THE CITY'S LARGEST walk-and-shop district. The picturesque streets include a combination of chains, independents, and boutique shops. And thanks to the crowds of teens and 20-somethings that hang out on Georgetown's sidewalks on weekends, many of these keep late hours for impulse shopping (which is, after all, another type of after-hours entertainment).

The central point of Georgetown's consumer compass is the intersection of M Street and Wisconsin Avenue NW; use the gilded dome of the PNC Bank at the intersection as a marker (it's hard to miss). Among the boutiques on M Street and Wisconsin Avenue are **Alex & Ani, Michael Kors, Free People, Hu's Wear, Kate Spade, COS, Dr. Martens Store, CUSP, Sterling & Burke** (sort of the Brit-style Louis Vuitton but with more for men), **Massimo Dutti, Hugo Boss, Rag & Bone, Kendra Scott, Onward Reserve, Patagonia, Rent the Runway, Rothy's, Tory Burch, Urban Outfitters,** and **Anthropologie.**

This is also the stretch where you can play around with cosmetics and spa products to your heart's content, thanks to chains such as **Sephora, Bluemercury, L'Occitane,** and the London-based, all-organic **LUSH.** Georgetown also has big-name bargain brands like **TJ Maxx** and **H&M Home.**

Jewelry junkies should visit **Ann Hand,** a Washington designer who makes statement pieces with a patriotic flare, and **Jewelers' Werk Galerie,** a gallery representing more than 50 established art jewelers, selling cutting-edge pieces from around the globe (located in Cady's Alley off M Street NW). For original jewelry designs, visit **AUrate.**

Georgetown is also quite the men's fashion warehouse. As if the previously named shops weren't enough, there is **Suitsupply** in the Four Seasons Hotel, as well as **Camper, Billy Reid, Brooks Brothers,** and **Ike Behar**—all on M Street—and **Everard's Clothing** and **Bonobos Guideshop** nearby. If you can't afford the flash, check out **Reddz Trading** on Wisconsin for high-style resales.

Anyone interested in home design and accessories should be sure to make it to the 3300 block of M Street and cruise Cady's Alley, which is actually a hidden minimall. The complex houses sophisticated furnishings that may upend your concept of environment. Among stops worth making are the super-chic Italian design stores **Boffi** and **Calligaris,** the two-story Danish-sleek **BoConcept, Room & Board, Ligne Roset,** and **Design Within Reach (DWR).** If you get hungry, the fine Austrian-style Leopold's Kafe & Konditorei is right in the alley's pedestrian intersection. And sticking with the theme, a large **CB2** store, an offshoot of Crate & Barrel, has parked itself on M Street just west of Cady's Alley.

ADAMS MORGAN

ADAMS MORGAN IS PRIMARILY a multicultural residential area adjoining exclusive Kalorama. It was known as the heart of the Hispanic and, a little later, the Ethiopian immigrant communities. For the last 30

*un**official* **TIP**
A particularly notable addition to the Georgetown shopping landscape is **Reformation,** where each curated piece is investigated in a very high-tech way. Look over the collection, pick out the ones you'd like to try, plug in your size, and then wait for the clothes to be delivered to try them on. All of the clothes are manufactured in responsible, fair trade conditions and cater to the young at heart. The fabric must have a low carbon footprint and be of the highest quality. It's pricey, but an experience.

years, Adams Morgan has offered eclectic nightlife and dining that caters to a slightly older audience than the Shaw and U Street neighborhoods.

Among **Adams Morgan's** melting pot of restaurants are boutiques along 18th Street NW and Columbia Road. **Tibet Shop** showcases striking Himalayan jewelry, clothing, furnishings, crafts, and painted altars. **Meeps Vintage** and **Mercedes Bien** are eclectic caches of vintage clothing and accessories. **Hart's Desire** is an adult entertainment store. **Le Bustiere Boutique** sells upscale lingerie. **Urban Dwell** has a hodgepodge of home goods, baby gear, and D.C.-themed gifts. **Fleet Feet Sports** is an athletic supply store specializing in sports shoes. **Lost City Books** sells new, used, and rare books.

unofficial **TIP**
With the rise of legal marijuana in Washington, D.C., the FunkyPiece Smoke Shop & Glass Gallery carries a cornucopia of merchandise for smoking the medicinal herb, along with weed-themed T-shirts and bags.

U STREET CORRIDOR, LOGAN CIRCLE, AND SHAW

IN RECENT YEARS, this historically distinct area has become Washington's epicenter for multicultural entertainment, attracting young, hip, and international crowds. It's also a busy strip of popular stores, including a number of home furnishings shops that cater to all kinds of tastes.

A commercial cluster runs along U and 14th Streets, with hipster boutiques and vintage shops. Among them are **Joint Custody,** a boutique that lines up vinyl records beside used men's clothing, with hats, coats, and shoes from the 1970s and 1980s. **Lettie Gooch** is an eclectic boutique that separates clothing by occasion. **Zawadi** stocks imported African art, textiles, books, and housewares.

Other impressive merchandise found here includes the beautifully displayed baby clothes, potions, dishware, hand-woven rugs, and leather poofs at **Salt & Sundry. Violet Boutique** is where the chic female executives get their show-stopping fashion finds. **Buffalo Exchange** is a hipster supply store, with fashions spanning the 20th century. The most lauded consignment shop in town is **Current Boutique,** stocking both new and used fashion finds for women.

unofficial **TIP**
Shinola in Logan Circle is a local favorite, selling the Detroit, Michigan–made watches and watch bands, handbags, notepads, dog leashes, and other fine leather items. They also sell classic bicycles.

Home furnishing stores are also grouped here along 14th Street. At T Street and 14th, **Room & Board** is almost its own big-box store, a four-story showcase for custom interiors from midcentury modern to contemporary, with an emphasis on green products. A few blocks down is **West Elm,** the chain of trendy furniture. Despite the vintage-sounding name (and some pieces are truly classic), **Miss Pixie's Furnishings & What-not** is a treasure trove of funky and classic furniture and spot-on tchotchkes, whose owner frequently dispenses cookies or perhaps a winter warmer. **Mitchel Gold + Bob Williams** features eco-friendly, luxurious furnishings in nostalgic designs. **Lori Graham Design & Home** spotlights slightly tongue-in-cheek glam in everything from chandeliers to armchairs, plus local artists' works. Over on U Street, **Good-Wood** has traditional furniture and contemporary accessories housed in an old-fashioned general store.

CHEVY CHASE

THIS ULTRALUXE NEIGHBORHOOD, with its slew of sophisticated shops, encircles the Friendship Heights Metro station, marking the boundary between Maryland and District jurisdictions. On the southwest corner of Wisconsin and Western Avenues is a stalwart source of fashion finds for grande dames everywhere, **Mazza Gallerie** (mazzagallerie.com). The mall is home to Neiman Marcus, Krön Chocolatier, Saks Fifth Avenue, World Gem Jewelry & Art Treasures, and an AMC multiplex.

unofficial **TIP**
There is a second, much larger, stand-alone **Saks Fifth Avenue** on Wisconsin Avenue. Located in a historic stone building, it's a 9-minute walk from the Friendship Heights Metro station, but this Saks has a broader collection of designer handbags and couture fashion.

Across the street is the **Chevy Chase Pavilion** (chevychasepavilion.com), which has its own Embassy Suites Hotel (so you can shop till you drop for a nap), as well as J.Crew, Old Navy, Cheesecake Factory, World Market, and three popular discount stores: Nordstrom Rack, Marshalls, and DSW Shoes.

A little north of Mazza Gallerie on Wisconsin Avenue between Western and Willard Avenues is the **Shops at Wisconsin Place** (shopwisconsinplace.com), which includes Bloomingdale's, MAC Cosmetics, Anthropologie, Cole Haan, Talbots, a huge Whole Foods, Capital Grille, and a wine bar. And just down Western Avenue is a full-size Lord & Taylor, with a BCBGMAXAZRIA inside. **The Collection in Chevy Chase** (collectionchevychase.com) is a revamped shopping center/park with quirky pop-up shops featuring jewelry and clothing.

You'll find a constellation of fine jewelry stores here, too, like **Tiffany & Co., Boone & Son,** and **Charles Schwartz & Son.** The diminutive perfume store **Santa Maria Novella** arrived in the D.C. market straight from Florence; some fragrances were custom blends made for Catherine de Medici.

DUPONT CIRCLE

ALTHOUGH IT IS PROBABLY BEST KNOWN for its restaurants and nightlife, Dupont Circle is also a draw for shoppers looking to enrich the mind—it's full of fine art galleries and bookstores. Most of the art galleries are clustered along R Street in the two blocks just west of Connecticut Avenue, leading you toward the Phillips Collection (see "Specialty Shopping" on page 288).

Founded in 1976 as a combination bookstore/café is **Kramerbooks & Afterwords,** located at Connecticut Avenue and Q Street. This neighborhood gathering place stays open until 1 a.m. during the week and 3 a.m. on weekends. Just off the circle at 20th and P Streets, you'll find

Second Story Books, a terrific source for used books. Next door, comic book collectors should check out **Fantom Comics.**

A few blocks north on 20th Street, **Tabletop** carries leather backpacks, distinctive glassware, notebooks, and art supplies. **Secondi,** on the upper level of 1702 Connecticut Avenue, has a loyal following of contributors and buyers of luxury consignment fashions, with experienced shopkeepers who are eager to assist. Also north of the circle, on 18th Street, **The Chocolate House** sells fine chocolate from all over the world.

South of the circle, on Connecticut Avenue NW, between N and K Streets, are several high-end retailers that cater to the area's law-and-lobby offices. These stores include **Brooks Brothers, Betsy Fisher,** and **Rizik's** (a prominent local women's shop). Find a wide selection of irresistible gifts (to give yourself or bring home) at **Proper Topper,** formerly a men's haberdashery but now catering to women, babies, and children.

Dupont Circle is also home to a fine estate-jewelry shop, **Tiny Jewel Box,** and precious gem specialists, **Boone & Sons.** For those who love unique costume jewelry with a rainbow of gemstones, check out **Bloom,** north of the circle on Connecticut. Across the street, **Looped Yarn Works** has a colorful collection of supplies for the crochet enthusiast.

QUICK STOPS

MOST SHOPS ON CAPITOL HILL are in and around **Eastern Market** (see the sidebar on "Flea Markets" on page 281) on 7th Street between Pennsylvania and Independence Avenues SE, and inside **Union Station,** which has dozens of name chains (see page 279).

Also on Capitol Hill, in the neighborhood known as **Barracks Row,** there is a women's boutique called Summit to Soul, the entertaining Labyrinth Games & Puzzles, the Toy Soldier Shop's mini-dioramas of historic battles, and the adorable pet store Howl to the Chief.

In **Penn Quarter,** the shopping tends to be chain clothing stores such as Macy's, Saks OFF 5th, UNIQLO, Urban Outfitters, J.Crew, Lou Lou Boutiques, Zara, and Anthropologie, with the exception of an international collection of shawls and tunics at PUA Naturally and the first Leica camera store in North America.

Many lavish stores have opened at **CityCenterDC,** especially those selling high-end handbags—Louis Vuitton, Gucci, Paul Stewart, Longchamp, Hermès, and Burberry. Acclaimed international brands, such as Bulgari, Loro Piana, Christian Dior, and Moncler, are also represented.

Bethesda shops are centered in **Bethesda Row,** an upscale mixed-use development near the Bethesda Metro station. Anchored by a three-story Anthropologie, the mini–street mall has a covered pedestrian shopping area and high-end boutiques such as the name-your-denim-brand Luna; Follain, for luxury skin care; Lilly Pulitzer; The North Face; Lululemon; Paper Source, for cards and gifts; the trendy eyewear store Warby Parker; and Sassanova, a designer shoe store. The block also includes an Apple store, a branch of the notorious Georgetown Cupcake (with usually a shorter wait than at the original), and one of the only Amazon stores in the country, where you can shop for books, home electronics, and a variety of Kindle models.

In **Old Town Alexandria,** the most interesting shops are along King Street. Independent boutiques include 3 Sisters, She's Unique Jewelry Boutique, Imagine Artwear, Bellacara, Bloomers, and Red Barn Mercantile. Other notables include The Shoe Hive, Mint Condition, and Christmas Attic on Union Street.

The artists at the **Torpedo Factory Art Center** in Old Town Alexandria create and sell one-of-a-kind pieces of wearable art.

In addition, many other town centers built around Metro stops—**Ballston, Clarendon,** and **Crystal City**—have shopping options. **The Mosaic District** in Fairfax County has a modern line-up of local boutiques and luxury fashion stores, including Alex and Ani, Erin Condren, Sophie Blake, and Sundance. For a couture collection of perfumes, stop in Arielle Shoshana Scented Luxuries.

SPECIALTY SHOPPING

ANTIQUES AND COLLECTIBLES

THE STRETCH OF WISCONSIN AVENUE north of M Street in Georgetown, where the clothing boutiques cluster, is also home to several notable antiques dealers, especially between O and Q Streets. Among the best are **Frank Milwee, John Rosselli & Associates, Cote Jardin, Pillar & Post, L'Enfant Gallery, Marston Luce, Cherub Antiques,** and the longtime Georgetown secret, **Christ Child Opportunity Shop,** where, on the second floor, you'll find china, paintings, and other cherishables on consignment from the best Georgetown homes. **Sands of Time Antiquities,** which deals in Roman, Greek, and Middle Eastern collectibles, is on P and 30th Streets NW.

One of the largest concentrations of antiques shops, about 30 in all, is on **Antique Row** in Kensington, Maryland, which is about 4 miles from the D.C. line. Most are along Howard Avenue, with smaller shops east of Connecticut Avenue and larger warehouses west of Connecticut. Whatever your era, country, or style, you're likely to find it here.

unofficial **TIP**
While some antiques neighborhoods thrive on weekends, Sundays are a toss-up; do a little web surfing before you hit the road.

Washington's *very* serious antiques-seekers drive an hour or more to the countryside of Maryland, Virginia, West Virginia, or Pennsylvania for the bargains. **Frederick, Maryland,** about an hour north of Washington, is particularly popular with area antiquers. The biggest single collection is at **Emporium Antiques** on East Patrick Street, with more than 100 dealers, though walking the Main Street neighborhood and the streets just off it will turn up scores of others. The charming town of **Leesburg, Virginia,** has a plethora of shabby chic and antique discoveries at **Vintage Magnolia, Rust and Feathers, Black Shutter Antique Center, My Wits End,** and, of particular note, **The Old Lucketts**

Store. **Gettysburg, Pennsylvania,** is heaven for Civil War collectors. **Rebel's Roost Antique Emporium, Union Drummer Boy,** and **The Antique Center of Gettysburg** are all must-visits. **Berkeley Springs** and **Martinsburg, West Virginia,** are nearby, quaint towns with antiques and Appalachian-craft shops. Historic **Annapolis, Maryland,** is another place to look for Navy-oriented and colonial-era treasures.

ART, PRINTS, AND PHOTOGRAPHY

WASHINGTON'S MOST CONCENTRATED SELECTIONS of art for sale—traditional, modern, photographic, and ethnic—can be found around Dupont and Logan Circles. The best shops are centered on the crossroads of Connecticut Avenue and R Street, where there are a dozen galleries within two blocks. Several of the galleries are affiliated with the Phillips Collection. Gallery openings are usually on the first Friday of the month. Highlights include **Marsha Mateyka,** who represents local art celebs Sam Gillian and Gene Davis; **Fondo del Sol** with Latin American art; and the nonprofit **IA&A at Hillyer,** which promotes many local artists.

In Logan Circle, you'll find modern and contemporary art by internationally known artists at **Gallery Neptune & Brown** and **Hemphill Fine Arts.** Nearby is the Warhol Foundation–endowed **Transformer. Foundry Gallery** opened in 1971 and has been a showcase for local artists with talks, receptions, and changing exhibits monthly.

Art enthusiasts who find themselves in Georgetown should concentrate their time on Wisconsin Avenue at the intersection of Reservoir Road. Top galleries there include **Calloway Fine Art, Addison Ripley,** and **Artist's Proof.**

The quickly changing neighborhood of Hyattsville, Maryland, is a suburban enclave where art is flourishing. Known as the **Hyattsville Arts District,** a number of warehouses-turned-galleries are scattered along US 1, including **Art Works Now, Gateway Arts Center, Brentwood Arts Exchange, Prince Georges African American Museum and Cultural Center,** and **Studio 3807.** If you're in the neighborhood, stop for a casual meal at Franklins Brewery, a multistory complex with whimsical gifts, toys, and candy.

One of the largest art "warehouses" is the former **Torpedo Factory Art Center** near the waterfront in Old Town Alexandria, where 82 artist studios on three floors feature a range of media—painting, sculpture, jewelry, and more. You can buy their work or simply watch; an estimated 700,000 visitors a year do just that. **Off the Beaten Track** is a cooperative art studio located inside a former post office; it's located in Northeast Washington near the National Arboretum.

BOOKSTORES

WASHINGTONIANS LOVE TO READ, and fortunately that's why so many independent bookstores are still in business. These local owners find success by hosting regular readings by famous authors, as well as children's events. One of the busiest is **Kramerbooks & Afterwords Café** in Dupont Circle. What makes this place special is the curated collection of tomes, especially their wide selection of travel books. It is also a delightful place to grab a cocktail or have a meal, as the bookstore is connected to the café. Shoppers are welcome to read while they eat!

Second Story Books, at 20th and P Streets NW in Dupont Circle, is among the city's oldest purveyors of rare books, and its Rockville warehouse boasts more than a million editions. **Lost City Books** in Adams Morgan also sells rare books, as well as new and used. Just north on Columbia Road, **The Potter's House** is an independent bookstore that features readings and community events.

U Street Corridor is the original home to D.C.'s beloved **Busboys and Poets,** a bookstore and café with a liberal bent, now with multiple locations. They host regular poetry slams and invite authors to give readings. Nearby on U Street, **Big Planet Comics** is a major source for graphic novels and comics. For religious-oriented books, try the **Gospel Spreading Bible Bookstore** on Georgia Avenue, as well as the **Museum of the Bible,** located near the National Mall.

In Georgetown, **Bridge Street Books** has a charming ambience and specializes in political writing and social commentary from both sides, as well as literary fiction, philosophy, and poetry. Nearby on P street you'll find **The Lantern Bookshop,** a used bookstore with proceeds funding college tuition for needy girls.

Solid State Books, on H Street NE, and **East City Bookshop,** near Eastern Market on Capitol Hill, are two of the newer independent bookstores in Washington. Both function as a gathering place for the community, thanks to the coffee bars and local author events.

The **Library of Congress** (bookstore.gpo.gov) is another place to pick up books, and don't miss the Smithsonian museum shops, especially the **National Building Museum** and the **National Gallery of Art.** Also in Capitol Hill, an amusing little shop called **Capitol Hill Books** carries a wide selection of mysteries, obscure biographies, and used books from all genres.

Politics and Prose, intellectual Washington's favorite hangout, specializes in psychology, politics, and the works of distinguished authors—and hosts many of their book-signing parties. They have an excellent kids' section and expert staff members who love to recommend books to satisfy every curiosity. They now have multiple locations, including the flagship on Connecticut Avenue in Cleveland Park, as well as more intimate locations at The Wharf and Union Market.

 HISTORY BUFFS WILL FIND A VARIETY OF BOOKS focused on the American Civil War at the area's nearby battlefields (**Manassas, Fredericksburg,** and **Monocacy National Battlefields**); as well as at **Ford's Theatre, Arlington National Cemetery,** and **The African American Civil War Museum.** For colonial-era tomes, check out Old Town Alexandria's museums and **The Shops at Mount Vernon,** which is the largest US bookstore dedicated to George Washington.

The younger set is well served by a handful of independent bookstores. **Fairy Godmother,** near Eastern Market in Capitol Hill, has both toys and books packed into a cramped space, but your kids will find some new favorites among their fanciful fiction and nonfiction literature.

The Children's Playseum, on Bethesda Avenue in downtown Bethesda, not only sells books and toys but also is a perfect place to bring your preschool-age kids to reward them for good behavior after touring D.C. With a few themed rooms, kids are free to interact and play, pretend, paint, try on costumes, and buy gently used books. In Chevy Chase, Arlington, and Rockville, you'll find **Barstons Child's Play** is stuffed full of games, toys, and books for all ages.

In the Virginia suburbs, check out **Kinder Haus Toys** in Arlington. Nicknamed "the Wonderland" by fans, it's packed with books, European toys, and designer kids clothing. **Hooray for Books** is in the main shopping area of Old Town Alexandria on King Street and hosts daily story time readings and book signings.

FOOD AND FARMERS MARKETS

IF YOU ENJOY SHOPPING FOR GOURMET FOOD, regional specialties, and unusual treats, you can't beat Washington's food and farmers markets. Year-round, stop in Capitol Hill's indoor **Eastern Market** (Seventh and North Carolina Streets SE) to sample international cuisine, find local produce, and peruse a variety of handmade arts and crafts. During the week, Eastern Market has a busy deli, fresh-baked goods, and local cheeses (it's known for having the best pancakes too). On weekends, the open-air flea market features handmade crafts, repurposed furniture, and antiques.

Union Market (1309 Fifth Street NE) opened in a historic market building originally constructed in the 1800s. The diverse market, attached to a number of wholesale food purveyors, has become a catalyst for the development of this once-blighted neighborhood. Today, Union Market, near the NoMA/Gallaudet University Metro station, hosts a concentration of curated vendors under one roof, selling everything from oysters to gelato to empanadas. You can dine in or take food home.

unofficial **TIP**
Within the Union Market complex is the new **La Cosecha,** an international market featuring Latin American vendors. The project is in coordination with Washington, D.C.'s Latin American embassies.

Near the Dupont Circle Metro, **Glen's Garden Market** (2001 S Street NW, facing 20th Street) is filled with prepared foods, beer and wine, local products, cheeses, and produce. The market regularly hosts wine and beer tastings on its outdoor patio.

 IN FAIR WEATHER, don't be surprised to walk through Washington right into a fresh-air farmers market. The vendors set up in different locations in the city on different days. To find out where they'll be when you visit, check the website freshfarmmarkets.org. The locations, which are usually near a Metro station, are currently in Dupont Circle, downtown Silver Spring, by the White House, Ballston in Arlington, and H Street NE.

VINTAGE CLOTHING

THE GREATER WASHINGTON AREA IS A MECCA for vintage shoppers. In D.C. head to U Street, Adams Morgan, Brookland, and Georgetown for the most options. Some standouts include **Meeps Vintage, Mercedes Bien Vintage,** and **Frugalista** in Adams Morgan; **Fia's Fabulous Finds** in Petworth; **Analog** in Brookland; **Crossroads Trading Co., Joint Custody,** and **Current Boutique** in the U Street Corridor; and **Ella-Rue, Pretty Chic DC, Inga's Once is Not Enough,** and **Georgetown Emporium** in Georgetown.

In Maryland, try **Chic to Chic** in Gaithersburg, **Remix Recycling Co.** in Bethesda, **Bespoke Not Broke** in Takoma Park, and **Reddz** (on Woodmont Avenue in Bethesda and Wisconsin Avenue in Georgetown).

In Virginia, vintage enthusiasts recommend **New to You** in Falls Church, as well as **Mint Condition** and **Elinor Coleman Vintage Mirage** in Alexandria.

WASHINGTON, D.C. SOUVENIRS

WHEN THE LEGIONS OF BUSES arrive in Washington, their passengers are often dropped off at **Souvenir City** (1001 K Street NW), a store full of D.C.-themed keepsakes such as shot glasses and postcards. Another popular tourist stop is the **Washington Welcome Center** (1001 E Street NW) near Ford's Theatre and the Old Town Trolley tour stop. This multipurpose facility sells tickets to various tours but also carries replicas of the White House, license plates, key chains, magnets, stuffed animals, and even presidential toilet brushes. Right next door is **Honest Abe's Souvenir** (506 10th Street NW), a shop with mostly kitsch items but often at a discount. **Ford's Theatre** carries an expansive collection of Abraham Lincoln–themed merchandise.

Adjacent to the Treasury Department on 15th Street, you'll find **White House Gifts,** which sells presidential and political candidate merchandise, including dolls, patriotic memorabilia, and Air Force One miniatures; it even has a movie set–style Oval Office where you may take your own photos posed at the president's desk.

You can easily find GOP- or Dem-leaning T-shirts and buttons in most quickie souvenir shops, but serious collectors might want to check out **Capitol Coin & Stamp,** near Farragut Square on H Street, which carries a broad selection of campaign items, posters, and ephemera.

unofficial **TIP**
In spring, nearly every gift shop has a collection of cherry blossom–themed gifts. Many of the Smithsonian and private museums have at least one table with merchandise featuring Washington, D.C.'s iconic puffy pink petals.

While D.C.'s street vendors sell T-shirts, sweatshirts, caps, and bags, **City Gifts and Souvenirs,** at 1300 Pennsylvania Avenue NW, has higher quality items such as president bobbleheads and patriotic teddy bears, as well as NCIS gear and Christmas ornaments. For Georgetown University–emblazoned clothing, check out **Georgetown Tees. The National Zoo** probably sells the most kid-friendly souvenirs, especially panda-mania gifts, stuffed animals, and toys.

 Shop Made in DC, in Georgetown and at The Wharf, carries unique Washington, D.C.-centric and locally made items like D.C. Metro maps, District of Columbia Flag merchandise, locally made jewelry and soaps, and other unexpected treasures.

Of course, the museum shops are the best source of high-quality souvenirs. Each museum has themed items; for example, at **National Archives** you'll find books on genealogy. At the **National Postal Museum,** collectors will find stamps from every era. We especially love the collection housed in the beautiful **White House Visitor Center** run by the White House Historical Association. Besides the clever interactive exhibits, you'll find ornaments, umbrellas, and pins, all with the presidential seal. For kids it sells playing cards, toys, models, and educational books.

WINE, CRAFT BEER, AND SPIRITS

ALCOHOL LAWS VARY IN THE DISTRICT OF COLUMBIA, Maryland, and Virginia; however, in all three consumers must be age 21 or older to order and buy alcohol. Each state varies in where they sell wine, beer, and spirits. In the two Maryland counties closest to D.C.—Montgomery and Prince George's—you can only buy wine, beer, and spirits in the private retail stores or ABC/state-run stores (with a few exceptions such as Rodman's and Balducci's, which sell wine and beer). In Virginia and D.C., wine and beer are available for purchase in grocery stores and convenience stores, while spirits are only available at state-run stores.

You'll find the biggest selection of wine and spirits in a few superstores located in Washington, D.C. Though it's not Metro-accessible, **MacArthur Beverages** (4877 MacArthur Boulevard NW) invests heavily and intelligently in wine futures and offers a strong catalog. **Calvert Woodley Fine Wines and Spirits** (4339 Connecticut Avenue NW, near Woodley Metro station) offers a huge selection of exotic, international wines and spirits, with knowledgeable salespeople eager to guide you. Other good sources for wine, beer, and spirits include **Magruder's** in Chevy Chase (5626 Connecticut Avenue NW), **Schneider's of Capitol Hill** (300 Massachusetts Avenue NE), and **1 West Dupont Circle Wines and Liquors** (2012 P Street NW).

unofficial **TIP**
For a sampling of the best American small-batch craft beer stores, visit **Craft Beer Cellar** near Union Station, **Cordial** at The Wharf, and the historic **Georgetown Wine & Spirits** in Georgetown.

PART EIGHT

EXERCISE *and* RECREATION

WORKING *a* WORKOUT *into* YOUR VISIT

MOST OF THE FOLKS IN THE *Unofficial Guide* family work out routinely, even when (or perhaps especially when) we're traveling. We walk, run, do yoga—the more transportable sports. It's not just a matter of offsetting calories (although those of us who review restaurants need extra help); it's also about easing stress and jet lag. But Washington's summer heat and humidity make outdoor exercise challenging. Washington, picturesque as it is, is also prone to high levels of allergens, especially in spring and fall. Although snow on sidewalks usually isn't a problem in the major tourist areas because of removal operations, cold air can also be hard on those with respiratory trouble.

The good news is there's less *work* in workouts these days and more *create* in recreation. With trapeze flying, zip lines, climbing walls, rowing, rafting, hiking, and horseback riding, the Washington region—whose sweep includes rivers, lakes, mountains, battlefields, and an admirable amount of public parkland—has plenty to entice you.

The BASIC DRILLS

WALKING AND RUNNING

THE MOST OBVIOUS METHOD OF EXERCISE —in fact, the almost unavoidable form for tourists—is walking. With its wide-open public spaces, long museum corridors, and picturesque neighborhoods, Washington is a walker's haven (in both senses of the word: security is very good around the National Mall at all hours).

Strolling (or running or biking) **the Mall** (nps.gov/nama) offers grand views of the **Lincoln, Jefferson,** and **Franklin Delano Roosevelt Memorials** and the **Washington Monument,** as well as the **Tidal Basin** and the

Potomac River. It's just over 2 miles from the Capitol steps to the Lincoln Memorial, with many memorable stops in between—World War II, Vietnam Veterans, Korean War Veterans, and Vietnam Women's Memorials, and of course, the Washington Monument. Crossing the bridge to **Arlington National Cemetery** adds about another mile. You can also walk north along the river past the **John F. Kennedy Center for the Performing Arts** and the **Thompson Boat Center** to the **Georgetown waterfront.** (This walk is especially nice when the cherry blossoms are in bloom; plan to have a drink or dinner at one of Georgetown's waterfront restaurants.) And within Georgetown, the waterfront and portions of the **Chesapeake and Ohio (C&O) Canal Towpath** are very popular; from the canal's beginnings near the Four Seasons Hotel to Fletcher's Boathouse is about 3 miles. Heading the opposite direction, from the Four Seasons to Union Station, going through the Mall and skirting the Capitol grounds, is about 3.5 miles, making a round-trip about 7 miles.

Contained within the city limits is the 32-mile trail system in **Rock Creek Park** (nps.gov/rocr), one of the oldest urban parks in the country. The best place to start your walk is at the park's nature center (5200 Glover Road NW) near the Cleveland Park Metro station. Other stellar walking trails are at the **U.S. National Arboretum** (usna.usda.gov), the **Anacostia Riverwalk Trail** (capitolriverfront.org/go/anacostia-riverwalk -trail), and **Kenilworth Park & Aquatic Gardens** (nps.gov/keaq), all in northeast D.C. The arboretum has miles of wide paved and mulched trails through various gardens, forests, and meadows. Kenilworth— where huge lotus flowers dot the elevated and land-based trails surrounded on all sides by a riot of water lily ponds—is a photographer's dream. The Anacostia Riverwalk Trail straddles both sides of the Anacostia River. On the Anacostia side, miles of scenic parkland offer lovely views of the city skyline, while on the Capitol Riverfront side, you can walk from Nationals Park to the 11th Street Bridge, which is in the process of becoming a bridge park, similar to the High Line in Manhattan.

Washington offers plenty of options to joggers as well. Most of the better running areas are relatively flat but visually stunning and centrally located, close to major hotels and attractions, making either a morning or late-afternoon run easy to fit into your schedule. Many hotels offer marked-route maps; check with the hotel concierge.

The **C&O Canal Towpath** offers what is probably the best running surface in town. Runners, cyclists, and hikers patronize this wide, dirt-packed trail that runs between the scenic Potomac River and the canal. Mileposts along the towpath keep you informed of your distance, but there are also several larger landmarks: **Fletcher's Boathouse** around mile 3 has restrooms and some vending machines. **Glen Echo Park** is about 7 miles out. (You may be able to get a restorative meal and/or drink at the Irish Inn at Glen Echo.) Another 7 miles out, near mile marker 14, is the enormous cataract at **Great Falls.**

In all, the C&O Canal, the entire stretch of which is a national park (thanks primarily to the efforts of US Supreme Court Justice William

O. Douglas), runs 184.5 miles to Cumberland, Maryland, offering hikers, bikers, and joggers another way to enjoy several bucolic and historic areas, including **White's Ferry,** where car commuters and recreational visitors still cross the Potomac toward Leesburg, Virginia; **Harpers Ferry,** where John Brown made his war-inciting stand; and Sharpsburg, Maryland, the site of **Antietam National Battlefield.** (This can be done in stages, of course; go to nps.gov/choh/planyourvisit.)

There's a second path that follows the C&O Towpath as far as Fletcher's Boathouse but then turns northeast toward Bethesda and Silver Spring. The **Capital Crescent Trail** (cctrail.org), based on the old Baltimore and Ohio (B&O) Railroad right-of-way (including a bridge over the canal), has both a wide biking trail and, in many places, a separate running path. More than a million walkers, runners, and bikers use the trail each year. From Georgetown to Bethesda—where the trail emerges at a convenient restaurant neighborhood not far from the Metro—is about 7 miles.

The **Mount Vernon Trail** (nps.gov/gwmp), a riverside route on the Virginia side of the Potomac, starts near **Theodore Roosevelt Island** off the George Washington Memorial Parkway; goes downriver through Old Town Alexandria, past wildlife refuges and marinas, monument views, jet takeoffs, and so on; and winds up 18 miles later at Mount Vernon itself. **Roosevelt Island** (nps.gov/this) is a sweet little wildlife and woodlands refuge designed by Frederick Law Olmsted Jr., with a 1.3-mile easy walking loop.

For an extensive guide to hikes in the area, check out my book, written with coauthor Rachel Cooper, *60 Hikes Within 60 Miles: Washington, D.C.* (Menasha Ridge Press, 2018).

BICYCLING

MOST OF THE TRAILS AND ROUTES ABOVE are great for cycling too. Adult cruiser bikes (plus helmets, baskets, locks, and so on) are available for rent on a first-come, first-serve basis at **Thompson Boat Center,** at the intersection of Rock Creek Parkway and Virginia Avenue on the Georgetown waterfront (thompsonboatcenter.com). **Fletcher's Boathouse** and **Washington Sailing Marina,** part of the same National Park Service concessioner, also rent a variety of bikes.

Bike and Roll rents Trek and tandem bikes from L'Enfant Plaza and Old Town Alexandria (☎ 866-736-8224; bikeandroll.com).

VISITORS MAY WANT TO RENT BIKES at one of more than 500 **Capital Bikeshare** stations (capitalbikeshare.com), located throughout the D.C. area and in Arlington, Virginia. A single pass is $2 per 30-minute trip, while a 24-hour pass costs $8. You must download the System Map through Lyft or Capital Bikeshare's mobile app, or purchase a pass at a kiosk, to rent one of the 4,300 bikes, then return the bike to another Bikeshare location.

FITNESS CENTERS AND CORE STRENGTHENING

MOST MAJOR HOTELS THESE DAYS HAVE A FITNESS ROOM with some cardio and weight lifting equipment. However, if you are a member of one of the national chains or are willing to buy a day pass, you have scores of options; many clubs have massage therapists, yoga instructors, and even hairstylists on hand. (If you check the companies' websites, you can sometimes find free trial memberships.)

Vida Fitness, a very trendy local chain, has six branches downtown (vidafitness.com) and most have salons on site, so if you want to break a sweat before that breakfast meeting, you're covered. **Equinox Sports Club** next to the Ritz-Carlton Hotel at 22nd and M Streets NW (equinox.com) offers Pilates, yoga, an indoor pool, a squash court, a restaurant named Blu, and a kids' club, as well as a handy deluxe spa for taking the ache out (it has a second location on Bethesda Row and another near Mount Vernon Square).

Balance Gym has four locations (balancegym.com) in the Greater Washington area (Thomas Circle, Foggy Bottom, Glover Park, and Capitol Hill) and wins top honors in the The Best of DC poll for its CrossFit program; ask about its Drop-in Pass. You must have at least three months of training in CrossFit to participate.

Intense fitness buffs should try **Solidcore** (solidcore.co), with seven locations in Washington, D.C., which emphasizes a 50-minute, full-body workout designed to work your muscles to "failure" to eventually rebuild them.

There are 10 **Sport & Health Clubs** (sportandhealth.com) spread out over D.C., Maryland, and Virginia. **Washington Sports Club** (washingtonsportsclubs.com), with six D.C. and three Maryland locations, is part of a company that also operates chains in Philadelphia, Boston, and New York City.

YOGA STUDIOS

WASHINGTONIANS LOVE THEIR YOGA, and you won't have to miss a day of practice when visiting, thanks to **Kimpton Hotels** (kimpton hotels.com), which provide a mat in each guest room. Several other local hotels emphasize healthful travel experiences, and one, **Avenue Suites** in Georgetown (avenuesuitesgeorgetown.com), offers complimentary yoga classes on its patio. Dozens of small neighborhood studios offer walk-in classes, so ask the front desk or concierge for recommendations, and inquire about discounts extended to hotel guests. Some especially popular studios in the District are **Yoga Shala** (theyogashaladc.com), **Georgetown Yoga** (georgetownyoga.com), **Flow Yoga Center** (flowyogacenter.com), **YogaWorks** (yogaworks.com/washington-dc) with six locations, **Down Dog Yoga** (downdogyoga.com) with four locations, and **Hot Yoga Capitol Hill** (hotyogacapitolhill.com). **Yoga District** (yogadistrict.com) has seven locations and fits in mindfulness. **Epic Yoga** (epicyogadc.com) offers both hot and barre-style classes.

◼️ RECREATIONAL SPORTS

TENNIS AND GOLF

WASHINGTON HAS SEVERAL PUBLIC TENNIS FACILITIES, but only two are likely to accommodate visitors. **Rock Creek Tennis Center** (rockcreektennis.com), which is home to the Citi Open tournament in late summer, has 25 outdoor hard and clay courts, plus 5 heated indoor courts. Tennis lovers may want to schedule their visit to watch the Citi Open (usually in early August), which draws many of the sport's biggest stars from around the world. **East Potomac Tennis Center** (eastpotomac tennis.com) is located in East Potomac Park across from the District Wharf and to the south of the Jefferson Memorial and the Tidal Basin. This National Park Service–run center has 24 hard courts, including 5 encased in a year-round white bubble. Make reservations for busy times at least one week in advance; walk-ups have a pretty good chance of getting a court on weekdays.

East Potomac Park also has one of three golf courses (golfdc.com) operated by the National Park Service; it's the only one easily accessible by public transportation, and it's the least expensive. Realize that this isn't a championship golf course by any stretch, but it offers one 18-hole course, two 9-hole courses, a driving range, and a very picturesque 1930s 18-hole miniature golf course (no cartoon characters here). In addition, East Potomac Park, which is more than 300 acres altogether, has an outdoor pool, a playground, Potomac Grille, and picnic facilities, so it's a good choice for family outings. But check before you go because the facilities are closed sometimes for maintenance. (☎ 202-426-6841; nps.gov/nama).

The other golf centers are **Langston Golf Course,** a serene public course near Kingman and Heritage Islands Park and the Anacostia River in Northeast D.C., and **Rock Creek Golf Course,** a 9-hole course for duffers of all skill levels located in the woods of Washington's largest park. **Old Soldiers' Home Golf Course** (afrh.gov/washington-residents) is open to members of the armed forces and is on the same grounds as **President Lincoln's Cottage.**

There are also many courses in Montgomery County (mcggolf .com) and Fairfax County (fairfaxcounty.gov/parks/golf). However, you'll have to know somebody to get into Bethesda's famed **Congressional Country Club** (ccclub.org), which lists scores of politicos and power brokers among its members.

The **Trump National Golf Club** (trumpnationaldc.com) near Algonkian Regional Park in Sterling, Virginia, is a championship-caliber course. The course has stunning views of the Potomac River, with greens positioned on the water's edge. In 2017 it hosted the Senior PGA Tournament. The club also has tennis courts. Ditto the **TPC Potomac at Avenel Farm** in Potomac (tpc.com/potomac), which has hosted numerous PGA tours over the years.

SWIMMING

LOCAL WATERS ARE UNSAFE except to kayak or sail, so unless you have time for a trip to the Atlantic beaches, stick to your hotel swimming pool, ask the hotel concierge to direct you to the nearest gym, or check out one of these popular aquatic centers.

unofficial **TIP**
Only a few hotels offer pool passes to outsiders, and most of those, of course, are open only Memorial Day–Labor Day.

One of the nicest is the free Olympic-size pool at East Potomac Park (see page 297), open June–early October (☎ 202-727-6523; nps .gov/nama). The year-round pool at **William H. Rumsey Aquatics Center** (☎ 202-724-4495; dpr.dc.gov/page/william-h-rumsey-aquatic -center) near the Eastern Market Metro station on Capitol Hill (also called the Capitol Hill Natatorium) and the **Wilson Aquatic Center,** located near American University and the Tenleytown Metro station (☎ 202-730-0583; dpr.dc.gov/page/wilson -aquatic-center-01), offer 30-day pool passes, but they're significantly cheaper for D.C. residents, so ask your friends to treat you like family. The **YMCA of Metropolitan Washington** (☎ 202-232-6700; ymcadc .org) has locations around the D.C. area, including Bethesda and Arlington. For those staying in Bethesda or Rockville, the completely accessible **Kennedy Shriver Aquatic Center,** where some of America's Olympic divers trained, is walking distance from the White Flint Metro station (☎ 240-777-8070; montgomerycountymd.gov/rec/facilities /aquaticcenters/kennedyshriver.html). Another option is a day trip to Annapolis to swim at **Sandy Point State Park** on the Chesapeake Bay in the shadow of the Chesapeake Bay Bridge; it has a small beach in the shadow of the 4.5-mile-long Bay Bridge that's popular with wind surfers (dnr.maryland.gov/publiclands/Pages/southern/sandypoint.aspx).

ROPES AND ROCKS

THERE ARE SEVERAL ELEVATED-ROPE ADVENTURE PARKS in the Washington area, though none are Metro-accessible. Each park has restrictions regarding minimum age, height, waist size (for harnesses), weight, minimal fitness levels, and so on. For the more challenging routes, you will have preliminary instruction, and most have courses that range from beginner to advanced.

Go Ape (goape.com) near Rockville was the first US location among the 16 Go Ape parks. In a space the size of seven football fields, it scatters zip lines, Tarzan swings, rope ladders, trapezes, and so on. Though farther away, **Terrapin Adventures** (terrapinadventures.com) in historic Savage, Maryland, is even more elaborate, with a 330-foot zip line 30 feet in the air, a giant tandem swing with an 80-foot arc, a multilevel ropes course, and a 43-foot climbing tower. It also offers kayaking, biking, caving, and backpacking tours. **The Adventure Park at Sandy Spring Friends School** (sandyspringadventurepark.org) has 13 separate trails and offers several levels of difficulty. The Labyrinth is a wooden structure with multiple bridges, ladders, and ropes sited for kids ages 5–10. To beat the heat of the day, try going during twilight hours when the park is magically lit with strings of LED lights.

The Trapeze School, in the Navy Yard neighborhood near Nationals Park, offers instruction for both adults and kids (age 6 and older) in all weather—it has indoor and outdoor facilities. To find out whether it offers a class during your visit, see washingtondc.trapezeschool.com.

Earth Treks (earthtreksclimbing.com), with locations near the Rockville and Crystal City Metro stations, boasts the largest indoor climbing facilities in the area, with 38,500 and 45,000 square feet of rock wall respectively. **Sportrock Climbing Center** (sportrock.com) in Alexandria will challenge climbers with its 150-plus routes and classes for different skill levels. At **Summit Ropes** (summitropes.com) in Sterling, Virginia, you can learn the techniques for via ferrata, a method that helps you ascend your favorite rock wall and gets you into serious shape. The new indoor adventure park features Scout's Landing, a children's course, and Zion Summit, a course for adults (named for the treacherous Angel's Landing in Zion National Park). Both are challenging but have elements that cater to beginner, intermediate, and advanced climbers.

The region also challenges outdoor rock climbers at parks bordering the Potomac River—**Carderock Recreation Area** in Maryland and **Romeo's Ladder** in Great Falls, Virginia.

BOATING, PADDLEBOARDING, FLOATING, AND WATER PARKS

IF YOU'RE ANYWHERE ALONG THE POTOMAC RIVER early in the day or around dusk, you'll see school rowing crews doing drills. The George Washington University Invitational regatta, which draws teams from all over the country during the National Cherry Blossom Festival, is only one of the many contests. And all forms of rowing are increasingly popular in the Washington area; some high-level competitors come here to train.

Canoes, rowboats, and single and double kayaks are available for rent at the **Wharf Boathouse**; it's a very picturesque place to tool around, despite the larger boats that dock at the marina there. The historic **Thompson Boat Center, Fletcher's Boathouse,** and **Key Bridge Boathouse** are all located along the Potomac in different parts of Georgetown. They rent two- and three-person canoes, single and double kayaks, and stand-up paddleboards. The **Ballpark Boathouse** in the Capitol Riverfront neighborhood rents canoes and kayaks. For a full listing of pricing, tours, locations, and hours of many Washington-area boating operations, visit boatingindc.com.

Paddlestroke SUP (☎ 301-442-6864; paddlestrokesup.com), just north of the city by the Old Angler's Inn in Potomac, Maryland, offers

unofficial **TIP**
Inspired by those rowing crews you see on the river? Or maybe you're just a fan of those British historical romance movies? Thompson Boat Center offers private hour-long or weeklong sculling lessons, and even sweep rowing courses, which draw out-of-town Olympic team wannabes.

rentals, as well as lessons in paddleboarding and river surfing with experienced instructors.

The Potomac River may look harmless, but please don't ignore warning signs about water conditions: swimmers, jumpers, and world-class kayak competitors have lost their lives here. Rescue crews have nicknamed the section near Little Falls Dam "the drowning machine" due to the frequent loss of life there.

For a perfect day trip, take a gentle float down one of the rivers close to Washington, such as **Antietam Creek** north of Harpers Ferry (river trail.com) or the Shenandoah River in Harpers Ferry (riverriders.com). Guides drive you to a drop-off point, and then the current pulls your inner tube through meandering and fast-moving rapids. Guided and whitewater trips are also available. This is the perfect family activity because it's safe for people of all ages and levels of fitness.

Prefer something family-friendly and closer to your hotel? Check out the **Tidal Basin paddleboats** (tidalbasinpaddleboats.com) on Maine Avenue near the Jefferson Memorial. The **National Harbor Marina** (nationalharbor.com/about/marina) rents pedal boats, paddleboards, and kayaks to paddle around on a gentle section of the Potomac River, across from Old Town Alexandria and close to Woodrow Wilson Bridge. Sunset tours are available during the summer.

If you've ever wanted to learn to sail, D.C. offers lessons and rents sailboats through **DC Sail,** part of the National Maritime Heritage Foundation located near The Wharf in Southwest D.C. In Virginia, you can rent paddles and boats from **Belle Haven Marina** in Alexandria, or **Columbia Island Marina** and **Washington Sailing Marina** in Arlington.

If you're looking to cool off and reward your kids for their sight-seeing skills, consider spending a few hours at one of the region's water parks. The biggest is at **Six Flags America** in Bowie, Maryland. In Gaithersburg, Maryland, **Bohrer Park,** on a historic farm, boasts a 250-foot double waterslide. **Ocean Dunes Waterpark,** located in Arlington's Upton Hill Regional Park, has a 230-foot open slide and 170-foot covered slide, along with a 500-gallon dumping bucket. **Splashdown Waterpark,** located in Manassas, is one of the largest water parks in the area and draws daring kids to its four-story Pipeline Tower, Tropical Twister, and Cannonball. Along with a lazy river, there's also a challenging log walk and a playground with fountains and sprays.

SEGWAY TOURS

THERE ARE MULTIPLE SEGWAY TOURS available in Washington, and frankly, this is a very efficient way to see a lot of sights and have fun doing it. Segways are two-wheel motorized vehicles that you can steer and propel forward with hand controls. They have an upright post and a platform on which to stand. D.C. law dictates that riders must be age 16 or older to operate one in the city.

Tours are offered in the daytime and evening by private guides; they involve a 10-minute training session and last about 2–3 hours. Guides usher riders around various monuments and attractions, including the Smithsonian museums, the White House, and the Capitol. Tours are usually limited to 8–10 people, so there are ample opportunities to ask questions and hear the guide's historical facts and interesting stories. There are limits on weight, and pregnant women are not allowed to ride. Reputable Segway companies include **Bike and Roll DC** (bikeandrolldc.com), **Segs in the City** (segsinthecity.com), and **Capital Segway** (capitalsegway.com), all of which offer tours of the National Mall; **City Segway Tours** (dc.citysegwaytours.com) bundles in bus tours or boat rides with some of its tickets. Capital Segway also offers tours in French and German. Segways may seem daunting at first, but they're fairly easy to ride and will allow you to cover a lot of ground during your tour. Older teens will love it.

ICE AND SNOW

THERE ARE A FEW ICE RINKS in the Washington area, but the two that would be the most fun for out-of-towners are the one on the Mall and the other at the top of the Watergate Hotel. Come skating weather—generally mid-November through mid-March—the **Sculpture Garden** of the National Gallery of Art (nga.gov/skating) between Seventh and Ninth Streets NW and Constitution Avenue NW and Madison Drive NW is transformed into a fantasy ice rink in the middle of the Mall, with the U.S. Capitol and all the Smithsonian museums lit up as a backdrop. It's open until a romantic 11 p.m. on Fridays and Saturdays, and the **Pavilion Café,** a lovely retro-Deco glass-sided eatery alongside the garden, serves until 9 p.m.

Several public rinks are accessible by Metro—and at Metro developments, in fact. The outdoor-café area at **Pentagon Row** (pentagonrowskating.com), part of the Pentagon City complex, and the **Rockville Town Square** (rockvilletownsquare.com) are iced during winter. **Canal Park Ice Rink** (capitolriverfront.org/canal-park/ice-rink), near the Navy Yard–Ballpark and Capitol South Metro stations (Second and M Streets SE), offers pretty city views. The newest addition is the **Wharf Ice Rink** (wharfdc.com/wharf-ice-rink), which opened in 2017. Not only can you skate here, you can also learn the Olympic sport of curling. After you're done, warm up at the bonfire by the Camp Wharf food truck parked nearby.

For hockey fans, however, the most intriguing facility might be **MedStar Capitals Iceplex** (medstarcapitalsiceplex.com) atop a seven-story building at Ballston Quarter (at the Ballston Metro) in Arlington; it's the practice rink for the National Hockey League's Washington Capitals.

Several downhill ski complexes are within a 2- to 3-hours' drive from Washington: **Whitetail** (skiwhitetail.com), **Roundtop Mountain** (skiroundtop.com), and **Liberty Mountain Resorts** (skiliberty.com), all in south-central Pennsylvania. In Virginia, check out **Wintergreen** (wintergreenresort.com), **Bryce** (bryceresort.com), or **Massanutten Resort** (massresort.com). In West Virginia, **Canaan Valley**

(canaanresort.com) and **Snowshoe Mountain Resorts** (snowshoemtn
.com) offer the highest vertical drops in the area. Maryland has the
popular four-seasons **Wisp Ski Resort** (wispresort.com) at Deep Creek
Lake. All are open to snowboarders and skiers. All of these resorts
also offer golf courses, rental cabins, lodges, and restaurants, and they
host regular events and festivals.

SPECTATOR SPORTS

BASEBALL

AT THE NAVY YARD METRO, the **Washington Nationals** (mlb.com
/nationals), the National League champions in 2019, play in an elaborate
stadium complex. Tickets can range well into the hundreds, but singles
start at less than $20 on some days, and all sight lines are good. Nationals
Park is more than just baseball; it's a D.C.-area meeting place and social
event. The park hosts the hilarious Presidents Race: four giant-headed
presidential likenesses (George Washington, Thomas Jefferson, Abraham
Lincoln, and Teddy Roosevelt) compete during the fourth inning by running around the stadium. In season, fans can take an hourlong behind-
the-scenes tour on days when the game is at night—or a 90-minute tour,
including the visiting team's clubhouse, on non-game days.

Prior to 2005, D.C. went 30 years without a baseball team, and
during that time, many locals became fans of the **Baltimore Orioles**
(mlb.com/orioles), whose retro-chic Oriole Park at Camden Yards stadium is only about an hour away.

For those who see baseball as a stepchild of cricket, Washington's
international community supports several cricket fields (wclinc.com),
but they're located in the suburbs of Northern Virginia and Maryland.

BASKETBALL

WASHINGTON'S PROFESSIONAL MEN'S BASKETBALL TEAM,
the NBA's **Washington Wizards,** plays at home at the Capital One
Arena, located directly above the Gallery Place/Chinatown Metro station. Wizards' games are high-energy entertainment, with lots of community involvement by local youth and military veterans. For visitors
staying in Penn Quarter, it's a fun night to schedule a pregame dinner
and then attend a Wizards game at the Capital One Arena. Its sister
team, the WNBA's **Mystics,** moved in 2019 to the St. Elizabeths East
Entertainment and Sports Arena. For schedules and tickets, go to nba
.com/wizards or mystics.wnba.com.

Georgetown University (guhoyas.com) also plays its home games at
the Capital One Arena. The **George Washington University** Colonials
(gwsports.com) also claim a host of devoted fans (watch for celebs
and media faces), and the team's Charles E. Smith Center home is
steps from the Foggy Bottom/GWU Metro stop. Two other university teams, with their own Metro stations, are **American University**'s

Eagles (aueagles.com), who play at Bender Arena, and **Howard University's** Bison (hubison.com), who play at Burr Gymnasium.

FOOTBALL AND SOCCER

GETTING TICKETS TO THE **Washington Redskins** (redskins.com) has gotten a lot easier in recent years, but attending a home game can be challenging. FedEx Field is located in the outer loop of I-495 in Landover, Maryland. Driving and parking can be quite hectic, so if you don't mind walking a mile, there's a dedicated walkway to FedEx Field from the Morgan Boulevard Metro station on the Blue Line. You can also take the Orange Line to Landover station, but it's 3 miles from the stadium.

The **Baltimore Ravens'** stadium (baltimoreravens.com), just south of the Orioles' Camden Yards, is accessible via the MARC train.

The Washington area is also home to the full-contact Women's Football Alliance **D.C. Divas** (dcdivas.com), who play at the St. James Sports Complex in Springfield, Virginia, April–June.

Pro soccer is *football* to the rest of the world. **D.C. United** (dcunited .com), formerly anchored by world-famous player Wayne Rooney, plays about 20 home games each season (February–October) at the new Audi Field, between Navy Yard–Ballpark and Waterfront Metro stations on Buzzard Point. The team has four MLS Cups and has been crowned the U.S. Open Cup champions three times, at this writing. D.C.'s women's soccer team, the **Washington Spirit,** plays a few seasonal games at Audi Field, though they play most at their stadium in Boyds, a Maryland suburb. Three of Spirit's players—Rose Lavelle, Andi Sullivan, and Mallory Pugh—are members of the U.S. Women's National Team who won the 2019 World Cup. Completed in 2018, Audi Field has a state-of-the-art facility with a capacity for 20,000 fans.

HOCKEY AND ROLLER DERBY

WASHINGTON'S PROFESSIONAL HOCKEY TEAM, the **Washington Capitals** (nhl.com/capitals), shares ownership with the Wizards and Mystics and also plays at the Capital One Arena. Washingtonians are fanatical about their hockey team, and it's nearly impossible to score a ticket to a matchup if they're having a good season. You may notice a sea of red jerseys if you happen to be around the arena on the night of a Caps game. The team won its first Stanley Cup in 2018, and the entire city came out in full force to show support for the team.

Although it's not quite the same sort of blades, D.C.'s four-team flat-track roller derby league, the **DC Rollergirls** (dcrollergirls.com), is pretty entertaining. Teams play a winter-spring season at locations around the area, including the DC Armory (Stadium-Armory Metro).

HORSE SHOWS AND HORSE RACING

RACING HAS A LONG HISTORY IN THE WASHINGTON AREA, particularly in Maryland, and both thoroughbred and harness racing are available at a number of tracks around Washington, though they're not easy to get to: only **Laurel Park** (laurelpark.com) is accessible by (MARC) train. It's a little run-down, but **Pimlico** (pimlico.com), outside Baltimore, is home to the Preakness Stakes, the middle contest of thoroughbred racing's Triple Crown, and the third Saturday in May is part of a huge celebration there.

There are several steeplechase courses in the Washington region, the most famous being the **Virginia Gold Cup** lineup in May (vagold cup.com). In October, the **Washington International Horse Show** (wihs .org) kicks off a week of festivities and features more than 500 horses and riders competing in Olympic-level events—classic equitation and show jumpers—held at the Capital One Area near the Chinatown/ Gallery Place Metro station in Penn Quarter. Highlights of the Tuesday–Sunday events are Barn Night, with an evening of competition among younger jockeys, and Kids' Day on Saturday, with kid-friendly activities and a free community event.

HORSE RACING
• **Rosecroft Raceway**   Fort Washington, MD; rosecroft.com
• **Hollywood Casino at Charles Town Races**   Charles Town, WV; hollywoodcasinocharlestown.com
• **Laurel Park**   Laurel, MD; laurelpark.com
• **Pimlico Race Course**   Baltimore, MD; pimlico.com

TENNIS

THE US OPEN TENNIS CIRCUIT includes a major tournament in late summer, the **Citi Open** (citiopentennis.com), at the Fitzgerald Tennis Stadium in Rock Creek Park. To get there, use the shuttle service from the Friendship Heights Metro station. Washington also has a World TeamTennis franchise, the **Washington Kastles** (washingtonkastles .com), coached by Murphy Jensen. The team, which features veteran Venus Williams, plays a three-week season in late July.

INDEX